GOOSE GREEN

GOOSE GREEN

a battle is fought to be won

mark adkin

CASSELL&CO

Cassell Military Paperbacks

Cassell & Co
Wellington House, 125 Strand
London WC2R OBB

First published in Great Britain by Leo Cooper,
an imprint of Pen & Sword Books Ltd., 1992.
This Cassell Military Paperbacks edition published 2000.

A CIP catalogue record for this book is available from the
British Library.

ISBN 0-304-35496-1

Printed and bound by
Guernsey Press, Guernsey, C.I.

CONTENTS

To Those Who Fought And Those Who Fell

MAPS AND SKETCHES

ABBREVIATIONS

AA	Anti-Aircraft
AAA	Anti-Aircraft Artillery
AOA	Out of Area
ATGW	Anti-Tank Guided Weapon
BC	Battery Commander
BM	Brigade Major
BMA	Brigade Maintenance Area
Bn	Battalion
Casevac	Casualty evacuation
CBAS	Commando Brigade Air Squadron
CBU	Cluster Bomb Unit
CCH	Camilla Creek House
Cdo	Commando
CP	Command Post
CPX	Command Post Exercise
CVR(T)	Combat Vehicle Reconnaissance (Tracked)
DF	Defensive Fire
DFC	Distinguished Flying Cross
DS	Directing Staff
DZ	Drop Zone
FAC	Forward Air Controller
FACE	Field Artillery Computer Equipment
FAME	Field Artillery Manual Equipment
FOO	Forward Observation Officer
FP	Firing Post
FUP	Forming Up Place
GMT	Greenwich Mean Time
GPMG	General Purpose Machine Gun
GPO	Gun Position Officer
GPMG(SF)	General Purpose Machine Gun (Sustained Fire)
GSO	General Staff Officer
HALO	High Altitude Low Opening
HF	High Frequency
IV	Intravenous

LAW	Light Anti-Armour Weapon
LCU	Landing Craft Utility
LCVP	Landing Craft Vehicle and Personnel
LMG	Light Machine Gun
LSL	Landing Ship Logistic
L2	Fragmentation Grenade
Medics	Medical orderlies
MFC	Mortar Fire Controller
MG	Machine Gun
MMG	Medium Machine Gun
MT	Motor Transport
MV	Motor Vessel
NGFO	Naval Gunfire Observer
O Group	Orders Group
OP	Observation Post
PD	Point Detonating
RAP	Regimental Aid Post
RFA	Royal Fleet Auxiliary
RV	Rendez-Vous
SAS	Special Air Service
SBS	Special Boat Service
SLR	Self Loading Rifle
SMG	Sub Machine Gun
SOP	Standing Operational Procedure
Tac	Tactical
VHF	Very High Frequency
WO2	Warrant Officer Class 2
WP	White Phosphorus

MILITARY SYMBOLS USED ON MAPS

Unit Sizes

A section

A platoon

A company

A battalion

A regiment

A brigade

A division

(−)   An understrength unit

Types of Unit

In defensive position

In open or on the move

Artillery

Infantry (Argentine)

Infantry (Para)

Infantry (Royal Marine)

A headquarters

△   An OP

Examples

12   D Coy

12 Platoon, D Company, 2 Para

C   12 Regt

C Company, 12 Argentine Regiment

Weapons

↑   GPMG or LMG

↑   Medium MG

↑   Heavy MG

↑   Medium mortar

⊓   Trench or bunker

Light artillery gun

Light anti-aircraft gun

Medium anti-aircraft gun

Milan FP

NOTE ON SOURCES AND
ACKNOWLEDGEMENTS

'Old soldiers never die, they only fade away'. They do,
however, get older and part of the fading process is the
inevitable dimming of the memory. Brigadier D.R.
Chaundler OBE, who took over command of 2 Para from
Major Keeble within a few days of the battle for Goose
Green, has earned the gratitude of historians interested in
2 Para's part in the Falklands campaign. While the
battalion was still at Stanley he instructed the then Captain
David Benest, the Regimental Signals Officer, to write up
a detailed account of 2 Para's activities during the entire
conflict. Benest spent many months interviewing his
comrades and recording their experiences, from the
voyage south to the voyage home. He did this before the
fading process had started, and was able to clarify issues
by questioning participants. The result was that Benest
put together a remarkable document, possibly the only
one of its kind.

Benest was told to give his manuscript to Major-General
John Frost CB, DSO, MC, who used it as the basis for
his book, *2 Para Falklands - The Battalion at War*, which
was published in 1983. As far as Goose Green is concerned
Frost was unable, I believe, to do full justice to the battle
for several reasons. Firstly, he had to prune Benest's
account drastically as his book was to cover the whole
campaign from start to finish. He was compelled,
therefore, to condense and omit in order to write a book
of manageable length. Then, because of the closeness of
events, he felt obliged to avoid describing or discussing the
more sensitive issues that Benest had included. He also,
for the most part, refrained from commenting on events
or the controversies of the battle. Lastly, he was somewhat
hampered by his inability, as the battalion was overseas in

Belize when he was writing his book, to interview or question many participants.

I wish to acknowledge my debt to Major D.G. Benest MBE for allowing me to use his original manuscript as my primary source document. I have referred to this in the Notes as the Benest Manuscript. With this as the framework I have been able to meet or correspond with some 45 persons who fought at Goose Green. That I was able to contact these individuals was due to the unstinting assistance given by the then Regimental Colonel of The Parachute Regiment, Colonel J.A. McGregor MC, and his staff. I offer them my sincere thanks.

This facility has enabled me, through the asking of questions, to amplify details, seek opinions, and correct misunderstandings on my part. Assistance of this sort has been freely given by the former commander of 3 Commando Brigade, members of 2 Para's main headquarters, Colonel 'H''s tactical headquarters, all the company commanders, six platoon commanders, several section commanders and various senior and junior NCOs and soldiers from every sub-unit within the battalion at the time. These have included members and former members of the Royal Artillery, Royal Engineers and Royal Marines who fought alongside the Paras. They all know who they are, and will probably recognize their contributions. To them all I offer my gratitude for their willing, often enthusiastic, help. I have been most impressed by the frankness and courtesy with which they have responded to my queries, questionnaires, telephone calls and correspondence.

I have been particularly struck by the quality and quantity of the written responses from people as far afield as Canada and Germany. These individuals, who I was not always able to meet, have devoted considerable time to setting down fascinating accounts of their experiences. I have made the maximum possible use of their stories. As a writer, I appreciate the effort that must have gone in to putting pen to so much paper.

I would like to record how helpful it has been to have

comments on various extracts of my first draft. These have been essential in preventing errors of fact and in the interpretation of events. Brigadier C.D. Farrar-Hockley MC, Lieutenant-Colonel J.H. Crosland MC, Lieutenant-Colonel P. Neame and Major R. Ash RA have all assisted in this way, while Major D.G. Benest MBE and Major R.D. Jenner have read and advised on the complete manuscript. My sincere thanks. Finally, although I drew the maps myself, credit for the two sketches must go to my former art master Mr W.R. Dalzell.

INTRODUCTION

The task of the Infantry is to close with the enemy and destroy him. To this end the Infantry battalion is equipped with the necessary weapons to give it the capability of sustained fighting as a self- contained unit. To carry out its task in battle the Infantry will normally be supported by tanks, artillery and engineers. Support may also come from naval and air force units.

A Ministry of Defence training manual.

The 2nd Battalion The Parachute Regiment's struggle for the tiny settlements of Darwin and Goose Green on 28 May, 1982, was intended to be as described in the above tactics manual. The event bore little resemblance to the theory. 2 Para fought continuously for over 14 hours to close with their enemy, making it the longest battle of the land campaign. The commanding officer's request for armoured (light tank) support had been turned down, artillery support was minimal and largely ineffective, the small detachment of engineers fought as infantry, only a fraction of the battalion's own heavy weapons were used until the latter stages of the battle, the solitary 4.5 inch gun of the frigate HMS *Arrow* broke down at a crucial time, while the Sea Harriers were unable to fly ground attack missions due to atrocious weather at sea until the fighting had virtually finished. All this left 2 Para on its own. It destroyed its enemy with the weapons that the paratroopers of the rifle platoons held in their own hands — SLR rifles, GPMGs, white phosphorous grenades,

1

66mm light anti-tank rockets, plus two out of their eight 81mm mortars and, towards the end, a few Milan missiles. The pressure, or as the Paras would say the momentum, was maintained until the Argentines had been driven back some six kilometres into Goose Green village itself. A surrender was then arranged.

2 Para achieved a number of firsts in the Falklands. It was first ashore on 21 May; it was first into action at Goose Green; indeed it was the first British unit to launch a full scale battalion night attack in 30 years.[1] It won the first land victory of the campaign, and two and a half weeks later it put the first troops into Stanley, some five hours before the official ceasefire. Perhaps appropriately these were men from A Company, 2nd Lieutenant Mark Coe's 2 Platoon, who had borne the brunt of the bitter, close quarter fight for the ridge west of Darwin that had almost stalled 2 Para's attack, and on whose slope the commanding officer had died. It was also the only battalion to fight twice during the war, and the only one to fight by day. For this one VC, two DSOs, three MCs, three DCMs, nine MMs and nineteen MIDs were awarded. A magnificent record.

There is a strange paradox about Goose Green. It was of paramount importance for both sides to win, but in itself it was a strategically unnecessary battle. It was the first land battle of the conflict, and as such its outcome was of profound importance, both politically and militarily, for Britain and Argentina. Success or failure would bring important international repercussions, probably affecting the outcome of the campaign, and would certainly affect the morale and determination of both armies. The result would set the tone for the remainder of the war. Nothing succeeds like success, or depresses like failure.

For Britain a win at Goose Green was even more essential than for the Argentines. Consider for a moment the consequences of a 2 Para defeat coming on top of a week in which the Royal Navy had been hammered by the Argentine Air Force, losing four ships and having five

2

badly damaged.[2] Apart from the inevitable slump in the Task Force's morale and the dismay at home, it would seem to the world that Britain's launching of Operation Corporate was a ghastly and expensive mistake.

In the Falklands such a setback would lose for the British that most precious of commodities in war — time. There would be delay. Gone would be the prospect of pushing forward immediately from the beachhead to Mount Kent. Instead of going on to the offensive against the main Argentine positions protecting Stanley, 3 Commando Brigade would have had to pull back 3 Para and 45 Commando, which had already started their 'yomp' (march) towards Stanley, and contract into a defensive shell around Ajax Bay to await the arrival of 5 Brigade. With the Argentines emboldened by their early success the likelihood of an uninterrupted march on Stanley would be remote. More importantly, delay could well have put paid to future prospects of any advance as winter approached. Snow fell after the battle for Goose Green. The capture of Stanley by mid-June brought the conflict to a close just in time. A week or so longer and General Winter could have combined with General Menendez to make coping with conditions in the open impossible.

At best a serious British repulse at Goose Green would have meant a stalemate, with the ground forces pinned into their foothold around Ajax Bay in dreadful conditions, with the bulk of the Argentines 80 kilometres away in Stanley. Not only would it have been militarily untenable, but politically unacceptable as well, with Britain hauled back to negotiate from a position of weakness. Such a scenario is hardly exaggerated. A great deal depended on the outcome of Goose Green.

Having said that, it was almost certainly unnecessary, from the military point of view, for the British to fight at Goose Green, although, once committed, they had to win for the reasons given above. 2 Para's attack was instigated, demanded, by the politicians at home against the military advice of the commander on the spot, Brigadier Julian Thompson RM. His forces had been ashore for nearly a

3

week, British ships were being crippled, and to the watching world it seemed that 3 Commando Brigade was sitting on its hands. As will become clear, this was far from true, and Thompson had his eye firmly fixed on the main objective — Stanley. But London wanted action, a quick victory to show the public that all was well, and that the sacrifices of the Royal Navy were not in vain.

To Brigadier Thompson, when he received his order direct from Northwood (the location of the British High command outside London) by satellite radio on the 26th to do so, launching a battalion at Goose Green seemed a needless complication, a distraction from his primary aim. As early as the 23rd Northwood had signalled that his objective was now to invest Stanley. This was fine; but two days later he lost three Chinook and six Wessex helicopters when the *Atlantic Conveyor* was sunk. Without them, to move on Stanley immediately meant marching. At that moment he was also instructed to attack Goose Green. It was a classic example of the military high command at home, under intense political pressure for some action to placate the public, dictating to the field commander how to run his war. Thompson was never enthusiastic about Goose Green; he obeyed his orders, but regarded it as unjustified interference which compelled him to deflect his scarce resources to what was, from his perspective, a redundant operation.

Thompson had little doubt that the capture of Goose Green, or the destruction of its garrison, was not essential for the prosecution of the war. The Argentines could have been left to wither on the vine with a small masking force watching their activities. The tiny grass airstrip was too exposed and useless as an airbase from which to attack the British landings, while the garrison was too small in terms of manpower and firepower to constitute a serious offensive threat.

Nevertheless the battle itself merits close examination, although it is not studied at the Army's Staff College at Camberley in the same depth as is 2 Para's second triumph 17 days later at Wireless Ridge. This is because Goose

Green was not a text book, all arms battle — too many things went wrong. It was a close-run thing. Viewed in retrospect, 2 Para had been asked to take on a task that the directing staff of most military colleges would have baulked at setting as a problem for their students. Every year key participants in the Wireless Ridge battle, including the former commanding officer and artillery battery commander, go to Camberley to lecture the students on the infantry battalion, all arms battle-group in the attack. Wireless Ridge was taken by 2 Para advancing behind, and in conjunction with, massive artillery fire support, naval gunfire, a bombardment by the mortar platoons of both 2 and 3 Para, and four light tanks. It all worked splendidly. Lessons had been re-learned at Goose Green, casualties to the attackers were extremely light (3 killed, one by 'friendly fire'), and within hours 2 Para had troops in Stanley.

Nevertheless, to my mind Goose Green is as equally deserving of attention as Wireless Ridge, if only because the latter battle is untypical of war. At Wireless Ridge most things went according to plan, there was no desperate crisis, no shortage of support, and no requirement for the attackers to face modern firepower in the open in broad daylight. Camberley has adopted Wireless Ridge as an example of what should happen. Goose Green was not like that. It was, I believe, more an example of what frequently happens, and as such deserves close examination. I first realized, that of all the six battalion attacks in the Falklands, Goose Green stood out as being of exceptional interest during the research for my book, *The Last Eleven?*, which tells the story of the eleven post-World War 2 winners of the Victoria Cross. It is not often these days that a lieutenant-colonel wins the VC, let alone gains it in a solo charge on an enemy position.[3] This is what happened at Goose Green. Lieutenant-Colonel 'H' Jones was shot within touching distance of an Argentine trench, with the nearest paratrooper, his bodyguard, lying some 25 metres from where he fell.[4] It is one of the controversies of Goose

Green. Why was the commanding officer the leading man of the entire battalion? Was he taking on the role of a section commander, and, if so, was his action warranted or misplaced? What effect did his leadership and example have on the outcome of the battle?

There is much more to interest the curious. Other questions arise. Was it meant to be a raid or the full scale battalion attack that actually took place? The word 'raid' has been used frequently to describe 2 Para's operation, yet in reality it was nothing of the sort. Why was there so much apparent indecision about mounting the attack? First it was to be undertaken on 25 May, but was cancelled with the leading company well on its way to the start line. Within 36 hours it was on again. The old Army saying, 'order, counter-order, disorder', springs to mind. Then why, with an operation that Northwood insisted on, was 2 Para sent alone with only one 4.5 inch naval gun and three 105mm light guns to support it?[5]

Queries also arise with the Argentines. What was the significance of Goose Green from their point of view? Was its defence fundamental to their strategy for defending East Falkland, and could it, or should it, have been heavily reinforced and used as a base from which to counter-attack the British landings before the arrival of 5 Brigade?

With hindsight it is sometimes possible when studying a battle to pin-point a particular moment and say: 'That was the turning point. There, for a few minutes, the issue was in doubt; either side could have snatched victory'. Although this moment may not be obvious to the leaders or their troops, the historian can usually see when the outcome hung in the balance, only requiring some small initiative to tip it one way or the other.

In these circumstances, when both sides have fought long and hard, it is the unit that has the greater will to win that triumphs. Such was the case at Goose Green. Looking back there can be little doubt that such a critical moment occured at around 9.30 am on 28 May, when both of 2 Para's leading companies had been halted by intense fire, and the commanding officer was mortally wounded. For perhaps fifteen minutes the Argentines had the opportunity of defeating their attackers. As the reader will discover, for a variety of reasons the chance went unnoticed or unheeded. Rather it was the action of one Para corporal destroying a bunker with a 66mm rocket that tipped the scales on Darwin Hill.

It has been said about the Battle of the Alma in the Crimean War that it was a 'soldier's battle', fought in a fog with great confusion and eventual victory stemming from the dogged determination of the infantrymen to keep fighting. Although the only fog at Goose Green was out to sea, where the weather was foul, much of the fighting was in darkness or smoke with, at the end of the day, 2 Para's triumph being due to the fitness, aggression and willpower of the Toms to keep at it.[6] There was no brilliant tactical manoeuvre, no sudden surprise and, in the event, no real alternative to the long, frontal attack down a narrow isthmus over open terrain.

Such an assault inevitably leads to gutter fighting, and to a series of crises that can only be overcome, in the absence of overwhelming fire support, by forceful leadership at low level. One of the most striking things I found about this battle was the number of occasions that quite senior officers, artillery FOOs, and indeed the commanding officer himself, had to involve themselves in actually firing weapons, throwing grenades, and generally participating personally in 'hands on' combat in order to maintain momentum.

The circumstances at Goose Green made it a difficult battle for 2 Para to win, particularly with the arrival of daylight. By night the average Argentine conscript fought poorly, often cowering at the bottom of his trench under a blanket praying the war would go away. But, come daylight, when he could see a considerable distance, it was a different story. Then he fought comparatively well, while his mortars and artillery kept firing to the very last.

In writing this book I have attempted to dispel several of the myths that have become, through media repetition, accepted as facts. I have not ignored controversies, or refrained from discussing possible errors of judgement, but I have attempted to present both sides of any argument, leaving it to the reader to decide whether things might better have been done differently. To appreciate exactly why a certain action was taken it is essential to try to see the situation through the eyes of the participants. One needs to know what events led to the situation developing, and what pressures were influencing those making decisions. In war it is seldom difficult to know what you want to do, or indeed how you would like to do it; the problem invariably lies with the means. This was certainly the case at Goose Green for both the commander of 2 Para and his opposite number, Lieutenant-Colonel Piaggi. The principles of war, of strategy and of tactics are similar, simple enough to understand; it is their application in practice that is the problem.

In most military operations Murphy's Law takes over long before a shot is fired. Things go wrong from the outset; confusion, sometimes chaos, are normal. Even before the enemy takes a hand a subordinate may make an error, a vital piece of equipment is lost or breaks down, expected support is not available, information is lacking and conflicting, there is insufficient time for reconnaissance or planning, the weather is bad, units are fatigued, or last-minute changes must be made. A host of unexpected and unremitting problems make up the friction of war. Fortunately both sides have their share — as at Goose Green. I have endeavoured to illustrate these stresses and difficulties through the experiences of both British and Argentine participants.

In order to give as balanced a view as possible I have included a lot of detail of the Argentine actions. With both sides I have tried to tell the story by using the experiences of individuals with differing ranks and tasks. Wherever possible I have made use of quotations of participants to illustrate how a task was done, why it was done, and the problems encountered. Throughout I have made extensive use of maps or sketches in which I am a

8

firm believer as a means of explaining military operations. While striving for accuracy I would ask the reader to regard the maps as showing approximate positions or movements. I have also made use of notes, not only to indicate references, although they have been used for this purpose, but also to elaborate on points of interest or add details. The comments and opinions not directly attributed are mine, and as such represent no official viewpoint.

During the Falkland campaign the British forces operated on Zulu time (GMT) which was four hours ahead of local time. This made dawn at 10.30 am and dusk at around 8.30 pm which I find confusing, so throughout the book all timings are local.

It is now ten years since Operation Corporate. This is long enough for the dust of battle to settle, long enough for personal animosities and prejudices to mellow, but not long enough for memories to fade completely. In interviewing or corresponding with over 40 participants, many of whom have long since left the Army, most were able to relive and describe events in which they took part with surprising clarity.

Soldiers serving in 2 Para are encouraged to remember Goose Green with an annual drum-head service, and sometimes in a more light-hearted fashion, such as when the Sergeants' Mess organizes a Goose Green Night. On one such occasion lamb stew was dispensed into mess-tins from a tent marked 'Fitzroy', and all the sergeants wore their Para combat smocks. To the majority of the Parachute Regiment Goose Green seems to represent both the best and the worst of the Falklands conflict. Best in the sense that they are intensely proud of what 2 Para achieved against the odds, and how it was at this unknown hamlet that they had been tested as professional soldiers and not been found wanting. Worst in that it was at Goose Green that they suffered severely in terms of comrades killed or injured, and that if it had to be done again it would undoubtedly be done better, with fewer losses.

The tenth anniversary of the battle, and the fiftieth of

the formation of the Parachute Regiment, in 1992 is surely an appropriate moment in time to take a closer look at the battle for Goose Green.

PROLOGUE

'Sunray is down.'

Sergeant Blackburn, Lieutenant-Colonel Jones's radio operator, at about 9.30 am on 28 May, 1982, near Darwin Hill.

'He was completely unconscious and the helicopter didn't arrive. For a few minutes afterwards I stayed there, trying to keep him warm with extra windproofs and his own quilted jacket. He died. I felt slightly numb because COs are not supposed to die.'

Sergeant Norman, Colonel Jones's bodyguard, Michael Bilton & Peter Kosminsky, *Speaking Out*.

He was not a difficult target to hit, the British paratrooper who had come running into view round the end of a spur that made up part of the ridge north-west of Darwin (see Sketch 1). He seemed to be on his own, carrying a sub-machine gun, helmeted, wearing only a belt with pouches over his uniform. These details were easily visible to the Argentine machine gunner in the trench, as he was only about 40 metres away. The soldier briefly disappeared from view as he continued to run up the small re-entrant, or gully, below and to the right of the gunner. At first it had looked as though he was making for the machine-gunner's own trench, but suddenly there was a shout, the paratrooper swung left and started up the bare slope opposite. He was heading towards another Argentine trench, the occupants of which did not seem to notice him.

COLONEL 'H'S SOLO CHARGE

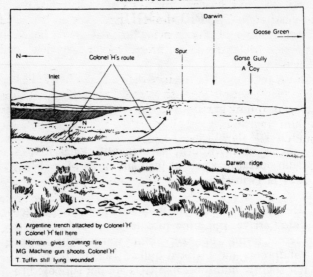

A Argentine trench attacked by Colonel 'H'
H Colonel 'H' fell here
N Norman gives covering fire
MG Machine gun shoots Colonel 'H'
T Tuffin still lying wounded

For a brief moment he seemed to stumble, crouch down and fumble with his weapon (he was changing magazines) before surging up the slope on his own.

As the Argentine swung his gun to the right he noticed that another man, who had followed the first soldier, was lying on the opposite slope firing frantically at the trench that was being attacked. These were the first British to get into this re-entrant since the battle had started in earnest at dawn, when some seven or eight paratroopers had also come under fire from his machine gun, and from other positions strung out to his left. At that time the heavy fire had driven them out quickly, but at least one was seen to fall, presumably dead, as his body was still lying on the slope of the spur[1]. The Argentine, who was probably a member of Lieutenant Estevez's platoon from C Company of the 25th Regiment, had only been in the line since just before first light. Prior to this the platoon had been held back in reserve just south of Darwin, but the rapid night advance of the British had led the

Argentine commanding officer, Lieutenant-Colonel Piaggi, to send forward Estevez's men, supposedly to counter-attack. This had proved impossible so they had occupied some of the trenches in what was the main Argentine defensive line protecting the airfield and settlement.

In the four hours or so since then a fierce fire-fight had taken place, with the British attempting to advance across the open, rolling grassland to his front (north), and up the (to him) invisible, gorse-filled gully the other side of the spur on his right. There had been much artillery and mortar fire, with the British using a lot of the dreadful white phosphorous mortar bombs which caused horrific burn wounds. Still, until this moment none of the attackers had come close to his part of the position since those first few minutes. Now it seemed that an attempt was being made to outflank the spur. When the machine gunner took aim at the back of the scrambling soldier he was getting close to his comrades' trench. It was a long burst. The rounds at first flicked up the dirt below the target; then, with a slight elevation of the barrel, they struck home, hitting the soldier in the small of his back, flinging him forward, almost to within touching distance of the trench. The figure lay still on the grass. The next ten minutes or so passed quickly for the machine-gunner; there was a lot of firing from the direction of the spur, and to his front, when suddenly a searingly vivid white flash and a vast explosion produced oblivion.

What this Argentine soldier never knew was that he had mortally wounded the commanding officer of 2 Para, or that he had been killed outright by a 66mm rocket, or that his death was the signal for the start of the surrender of seventy-four of his comrades on the ridge north-west of Darwin. This line had consisted of twenty-three trenches in which ninety-two men had been dug in, eighteen of whom had died. The vital ground overlooking the airfield and Goose Green had at last fallen.

It had been nearly 9.30 am when Colonel 'H' (he disliked his name of Herbert and was always known and referred to throughout the Regiment as 'H') made the decision that cost him his life. By that time he had been crawling around a gorse-filled gully with A Company of 2 Para for over an hour. This gully separated Darwin Hill proper from the slightly lower ridge that ran north-west for 1000 metres until it almost touched the shore overlooking Brenton Loch. The central part of the ridge had turned out to be the main Argentine position, in front of which 2 Para's advance had been halted for over three hours. Only a few minutes before, the by now utterly frustrated colonel had seen an attempt to storm the crest of the spur beaten back by intense machine-gun and automatic rifle fire. Three paratroopers had died, including the second-in-command of A Company, Captain Dent, and the adjutant, Captain Wood. Although Colonel 'H' probably saw these men fall, he could not have known for certain who they were. The officers were dressed identically to the soldiers, with badges of rank only visible from the front at close range. That he could not have known that Wood had been killed was a kindness — of sorts.

The relationship between Colonel 'H' and his adjutant was a close one. Although the gap of years and rank between them was substantial, there was a bond of friendship between these two like-minded professional soldiers. This had developed during their working relationship in the year that Colonel 'H' had commanded 2 Para. An adjutant is the commanding officer's staff officer, and as such has more direct dealings, more personal contact, with him than any other person in a battalion. In war it is normal for the adjutant to remain at the main battalion headquarters, while the commanding officer goes forward to command. This did not happen at Goose Green. Captain Wood went with his commanding officer, and was with him in the gorse gully that morning. In fact, the adjutant was following normal practice in 2 Para at the time. During training in Kenya in December, 1981, Colonel 'H' had invariably been accompanied by Wood whenever he left his main headquarters. At Goose

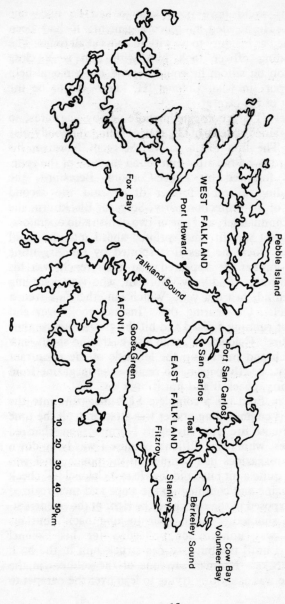

THE FALKLAND ISLANDS

Map 1

WEST FALKLAND

Fox Bay

Port Howard

Pebble Island

Falkland Sound

LAFONIA

Goose Green

San Carlos

Port San Carlos

EAST FALKLAND

Teal

Fitzroy

Stanley

Cow Bay
Volunteer Bay

Berkeley Sound

0
10
20
30
40
50 km

Green it would have been strange had he not gone forward. He needed no encouragement; it had been established as his duty to be with his boss at all times. The commanding officer took him with him as a close companion on whom he could depend for personal help and support in what Colonel 'H' knew was to be the highlight of his career[2].

Colonel 'H''s action caught those nearby unawares, so he had gained a lead of 25 metres before anybody else reacted. The first to do so was Sergeant Norman, his bodyguard, who ran after him round the base of the spur. He was followed by Lance-Corporal Beresford, the commanding officer's former driver and the second member of his protection party, Sergeant Blackburn, the battery commander, and one or two of his radio operators. The Colonel was fit, and sprinted ahead into the small re-entrant where he was first spotted by the Argentine machine-gunner. It appeared that this trench was his initial objective. Suddenly, Norman, who was pounding along behind, heard a yell, 'Watch out, there's a trench to the left'. On hearing this, 'Instinct took over and instead of running I dived and hit the ground just as they opened fire'. Colonel 'H', who also heard the shout, saw the trench and turned up the left side of the re-entrant towards it, briefly pausing to remove the magazine from his Sterling, check it and put it back on.

Norman fired off a complete SLR magazine into the trench his commanding officer was attacking, all the time under intense fire from his right. Norman then 'changed magazines, which was difficult because I was lying down and the magazines had jammed in the pouch, so I was flapping quite a bit but I did it'. He saw Colonel 'H' check his magazine and continue up the slope and then realized he was exposed to the trench on the right of the re-entrant. Norman shouted, 'Watch your fucking back', but his warning was unheard or unheeded for his Colonel continued until the burst of fire struck him in the back and buttocks[3]. Norman saw one of the soldiers in the trench he was assaulting trying to lean over the parapet to finish him off, but he failed as Norman continued to fire rapidly and accurately. He later described his thoughts during the next few minutes: 'Then I had a choice of staying there and firing, or I had a grenade. I thought: if I throw the grenade I'll neutralize the CO at the same time. I continued firing for what seemed like a lifetime.' Colonel 'H' died some 30 minutes later, without regaining consciousness, while awaiting a helicopter to fly him out, although those who were with him during that time were certain he was mortally wounded.

Colonel 'H''s gallantry was to make him the 41st lieutenant-colonel to be awarded the Victoria Cross out of the 1350 awarded since its institution by Queen Victoria after the Crimean War. The most recent was thirty years earlier, when the commanding officer of the Glosters had received it for his actions at the defensive battle on the Imjin River in Korea. It was in recognition of the way that Colonel 'H' always led his battalion – from the front. It reflected the success of his leadership as well as his personal courage. It had been Colonel 'H''s drive and determination that had made 2 Para the well trained, aggressive battalion that it was. It was his plan, his example, and finally his sacrifice, that gave 2 Para their will to win. Regrettably, he died without knowing that his battalion won the day.

The importance of a commanding officer cannot be over-emphasized. It is his character, his personality, that is reflected in his command, for good or ill. In any army it is these officers who have the greatest influence on morale and the standard of training. At no other level within the military does one man have such direct and personal influence on the spirit of a unit. In war he bears a dreadful responsibility. It is then that all he has achieved is revealed on an unforgiving battlefield. An American, Colonel David Hackworth, put it well when he stated of the infantry, 'I cannot think of a profession that is more demanding, deadly, and where the responsibility is more awesome'.

The strain of commanding in action is increased by the

17

closeness of a commanding officer to his men. It is the most senior level within an army at which all subordinates, even down to individual soldiers, are known personally. Jones was known throughout the battalion not as the commanding officer, or Colonel Jones, but as 'H'. In the year he had commanded them prior to Goose Green he had imprinted his personality and enthusiasm on all ranks of 2 Para.

Unlike more senior commanders, this close familiarity with his men makes many battlefield decisions infinitely more painful and stressful. When a commanding officer sends his men into a dangerous situation the weight of responsibility is keenly felt. The only way of lessening it is to share the risks himself, to be well forward to encourage, to influence, to show by example and, if necessary, to drive. At this type of leadership Colonel 'H' excelled. I believe it is highly likely that at that moment in the gorse gully, when all else he had tried seemed to have failed, when men he knew so well were dying carrying out his direct orders, that he instinctively reacted to put himself to the fore. For Colonel 'H' the objective was everything; the success of his battalion was a very special matter; the battle for Goose Green was the supreme test, the culmination of all his life in the army and the moment for which he had prepared himself for so many years. His cry of 'Follow me' and the desperate dash up the re-entrant was typical Colonel 'H' style leadership. Lance-Corporal Beresford summed it up afterwards: 'He always led from the front and never had anybody do anything which he couldn't do himself .... He was very close to everybody and they all respected his judgement, and I think everybody was quite happy to follow him to the end.'

His style of leadership has been described by several who served under him as 'Wellingtonian'. By this it is meant that he gained respect rather than affection from those under him. He could be extremely hard and unforgiving with his officers, and only seemed to trust one or two whose experience was greater than his. His anger

18

could be frightening, and his bawling out in public of sometimes quite senior officers could be a humiliating experience. Major Keeble, who took command on his death, later said of Colonel 'H': 'He was the originator and the source of everything that happened to 2 Para. The way the unit was constructed, the training, the emphasis, and speed, and the offence, all stemmed from him.' Colonel 'H' wanted nothing more than to take 2 Para to the Falkland Islands. As his wife Sara was to say, 'Had he failed he would have been impossible to live with'. The outbreak of hostilities found Colonel 'H' and his wife on a ski-ing holiday in Europe and 2 Para kitted up ready for a tour of duty in Belize. An advance party was already there doing jungle training. Colonel 'H' instantly abandoned his holiday and drove non-stop back to Britain, only pausing briefly on the motorway to telephone the Ministry of Defence to say he was on his way and that 2 Para must go. 3 Para had already been earmarked to join 3 Commando Brigade (Royal Marines), and to the commanding officers of 1 and 2 Para the prospect of being left behind was unthinkable. While Colonel 'H' raced home by car to plead his case, his counterpart in 1 Para, who were doing a four-month tour in Northern Ireland, flew to London for the same purpose. Ordinary soldiers wrote to Mrs Thatcher begging to be sent. In the end Colonel 'H' got his way, although it was, in practice, far simpler to cancel the forthcoming Belize move than replace 1 Para on operations in Northern Ireland. Ten years on it is still a sensitive subject with 1 Para that they never made it.

Colonel 'H' was 42 when he died at Goose Green. After education at Eton and Sandhurst, he was commissioned into the Devon and Dorset Regiment in 1960. He served in Australia, and what was then British Guiana; was adjutant of his battalion; served on the staff; obtained a secondment to the Parachute Regiment where he commanded the Mortar Platoon of 3 Para. He attended the Staff College at Camberley, and in 1975 he was the Brigade Major of the 3rd Infantry Brigade in Northern Ireland, for which he was later awarded the MBE. This was followed by a spell as an instructor on the Company Commanders' Division at the School of Infantry at Warminster. Then another staff post as a lieutenant-colonel in the UK. In this capacity he played an important part in planning operations for the peace-keeping force in Zimbabwe. His efforts were rewarded with an OBE. In April, 1981, he took command of 2 Para.

Colonel 'H' was an enthusiast. His year in command moulded 2 Para into a formidable fighting unit with a zest for soldiering that mirrored his own. He was a fervent advocate of fitness and shooting, probably the two most crucial and basic requirements of successful infantry soldiering. He encouraged all sport, and made the sniper section into an effective weapon system. The Padre, David Cooper, who is a Bisley shot and supervised the snipers' training as well as attending to the battalion's spiritual needs, thought extremely highly of the new commanding officer. He respected his ability both to give and inspire loyalty. He demanded exceptionally high standards, an individual's absolute commitment to soldiering, and to 2 Para in particular.

Padre Cooper, who got to know Colonel 'H' well, and in whom he frequently confided on their way to war, speaks of his dedication, of his quick brain, and above all his tremendous zeal. He tells of his commander's ability to establish a bond between himself and his soldiers by his example, and his way of conversing with them in a blunt and forthright manner which they readily understood. If some did not like him it was because they could not live up to his standards, but every man in the battalion grew to respect his professionalism.

Colonel 'H' was a black or white person who did not recognize compromise. He was certainly an impatient man, quick to anger when he felt he was being thwarted or frustrated, a characteristic that comes across clearly in the battle for Goose Green. Sara illustrates his impatience by recounting how, when playing a board game at home (invariably a wargame), he would move everybody else's counters to speed things up. He had a tendency to want to jump in and do things for himself if he felt something could be done better. On exercises he was always to be found at the front, often with the leading section, wanting to know what was happening, wanting to see for himself, and always pushing to keep things moving. On several such occasions the exercise umpires had ruled him 'dead'. There is no doubt that the way he died at Goose Green was typical of the man.

I

2 PARA

'... we are a body of people welded together by our traditions, by our regiment, by a feeling of togetherness. We're a family of people and you have to remember that. We all know each other, we know each others families. This is a body of people who would die for each other....We have to win, the mission is paramount. It is more important than anything else.'

Lieutenant-Colonel Chris Keeble DSO, 2 Para's second-in-command at the start of the battle, in an interview with Michael Bilton and Peter Kominsky for their book *Speaking Out*.

Most civilians do not realize that the great majority of young, single, soldiers welcome a posting to Northern Ireland. Over some 23 years to date it has provided every infantry battalion in the British Army with a training area where the targets sometimes strike back. Certainly, as professional soldiers they complain of the restrictions under which they must operate, or the often squalid conditions under which they must live, but they acknowledge that it is probably the only place where they can test their competence and their 'bottle'. The average infantryman in today's small, all-regular Army, feels decidedly naked if he is not eligible to wear the General Service Medal with the Northern Ireland clasp. 2 Para know Northern Ireland well. At the time of writing it has completed nine emergency (short) tours, and one 20-month tour. On 27 August 1979, the day the IRA assassinated Lord Mountbatten, 2 Para was ambushed at Warrenpoint suffering sixteen dead - precisely the same number who would later die at Goose Green.

2 Para went to war in the Falklands at full strength, some 650 all ranks. After it had sailed on 26 April the Regimental Sergeant-Major discovered several stowaways on board. They were soldiers who, due to age or minor physical afflictions, should not have gone but who could not contemplate being left behind. It was an early indication of the tremendous spirit within the battalion. For their unit, their mates, to sail off without them was unthinkable. An all-regular infantry battalion in the British Army is, or should be if it is well led, a family. The only difference with the Parachute Regiment is that it is a larger family than most as it extends to three regular battalions and three Territorial ones. As with any happy family, separation is hated and avoided. When 2 Para (3 Para was the same) knew they were to join the Task Force the easiest part of the preparation was filling vacancies. Officers, NCOs and Toms who were on courses, on postings away from the battalion, or instructors at the depot or other military schools, clamoured to join. Lieutenant Jim Barry was about to leave on a sailing selection trial for the famous America's Cup yacht race, but rejected it so as not to miss taking his platoon to war. No less than fourteen pairs of brothers were to fight at Goose Green.

Those who have never served in any of the Services find it difficult to understand how soldiers can sometimes relish the prospect of action, with the possibility of death or terrible wounds. To spend one's life, year after year training, but never to test one's stamina and skills against a real opponent can be most frustrating. A professional football team which has reached its peak performance needs a real match, preferably an international one, to prevent staleness, boredom and declining morale. So with soldiers. Not that they want a major conflict, with its attendant horrors and enormous loss of life, but the odd skirmish or small-scale battle every few years is a different matter. This hankering for action is illustrated in the average young soldier's willingness to serve in Northern Ireland, or the bitter disappointment felt within the Parachute Regiment in not being selected to serve in the recent Gulf conflict. For over two decades Northern Ireland has provided almost every infantry battalion in the British Army with a training area par excellence.[1] It does exactly the same for the modern army what the North-West Frontier did for the British Army in India up to the outbreak of World War 2 — sharpens up the infantryman's basic skills in a dangerous environment.[2]

When 2 Para sailed on the MV *Norland* they were going to join an elite formation, 3 Commando Brigade, which consisted of 40, 42 and 45 Royal Marine Commandos, plus their sister battalion, 3 Para. All these units had earned a reputation for fitness, fighting ability, and toughness second to none. Every man had come through a gruelling selection process with a pass rate of only 40 per cent. Everybody in 2 Para had earned their maroon beret, not by leaping out of aircraft, although they had all done that, but by passing test week in P (Pegasus) Company, which is done before parachute training.

P Company comes as the culmination of weeks of the most intensive physical and mental training schedules in the modern Army. The training is specifically designed to develop fitness, nerve, aggression, team spirit and a mental attitude that refuses to accept failure, an attitude that puts achieving a mission above all else. For five days the testing goes on, relentlessly, without let-up, every event done against the clock. Apart from the steeple chase, log race, speed marches, endurance march, assault course and stretcher race, there is 'milling' and the confidence course. Milling means fighting, not boxing. For one minute two soldiers flail away at each other giving and receiving punishment under the critical eyes of their instructors. They are looking not for skill, but for aggression and guts. The confidence course consists of a huge piece of scaffolding, called the Trainasium, on which the soldier's nerve is assessed.

The shuffle bars can be terrifying. They are two parallel, shoulder-width, scaffolding poles 45 feet above the ground along which the soldier has to walk, or rather shuffle, with arms outstretched. At intervals along the four-metre poles brackets have been attached so the man must lift his feet. Just before completing this he is ordered to stop and touch his toes. It is the standing jump, however, which causes more failures. It is designed to test instant obedience to orders, despite fear. From a platform 12 feet up the soldier must leap onto a similar one some six feet away. Once on the platform it looks impossible for a standing jump. But it seems far worse than it is as the second platform is about three feet lower, so the momentum of the jump carries the soldier across comparatively easily. On the command 'Go' from the instructor on the ground the man must hurl himself across. Three refusals and he is finished. The course is perhaps summed up in the phrase, 'There's no gain without pain'. Men who have been through this type of fitness and confidence training feel, and rightly so, that they are part of an elite. They belong to a brotherhood.

For the leaders there is much more. Section commanders, platoon sergeants and platoon commanders must all qualify on 'battle' courses run by the School of Infantry mainly on the Sennybridge training area in Wales, or on Salisbury Plain. It is on these exacting courses that the junior leaders within the rifle platoons gain the confidence that was to contribute so much to winning the battle at Goose Green.

2 Para, as it drew slowly out of Portsmouth harbour that spring day, was undoubtedly a highly professional battalion, but their average age was only 20, and with the exception of the officers commanding HQ Company, Major Mike Ryan, and B Company, Major John Crosland, none had real battle experience. Many had patrolled the streets of Belfast; some remembered the day, almost three years earlier, when their battalion was hit by the radio-controlled bomb attack at Warrenpoint;

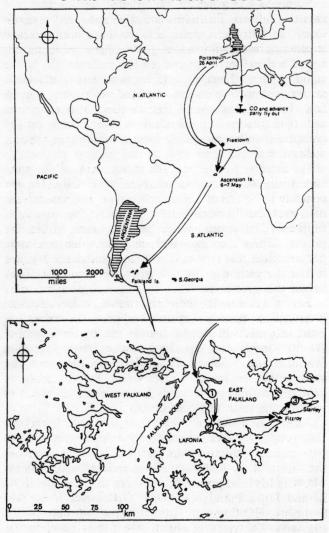

Portsmouth
26 April

CO and advance
party fly out

Freetown

N. ATLANTIC

PACIFIC

Ascension Is.
6-7 May

ARGENTINA

S. ATLANTIC

0   1000   2000
miles

Falkland Is.   S. Georgia

WEST FALKLAND

FALKLAND SOUND

EAST
FALKLAND

Stanley

Fitzroy

LAFONIA

0   25   50   75   100
km

26

but the Falklands was likely to be a full-scale conflict against a well-equipped modern army. A different matter.

No apology is made for the detailed introduction to 2 Para that follows. To understand what happened at Goose Green, and why, it is essential to know something of how an infantry battalion fights, and how 2 Para was organized, armed and prepared for battle. The basic tactics of the infantryman's offensive battle are simple to understand; they consist of two elements - fire and movement. His aim is to close with the enemy, destroy him, in order to seize and hold ground. Fire without movement is usually indecisive, while exposed movement without fire support is disastrous.

The attacker has the problem of advancing while at the same time nullifying or avoiding defensive fire. This was certainly to be one of 2 Para's dilemmas at Goose Green. An attack can be screened by darkness, fog or smoke, while every effort can be made to use covered approaches to get within striking distance of enemy positions. Achieving surprise is usually sufficient to win the day, but in war the ground or the situation sometimes precludes any of these methods. Then the enemy's defences must be beaten down by the attackers' fire while they advance. If an attack lacks surprise or superior fire-power, an increase in men will usually mean an increase in casualties. For the infantry there comes a time when other supporting fire must cease. For the last 100 metres their own fire must get them forward. Then a series of short dashes by small groups and individuals, covered by close-range fire from their mates, finally brings the attacker to grips with his enemy. Goose Green saw a lot of this type of fighting.

Appendix 1 shows in outline 2 Para's organization and approximate strength at the start of the battle, together with its artillery and engineer support. Under Colonel 'H', with his headquarters, were three rifle companies (A, B, and D), a Patrols Company (C Company), Support Company, HQ Company, plus the attached gunners and engineers. In terms of the fire and movement tactics discussed above, A, B, and D Companies constituted the

27

movement element, while Support Company and the artillery provided the fire support. C Company was primarily the battalion's reconnaissance sub-unit, and HQ Company looked after logistics.

One of the least understood aspects of a military attack is the numbers game. To be told that 2 Para, who went ashore with a strength of 620 men, attacked Goose Green means, to the uninformed, that 620 soldiers assaulted the Argentine positions. Far from it. It is the task of the three rifle companies, which at Goose Green contained a total of some 270 men, say 300 with attachments, to close with the enemy.[3] But not all three companies could, or should, have attacked simultaneously. An advance with two companies forward would mean probably four rifle platoons in the leading wave, so at most the cutting edge of the assault would consist of some 100-120 bayonets, perhaps a fifth of the battalion's actual strength. Such is the real arithmetic of a battalion attack. The bulk of the remainder of the unit exists to get these leading troops on to the enemy position. They command, control, support, or administer the rifle companies.

Appendix 1 shows battalion headquarters as fifty-six strong, and if other attached sub-units such as the Defence Platoon, medics and provost staff are added, a seemingly cumbersome organization of well over 100 men results - enough to provide another rifle company. Although swollen slightly by the addition of a Royal Marine and brigade liaison officer, an interpreter, a forward air controller, a naval gunfire liaison officer and two media representatives, Colonel 'H''s headquarters was not exceptionally large. It had two distinct functions — to command and to control. An important element of the Goose Green story is how 2 Para was commanded and controlled, so the method by which these functions were achieved needs to be clear.

Command was entirely the responsibility of the commanding officer, Colonel 'H'. He made the decisions, issued the orders and supervised their implementation. That was his job. He had to make his decisions regardless of the fact that the situation might be vague, confused, or illogical. Each event that occurs, each piece of information received, causes the commander to ask himself questions requiring decisions. Shall I continue with my present plan? Are new orders necessary? Should I commit my reserve now? Possibly the most worrying problem is the timing of the decision. Not what to do, but when. Certainly Colonel 'H' was to be acutely concerned about timings at Goose Green. In order to command, to make decisions, the commander needs to know what is happening. It is interesting to compare the British method of achieving this with that tried out by the US in Vietnam. American commanders often resorted to commanding from the air, in a helicopter, a system that came to be known as 'the great squad leader in the sky' method. It was fine in that they had absolute control of the air, and it gave a splendid view of the battlefield, but its great weakness was that it divorced the commanding officer from his men. There was no personal contact; he did not share the same fatigue or danger, and above all he could not effectively impose his leadership on his command. He was only a voice on a radio, heard by a few, but seen by nobody.

The British system, of which Colonel 'H' was a dedicated exponent, was to move forward, on foot in this case, close behind the leading companies with what is called Tac 1. This is a comparatively small group (about thirteen at Goose Green) consisting of the essential officers or men that the commander needs to help him make or implement his decisions, and influence the battle quickly. In Tac 1 with Colonel 'H' would be his adjutant and friend Captain Wood, two 'minders' (Sergeant Norman and Lance-Corporal Beresford), his mortar officer to bring down mortar fire (Captain Worsley-Tonks), the artillery battery commander to control gun support, (Major Rice RA), plus some seven signallers, without whom no decisions could be communicated.

As there is always a possibility of a commanding officer and his Tac 1 becoming casualties the command function is duplicated. There is a Tac 2, an alternative command element within the battalion headquarters. With 2 Para this was under the second-in-command, Major Keeble. With him were a Royal Artillery party, a mortar platoon party, and more signallers. In all about ten men.

The rest of battalion headquarters is known as Battalion Main (Bn Main), over thirty people whose primary function is to facilitate control, not command. Here, under an experienced major, in this case Major Miller, are found the operations officer, watchkeeping officers, the intelligence section, liaison officers, the signals officer, clerks, and more signallers. One of its tasks is to man radio links, both forward to Tac 1 and the rifle companies, and back to brigade headquarters. During any battle Bn Main would be required to co-ordinate the progress of the operation, communications, external fire support, resupply, and deal with prisoners of war. The large numbers making up the headquarters are essential if duties are to be maintained indefinitely on a 24-hour basis. For example, it is normally considered necessary to have at least two, preferably three, radio operators available to keep one set continuously open.

Making up the numbers to well over 100 at Goose Green would be the Defence Platoon made up from MT drivers without vehicles, and an RAP split into two with two doctors and their assistants. The Defence Platoon under Colour Sergeant Caudwell was, theoretically, responsible for the close defence of battalion headquarters but, as will become clear, he had other more pressing tasks at Goose Green.

Colonel 'H''s manoeuvre element was the three rifle companies. Each had a headquarters and three rifle platoons which provided the actual assault troops in any attack. This gave nine platoons, plus two more in C Company which could be made available as rifle platoons in some circumstances. A Company was under Major Dair Farrar-Hockley, whose father, General Sir Anthony Farrar-Hockley was then the Colonel Commandant of the Parachute Regiment. By a remarkable coincidence,

General Farrar-Hockley had been the adjutant of the Glosters in Korea when his commanding officer got the Victoria Cross for his outstanding leadership at the Imjin River battle. Now, 30 years later, his son was to be the company commander most involved when Colonel 'H' won his.

B Company's commander was Major John Crosland, whose special aura of authority and experience had been earned by service with the SAS in Oman. He was held in immense respect by his men, who were amused by his habit of wearing a black, woolly hat in the field instead of a helmet. Despite Colonel 'H''s explicit orders that helmets must be worn Crosland was still recognizable at Goose Green by his hat. His fund of ribald comments, which he brought out to emphasize a point, did a lot to raise laughs and spirits. In a tight situation he was fond of saying, 'I know I've got the right initials but even I can't walk on water,' or in the Falklands, 'This thing isn't over until I've got Menendez's balls on the end of my barrel'.

The third rifle company, D Company, was commanded by Major Phil Neame, who, like Farrar-Hockley, came from a distinguished military family. His father, Lieutenant-General Sir Philip Neame, won the Victoria Cross as a Royal Engineer lieutenant at Neuve Chapelle in 1915. Before he died, at the age of 90 in 1978, General Neame had also received the KBE, CB, DSO, Croix de Guerre (France), Croix de Guerre (Belgium), was a Chevalier of the Legion d'Honneur, a Knight of the Order of the White Lion (Czechoslovakia) and the Order of St John. His son had come to the Paras by way of the RAF Regiment. He was an enthusiastic and successful mountaineer as well as soldier, having climbed Everest and pioneered several new rock routes in Britain.

Each of these companies split their headquarters into two groups, similar to battalion headquarters, and for the same reasons – to facilitate command and to provide an alternative to take over if necessary. Company Tac usually consisted of the officer commanding, his escort/runner, and two signallers, one manning the forward link to the platoons, the other on the battalion net. Also moving with this group would be the artillery Forward Observation Officer and his signaller, with the task of calling for and adjusting gunfire support. In total Company Tac would contain about six men. The rest of company headquarters would move a tactical bound behind under the company second-in-command, usually a captain. His task was control and coordination. With him would be two signallers, one listening to what was happening on the company net, the other doing the same on the battalion net, plus the company sergeant-major. His main responsibilities in action included ammunition resupply, casualty collection and handling of prisoners. A Mortar Fire Controller, a junior NCO with a signaller, accompanies the headquarters to direct mortar fire support, and a similar party of two gunners make up the alternative FOO party. Finally, two or three medics and a pair of snipers might be attached. At Goose Green this total of eleven was boosted to fifteen by a small group of Royal Engineers.

Like most headquarters the problem on the move was the small forest of radio antennae waving in the air which announced the importance of the group from a considerable distance. 2 Para had the new Clansman radio sets which had shorter, low-profile, antennae but, in the words of the signals officer, they 'invariably impaired communications and were little used'. A signaller's job is not always a popular one, as not only does the soldier or junior NCO have considerable responsibility to get things right on the radio under stress, but he is a tempting target, and invariably bowed down by the weight of his set.

Lieutenant Ernie Hocking commanded a typical rifle platoon, (4 Platoon, B Company) at Goose Green. As a young man with a BSc in maths and physics, he had been commissioned from Sandhurst in 1981 into the Parachute Regiment. He had married exactly a week before boarding the *Norland*. 4 Platoon was his first command so some apprehension at being sent to war so soon was understandable. As at battalion or company level, as the senior member of in the platoon, Hocking's job was to command, so he carried a radio with which he could talk forward to each of his three section commanders who also had their own small sets. His number two in platoon headquarters was Sergeant O'Connell, again with a radio, so he could take over if Hocking was hit. There was also another signaller who humped the larger set and listened in to the company net. Also in the platoon headquarters were soldiers carrying the 2-inch mortar and 84mm Medium Anti-Armour Weapon. The small light mortar, with a range of 500 metres, gave the platoon the ability to put down an instant smoke screen or to illuminate the surrounding area at night with flares. As such it was a valuable weapon. Its drawback was the need for others to carry the bombs, and the lack of any HE ammunition. The 84mm, with its ammunition, was heavy and cumbersome, and Private Arpinio who was carrying it did not relish the prospect of long tabs. It was a good weapon in defense, but its suitability in the attack was something of a question mark.

Hocking's three sections were numbered 1, 2 and 3, each under a corporal. Corporal Montgomery with No. 1 Section only had five men instead of seven, with one GPMG group and one man carrying an M79 grenade launcher. The other two sections, No. 2 under Corporal Kenyon, and No. 3 under Corporal Norton, each had two fire teams of four men, with a GPMG to each team. The corporal commanded the section and one of the fire teams, while the lance-corporal commanded the second. At Goose Green most rifle sections had two GPMGs, double the normal allocation. While preparing in the UK, Colonel 'H' had demanded, and received, these extra machine guns. He believed that the SLR, which did not fire automatic, would not give sufficient volume of fire in the attack. Events were to prove him right. On the battlefield the most valued weapons in the assault proved to be the GPMGs, the 66mm LAW and the WP grenades.

Like the other platoons 4 Platoon had some twelve 66s,

and each man carried two WP grenades and two HE grenades. Although the 66 required the firer to expose himself by kneeling to get a good sight picture, it was light and produced the 'biggest bang for the buck'. It was to prove the decisive weapon for A Company on Darwin Hill as a bunker buster. The WP grenade could be used to produce a small, but instantaneous, smoke screen to get out of trouble, or as an anti-personnel weapon. Exploding in a confined space such as a trench, its effects were spectacular, usually lethal, and always agonizing and demoralizing, as phosphorus continues to burn despite every effort to extinguish it. In contrast the HE grenades were to prove ineffective. In the open men five metres from the explosion had a good chance of walking away unscathed.

C Company was small, only some fifty-five strong, with two platoons. It was commanded by Major Roger Jenner who, by 1982, had been in the Parachute Regiment for 20 years. Within that time he had done exceptionally well to have risen from private to RSM of 10 Para (V) before being commissioned as a combatant officer. At Goose Green he would be commanding a company of the same battalion he had joined as a soldier all those years before.

C Company's other name was Patrols Company, and this more adequately describes its role. It provided Colonel 'H' with his eyes and ears. Such a company is special to a parachute battalion. Under Major Jenner's small headquarters were the Recce Platoon and Patrols Platoon, each of six four-man patrols, identically equipped and organized. This interchangeability was adopted specially for the Falklands as each platoon normally had a different method of operating, and slightly differing tasks. The Recce Platoon, then under Lieutenant Colin Connor, would normally expect to operate with six stripped-down landrovers to provide fast forward observation posts, convoy protection and, as Connor put it, 'to furnish the battalion taxi service'. Although the platoon's vehicles were loaded on the *Norland* none were put ashore in the Falklands. Patrols Platoon, commanded by Captain Paul

Farrar, were more accustomed to being footbound. Their function was to man static OPs out in front of a defensive position to report movement or give early warning of enemy activities. Their more exciting duties involved the marking out and protecting of DZs ahead of a battalion parachute drop. For this every man was HALO qualified. In other words he was a military free-fall parachutist.

Colonel 'H' attached considerable importance to C Company, and as such had insisted that the platoons were commanded by more experienced officers than their size perhaps warranted. For example, Patrols Platoon was under a captain, whereas the company second-in-command was a lieutenant. The commanding officer had every intention of making the maximum use of these twelve small patrols to probe deep into enemy territory. They were the main means of seeking information over which he had personal control.

Patrols could have their radios on the battalion net, or could report to their company commander when he was co-located with battalion headquarters. Each was armed with SLRs, a GPMG, and grenades. Several M79s were carried within each platoon. Captain Farrar was, like many in the rifle companies, concerned with the fact that the SLR magazine only held 20 rounds and could not be fired on automatic. The conflict was going to be essentially offensive, to recapture the islands, so a high rate of fire was vital, which in turn posed resupply and carriage problems. He explained part of the dilemma:

Before the landings there was a lot of discussion about the use of the 30 round LMG magazine with the SLR. This had the obvious advantage of more rounds per reload, but there was some concern that the 'W' spring in the magazine would not be strong enough to ensure a reliable feed upwards into the SLR breech, rather than its designed [function] downwards into the magazine housing of the LMG. The quandary was resolved by intense test-firing at last light over the rear deck of the MV *Norland* - the so called 'gash shoot' i.e. shooting at bagged rubbish.... Every man put at least four LMG mags through his weapon without a single stoppage. It was then left largely to individual preference as to what to carry on landing. In my case I opted for a normal 20-round mag for starters, but if in a fire fight could use the 30-round mags in which I carried the bulk of my remaining ammo. Each patrol carried in the region of 1300 rounds of ammunition. All bar about 200 was loaded in magazines. In my case I started with 330 rounds - I have a note of this figure. I fired 169 at Goose Green.

Support Company, as its title implies, was designed to sustain the rifle companies, not with ammunition or food, but with firepower. Within this company were the battalion's own heavier and specialist weapons. In any battle this company was likely to play a key role in dissuading the enemy from offering prolonged opposition. One of the controversies of Goose Green involves the use and effectiveness of Support Company so its composition and capabilities need explanation. It was under the command of Major Hugh Jenner (no relation to Roger Jenner), an officer who had spent most of his previous service in the Cheshire Regiment. He had volunteered for secondment to the Parachute Regiment much later than most, and found himself having to complete the Pegasus Company course at the age of 36. That he did so successfully speaks volumes for his stamina and determination. His three main platoons had mortars, medium machine-guns and Milan anti-tank missiles.

The Mortar Platoon, under Captain Worsley-Tonks with 44 men, was the strongest platoon in 2 Para. It had to be, as not only did it have to provide crews for eight 81mm mortars, but also an MFC party to accompany up to four company headquarters, plus the one moving with Tac 1, and a reserve party available to Tac 2. All eight tubes firing together packed a heavy punch. The 81mm mortar has a maximum range of 5,650 metres with HE using supercharge, 5000 with normal ammunition. It can also fire WP (smoke) or illuminating rounds. Each of the four sections of two mortars is under a sergeant with a crew of three. They fire from what is called a baseplate position, which is usually split, for security reasons, into two groups of four mortars. Their fire, which is highly lethal to infantry in the open, is controlled and adjusted by the MFCs well forward with the advancing troops, or from a forward trench in a defensive situation. To support a lengthy advance they would again expect to be divided into groups of four, each leap-frogging forward alternatively so that at least half the platoon could be firing at all times.

Their rate of fire is only dependent on the speed the crews can drop bombs down the barrels — eight rounds per minute is normal, twelve the top rate. With the entire platoon firing at maximum speed it is possible to have sixty or more bombs in the air at one time. But there are serious drawbacks to the 81mm mortar, all related to its weight. The platoon has vehicles (landrovers for parachute battalions) on its establishment to carry the mortars and ammunition. Although the mortars can be broken down into barrel, bipod and baseplate loads of around 12 kilograms each (26lbs), to expect a soldier to move far or fast with this added to his normal equipment is unrealistic. Then there is the ammunition problem. Each HE round weighs 4.5 kilograms (10lbs). If no transport is available, how are the hundreds of bombs needed to be got forward? Half an hour's normal firing by half the platoon could require nearly 1000 bombs - about two for every man in a battalion. 2 Para had no vehicles ashore for the mortar platoon. Colonel 'H' and Worsley-Tonks were both acutely aware of this looming difficulty. After the landings and march to Sussex Mountain, during which every soldier had indeed carried two bombs, Colonel 'H' said, only half-jokingly, to Colour-Sergeant Cotton, the second-in-command of the platoon: 'Your mortars almost killed my battalion'.

One of the new concepts being tried out by 2 Para was

the grouping together of six GPMGs in the sustained fire role into a machine-gun platoon. The standard practice was for the tripods, special heavy barrels, and other kit, to be held by the rifle companies for use at their discretion. This setting up of what was, in effect, a medium machine-gun platoon was harking back to the days of over 20 years earlier when battalions had the old Vickers machine-gun. The GPMG had been the infantry's machine gun since it replaced the Bren gun in the light role, and the Vickers in the sustained fire role, in the early sixties. In this latter capacity, on its tripod, it could produce a heavy volume of fire for prolonged periods to a range of 1800 metres. One snag was that spotting the strike at this distance was difficult as tracer rounds burn out at 1100 metres.

This platoon was under Lieutenant Lister, whose main worry was, like the mortars, weight – how to carry everything without vehicles. One gun with 50 rounds weighs nearly 13 kilograms (28lbs). Fifty rounds would disappear in a few seconds. What was needed was tens of thousands of rounds in belts up with the guns. A machine gun acts by fire alone. Movement serves no other purpose than to secure a better fire position. It was movement that was likely to be difficult with only eighteen men in the three gun sections, but vital if the platoon was to keep up with the rifle companies as they advanced, and then support them on to their objectives. On the MV *Norland* the plan was for each gunner to carry the gun, plus up to 800 rounds; the Number 2 the tripod, spare barrels, other accessories, and more ammunition; while the NCO section commander had his rifle, with as many belts and bandoliers as could be festooned about his body.

Major Hugh Jenner's third main support platoon was the Anti-Tank Platoon under Captain Ketley. Each of his three sections, led by corporals, had two Milan launchers (Firing Posts or FPs) with each Milan having a team of three men. The Milan is a wire-guided anti-tank (armour) weapon and comes in two pieces - the launcher and the missile. It is a simple matter to clip both items together, thus making the system ready to fire. Its maximum range is 2000 metres, rate of fire 3-4 missiles per minute, and it can penetrate 352mm of armour plate. It made a nasty mess of anything at the receiving end, although it did not pack the punch of the former anti-tank gun, the wombat. It was, nonetheless, a useful weapon, which was going to be fired in action for the first time in the Falklands. 2 Para was to have this honour, although not against tanks.

Like all weapons, Milan was not perfect. It was expensive to fire — £8000 per missile at 1982 prices. If the target was at extreme range the firer had to keep the cross hairs of the sight aligned for up to 13 seconds, which was the time of flight of the missile. If the target was static this was not always necessary as the tripod could hold it in the aim unassisted. 2 Para had not been issued with the night sight, so it was only a daytime weapon, unless there was considerable illumination. Finally, it was cumbersome to carry, and heavy. The launcher had no special carrying frame, and as it had to be carried with the tripod attached for quick reaction, it made an extremely awkward load. The intention was that one man would take the launcher, another two missiles, and the third one missile and the radio. None could be expected to go far and fast over any distance or rough terrain. Without transport of some kind Support Company were under no illusions — they were going to have a hard war.

Making up the remainder of the company were the Assault Pioneer Platoon, some twenty-four strong, under Sergeant Bell, and the Sniper Section of twelve men, commanded by Sergeant Head. The former, whose expertise included basic field engineering, mine-laying and lifting, construction work, and booby-traps, had little inkling that most of their time in action would be spent as beasts of burden humping other people's ammunition. The latter, who operated in pairs, could be attached to companies, or their activities centrally coordinated by the commanding officer, through the intelligence officer, to supplement the battalion's information gathering capacity. As mentioned earlier, the padre, Captain David Cooper, spent a lot of his time assisting with their training.

HQ Company normally contains more men than any other company in a battalion. It is a reflection of the fact that, for every man in the firing line, there are infinitely more behind him supplying his needs. In this company is the Signals Platoon, whose signallers are to be found at every company, and at battalion's headquarters; the drivers and mechanics for the battalion's vehicles, who in this case were to become ammunition carriers; the MO and his staff who form the RAP, and the numerous cooks, orderlies, clerks, storemen, and regimental police.

At Goose Green Major Mike Ryan was the company commander. He was the same age as Colonel 'H' and the most experienced combat officer in 2 Para. He had joined the Army in 1962 but resigned when he was refused permission to try for the SAS. He then served with the Rhodesian Army and later in Oman as a contract officer where he participated in the tough campaign against the rebels in the Dhofar. He had rejoined the British Army in 1971. Colonel 'H' nominated him as third-in-command of the battalion. His responsibility was to keep 2 Para supplied with the means to fight — food and ammunition. Doing this without transport over long distances, dependent on infrequent helicopter lifts, was to be something of a nightmare. The system adopted was to split the logistic effort into two parts called, in military terminology, 'A' and 'B' Echelons. 'B' Echelon, under the quartermaster, Captain Godwin, would have responsibility for getting the battalion's needs forward from the MV *Norland* (afterwards from the brigade beachhead) to the area of 2 Para's operations. It was to be a testing task for the quartermaster. Upon his skill and initiative in begging and bargaining for helicopters depended 2 Para's ability to function.

At, or near, Bn Main 'A' Echelon took over. It received all the ammunition, food, equipment, or other supplies, broke them down into company requirements, and then had to get them forward to the consumers. Coordinating all this was 2 Para's technical quartermaster, Captain Banks Middleton.[4]

So much for 2 Para. It is time to look at their enemy and to examine the situation confronting the Argentines as the MV *Norland*, and the rest of the task force steamed south. The reader is asked to remember that these details of the opposition are considerably more revealing than the information available to 2 Para. Goose Green was no exception to the battlefield norm, when both sides fight in varying degrees of ignorance about each other.

II

TASK FORCE MERCEDES

'Some of my relatives come from Britain, and knowing the British character I was not surprised that they decided to send a Task Force to the South Atlantic. My feeling was that if you tread on the lion's tail, it sometimes turns round and bites you'.

2nd Lieutenant Pelufo, a former Argentine platoon commander in the 12th Regiment, who fought on the ridge NW of Darwin. *Speaking Out*

1st Lieutenant Carlos Estoban arrived at Goose Green within 36 hours of the Argentine capture of Stanley. On 2 April, 1982, Stanley fell to a marine landing force, consisting of an amphibious commando company, a few guns, and a platoon from C Company 25th Infantry Regiment. Estoban commanded C Company. Within hours of their success the bulk of the Argentine 9th Brigade were on their way to the islands as the occupying garrison. The leading unit was the remainder of the 25th Regiment, to be followed later by the 8th Regiment and a marine battalion. The Argentines' initial deployment was in no way intended to defend the Falklands from any counter-attack. It was dispersed to establish a presence, to raise the flag, and to demonstrate to the population that the Falklands were now the Malvinas. The 8th Regiment went to Fox Bay on West Falkland, while the marines and the 25th Regiment stayed at Stanley on East Falkland. The only exception was C Company.

Estoban was 27 years old, the son of a former Air Force NCO, who had done exceptionally well to graduate second in a class of 250 from the Army Military Academy. He was to be described by the Goose Green manager as 'a real soldier'. This was his first independent command. His commanding officer, Lieutenant-Colonel Mohamed Ali Seineldin, was 100 kilometres away in Stanley.[1] In the event Estoban was to be on his own for over three weeks, only linked to his superiors by radio and telephone, and the occasional helicopter visit. His role was to secure the small grass airstrip, ensure the locals understood and complied with the new Argentine administration, and to send patrols to probe north to the settlements of San Carlos and Port San Carlos. For the present his tasks were more concerned with civil and administrative affairs than military.

Although delighted and proud to be in the Malvinas, Estoban was not particularly impressed with the settlement of Goose Green. In fact the remoteness and lack of people reminded him of Chubut Province in southern Argentina, where his regiment had recently been based. Goose Green, with its even tinier neighbour Darwin, sits on an extraordinary freak of nature − a land bridge between the large islands of East Falkland and Lafonia. This bridge, or isthmus, is a mere ten kilometres long and two wide. It is a narrow, bare, windswept strip of land on which scarcely 100 people live.

It blocks the channel between the two larger islands, adding 150 kilometres to the sea journey from Stanley to the settlement of Port Howard on West Falkland. It also sits on the southern land route from Stanley to San Carlos. To travel by land, and few islanders chose this method, from Stanley to San Carlos or vice versa you must drive along the tracks north of the central mountain chain via Teal Inlet, or take the longer, southern, route through Fitzroy and past Goose Green.[2] Neither Estoban nor anybody else, Argentine or British, had any inkling that this soggy soil, these low ridges and open grassland, would be the scene of the first and longest battle of the conflict.

Goose Green is typical of any of the larger settlements dotted round the coast of the 'camp', as everywhere other than Stanley is called. Its sole purpose is to shelter sheep farmers. There is a manager's house, bunkhouse, store, community hall, a small school, a handful of houses and a scattering of shearing sheds or barns. During the battle the entire civil population of Goose Green and Darwin, 114 people, crouched on and under the floor of the community hall.[3] The only facility of significance is the landing strip. It is the main one in the west of East Falkland. For this reason Goose Green merited a permanent Argentine garrison.

One Argentine regiment approximately equates to a British battalion in that they are both between 550-650 strong and have three rifle companies as their striking force. Like their British counterparts Argentine companies have three platoons each, although these platoons tend to be larger, as they often include supporting weapons such as heavy machine guns and are organised on American lines with stronger squads under sergeants, rather than the British system of eight men sections under corporals.

C Company was to play a crucial part in the fighting; Estoban was to come through unscathed and win the al Valor for his actions. It had been one of Estoban's platoons that had represented the Army in the assault on Stanley. 2nd Lieutenant Roberto Reyes had almost fifty men with him when he occupied Stanley airport on the afternoon of 2 April. He had clambered up the spiral stairs of Cape Pembroke lighthouse to tie the Argentine flag to the rails, giving firm orders to the keeper that it was not to be touched. Reyes was also destined to be the first officer into action against 3 Commando Brigade, just prior to their landings on 21 May.

A fellow platoon commander was Lieutenant Roberto Estevez who was to be pitted against A Company of 2 Para in their struggle for the ridge NW of Darwin, and whose machine-gunner was, in all probability, the one who shot Colonel 'H'. Estevez himself was also to die on Darwin Hill, the only Argentine officer to be killed in the battle. Like Colonel 'H', he received a high decoration posthumously – the Cruz La Nacion. His friend, the third platoon commander, 2nd Lieutenant Gomez Centurion was also to win the same decoration, although he lived to wear it. Centurion himself was commando-trained, but although all of C Company wore a distinctive green beret it was of no real significance. It was to be this officer, who spoke excellent English, who conversed with Lieutenant Barry of D Company, 2 Para, just before Barry was shot dead in a 'surrender' incident.

Estoban's soldiers were all conscripts. There is no such thing as a regular private in the Argentine Army. The professional soldiers are the officers and NCOs. The former are an elite class, many belonging to families with military traditions stretching back for generations. Brigadier-General Menendez, the Argentine Governor and overall commander in the islands, had a son serving in the 5th Regiment which went to Port Howard at the end of April. The social gulf between the officers and conscripts is seldom, if ever, bridged, even when units live in the field. The officers have, by right of rank, numerous privileges denied their soldiers. Even their rations are better, with special officers' packs containing a variety of meat dishes, toilet paper and small bottles of brandy.

The Argentine officer corps came under heavy criticism by the British for their behaviour and lack of control over their men in the Falklands. Sergeant Norman, of 2 Para, was particularly forthright after Goose Green when speaking about the condition of the houses in the settlement.

The Argentinians had left Goose Green a pigsty. We went into some of the houses and they had deliberately shit in the bath.... The houses stank, and I couldn't understand how any army ... could allow themselves to degenerate into living in a pigsty. I could not feel less for the officers if I tried. They were contemptible for allowing their

men to suffer the way they did. They had a lot of
food and comforts whereas the soldiers had very
little ... they treated their men in the most
unprofessional way.[4]

After the surrender many officers objected vociferously to
being detained with their men, even demanding to keep
their pistols to protect themselves.

Nevertheless, the subsequent accusations that the
officers at Goose Green deliberately skulked in the rear
during the fighting were mostly baseless. The company
and platoon commanders fought from their trenches
alongside their men, and four officers and two conscripts
received decorations for gallantry, one platoon
commander (Centurion) for rescuing a wounded NCO. It
was the cadre of regular NCOs that formed the second of
the three classes within the Argentine Army. They were
men who had volunteered for a military career but did not
have the education or upper class background to gain
acceptance at the officer school. They did not have to serve
as privates, but rather went straight to NCO training
establishments. The successful completion of these
courses secured the rank of corporal. Many also went on
to become specialists on a variety of equipment and
weapons such as radios, or heavy support weapons. Like
the officers they had little in common with the conscripts,
although it was they who, year after year, had to carry out
most of the training of these reluctant soldiers.

The nine brigades in the Argentine Army are composed
of regiments whose main preoccupation is to act as
training units for the nation's young conscripts. Every
male youth is liable for a year's military service on
reaching the age of 19. These boys (chicos) start their
training every January, when up to 600 are assembled at
each regiment's barracks. In practice most are only in
uniform for ten months as it is often February before all
are assembled, and to release everybody by Christmas
means some start trickling away in late November. It is a
surprisingly relaxed regime, with many recruits able to go

home at weekends, and sometimes at night during the week if they live close to their camp. It also has some serious drawbacks which the Falklands campaign immediately underlined.

The regiments are perpetual basic training institutions. Only at the end of a year are they reasonably trained, or able to undertake anything but the simplest tactical exercise. Then, almost overnight, they become completely untrained units filled with raw recruits. This is no way to fight a war, especially as in this case the conflict started in April, with the conscripts only a few weeks into their training cycle. These were men born in 1963. The only solution was to recall reservists. There was a desperate rush to do so as extra units were earmarked for the Malvinas when the crisis mounted, and it became certain that Britain would make a landing to try to retake the islands. Men who had left the Army the previous December found themselves recalled. As Major Cuillermo Berazay, of the 3rd Regiment, explained to the British author Martin Middlebrook:

> We had to be in the Malvinas in thirty-six hours! So we returned [from an exercise] to La Tablada to start recalling reservists ... We managed to change two thirds of our new men for reservists and off we went. We were even processing reservists right up to the last minute. I remember a convoy of lorries loaded up with men to go to El Palomar airport, with reservists still coming in, hurriedly changing their civilian clothes for uniforms, and jumping on the lorries.[5]

The contrast with the fitness and professionalism of the Royal Marines and paratroopers of 3 Commando Brigade could not have been more marked.

The sailing of the British carriers *Hermes* and *Invincible* packed with aircraft on 5 April, followed by the *Canberra* with three Royal Marine Commandos and 3 Para on board on the 9th, came as a shock to the Argentine Junta coming, as it did, so quickly after the UN resolution for Argentina to withdraw. With only three regiments in the islands, reinforcements were required at once. From 11 to 16 April 9 Brigade, under Brigadier-General Oscar Jofre, flew into Stanley. Jofre, whose nickname was 'the Horse' due to the shape of his features and bulky appearance, commanded a mechanized brigade consisting of the 3rd, 6th, and 7th Regiments. However, apart from the 10th Armoured Car Squadron, the bulk of the vehicles, including the armoured personnel carriers, had to be left behind. Jofre had been woken at one in the morning on the 9th with the news that he was to take his men to the Malvinas. He was delighted, but it was the start of the most frenzied few days of his life. He was appalled at the prospect of going to war with recruits, so absolute priority was given to replacing them with reservists. It was only early April so none of the recruits had received any training on the heavier support weapons, the machine guns, anti-tank guns, or mortars. These were locked away in armouries and had now to be handed out to the reservists as they came in. What a way to go to war. Although they were more fortunate than the troops already in the islands, or indeed than subsequent reinforcements who were forced to fight with far higher proportions of recruits. All units of 9 Brigade were deployed around Stanley, and Jofre, who became the land forces commander under Menendez, issued instructions that all units must be ready to defend the islands by 18 April. This was also the day on which Buenos Aires received confirmation that the British Task Force had sailed south from Ascension Island.

On 22 April an important planning conference took place at Moody Brook barracks just west of Stanley. Earlier that day Menendez and Jofre had escorted General Galtieri in a long helicopter ride around East Falkland; now they reviewed their defensive plans for Galtieri. As with all military plans, their first task was to agree an objective, which in the widest sense was to prevent the British retaking the islands, but for planning purposes had to be refined into something less vague. Galtieri accepted that in the end the retention of Stanley was the key. It was appreciated that Stanley would become the main British objective; that whoever held Stanley held the Malvinas. Other places, like West Falkland, or the larger settlements such as San Carlos or Goose Green, were of secondary importance. The Argentines' basic strategy would be to hold Stanley and fight their main defensive battles on the approaches to it.

They really did not have any other option as far as a land battle was concerned. There was no way of knowing where the British would come ashore, although it was felt that the main landing would be as close to Stanley as possible. Concern was expressed at the Moody Brook meeting at the large numbers of helicopters that would give the British both speed and flexibility in choosing landing sites. The age old problem of the defender, lack of the initiative, manifested itself. Even by confining their efforts to the defence of Stanley the Argentines could not be strong everywhere; they could not know from which direction the main enemy thrust would come, and they were worried that at least one diversionary landing might take place.

On his map Menendez tapped several possibilities. Uranie Bay, Berkeley Sound, Stanley harbour, the beaches south of Stanley, even Fitzroy-Bluff Cove were feasible. Jofre later stated that San Carlos was mentioned but rejected because of the distance (90 kilometres) from Stanley. At that time four infantry regiments, less C Company 25th Regiment at Goose Green, were earmarked for holding Stanley, with the fifth isolated on West Falkland. Galtieri brought up the obvious problem — there was no strong central reserve.

That night Galtieri flew back to Buenos Aires promising to send a regiment to make good this deficiency. He went one better and sent a brigade, although so many more troops would compound the critical logistic difficulties confronting Menendez's staff. While the men and some equipment could be flown in, the bulk of the heavy stores, food and ammunition needed ships. Jofre's men had arrived by air, but all their cooking equipment, for example, took twelve days to arrive by sea. At that time he only had fifteen days reserve of rations and ammunition sitting on the *Formosa* in Stanley harbour. With the rapid approach of the British ships to tighten the blockade and enforce the total exclusion zone around the islands, plus the certainty of heavy air attacks on Stanley airfield, the prospect of keeping an enlarged garrison supplied seemed bleak.

The additional, and as it transpired the last, infantry reinforcements were the 4th, 5th and 12th Regiments of 3 Brigade under Brigadier-General Omar Parada. Of all the remaining seven brigades still in Argentina it was probably the least battleworthy. Its normal location was near the Uruguay border, in the sub-tropical north, and it departed in such haste that insufficient reservists could be recalled in time to replace the recruits. Men literally climbed aboard their transport aircraft in the clothes they stood up in carrying only their personal weapons. Radios, vehicles, support weapons, spades, even rifle cleaning kits, had to be left behind to follow by sea. The vessel on which these items were loaded never sailed.[6] The thoughts of some of these young recruits are not hard to imagine as they saw their units frantically rushing round local shops buying up spades to take on the aircraft. These regiments arrived lacking the two basic essentials needed to fight – training and adequate weapons. Why, one wonders, did such ramshackle regiments get sent to the war at all? The 6th, 8th and 11th Brigades were all better equipped, with the latter stationed in the south of Argentina kitted out and trained for winter warfare. The answer lies in the fact that Argentina did not dare remove any of these frontier formations from the Chilean border. For years Chilean and Argentine relations had been strained, particularly over ownership of two islands in Tierra del Fuego. To weaken these frontier defences might tempt Chile into taking advantage of the Falklands conflict.

Of the three new regiments it was the 12th that was to fight at Goose Green. Under the command of Lieutenant-Colonel Italo Piaggi, it arrived at the settlement on 24-25 April. Estoban lost his independence and thereafter came under Piaggi's command, his company replacing the 12th Regiment's B Company which had been detached at Stanley to become Menendez's heliborne strategic reserve force.

Before looking at the situation facing Piaggi at Goose Green, it needs to be stressed that this settlement had no critical importance, from the Argentine point of view, in the forthcoming ground operations. Like San Carlos it was a long way from Stanley, its loss would in no way affect the Stanley defences, and nobody in Menendez's headquarters thought the British would go anywhere near it. It was reinforced because Goose Green airstrip was the best practical alternative to Stanley for Pucara aircraft.

The Pucara played an important role at the start of the conflict. It is not generally appreciated that this aircraft was the only fixed wing plane that could be deployed in, and operate satisfactorily, from the islands. Even Stanley airport was unsuitable for combat aircraft, and an obvious target for British bombers. The Pucara, named after an Inca hilltop fortress, was to make several appearances over the Goose Green battlefield, gaining the reputation as being particularly effective against helicopters. It was designed as a two-seater ground attack counter-insurgency aircraft, but in the Falklands it was normally only crewed by the pilot. Its advantages were its manoeuvrability, low stall speed of 78 knots, coupled with its formidable firepower. It had two 20mm cannons, four 7.62mm machine guns, and could additionally carry either three Bullpup air to ground missiles, napalm, or bombs.

Four Pucaras were deployed to Stanley on the day of the Argentine invasion. They came from the thirty-five operational aircraft of Grupo 3, and by 9 April an entire squadron of twelve, under the command of Major Navarro, had been based at Stanley. The Argentine Air Force staff became increasingly concerned about the

Pucara's vulnerability on the ground, and the likely damage that would be inflicted on the Stanley runway. There was also the growing problem of air traffic and ramp congestion. They searched the islands for alternative strips. Their reluctant conclusion was that the spartan strip at Goose Green was the best of several poor options. The grass runway was only 450 metres long, totally exposed to the wind and weather, with a disconcerting undulation on the strip which made take-offs something of an adventure. Despite these drawbacks Goose Green was considered preferable to Pebble Island, whose runway was longer but was liable to become waterlogged. Pebble Island was, however, earmarked as the alternative to Goose Green.

By mid-April Goose Green had been designated as Air Base Condor under the command of Vice-Commodore Wilson Pedroza. Major Navarro was instructed to be prepared to deploy most of his squadron to Goose Green by 14 April. Meanwhile the Air Force contingent at the settlement was steadily built up. This included several helicopters, anti-aircraft guns, plus associated Air Force personnel, many of whom were cadets flown in to act as observers in remote areas but, as yet, no Pucaras. Air defence was based around two twin 35mm Oerlikon and six twin 20mm Rheinmetall guns. The former had a range of 4000 metres and were equipped with Skyguard radar with three man crews from B Battery of the 601st Anti-Aircraft Regiment. The 20mm guns, manned by Air Force personnel, had only half the range but almost twice the rate of fire, 1000 rounds per minute. Both weapons could fire armour piercing ammunition with tracer or HE shells. Like the old German 88mm anti-aircraft gun of World War 2 vintage, these weapons were to prove highly effective against ground targets.

It was not until 29 April, with the British warships approaching the 200 mile exclusion zone, that Navarro moved all his twelve Pucaras to Goose Green. Prior to this, on the 24th, the inhabitants and soldiers at the settlement had merely been treated to a Pucara firepower demonstration when several planes strafed one of the small, empty islands in the channel to the east of the village.

With the arrival of 3 Brigade the Argentines' build up was virtually complete. They had some 13,000 men in the Malvinas, the infantry component being eight regiments with between 5000-6000 men. The British landings would see five battalions ashore, with another three arriving nine days later. The Argentines' advantage in numbers of men was slightly more marked with artillery. They had assembled two complete artillery regiments, each with eighteen 105mm pack howitzers, plus another six with B Battery of the Marine Field Artillery. Additionally there were four 155mm guns, also in the Stanley area – forty-six artillery pieces opposed to the thirty-six guns the British ultimately brought ashore. On the ground the Argentines were numerically superior, but not overwhelmingly so. In terms of training, morale and aggressiveness, the British were far superior although neither side had experienced a major conflict, and they remained uncertain of each other's qualities until after Goose Green.

The Argentines' deployment of major units at the end of April is shown on Map 3. There were to be no significant changes throughout the conflict. The commander-in-chief and governor of the Malvinas was Menendez and, with the arrival of 3 Brigade, he assumed direct control of the forthcoming operations by also acting as Land Forces Commander. Because the Argentine Army has no divisional system there was a surfeit of brigadier-generals at Stanley. In addition to Menendez, there were the three brigade commanders – Daher of the 9th, Jofre of the 10th, and now Parada with the 3rd. With the best part of three brigade headquarters staff officers were not scarce either. Menendez sorted out the seniority problems by confirming Daher as his chief-of-staff and dividing the islands by an arbitrary vertical line some 25 kilometres west of Stanley. Jofre got the Stanley Sector with his own brigade plus the 4th and 25th Regiments. All units west of the line, in what was termed the Coastal

Sector, went to the new arrival, Parada, who was told to move himself and his staff to Goose Green. This would relieve some of the officer congestion in the capital, and should enable Parada to come to grips with his scattered command – he had the 12th Regiment at Goose Green, the 5th at Port Howard, and the 8th at Fox Bay. Parada dragged his feet over the move so that when the battle took place he was still at Stanley. His tardiness was the subject of criticism after the war.

Lieutenant-Colonel Piaggi arrived at Goose Green the day before 2 Para sailed from Plymouth. He was a tall man, with a shaven head and a striking resemblance, according to Martin Middlebrook who interviewed him, to the television detective Kojak. His command was a mixed bag, which henceforth was called Task Force Mercedes after the town at which the 12th Regiment had been based. As noted earlier, Piaggi had lost his B Company at Stanley, together with several of his staff. Estoban's C Company of the 25th Regiment filled this gap numerically, but the officers and NCOs were unknown to him. Then there was the Air Force. Vice-Commodore Pedroza was of the same rank, but slightly senior, which could have caused problems. In the event it did not, and the two officers worked amicably together with Piaggi controlling the ground operations, which eventually included using Air Force personnel as infantrymen.

In the rush to leave Argentina insufficient reservists had arrived to replace all the recruits. A large proportion of the 12th Regiment were boys of nineteen, with just four months' service, from the Class of 1963. The Argentine equivalent to 2 Para's C Company (Patrols Company) was their Reconnaissance Platoon of some thirty men under Lieutenant Carlos Morales. It was not a part of a rifle company, but came directly under Piaggi's control. The two rifle companies of 12 Regiment present at Goose Green from the end of April until the end of the battle were A Company, commanded by 1st Lieutenant Jorge Manresa, and C

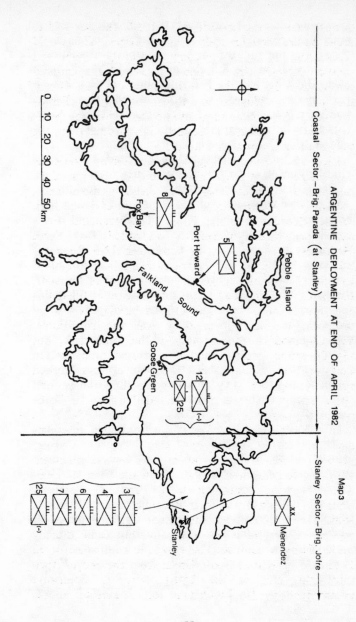

ARGENTINE DEPLOYMENT AT END OF APRIL 1982

Map 3

Coastal Sector — Brig. Parada (at Stanley)

Stanley Sector — Brig. Joffre

0 10 20 30 40 50 km

Fox Bay

Port Howard

Falkland Sound

Pebble Island

Goose Green

Stanley

Menendez

55

Company under 1st Lieutenant Ramon Fernandez, both with three platoons. Adding to the ad hoc nature of Piaggi's command was a platoon from yet another C Company, from the 8th Regiment, based 50 kilometres away the other side of Falkland Sound at Fox Bay. Its platoon commander, 2nd Lieutenant Guillermo Aliaga, had been one of the recent batch of cadets commissioned in a hurry at the beginning of the month. Quite how he ended up at Goose Green is uncertain, but he must surely have felt somewhat bewildered by the speed of events, and finding himself so far from his own unit.

Piaggi had other worries apart from the inexperience and hotch-potch nature of his command. These were in the realm of equipment deficiencies. Virtually all his heavier equipment and weapons had been left in Argentina in the scramble to get away. It was supposed to catch up eventually, but never did. Like 2 Para, 12 Regiment lacked vehicles, the only ones available at Goose Green being a few locally commandeered landrovers. He allocated one each to A and C Companies of his regiment, to carry the only radio sets available for his rifle companies. One other went to Morales with the Recce Platoon.

His men also lacked training, unit esprit-de-corps, mobility and radio communications. They had inadequate support weapons. Out of an establishment of ten 81mm and four 120mm mortars, Piaggi claims to have had two of the former and only one of the latter. He also stated later that of thirteen 105mm recoilless rifles he had one, which had no sight. Even with the light machine guns he maintained he could muster less than half the normal allocation of 25.[7] Apart from the anti-aircraft guns there was no artillery at Goose Green.

Piaggi's orders were to guard Goose Green, Darwin and the airstrip. Deterring attack from the air was the responsibility of the Air Force and AA gunners; his role was to protect them from assault from the land or the sea. Brigadier Parada had told him to concentrate on dealing with a seaborne landing. It all seemed somewhat far-fetched. Nobody felt Goose Green to be of great strategic value, it was possible that a small force might be sent to capture the airfield, but the main British landings and thrusts would certainly be aimed at Stanley, or in its vicinity. Piaggi was also puzzled by the emphasis on the seaborne threat. Why and how would an enemy force navigate up the treacherous channels to the NW or SE of the isthmus? If they did there were some 10-12 kilometres of beach on either side on which they could land. There was no way he could spread his three companies to cover all this ground and provide close protection for the settlements and airstrip. Surely an attack, if it came, was more likely to arrive by helicopter. Piaggi attempted to resolve his dilemma by deploying Manresa's A Company about three kilometres north of Goose Green, on the general line of the high ground west of Darwin, and Fernandez with C Company (12th Regiment), on the low hill feature one and a half kilometres SW of Goose Green. Both these companies could watch the beaches on either side of the isthmus adjacent to their positions and, at the same time, block it to approaches from the north and south.

Aliaga was posted to overlook Salinas beach directly west of Goose Green, while Estoban's company was kept in reserve at the settlement (see Map 4). Priority would be given to laying mines along likely beach or land approaches as soon as they could be ferried forward from Stanley.

The 1st of May 1982, is the date the Argentines claim the war started. For them it began at 3.46 am with a stick of twenty-one bombs falling from an RAF Vulcan attacking Stanley airfield. Within fifteen minutes the Argentine Air Force commander, Brigadier Luis Castellano, was on the radio to Major Navarro at Goose Green. The major was instructed to launch Pucara sorties from first light, with the task of locating any British troops who might have landed by helicopter during darkness.[8] Navarro was also told to be prepared to move his entire squadron to Pebble Island should Goose Green become untenable. He briefed his pilots for what was to be a disastrous day at Goose Green.

Navarro's intention was to launch two flights of four aircraft in rapid succession starting at first light (6.30 am). The Pucaras always flew in pairs, or sections. The first flight leader, Captain Ricardo Grunert, with his wingman Lieutenant Calderon, would head south, while the second section with Lieutenants Russo and Cimbaro checked on a possible heliborne landing in the Stanley area. Due to a technical hitch with Grunert's aircraft at the last moment, the second pair was cleared to take off first. Russo surged down the short strip with throttle wide open, hit the undulation which lifted the aircraft slightly, causing Russo to believe he was airborne and start to rotate (pull up) prematurely. After a few moments the Pucara came down heavily. Only with enormous effort did Russo clear the fence at the end of the runway, although not before the nosewheel leg had struck a landing light. Cimbaro took off without mishap. Worse was to befall the next section.

This time it was Calderon's machine that was slowed by the nose wheel dragging in a patch of deep mud. The Pucara pitched forward before standing on its nose with the tail high in the air, blocking the runway. Clearing the obstruction took twenty minutes, delaying the take off of the next section with Lieutenants Hernandez and Jukic. As these two aircraft taxied out to the strip at about 7.25 am three British Sea Harriers screamed into attack.

They came from No.800 Squadron on *Hermes*, carrying parachute retarded and cluster bombs, led by Lieutenant-Commander 'Fred' Frederickson. All three approached low and fast down Falkland Sound to attack Goose Green from the NW. These raiders were totally unexpected. A few bursts of small arms fire were all that could be brought to bear as the Sea Harriers rose sharply up to drop their ordnance before wheeling away out of sight. The AA gunners could not fire in time. Staff and ground crews made a desperate dash for cover but many failed to make it. A cluster bomb struck Antonio Jukic's

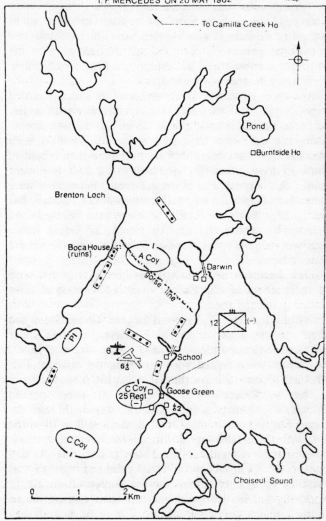

Pucara which was blown apart and burst into flames killing the pilot instantly. The Sea Harriers left the airfield in chaos with one Pucara destroyed, two seriously damaged, several fires burning, an ammunition dump in danger of exploding, and five dead and fourteen wounded Air Force personnel. Two of the injured were to die during the subsequent helicopter evacuation to Stanley. The Army escaped unscathed.

An hour later the three airborne Pucaras returned expecting to land. Grunert was turned away with orders to fly to Pebble Island; Goose Green airfield was closed. Over the next few days four more of Goose Green's Pucaras were sent to Pebble Island where they remained until 15 May, when D Squadron of 22 SAS Regiment raided that airstrip and destroyed them. Four more were flown into Goose Green on the afternoon of 15 May, but by the 20th they were back in Stanley as the Pebble Island disaster had convinced the Air Force that Goose Green was too vulnerable to commando attack. By the time 2 Para advanced on the settlement only three damaged aircraft were left near the strip as decoys, together with large numbers of Air Force personnel with no obvious duties to occupy them.

Within three days the ground forces at Goose Green had their revenge. Again three Sea Harriers, this time under Lieutenant-Commander Gordon Batt from No.800 Squadron, were tasked with attacking the airstrip. Batt planned to run in from the SE, with his second aircraft piloted by Lieutenant Nick Taylor, to attack parked Pucaras with cluster bombs. Once they were through the target Flight-Lieutenant Ted Ball would follow from the SW with three 1,000 pound bombs to crater the runway. This time the AA gunners were alert and waiting. As Ball banked for his approach he 'caught sight of him [Taylor] running in exactly where he was supposed to be ... Suddenly his Sea Harrier burst into flames; it continued flying for some way then it crashed into the ground with a huge ball of fire. Probably he was killed before he hit the ground, otherwise he would have had time to eject.'[9]

The AA defences had been warned to expect air attack by the radar controllers in Stanley. The Skyguard radar of the 35mm Oerlikons picked up the Sea Harriers as they flew up Choiseul Sound. As the leading pair flew straight in all the guns opened up. Cannon shells ripped into Taylor's aircraft and it impacted just short of the airstrip to the yells of triumph from the gun crews and watching troops. First Lieutenant Estoban was the first to reach the wreck:

It was in pieces along the airfield. The pilot was dead, still in his seat, with his parachute partially open. I think he died on impact. His body appeared to be quite intact externally, and his flying helmet was OK. I had a camera but out of respect I decided not to take a photograph. I found a piece of paper near him with navigation notes showing the location of the task force. I think that was a big mistake.[10]

Taylor was given a military funeral by the Argentines before being buried near the graves of their own men killed on 1 May.[11] The ceremony was shown on television. It was the first Sea Harrier lost by the British.

On 12 May Goose Green's Oerlikon gunners were again in action. Once more they were successful, although this time with tragic results for the Argentines. It was to be what the British term a 'blue on blue' incident, when a unit accidentally inflicts casualties on its own side. On this occasion the pilot of a Skyhawk, 1st Lieutenant Gavazzi, returning from an attack on HMS *Glasgow*, in which he had put a bomb which failed to explode clean through the ship, strayed too near Goose Green. He took a route which was forbidden to Argentine pilots, and he paid for his error with his life. On the ground the initial elation at seeing the aircraft spin down into the ground turned to tears when the troops went to examine the wreckage.

For the first three weeks of May all the action at Goose Green had been by, or against, aircraft, in which Piaggi's troops had been merely interested spectators. Nevertheless they had work to do. On 1 May, after the destructive Sea Harrier attack, the Argentines adjusted some of their defensive positions nearer to the houses at Goose Green in the belief that British aircraft would avoid attacking the settlement directly. Estoban later put it bluntly: 'I had already decided that, if air attacks came, I would move my defences from around the school, which was separate from the settlement, to new positions around the houses, with the idea that the British would never bomb the settlement area.' Helicopters were also parked between houses for the same reason.

As part of this policy of using the civilian houses as protection from attack was the decision, also taken on 1 May, to centralize all the civilian inhabitants in the community hall, and to use the empty houses for troop accommodation. Estoban had become exasperated with the uncooperative activities of some civilians: 'They left lights on at night, let animals out onto our minefields, and sometimes cut off the water and petrol. I thought it better to concentrate them all in one place in the centre of the settlement, with a red cross painted on the roof.'[12] June McMullen, the wife of a shepherd, who was born in Goose Green, described it thus:

> When we first went into the hall we were told it was for a meeting. We thought they simply wanted to talk to us and then we would go back home .... We just had what we stood up in. The first night was pretty cold .... Then we were able to sort something out and go and get mattresses and blankets. Conditions in the hall were pretty grim. There were 114 of us in there and only two toilets and two wash basins.[13]

During May the Argentines were alert to the certainty of a British landing, but it was impossible to know exactly where. Neither Piaggi nor his superiors had any reason to suppose it would be near Goose Green, or that their enemy would ever mount more than air attacks, or possibly a commando raid, on the garrison. For the weeks preceding the landings Piaggi's men dug bunkers and trenches, laid extensive mine fields, carried out some patrols, and watched with mounting excitment as the air war came to Goose Green. But there was no redeployment of troops.

On 15 May Estoban was summoned to his commanding officer. Piaggi explained that the high command at Stanley was concerned with the apparent ease with which HMS *Alacrity* had sailed unreported through Falkland Sound on the night of the 10/11 May, during which she had sunk the supply ship *Isla de Los Estados*. Weapons, vehicles and 325,000 litres of helicopter fuel had gone to the bottom. Piaggi told him he was getting his second independent command. He was to assemble a force of some sixty men from his own company, together with others from A Company of the 12th Regiment, to form what Piaggi called 'Eagle Detachment'. There was now concern that no troops were positioned to keep watch on Falkland Sound's northern entrance. Estoban, with Eagle Detachment, was ordered to take on responsibility for observing the Sound, giving early warning of any landings in the area, and controlling the settlement of Port San Carlos.

Estoban set off immediately. With him went 2nd Lieutenant Reyes with his platoon, plus men from Manresa's company. Piaggi could only spare two 105mm anti-tank guns and two 81mm mortars, hardly sufficient to deter a landing but then at that stage such a possibility near Port San Carlos was still considered remote. Estoban established himself in Port San Carlos with a detachment ten kilometres away to the NE on Fanning Head, an 800 feet high, windswept, rain lashed promontary jutting out into the Sound. This detachment had the heavier weapons, a radio, a stunning view of Falkland Sound, and one of the most uncomfortably exposed locations in the islands. Although Estoban rotated the soldiers the weather on Fanning Head was so appalling that a number had to be evacuated by a borrowed landrover, suffering from exposure.

What neither Menendez, Parada, Piaggi, nor Estoban could know was that they had picked the spot that had been selected for the landing of 3 Commando Brigade five days later. Eagle Detachment was to have the first ground skirmish of the conflict.

III

OPERATION SUTTON

'David, this is a bloody shambles'.

Lieutenant-Colonel 'H' Jones OBE to his Royal
Marine liaison officer, Captain David Constance, as
2 Para moved towards the beach in its landing craft
in the early hours of 21 May, 1982.

The one thing above all else that commanders and troops
taking part in an amphibious landing dread is opposition.
As men and equipment are packed shoulder to shoulder
in landing craft they are acutely aware of their
vulnerability during the slow, seemingly endless approach
to the beach. A direct hit on the craft by virtually any
weapon heavier than small arms can cause carnage. If the
vessel strikes a mine, if it capsizes for any reason, the
troops, weighed down with equipment, stand little chance
of surviving. Modern landing craft can carry up to 200
men. The destruction of one before it hits the beach means
the loss of at least an entire company, perhaps more, some
25 per-cent of a battalion at one stroke. When the LCU
reaches the shore the ramp is lowered allowing the soldiers
to pour out onto the beach. At this moment, too, their
vulnerability is acute. They are bunched together, moving
ponderously under the weight of their kit, anticipating the
possibility of a machine-gun opening up on a perfect
target. Opposed beach landings are usually expensive in
terms of casualties.

For these reasons the overriding problem for the British
in Operation Sutton, the actual landings in the Falklands,
was how to achieve surprise, how to get ashore, if not

unobserved, at least with sufficient time to prepare defensive positions to protect the beachhead before any counter-attack could be mounted. Brigadier Thompson and his planners needed a landing place that was within striking distance of Stanley, had suitable beaches for the LCUs, could be approached during darkness, and was unoccupied by the enemy.

On 13 May, in the wardroom of HMS *Fearless*, Thompson issued his orders for Sutton. The assembled commanding officers had already seen the brigade's lengthy (47-page) written operation order the previous day, so they all knew what was involved, but the 'O' (Orders) group, as this gathering was called, was essential for the brigade commander to put across personally to his unit commanders what he expected of them. The mission of 3 Commando Brigade had been sent to Thompson by Major-General Moore RM in a signal from the UK. Moore intended to take command of all the land forces about a week after the initial landings, by which time 5 Infantry Brigade would be due to go ashore. In the light of the doubts later expressed about the need to attack Goose Green Moore's directive is given below:

> You are to secure a bridgehead on East Falkland, into which reinforcements can be landed, in which an airstrip can be established, and from which operations to repossess the Falkland Islands can be achieved. You are to push forward from the bridgehead area so far as the maintenance of security allows, to gain information, to establish moral and physical domination over the enemy, and to further the ultimate objective of repossession. You will retain operational control of all forces landed in the Falklands until I establish my Headquarters in the area. It is my intention to do this, aboard *Fearless*, as early as practical after the landing. I expect this to be approximately on D+7. It is then my intention to land 5 Infantry

Brigade into the beachhead and to develop operations for the complete repossession of the Falkland Islands.

Colonel 'H' had only been re-united with his battalion for six days as he had flown ahead to Ascension Island and come onboard the *Norland* there. This had meant that the responsibility for getting 2 Para ready for war on the voyage south rested with the second-in-command, Major Chris Keeble. A comprehensive training programme had filled every working day. Honing up on individual military skills such as shooting, weapon handling, map reading and fitness were very necessary. Much of the fitness effort involved running round the ship in soft shoes to spare the deck and reduce the noise. When Colonel 'H' joined at Ascension Island he immediately insisted on continuous running in combat boots by all companies in rotation. From then on the ship reverberated to the thunder of pounding feet. A number of special subjects, however, merited extra effort.

The most crucial of these was training in how to stay alive. The point was that casualties were going to occur and, unlike Northern Ireland, an operation was not going to stop immediately a soldier got hit. In the Falklands achieving the objective would take priority over treating, or evacuating, wounded. Looked at from the enemy point of view it is often better to wound rather than kill. A dead man is left, and the unit is one man short. An injured soldier demands attention by others to treat his wounds, and to carry him away to safety. Up to four comrades may be involved in evacuating one man - result five men no longer fighting. Similarly, it is a common tactic of snipers to wound a soldier in the expectation that his friends will expose themselves in their efforts to drag him behind cover, thus presenting the marksman with more targets. These things can break the thrust of an attack. It was appreciated that the Toms would have to learn self-aid rather than first-aid. The medical officer, Captain Steven Hughes, instituted a crash programme of what he called basic 'battlefield resuscitation'.

Every soldier had his 'puncture repair kit'. Not just the usual single field dressing but two or three, as high velocity bullets make two wounds, one at entry and a bigger one on exit. Crepe bandages were issued to ensure elasticity and effective pressure to stop bleeding. There were obviously going to be wounded who could not care for themselves, so Hughes concentrated on teaching at least three or four men in each platoon to be combat medics. 2 Para's solution to the problem of the badly injured was based on the letters ABE - Airway, Bleeding, Evacuation. With extensive loss of blood just stemming the flow is often not enough, the fluid loss has to be replaced. The combat medics were trained to set up an intravenous drip, using the half-litre bag of Hartmann's solution that every soldier carried inside his smock to keep it warm. Many of the trainees, however, found locating a vein difficult. Hughes later described his answer to this problem:

> As a last resort, unsure how effective a method it is, we taught the guys to put the end of the IV tube (not the needle!) into the casualty's anus - rectal infusion. Lots of criticism followed the teaching of this technique. No one has yet proved whether it works or not, but if there's no one to put in a drip and you've got a ready-made hole, what have you got to lose?[1]

Battlefield resuscitation and self-aid proved their worth at Goose Green when wounded often lay in the open for many hours before evacuation. Not one member of 2 Para who reached the RAP died of his wounds.[2]

Another aspect of warfare was unfamiliar to the paratroopers - an amphibious landing. Leaping ashore from landing craft is normally the job of the Royal Marines, but as 2 Para was now in their brigade, Captain

Antrim

'Fanning Head
Mob'

③

SBS

Intrepid

3 Para

42 Cdo

Fearless

⑤   Port San Carlos

San Carlos Water

40 Cdo

45 Cdo

San Carlos

⑥

2 Para   Sussex Mt.

②?

SAS

①   ④

Goose
Green

Ardent

KEY

① Suspected Argentine strategic reserve

② Possible Argentine thrust for Sussex Mt.

③ SBS land and attack Fanning Head Mob with Antrim's support

④ D Sqn 22 SAS' diversionary raid on suspected reserve

⑤ Assault ships launch first and second waves of landings

⑥ 2 Para moves from beach to Sussex Mt.

3 Cdo Bde units' final locations

0   5   10 km

David Constance RM was attached to 2 Para with particular responsibility for developing and practising drills for getting the entire battalion off the ship, either through the side doors or from the two helicopter decks. Constance had attended a crash course prior to joining 2 Para and was able to supervise one daylight practice of disembarking into landing craft during the *Norland*'s brief stop at Ascension Island. Jumping from a ship into an LCU is often worse, in terms of danger, than leaping into the water on the beach. In anything other than a flat sea the LCU moves up and down with the swell like a yo-yo so that the soldier must time his jump exactly right to avoid falling up to 20 feet. It is also an incredibly slow process, which was not helped by the lack of scramble nets on the *Norland*.

The third priority was to train everybody, but in particular the officers, NCOs and radio operators, in the use of the new radios. The 'Clansman' series of radios were brand new, the latest sets, produced with increased range and reliability for the infantry, but which 2 Para only received on the *Norland*. The fact that they had been on issue to the rest of the Army for several years is an indication of the low priority given to 'Out of Area' (out of Europe) operations. They were to prove excellent radios.[3]

Finally, every effort was made to maintain morale. The occupants of the *Norland* were mostly paratroopers, plus a few gunners, a small Royal Navy detachment, with the Merchant Marine officers and crew. There was none of the friction, inter-Service or inter-unit rivalry, that was evident on the *Canberra*. Major Keeble ensured a happy ship, with training interspersed with sports days and recreation. The Toms were usually able to get a more generous ration of beer than the official limit of two cans a day, and emphasis was given to preparing the troops mentally for the trauma of battle.[4] In this the padre played a key role. He had the happy knack of being able to talk to the men in their own language, as an equal. The Toms respected him as a soldier, knew of his ability as a marksman, and found discussing their feelings and fears with him wholly beneficial. In one of his shipboard sermons he said: 'Okay, on the way down you're going to book in for some credits by coming to church, but I can't guarantee it's going to give you any luck; because some of you will not be coming back. All I will guarantee is that you will be looked after whether you come back or whether you don't.'

Throughout the voyage the British serviceman's unique sense of humour was always evident. When the *Norland* crossed the equator around midnight in mid-May the ship's naval duty officer made the following announcement on the tannoy: '... and if you care to observe from the starboard bow you will notice the illumination of the line of buoys that marks this particular latitude across the Atlantic Ocean'. Sure enough, a number of gullible persons emerged to see this eighth wonder of the world.

Brigadier Thompson and Commodore Mike Clapp, who commanded the Amphibious Task Group that would actually put the troops ashore, together with their staff, had been responsible for selecting San Carlos as the landing point. The selection process had involved spending a lot of time on their hands and knees peering over a large map spread out on the floor of Thompson's cabin. There had been nineteen possible beaches before these had been reduced to three — Cow Bay/Volunteer Bay, Berkeley Sound and San Carlos. As Thompson said: 'San Carlos was the favourite. It provided everything that Clapp and I wanted. Its only drawback was the distance from Stanley.'[5] The three alternatives were put to General Moore, who consulted Northwood, who in turn had them considered by the Chiefs-of-Staff and the Cabinet. San Carlos was accepted.

For Thompson the planning process had not been without its frustration. To him, his superiors at Northwood did not seem to grasp the problems of an amphibious landing. On board HMS *Fearless* he would often be summoned to the telephone to be asked:

71

'What's your plan now?' and I would give the plan and be grilled about it and asked why I wanted to do it in that particular way. Often the ship would be in rough seas, so one was clinging on to something to avoid being thrown about while talking over a rather bad and crackly line . . . . Frequently, in order to have a five or ten minute conversation, I would be in this little shack . . . for half an hour, scribbling frantically with my notebook balanced on my knee, trying to remember what had been said to me.

Northwood's ignorance of what an amphibious landing involved was not reassuring. As Thompson explained:

I put over the points I wanted covered only to be grilled about why this or that had to be done. I assumed the reasons were pretty obvious. Plainly they didn't understand how an amphibious operation should be carried out. It was quite a low point.[6]

As Colonel 'H' listened to the opening remarks of Thompson's intelligence staff officer, Captain Rowe, it became clear that one of the primary reasons for selecting San Carlos was the apparent absence of the enemy from the vicinity. The nearest Argentine troops were at least 30 kilometres away at Goose Green. The British intelligence on the Argentine locations on 13 May is shown on Map 3. A reinforced brigade (10th Brigade) was centred on Stanley, with artillery, engineers, anti-aircraft guns, Tiger Cat and Roland missiles, plus some helicopters and armoured cars. Their 3rd Brigade was occupying West Falkland, with a regiment and guns at Port Howard, and another, plus engineers, at Fox Bay. Pebble Island, Fox Bay and Goose Green were identified as operating airbases. At Goose Green/Darwin Rowe indicated an understrength regiment of 300-500 men, possibly supported by some artillery, anti-aircraft guns and/or missiles, logistic troops, and a number of Air Force personnel. Of considerable interest was the possibility of the enemy's heliborne mobile reserve of an infantry regiment, artillery and a special forces company being based near Fitzroy. At San Carlos, nothing. As to Argentine morale the intelligence assessment was that they were likely to be hungry, indeed it was thought they would run out of rations by 18 May, that they had suffered heavy losses from British air attacks, and that consequently they were somewhat demoralized and unlikely to fight well.

After hearing details of the air and naval support available for the landing, Thompson stood to outline his mission and plan. The objective and general outline were crystal clear:

> Mission: To land at Port San Carlos/Ajax Bay complex and establish a beachhead from which to launch offensive operations.
> Execution: General outline. A silent landing in three phases. Phase 1 - a simultaneous beach assault by two commandos to secure San Carlos Settlement and Ajax Bay complex. Phase 2 - two battalions concurrently to secure San Carlos Settlement and a defensive position on the reverse slope of Sussex Mountain. Phase 3 - the move ashore, by helicopter, of the artillery and air defence systems to cover the beachhead.[7]

As the British lacked air superiority it was vital that the troops were landed by night, with sufficient hours of darkness left to occupy defensive positions from which to repel anticipated enemy ground or air attacks in daylight. As the helicopters could not operate at night there would be a dangerous period immediately after first light, as the guns and Rapier anti-aircraft batteries were flown to their positions ashore, but it was unavoidable. The Phase 1 landing would be by 40 Commando at San Carlos Settlement and 45 at Ajax Bay, which was to be the brigade's main logistic base. In phase 2, 3 Para would secure Port San Carlos, while 2 Para went for Sussex Mountain. Both battalions would use the LCUs returning from the first phase. The primary aim was to seize and secure the beachhead area as a base from which to launch an advance on Stanley. At this stage it was still the intention that 5 Infantry Brigade would be landed in Ajax Bay to reinforce 3 Commando Brigade before the ground forces moved east in strength.

As the commanding officers boarded their helicopters for the flight back to their own ships there was only one critical piece of information lacking. The D-Day date, and the timings of the landings, such as H-hour - the time the first wave of LCUs hit the beach. These were to follow by signal. Like the others, Colonel 'H' had been given the outline of the signal, the various headings designated by letters, so that the message could eventually be sent as a list of coded figures and timings, easily decipherable by the receiver using his formatted outline.

Colonel 'H' now devised his own plan to get 2 Para on to Sussex Mountain which, in the worst scenario, might have to be assaulted. On that assumption he decided on the allocation of the four available LCUs to the companies, the order of march from the beach, the equipment loads to be carried, and an outline plan to take the mountain. The first LCU was to contain C Company, to lead the way to Sussex Mountain, lay out a suitable start line and secure it for any necessary attack. If all went well this company would then deploy well forward of the mountain in a number of OPs. A Company, also in LCU1, would follow C Company in the move forward to be the right assault company in any attack. Tac 1 would be in this LCU, together with a small engineer recce party. In all nearly 180 men.

LCU2 would have B Company as the third company in the line of march, and the left assault company onto the mountain. The remaining load was made up of two 81mm mortars, Support Company headquarters, the Assault Pioneer Platoon, and half of Bn Main HQ — some 170 troops. LCU3 had D Company as the reserve, half the

RAP, half the air defence detachment, the MMG Platoon and another two mortars, making a total of over 150. Finally, LCU4 carried the remainder of the RAP and air defence detachment, the Anti-Tank Platoon, the Defence Platoon, snipers, two sections of mortars, Tac 2, and the rest of Bn Main, totalling about 120 men. 2 Para would leave the *Norland* around 620 strong, the craft loaded in such a way that the loss of one would not completely destroy the command, control, fire support or fighting ability of the battalion.

A major cause for concern was the weight of equipment each man had to carry. Helicopter lifts would be for the artillery, Rapiers, bulk ammunition and stores, the infantry having to hump everything they would need to live and fight for the first two days. Riflemen had their own weapon with at least seven full magazines, four grenades, rations, two full water bottles, entrenching tool, web equipment and bergen stuffed with arctic clothing, sleeping bag, washing kit and spare boots. Then they had to find room for the extras - two or more bandoliers of ammunition for the GPMG, individual weapon sights, spare radio batteries, bombs for the platoon 2 inch mortar, rockets for the 84mm rocket launcher, 66mm rockets, shells for the M79 grenade launcher. Every man had to carry some of these items. Then, finally, two 81mm mortar bombs weighing nine kilograms were given to each soldier just prior to disembarking. Captain Farrar described it thus:

> The equipment was distributed as evenly as possible; nevertheless the weight was incredible. I would not like to put a figure on it, but it was certainly the heaviest weight I have ever carried .... My webbing and bergen were so tightly packed that it was impossible to include anything else. I honestly believe it would have been impossible to wedge in even a clip of 5 rounds of ammunition.[8]

In fact most loads weighed about 110 pounds, some more.

Once on to Sussex Mountain trenches would have to be dug, overhead cover provided, barbed wire erected, and mines laid. For the landing, and indeed for the final approach into Falkland Sound in the ships, there was to be complete radio silence. Colonel 'H' ended his orders with advice on the treatment of prisoners. 'If anyone mistreats prisoners in any way at all they will be removed from the Regiment, regardless of what legal action may also be taken.'[9] Nobody was in any doubt as to his views on that subject.

On 16 May Thompson received bad news. Fresh intelligence reports now put an Argentine company on Fanning Head, while the mobile reserve force appeared to have moved to the north of Darwin. Serious difficulties could ensue for the landings. Not only would the 'Fanning Head Mob', as they were now called, have a grandstand view of the ships as they approached the entrance to San Carlos Water, but a few anti-tank guns could wreak havoc with the landing craft. Then, supposing the Argentine reserve force moved up to Sussex Mountain as soon as the landing was spotted. With the enemy in a position from which they would dominate the whole of San Carlos Water Operation Sutton's success would be in doubt. To meet these new threats Thompson both added to, and changed, his plan.

First, thirty-five men with twelve machine guns, plus an NGFO, would land by helicopter during the night of 20 May behind the company on Fanning Head. This group would, with the aid of gunfire from HMS *Antrim*, destroy or distract the Fanning Head Mob. Similarly, special forces, this time D Squadron 22 SAS with the help of HMS *Ardent*, would carry out a heliborne raid on the strategic reserve near Darwin to keep them busy during the crucial hours during, and immediately after, the landings. But this might not be enough. With a strong mobile enemy force so close to San Carlos Water Sussex Mountain became the vital ground as far as securing the beachhead was concerned. Whoever sat on Sussex Mountain controlled the whole area. To ensure 3

Commando Brigade got there first Thompson changed his plan by putting 2 Para in the leading wave of LCUs. The southern flank of the landing had to be secured quickly.

On 17 May Thompson flew around to explain the changed plan to his commanding officers. On the *Norland* Colonel 'H' summoned his 'O' group once more. The SAS and SBS patrols ashore were continuing to downgrade the qualities of the enemy. The attack on Pebble Island on 15 May had been a pushover. Argentine morale was low, food was short, they lit bonfires at night to keep warm, and did not bother with sentries. So the commanding officer's final message, having detailed the changes and making it quite obvious that he was delighted 2 Para was to be the first ashore was, 'Hit the enemy really hard and they will fold'.[10]

On the basis that an Argentine regiment approximately equalled a British battalion, the situation on 20 May was that five British battalions were about to seize a beachhead against an occupying force of eight or nine. But numbers alone give a totally false picture. Despite the disparity, the Argentines were at a disadvantage at the outset. They did not have the initiative, they did not know where the landings would be, they could not be strong, or even watch, everywhere. For a while at least after any landing they would be uncertain if it was a diversion. This is the age-old problem of the defender. The attacker has the ability to concentrate, choose his point of attack, confuse his opponent with diversions, and so achieve the key to success - surprise. Although the Argentine High Command were well aware of this strategic problem their deployment to meet the threat was a compromise between dispersion to watch everywhere and concentration to secure Stanley. This was partially the result of the Junta in Buenos Aires refusing, after the seizure of the Falklands in early April, to believe that Britain would actually use force to retake them. As Brigadier-General Menendez put it:

There was really no structured plan for the defence of the Island because the original plan for the occupation of the Malvinas did not contemplate the possibility of a British military reaction. Naturally this caused serious problems later on because we had to improvise a defence plan, and when other military units started arriving in the Malvinas sometimes they didn't have proper logistical support .... We tried to organize a defence as best we could.[11]

The actual deployment on the eve of the landings had not changed from that shown on Map 3. Although the Argentines expected, and indeed wanted, the main battle to be in the hills west of Stanley a large proportion of their infantry was well away from the capital. The 12th Regiment was at Goose Green, while the 5th and 8th were on West Falkland; a third of the infantry could not, realistically, be expected to play any part in the critical battle.

This scattering of their forces is all the harder to understand when it is realized that these outlying garrisons lacked mobility or artillery support. Despite the British intelligence to the contrary, there were no guns at Port Howard, and neither were there sufficient helicopters to lift more than 200 men at a time. Even if the British intended to land on West Falkland in strength, and the Argentines thought this highly unlikely, the 5th and 8th Regiments, themselves separated by nearly 50 kilometres, could not have offered more than token resistance. They could not be quickly reinforced either, so the Argentine High Command was failing to concentrate its forces for the defence of the vital area, in effect abandoning two regiments.

Another error of British intelligence was in placing an Argentine strategic mobile reserve of more than a regiment north of Darwin. No such reserve existed. The best Menendez could do was to hold back B Company of 12 Regiment from Goose Green, and keep them 18 kilometres west of Stanley just north of Mount Kent. Piaggi's company acted as both strategic reserve and guard unit for the helicopters when they were not being used for other duties. This was the only mobile reserve for use on East Falkland. It was small because that was the maximum number that could be moved at one time in the available helicopters. The 601st Combat Aviation Battalion, under Lieutenant-Colonel Juan Scarpa, only had nineteen aircraft in the Falklands at the outset. These consisted of two Chinooks, three Augustas, five Pumas and nine Hueys. Lack of sufficient helicopter lift capacity was to be the bane of both British and Argentine commanders. For the former it was to mean the breakout from the beachhead would be primarily on foot, while for the Argentines it restricted their ability to switch units quickly to meet the unexpected. As the conflict progressed the British superiority in helicopters became progressively more marked.

At Goose Green Piaggi was alert to the likelihood that a British landing somewhere was imminent. On the evening of 20 May his defensive positions were as shown on Map 4. He had, over the past weeks, been able to lay a considerable number of mines in the centre of the isthmus north of Darwin, behind the beaches on the western side, north of the school bridge in the east, and protecting the airstrip and Goose Green settlement from the north. There were more on the tips of the Goose Green peninsula and further south. His main worries continued to be his lack of his proper scale of support weapons, and the absence of any ground artillery. His persistent requests for guns had so far gone unheeded.

2nd Lieutenant Reyes was commanding the platoon up on Fanning Head on the night of 20/21 May. With him were about half of Eagle Detachment, some thirty men, plus the two 105mm anti-tank guns and two 81mm mortars. Estoban, with the remaining men, was billeted down at Port San Carlos. Life on top of the hill was a losing battle against the weather, particularly the wind. It was, as 2 Para would later describe it, a 'lazy' wind — it went through you rather than round you.

Most of his men had only one threadbare blanket in which to wrap themselves. There was no shelter except in the lee of the summit, but some men had always to be on watch. No attempt had been made to dig in. Throughout the day the weather had been particularly unkind, with driving rain and poor visibility. This changed at dusk when the clouds cleared and visibility improved. Reyes remained concerned about the cold. Already, since leaving Goose Green, several men had succumbed to exposure. The gruelling climb up from the settlement was exhausting, making everybody sweat. This was followed by the long period of inactivity on the bare summit which the conscripts had found so debilitating.

Reyes was huddled down near the radio set shortly before midnight on the 20th trying to doze, thinking enviously of his brother officer asleep in the comfort of a house, when he heard a yell from the nearby anti-tank guns. He went across and stared down into the Sound in the direction indicated by the excited soldier. It was a ship. Through his binoculars Reyes could see it quite distinctly, with several others nearby, exactly opposite the entrance to San Carlos Water. The British had arrived. Reyes' men were about to fire the opening shots of the Argentine Army in the land battle for the Falklands. Both anti-tank guns opened fire, followed a little later by the mortars. Reyes dashed back to his radio, but despite repeated attempts he could not get through to Estoban.

At about the same time at Goose Green Piaggi was awakened by heavy automatic and mortar fire from north of Darwin. It was the SAS diversionary attack on what they thought was the Argentine strategic reserve. Some forty men had landed by helicopter and advanced rapidly towards Darwin. They halted in front of Manresa's A Company and proceeded to shoot up his position. No attack was made and no casualties inflicted. Piaggi stood everybody to and reported what was happening to Stanley. Some sort of raid was taking place but the firing was ineffective and, as yet, there was no reason to think the British were landing in force nearby.

On the afternoon of 20 May Colonel 'H''s meagre reserve of patience was being rapidly eroded. The Task Force had changed course westwards, with obvious significance for everybody, but as yet the *Norland* had not received the signal giving the date and critical timings of D-Day. The situation was becoming farcical. With the landings obviously about to take place the battalion that was to be first ashore did not know when it was supposed to happen. As there was now complete radio silence between ships it seemed nobody was going to be able to tell them.

What Colonel 'H' did not know was that the signal had been sent out on 19 May with the usual 'Ack' at the end, indicating the recipient should immediately acknowledge receiving it. When *Norland* did not acknowledge, a lamp signal querying the problem was responded to with the answer that the *Norland*'s literalizer, the equipment that decodes secret signals, had broken. HMS *Broadsword* was ordered, by lamp, to shoot a copy of the signal across to *Norland* by gun-line. As she approached, *Norland* flashed, 'Do you know something we do not?' *Broadsword* replied, 'Yes, stand by for line'. Thus, only eight hours before they were due to hit the beach, 2 Para got their timings.

A final hurried 'O' group assembled. 2 Para learned that H-Hour was 2.30 am on Friday, 21 May. This was the time their LCU's bows should go down onto Blue Beach 2 at San Carlos Settlement. It would give them four hours of darkness to climb up Sussex Mountain, dig in and be prepared to receive any counter-stroke from Goose Green/Darwin. A rush of last-minute preparations ensued — the priming of grenades, the breaking open of mortar ammunition and its distribution, the final check and cleaning of weapons, the loading of magazines, packing of bergens, the eating of meals and the holding of a church service. There was little, if any, time to sleep, especially as four hours were lost when everybody had to convert to Zulu (GMT) time and put their watches forward.

2 Para would go ashore on the four LCUs coming from HMS *Intrepid*, and this would mean the troops assembling in their disembarking groups at 10.00 pm. Colonel 'H' was in his cabin trying to rest when suddenly he was called to the radio to speak to the operations officer of *Intrepid*. Now what? Something must be horribly wrong for radio silence to be broken at this stage. 'Are you aware that in three hours time the brigade is due to go ashore?' he was asked. 'Has the battalion broken out its first line scales of ammunition yet? Can the battalion make the deadline?'[12] At the last moment the ship that was shortly to send its LCUs to collect 2 Para did not know if they were ready. It was not a good omen. Murphy had already appeared with his law. The two assault ships (*Fearless* and *Intrepid*) were almost an hour late anchoring outside the entrance to San Carlos Water due to navigational problems, caused by thick mist as the amphibious group had sailed into Falkland Sound. It was nearly midnight when the flash and bang of gunfire was seen and heard from up on Fanning Head. The Fanning Head Mob had fired first.

There was some concern, as the SBS, with Captain McManners RA directing the guns of HMS *Antrim*, were supposed to be engaging this enemy group. The Argentines continued to fire ineffectually for some time with no response from on shore. What Thompson could not know was that the SBS approach to Fanning Head was also running late. When Reyes' guns opened up the Marines were still out of range of the Argentine position. McManners called for fire from *Antrim*, which promptly had trouble with one of her twin-turreted 4.5 inch guns. Eventually she got off twin salvoes, soon followed by 20 more. The Fanning Hill Mob appeared to lose interest in what was happening at sea - but the ships had been seen.

Back on the *Norland* things were not going smoothly either. The LCUs had arrived slightly late and Colonel 'H' was far from happy when the leading one, with the senior naval officer onboard, started picking up the troops destined for the second, and vice versa. This meant that B Company would be first ashore instead of C Company, A Company, and Tac 1. An exasperated commanding officer redesignated the order of march.

The loading itself was much slower than anticipated. Getting the grossly overburdened soldiers into the heaving LCUs could not be rushed. More delays resulted when the life boats, which had been lowered to the half-way position, snagged on headropes. Once loaded, the LCUs moved away from the ship's side to wait, or rather circle, as the next ones loaded up. For an hour and a half Colonel 'H' went round and round the *Norland* waiting for the rest of his battalion. The move ashore was supposed to be done in silence, but this instruction did not seem to have been passed to the Royal Marine crews of the LCUs. The frequent flashing of torches and shouted orders did little to inspire confidence that the long-delayed move to the beach would be uneventful. Major Ryan put it tersely in his written report on the operation: 'The main lack was no beach assault training. RMs running the LCUs were ill-disciplined and noisy, shouting, lights.'

On *Fearless* 2 Para's slow start was causing anxiety. As Thompson later described it:

> Because of various problems it became quite clear that the landing was getting later and later and we could be running into daylight if we weren't careful. Someone said to me: 'Why don't we speed things up?' I said: 'No, we won't do that'. I could imagine the chaos it would cause in the night. We were trying to maintain radio silence .... A lot of chatter on the radio to a chap standing on a landing craft in the dark trying to take down orders, would have resulted in worse chaos than there was already.[13]

Thompson was rejecting the suggestion that he let 40 Commando go ahead of 2 Para.

Inside the LCUs life was pretty miserable with the

troops jammed together like sardines, absolutely helpless as the boats wallowed around in the swell waiting for the last craft to fill up. Luckily it was a calm, clear night with an occasional satellite passing overhead. Men started to cock their weapons. Then came the unmistakable crack of somebody accidentally firing a shot from a Sterling sub-machine gun. Miraculously the bullet went into a soldier's boot, only bruising his foot, but it was not a good beginning. Eventually the line of landing craft sorted themselves out and departed for the shore. 2 Para had now reverted to the original order of march again, so the line was led by Colonel 'H', with Major Southby-Tailyour RM, who knew the bays and inlets intimately, responsible for navigation to Blue Beaches 1 and 2. Behind came the other three 2 Para LCUs, followed by 40 Commando in four more LCUs and four LCVPs (small landing craft able to carry a platoon of thirty men). These extra craft were essential as 40 Commando were accompanied by two Scorpion and two Scimitar CVRs(T) (light tanks) of the Blues and Royals. Suddenly, as they moved further into San Carlos Water the alarm bell on an LCU rang shrilly. Another accident, which prompted Colonel 'H' to snap over the radio: 'David, this is a bloody shambles'. All eyes watched for the expected light signal from the SBS patrol ashore which was supposed to indicate the enemy's presence or absence. There was no signal. Apprehension remained.

In the Colonel's LCU A Company had been first onboard. Packed up against the ramp at the front was 2nd Lieutenant Mark Coe's 2 Platoon. He later described boarding the LCU through the *Norland*'s side door:

> There was a large swell and you either met the LCU on the way up or way down. We were right at the front as we were the leading platoon. The first section's bergens were submerged in the water at the bows. At this stage it was fairly quiet except for the CO who kept yelling: 'Push forward at the front.'[14]

As the LCUs approached the beach several grated on submerged rocks. The one carrying A Company tried to beach twice before finally succeeding, by which time B Company were ashore. In 2 Platoon Lance-Corporal Gilbert's pre-occupation was, like most of his comrades, with keeping his feet dry. It was an important but impossible task.

> I was sitting on my kit [bergen] with my feet on the ramp. When the boat went fast it kept the wash out, but when it slowed or stopped the water came in. As we neared the beach there was a lot of slowing and stopping and starting. Then people were standing up, and my bergen floated, and then sank. My feet and kit were soaked before I left the landing craft.[15]

His concern was a common one. In B Company Private Ferguson, on seeing a foot or so of water when the ramp went down, summed up the feelings of many when he said: 'Oh fuck, I'm going to get my feet wet before I even start'.[16] Sergeant Norman was equally unhappy with his arrival:

> So we stepped off on to what we thought was the beach. We went straight up nearly to the waist in water which, being the South Atlantic, was quite cold. I was not amused. Even at this stage people thought it was like an exercise: 'We're wet; we get wet when we are on exercise.'[17]

The Toms expected the 'Booties', as they called the Marines, to put them on to a beach. They wanted to walk down the ramp on to dry sand, so when they saw some 20 metres of water between them and the shore there was some reluctance to move. In B Company's boat the Royal Marine colour-sergeant yelled, 'Off troops'. Nobody moved. Another shout, but still no reaction. One of his crew scurried back from the bow to tell him, 'There's still two or three feet of water'. 'I don't give a damn! They'll have to get their feet wet. Get off'. It was probably the sergeant-major who solved the problem — by simply yelling 'GO'.[18] They went. Gingerly, slowly, they stumbled into the icy sea.

As B Company waded ashore there was a shout from the darkness: 'Who the hell are you?' To which Major Crosland responded: '2 Para. Who are you?' It was the SBS. 'God, we thought you were coming on the 24th'. 'Par for the night', replied Crosland.[19] It explained the absence of torch signals, but for Colonel 'H' it was a relief to know that there were no enemy in the area as his men piled ashore. Now it was a question of getting up on to Sussex Mountain before any Argentines from Goose Green could do so.

A number of factors mitigated against 2 Para getting into their defensive positions by first light. Firstly, the landings were late. It was not until about 4.30 am that 2 Para hit the beach, a good two hours behind schedule. With first light at 6.30 there was no chance of securing Sussex Mountain in darkness. Secondly, there was chaos on the beach as men milled about trying to sort themselves out into their companies and platoons, and into the correct order of march. Colonel 'H' fumed, causing consternation to his signals officer with his breaches of radio silence. When the troops finally shouldered their enormous packs another half an hour had been lost. Thirdly, they had a long way to go — some eight kilometres to the top, much of it uphill. Added to this was the inability of anybody to move faster than a slow walk. The battalion snake uncoiled itself in slow motion, stumbling and staggering under the ache of overloaded bergens.

C Company was in the lead, followed by B and A Companies. D Company was the last to leave. As it waited its turn, 40 Commando began coming ashore adding to the confusion. The proximity of the two units demanded liaison which was not forthcoming. Corporal Abols in 1 Platoon of A Company described part of the problem of this tab thus:

The ground was bloody to march on; pea[t]
thick tufts of grass that jarred at the ankles. [...]
biggest problem was keeping the blokes moving.
The pace was slow but a lot of gaps formed during
the night and early morning because when a man
fell over he had to wait for the next bloke to pull him
to his feet.[20]

Many Toms considered this the most gruelling march they
had ever done, surpassing P Company's worst. For those
carrying machine-guns, Milans, mortars, or Blowpipes,
the burden was almost unbearable. The folly of attempting
to carry the Blowpipes became apparent within 500
metres. These men, who were artillerymen not Paras, had
no hope of keeping up, and some ended up at the rear of
the column dragging and bumping their Blowpipes along
the ground rather than lifting them.

As D Company struggled to overtake the Mortar
Platoon they stumbled across a mortarman, Private
Hemphill, who had fallen unconscious in the darkness
unknown to his comrades. Captain Steven Hughes came
forward with his team to assist. In doing so they had to
cross an icy stream into which one of the medics, Private
Clegg, had the misfortune to fall. The repercussions of
being soaked in freezing water with no chance to dry out
were extremely serious. Unless Clegg could be kept warm
he would quickly become a victim of hypothermia. There
were now two casualties. The medical officer opted to
keep Clegg moving while at the same time giving him a
long swig of hot, sweet drinking chocolate that he carried
in a thermos for just such an occasion.

There was no option but to stagger on, with Hemphill
still unconscious, wrapped in one of the carrying sheets
prepared on *Norland*. The medics took turns at the carry,
with the padre, David Cooper, also doing more than his
fair share. The march slipped further and further behind
schedule. Colonel 'H' later admitted to Hughes that he
had made an error in insisting such heavy loads were
carried.

few dropped out; some kit was
.e Platoon suffered particularly as
.nics did not have the fitness of the
not surprisingly, five collapsed.
: was no enemy interference with this
, and luckily it was not raining. Had 2
.ed to assault Sussex Mountain, as had been
.ossibility, there could have been a serious
.o the landings. Captain Farrar, the Patrol
Pl. commander, was at the foot of the mountain as
dawn was breaking, on what would have been the start
line for an attack. To him, 'It was just as well that this (an
attack) wasn't the case, for watching the heavily laden
battalion stagger by our start line there was no way that
an uphill assault would have worked'.[21]

As dawn broke the rifle companies began the long
ascent up the 800-foot high hill, having gratefully dropped
off their two mortar bombs at the battalion RV. Despite
all the effort the Toms still retained their sense of humour.
The sight of the medical officer falling flat on his back
raised a laugh. As Hughes explained, 'I provided some
entertainment when both feet went out from under me and
I went down on my back with an explosive 'Fuck!' This
was to prove most people's favourite word for the
campaign, and we meant it every time we said it.'

Although no Argentines occupied Sussex Mountain, 2
Para's presence was spotted from the air. Their first sight
of the enemy was a Pucara pilot floating gently down into
the valley south of the mountain, his aircraft having been
downed by the SAS on their way back from their
diversionary raid. Another plane was seen in the distance,
then another Pucara screamed low overhead. Later a
Macchi 339 attacked D Company. Captain David Benest,
the signals officer, described battalion headquarters
reaction — 'Colonel 'H' fired his sub-machine gun at the
plane and everybody took cover'.

First Lieutenant Estoban was awoken by the sound of
the muffled crump of the shells landing on Fanning Head.

Reyes was obviously in trouble, but try as he might he could not raise any response on his radio. For three hours he kept trying without success, every moment hoping a runner would arrive to let him know what was happening. Nobody came. At daylight he sent some soldiers with binoculars up on to the high ground north of the settlement to establish an OP.

The 4.5-inch shells from HMS *Antrim*, bursting 50 feet above ground, turned night into day with the flashes of their enormous explosions. On the ground Reyes' men dived for cover, regretting the lack of even shell scrapes. Within the first few minutes twenty shells came crashing down, putting an end to any thoughts of continuing to fire on the ships below, but, strangely, causing no casualties as yet. Reyes regrouped his men in the lee of the ridge north of Fanning Head as the shelling slackened off to about one round every minute. This slight respite was used to start some belated digging. Reyes could still not contact Estoban. Some time later troops were seen approaching from the east, then some bursts of red tracer came their way. Reyes considered it was time to withdraw. He succeeded in slipping away to the north and east with the bulk of his men. When the SBS group finally arrived they secured six prisoners and four wounded.

It was not until shortly after 8.00 am that the early morning mist cleared sufficiently to reveal to Estoban's OP an amazing sight. At the entrance to San Carlos Water was a large white ship, the *Canberra*, busily offloading troops into a boat. Nearby were three warships. Clearly the British had arrived. Finally, as visibility further improved, an excited message reached Estoban that troops had been spotted advancing towards Port San Carlos. These were the leading elements of 3 Para. Estoban had reported what was happening to Goose Green and suggested an air attack. By about 8.20 Estoban withdrew all his men to the east of the settlement.

Within a few minutes three helicopters came swinging in from the sea. One was a Sea King with an underslung load of a Rapier anti-aircraft firing post, the others escorting Gazelles. Estoban's group opened up with machine guns, causing the Sea King and one Gazelle to veer off the way they had come. The other Gazelle came down gently into the water. That it had not crashed was due to the incredible skill of the mortally wounded pilot, Sergeant Evans RM. In the water his crewman, Sergeant Candlish, struggled to bring his comrade ashore - under fire from Estoban's soldiers.

According to Estoban, when describing this incident to Martin Middlebrook in 1987, he shouted at his men to stop firing but:

> The men who were firing were some distance away and did not hear my order. You must understand that they were only conscripts with 45 days' service and knew nothing of the Geneva Convention .... Instruction on the Geneva Convention is now part of the basic training of our conscripts because of this incident.

As Estoban pulled back on to higher ground another Gazelle flew inland to within 40 metres of the Argentines, who once more opened up with a hail of fire. The bubble of the Gazelle was shattered and the helicopter fell like a stone, killing Lieutenant Francis and his crewman, Corporal Giffen. It had crashed within ten metres of where Estoban was standing. He now took his party on a four-day trek to Douglas Settlement from where he was lifted by helicopter to Stanley. He was to reappear at Goose Green to play his part in the battle with 2 Para.

Shortly after daylight at Goose Green Vice-Commodore Pedroza ordered four of the six Pucaras into the air to find out exactly what was happening at San Carlos Water. As the first pair, flown by Captain Jorge Benitez and Lieutenant Brest, taxied out for take-off HMS *Ardent* began shelling the airfield. This prevented Brest getting airborne. The second pair took off despite the gunfire. As Benitez sought a suitable target, his starboard engine was hit by a Stinger missile fired by D Squadron 22 SAS.

Initially the Pucara climbed sharply, then went into a spinning fall over which Benitez had no control. At 300 feet he ejected. It was his parachute that was seen by 2 Para as they reached the summit of Sussex Mountain. He spent the rest of the day walking back to Goose Green.

The other two Pucaras, flown by Major Carlos Tomba and 1st Lieutenant Juan Micheloud, were pounced on by two Sea Harriers over San Carlos. Micheloud escaped, but Tomba was not so fortunate:

> I felt an impact on my plane. I looked at the wings and saw a pretty large hole, like a rose with open petals ... the aircraft was still under control although shaking violently. The engine and controls seemed to be working properly so I went down very low .... I was then hit by another burst of machine-gun fire ... this time one engine caught fire .... I lost control .... Soon the whole plane seemed to be on fire and that was when I decided to eject. The aircraft and I practically fell together.[22]

Tomba, like Benitez, had a long walk back to Goose Green where, a week later, he assisted in the defence of the settlement as an infantryman.

By mid-morning on the 21st it was clear to Menendez in Stanley and Piaggi at Goose Green that a substantial landing was taking place at San Carlos. The questions they sought to answer were — was it a diversion? If not, what should they do about it?

IV

IT'S ON – IT'S OFF – IT'S ON AGAIN

'I've waited twenty years for this, and now some
fucking marine's cancelled it'.

Lieutenant-Colonel 'H' Jones OBE on being told
the brigade commander had cancelled 2 Para's raid
on Goose Green.

Brigadiers Thompson and Menendez had a number of
things in common apart from their rank. Both were under
close scrutiny by their respective governments in London
and Buenos Aires. After the successful British landings
both were subjected to strategic and, in Thompson's case,
tactical instructions on how they should conduct ground
operations. Both were to be exasperated by what they saw
as their high command's unjustified and unrealistic
interference with their actions as the commanders on the
spot. Both were clear in their own minds as to the strategic
objective of the conflict – for the British the recapture,
and for the Argentines the retention, of Stanley. All their
actions had to be assessed in the light of whether they
furthered these aims. Thompson, who was forced to spend
long spells on the satellite telephone link to Northwood
explaining and justifying what he was doing, recalled: 'On
one occasion, after a particularly irritating telephone
conversation, I remember walking out of the tent and
saying to myself in something of a temper: I shall win the
war for these buggers and then I shall go.'[1] Goose Green
was to feature prominently in the communications that
flashed back and forth between Thompson and
Northwood, and Menendez and his newly established

equivalent superior joint headquarters at Comodoro Rivadavia. The difference was that Menendez was able to avoid getting distracted by Goose Green, whereas Thompson was not. The result was a battle whose outcome was of enormous political and psychological importance to both nations, and all the forces committed to the conflict, but was perceived as unnecessary by the British commander in the field.

Thompson's job was clear. He had to hold and secure the beachhead and prepare the way for a future advance on Stanley. With only five battalions to hand he rightly anticipated staying around San Carlos until the arrival of the three battalions making up 5 Infantry Brigade, which were expected by the end of May or early June. With eight battalions an advance, with a major battle at the end of it, against the Argentine defences around the capital, made military sense; with five it did not.

As always, logistics dictated to strategy. There was no way 3 Commando Brigade could move any distance from the beachhead prior to the off-loading of the thousands of tons of ammunition, food, and fuel packed into the RFA supply ships. A Brigade Maintenance Area, a supply base, had to be established ashore. To do this every available medium-lift helicopter had to be used, which at that stage meant all eleven Sea Kings plus the five Wessex. Thompson's worries were compounded by the fact that helicopters could only work in that environment by day, as only four had crews trained and fitted with night-vision goggles. Daylight meant they provided slow, vulnerable targets to air attack — hence the priority of placing the Rapier battery into position on D-Day, and the urgency of wresting air superiority from the Argentines in the days following the landing.

Thompson was well aware of the logistic problems of an advance of 80- 100 kilometres to Stanley, across an inhospitable and unforgiving countryside with the onset of winter not far away. Helicopters would again be the single most important element in getting troops and supplies forward. He earmarked Teal Inlet as a likely forward base, situated as it was about half-way to Stanley. Modern technology has not changed the principles of military strategy, particularly the one that states that the further an army moves from its supply base, the weaker and more vulnerable it becomes. All its supplies have to be moved that much further, which demands an increasingly greater administrative and transport effort. The longer the link between troops and base the more vulnerable it becomes to attack or destruction by the enemy, especially from the air. This in turn often leads to units having to be deployed to protect lines of communication, units that would otherwise be available at the front.

Helicopters were also essential to move the artillery forward. No gun could be moved in the Falklands unless it was slung underneath a helicopter. The effort required was massive. Thompson quotes an example of moving one battery of six 105mm guns to Mount Kent. It took 85 Sea King sorties of a round trip of an hour each – three days to move a battery with 500 rounds per gun. There were four such light batteries to be deployed. If the infantry advanced they needed artillery support, so the guns must advance as well. The feasibility of any strategic or tactical move was calculated in terms of its logistical needs and helicopter lifts. Thompson sometimes wondered if his military and political masters in London appreciated this basic constraint.

While 3 Commando Brigade stocked up and secured the base area for future operations, the key battle of the campaign would be fought in the sky for air superiority. Without that superiority a ground advance might prove an impossibility.

Although Thompson knew that in the first few days after the landing his aim was to prepare for, rather than undertake, an advance, this did not preclude aggressive action. As Moore's directive had said, he was to 'push forward from the bridgehead area so far as the maintenance of its security allows, to gain information, to establish moral and physical domination over the enemy'.

With this in mind he arrived to visit 2 Para early on the morning of 22 May.

He found Colonel 'H' well forward in an OP with B Company, on the left of the battalion position. The two discussed the situation while gazing south over the rolling, grassy peat and the glistening water of Brenton Loch which was blocked by the Goose Green isthmus some 20 kilometres in a straight line from where they sat. It was a dull day, but a high cloud base allowed aircraft to operate. Despite the good visibility, distance and intervening hills prevented the watchers from seeing the isthmus where they knew the enemy to be. Thompson told an enthusiastic Colonel 'H' that he intended to use 2 Para to raid Goose Green. The Argentines down there were the nearest enemy to the landings, and 2 Para was the closest unit to them. Such an operation would be in accordance with Moore's orders to dominate the enemy.

For reasons that will became apparent as the story unfolds, it is necessary to emphasize that Thompson intended 2 Para to conduct a raid. Two points on raiding need clarification. Firstly, such an operation implies a sudden, surprise attack, followed by a withdrawal. It is not the object of a raid to seize, hold, capture and remain on the enemy position for longer than necessary to inflict damage. Secondly, the aim of a raid - and the military like to have their aim clear and unambiguous - is often unavoidably less than precise. It is sometimes not possible to be more specific than to indicate the location to be attacked and instruct the raiders, as Thompson later wrote, 'to cause as much damage as possible to the garrison and its equipment, including air defence guns and missiles'.[2] The brigade commander was also to describe the operation in more down-to-earth language: 'We had planned to raid Goose Green before 5 Brigade arrived — a battalion raid by 2 Para, with gunfire support, wellie-in, duff-up the garrison and bugger off, that's all'.[3]

A raid relies on surprise for success. It is normally a quick 'in out' job, often by a much smaller force than that being attacked. The concept is well known to the Royal

Map 6
STANLEY'S NATURAL LINES OF DEFENCE

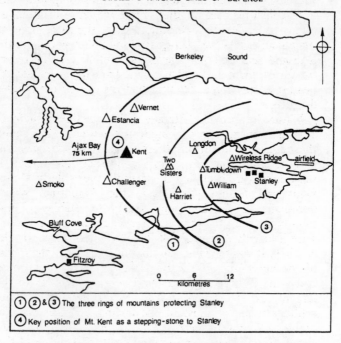

① ② & ③ The three rings of mountains protecting Stanley
④ Key position of Mt. Kent as a stepping-stone to Stanley

Marines, who had 1 Raiding Squadron deployed as part of 3 Commando Brigade, but possibly less so by the Army who, although it had perfected raiding techniques during World War 2, had since become more accustomed to attacking with a more specific objective of seizing and holding a position. At the time these tactical niceties were of no significance. Colonel 'H' was delighted his battalion was to be given a worthwhile task. 2 Para was to have first crack at the Argentines. It was exactly what he wanted. Thompson had given Colonel 'H' a 'Warning Order', which he said would be confirmed with more specific details later.

On the day following the landings, despite favourable weather, the air attacks of the 21st were not repeated. The respite allowed the continued movement of supplies to shore by boat and helicopter. Thompson's top priority was to establish his base of supply from which to maintain an offensive on Stanley. He intended, at the same time, to sustain an aggressive, deep-patrolling policy with both the SAS and SBS, to obtain the tactical intelligence necessary for future planning, and to use 2 Para to intimidate the nearest enemy force. He also had his eye on the Stanley defences.

Nature has provided Stanley with three lines of defence against an enemy approaching from the west. Map 6 shows these lines of hills in simplified form. It was the western, or outer, line that particularly concerned Thompson. If these hills were occupied in strength, particularly Mount Kent and Mount Challenger, the Argentines would dominate all the land approaches to Stanley. These mountains were the highest, and would be formidable to seize if heavily defended. Of the two Mount Kent was the real key. It was the vital, dominating ground, in the centre of the outer line. If the British could take it, it would make the hills to its north and south untenable to the Argentines. It would provide a springboard within artillery range of most of the enemy defences west of Stanley. Thompson needed to know everything he could about Mount Kent. He saw the eventual securing of this mountain as a crucial objective on the road to the capital. In comparison Goose Green was of little significance.

Unbeknown to Thompson, pressure for a speedy ground advance had started in Britain even before a landing had been made. The Chiefs-of-Staff had assured the government that once troops were ashore they would advance quickly. Admiral Sir Terence Lewin, Chief of Defence Staff, had stated on the day that Thompson first mooted the raid to Colonel 'H': 'We're going to move and move fast'.[4] On the following day, the 23rd, Thompson was somewhat peeved to be told, in a signal from Northwood, that his objective was now 'to invest Stanley'.[5] A number of not unreasonable queries sprang to mind. Was he no longer to await the arrival of General

Moore and 5 Infantry Brigade? Were five battalions now considered sufficient to attack the main enemy defences and secure the bridgehead? And how, with all his helicopters committed to the logistic effort of setting up his base and the air war still undecided, was he physically to comply with this new instruction? Perhaps, once the dumping and movement of supplies in the base area, and with the additional four Chinook and six Wessex helicopters due to arrive in two or three days on the *Atlantic Conveyor*, a start could be made.[6] In the meantime he confirmed the raid on Goose Green, and began to concentrate on how to get to Mount Kent.

On the 23rd and 24th Colonel 'H' considered his options for the raid. He had been told to submit his plan to Thompson for approval. To assist, Lieutenant Thurman RM was attached to 2 Para to provide detailed knowledge of the Goose Green area. He had been the second-in-command of the Royal Marine Falkland Island detachment and had spent much of his time walking around the settlements.[7] Colonel 'H''s intelligence officer, Captain Alan Coulson, was given a rosy picture of the opposition by the SAS who had carried out the recent raid. According to them there was now no regiment, no strategic reserve, in fact probably only one company of infantry that could easily be defeated by two Para companies. How they came to this conclusion was not explained, especially as the SAS efforts on the 21st had involved little other than firing into the night at suspected positions. Coulson was unconvinced.

Colonel 'H''s initial ideas were turned down. His main difficulty was the distance to the enemy, at best 20 kilometres by air, and nearer 25 on foot. How could he close up to the Argentines, surprise them, hit them hard and then get out again? Up till then the only raids carried out had been with the troops being inserted by helicopter, such as at Pebble Island, or the diversionary attack on Goose Green on the 21st. It was the obvious way to solve the distance problem, but Colonel 'H' was firmly told that no helicopters could be made available for troop lifts, although the four Sea Kings with PNG equipped and trained pilots could be used to position three guns and ammunition. He then proposed a seaborne approach in LCUs from Port Sussex, up Brenton Loch, to land on Salinas beach opposite Goose Green. It would have to be a night operation. Once again this proposal was vetoed, this time on the grounds that the precise navigation required among the rocks and shallows of the loch would necessitate the use of radar, and this risked being picked up by the enemy. Without air superiority both a heliborne or seaborne approach by day constituted too serious a risk, even supposing the helicopters were available. 2 Para would have to go in on foot.

During the 24th Colonel 'H''s final plan was agreed. As forward OPs from C Company had earlier reported up to sixty enemy with a troop carrier in the vicinity of Cantera House, these would have to be eliminated first, otherwise they might discover or delay the long approach march. On the 23rd Lieutenant Jim Barry, with his 12 Platoon of D Company, was sent to investigate. A Sea King was made available to lift these men to within two kilometres of Cantera House. It took Barry four hours of night marching, and the use of artillery fire to help locate the house, before he was able to assault the empty building. The platoon remained at Cantera House as it fitted in with the plan for the raid on Goose Green. This small operation graphically illustrated two important lessons. One was that even 'mark one eyeball' intelligence can be incorrect or quickly outdated and thus needs verification by other means. The other was the inordinate time needed to move and navigate across the 'camp' at night.

2 Para's raid involved two phases, or rather the approach to the enemy was in two phases. The actual plan for attacking the enemy had, of necessity, to be left to the moment of contact. That was the problem with the rather 'woolly' objectives of a raid: there was no clear enemy position to seize or building to destroy. Major Phil Neame was briefed by the commanding officer on the afternoon

of the 24th. His D Company's task was to move out after last light, march to Camilla Creek House, picking up 12 Platoon on the way, and secure the area as the start line for the raid proper to be carried out by A and B Companies the following night, the 25th/26th. Three guns, with 200 rounds of ammunition each, were to be flown to Camilla Creek House to be in position before dawn on the 25th. This artillery was seen as the critical support for the otherwise unsupported, lightly armed paratroopers who would be going in without their own supporting heavy weapons. With Camilla Creek House secure A and B Companies would move down to join D Company. They would carry out the raid on the next night. Thompson and Colonel 'H' both knew this was not the best option; both appreciated that without artillery support the operation was a non-starter, and that without the four PNG Sea Kings the guns could not move.

The D Company move got under way on time shortly after dark. They plodded steadily down the track in a long, silent snake, at the start of a 15 kilometre tab. It was an uneventful march, on a cloudy, pitch black night, until they had got about half way to Camilla Creek House. Major Neame's radio operator received the message: 'Fetch sunray'. When Neame picked up the handset it was the unmistakably frustrated voice of his commanding officer. Colonel 'H' told him to about turn and come back. The operation was cancelled. There could be no explanation over the radio, just the terse order. 12 Platoon returned to Cantera House, while the rest of the company trailed back up the long slope to Sussex Mountain. It reminded some of the nursery rhyme of the 'grand old Duke of York' who had been fond of marching his men up and down hills for no reason. It had been a tiring march, a night's sleep had been lost, all to no avail.

What had gone wrong? The problem was the worsening weather and the consequent inability of even the PNG-equipped helicopters to fly. Soon after dark they had been used to take reconnaissance elements of D Squadron 22 SAS to Mount Kent, which had been reported as possibly unoccupied or only lightly held. Mount Kent overlooked Stanley. Stanley was the goal of the entire campaign, so Thompson was keen to occupy it by a helicopter-borne coup-de-main if at all possible. The first step in this direction was to get recce parties in who could later secure an LZ for follow up units. On this occasion, by the time the Sea Kings were available to lift the guns for 2 Para's raid the awful weather had closed in making it too risky. Without artillery support a raid would be foolhardy, hence the cancellation. As Thompson later explained:

> The raid was not a starter without artillery support so, to Jones's intense annoyance, I cancelled it. It was either that night or not at all as far as I was concerned. The main objective was still Stanley, so establishing a strong force on the vital ground of Mount Kent and the nearby features was the most important task ahead.[8]

He had intended to lift 42 Commando complete, plus the remainder of D Squadron but, with lousy weather and only four helicopters available, putting the recce parties in place by the morning of the 25th was the most that could be achieved.

Colonel 'H' was fuming. In his usual forthright manner he let everybody know his feelings, best summed up by his remark quoted at the start of this chapter. But he did not abandon efforts to try again. He arranged for the helicopters to arrive at 6.00 am on the 25th, the idea now being that D Company should be flown to Cantera House, link up with 12 Platoon and continue on foot as far as Camilla Creek House for a watered-down version of the original plan. He was bent on having a go at the enemy if remotely possible, even if, as this plan entailed, it meant moving by day without artillery support. Major Neame would have preferred to walk, even with his weary men, as without proper air cover helicopters make tempting targets. Nevertheless, the arrangements were tied up and, at the appropriate hour, D Company huddled in the gloom awaiting their lift. It never came. The weather had got steadily worse. Colonel 'H' was told only one helicopter could be made available, then none. The raid was definitely off.[9] Barry's platoon were recalled from Cantera House for the long trek back to the battalion. They had been away for 48 hours, had run out of food, and by the time they reached Sussex Mountain that evening all were exhausted. D Company needed some rest.

In London signs of impatience were growing. On the 23 May Bernard Ingham, Margaret Thatcher's press secretary, had held a press conference at which he claimed, 'We're not going to fiddle around'.[10] Having seen the landings go in with no casualties and no counter-attack by ground forces, having seen the mounting losses to ships and personnel from air attack, press, public, and parliament felt it was high time the force ashore got moving. The Chiefs-of-Staff, and the military high command at Northwood under Admiral Fieldhouse, shared this view. Thompson appeared to be excessively cautious; it was important to seize the initiative; the War Cabinet wanted action; there was mounting international pressure for a cease-fire. Lord Whitelaw, then a member of the War Cabinet, later described the concern:

> I think there were many of us who were worried initially that having got a beachhead at San Carlos, we were going to get stuck there. ... There were memories of the time we took to break out of the beachhead in Normandy ... just to be stuck in a very small area and confined there, we'd have had all sorts of troubles. In every way not least on the diplomatic front because ... all the proposals for ceasefires would become stronger. ... So a breakout was very important.[11]

Over the satellite radio Thompson's superiors repeatedly urged action. Break out, press on, give us some sort of advance or victory was the message.

102

It was not that Thompson did not want to get on — he was determined to do so — but he was constrained by what was physically possible with a limited helicopter lift capacity. London did not appear to appreciate his problems. Thompson was relying on the arrival of the *Atlantic Conveyor*, due on the evening of the 25th, with the extra helicopters, particularly the squadron of four Chinooks, to triple his lift capability. At 6.00 that evening Thompson's planning conference, which was discussing getting the brigade forward, was interrupted with the disastrous news that the *Atlantic Conveyor* had been burnt out, gutted, totally destroying three Chinooks, six Wessex, one Lynx, a huge stock of spares, hundreds of tents, trucks, material to build an airstrip for Harriers, and a water distilling plant. The fourth Chinook was saved as it happened to be airborne at the time.[12] An Exocet missile had made a hole the size of a house in her side, and exploded on a deck packed with 4-ton trucks with full fuel tanks - hence the massive fire. Thompson ordered his staff to investigate what, if anything, could be done to salvage the wreck of the plan using existing helicopter and landing craft assets. As the R Group (his staff) dispersed somebody said, 'We'll have to bloody well walk'. Goose Green had been forgotten. As the Brigade Commander later wrote, 'The Brigade's energies must be concentrated on getting on to Stanley. Darwin and Goose Green did not lie on the route I intended to take and any effort in that direction would be a diversion from the aim.'[13]

It is important, if what happened at the battle for Goose Green, and why, are to be fully understood and not taken out of context that Thompson's position early on the morning of 26 May is clear. First, his intention had been to get 42 Commando on to Mount Kent together with a battery of six guns. With the *Atlantic Conveyor*'s additional helicopters this would not have been a problem. Nor would the follow-up of the rest of the brigade. This plan was now impossible. Next, he considered using the existing helicopters plus the surviving Chinook to ferry 42 Commando with the guns and ammunition forward while the rest walked. Some quick staff calculations showed that one night would be needed per rifle company and half the guns, with a small amount of ammunition. The 42 Commando battle group would need three nights of uninterrupted flying to consolidate on Mount Kent. This meant these companies would be isolated 65 kilometres from the beachhead, exposed to Argentine counter-attack with no possibility of support until the other units could march to join them. Implementing such a scheme was a gamble. Was it justified when 5 Infantry Brigade were expected in about five days time? Thompson thought not. As he wrote: 'I therefore favoured waiting for the arrival of 5 Infantry Brigade and, far more important, more helicopters before moving anybody other than D Squadron. Certainly there was no question of flying 42 Commando and the guns until the landing zone on Mount Kent was in the hands of our own reconnaissance.'[14] Having just made up his mind, and told his staff to look at the logistics of using the helicopters to support a march on Mount Kent, Thompson was summoned to the satellite communication terminal which had been set up in the BMA at Ajax Bay.

Northwood wanted to know why there was no movement? What was he doing? What had happened to the raid on Goose Green? Thompson replied, 'Recceing Mount Kent, and I can't move the guns to support 2 Para, so the raid on Goose Green is cancelled.' That his military superiors had subordinated their professional judgement to political pressure was clear from their reaction to this explanation. 'You don't need recces for Mount Kent, and you don't need guns to assault Goose Green.'[15] Thompson was staggered. Here was a headquarters 8000 miles away dictating to the commander on the spot the minor tactics of his operations. Warfare is full of examples of disasters that can be attributed to failure to reconnoitre or attack without adequate fire support. Such remarks left Thompson inwardly seething. Northwood brooked no argument. 'I was given a direct order to attack Goose Green, so I sent 2 Para against it,' was how he summed up this extraordinary conversation. He was also told to move out of the beachhead without further delay. It was after putting down the radio telephone on this occasion that he muttered the remark quoted earlier about winning and quitting. There can be little doubt that if Thompson had argued further, or not immediately complied with his orders, he would have been putting his career 'on the line'. His judgement had been overruled; he had to get on with it or get out. He chose to get on with it, the getting out could come later if necessary, at a time of his own choosing.

The helicopter move of 42 Commando was postponed, but by early on the 27th three of his five units were advancing — on foot. Map 7 shows the resultant dispersal of 3 Commando Brigade on 28 May, at the time when 2 Para were in some difficulties at Goose Green, and 5 Infantry Brigade were still four days away. Fortunately, 2 Para eventually succeeded in their attack, and the Argentine high command was unaware or unable to seize the operational window of opportunity that had presented itself.

Colonel 'H', who had been complaining bitterly that 'We are not winning. We are losing'[16], was delighted when told on the 26th that once again the raid was on. As he left the brigade command post the brigade major, John Chester, who was feeling somewhat guilty at the way 2 Para had been mucked about by the recent order, counter-order routine, said: 'Colonel, I'm sorry you've been fucked about so much'. To which Colonel 'H' responded cheerfully, 'John, life's too short to worry about things like that'. He was about to lead his battalion into battle, which was precisely what he had always wanted but, regrettably, his remark was to prove uncannily accurate. That it was still Thompson's intention that 2 Para should conduct a raid was confirmed when he later wrote: 'Jones was told to carry out the raid on Darwin and Goose Green, using the same plan that had been agreed before.' By that night 2 Para was on the move.

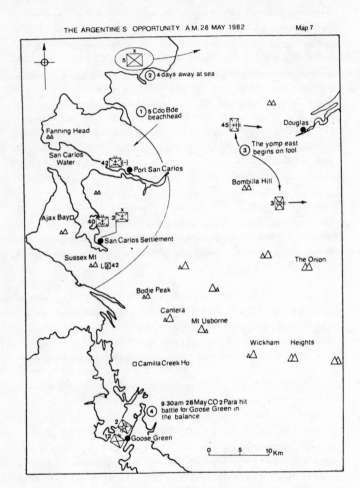

① 5 Cdo Bde
beachhead

② 4 days away at sea

Douglas

45 →

③ The yomp east
begins on foot

Fanning Head

San Carlos
Water

42 (-) Port San Carlos

Bombilla Hill

Ajax Bay

40 3

San Carlos Settlement

3 →

Sussex Mt L 42

The Onion

Bodie Peak

Cantera

Mt Usborne

Wickham Heights

Camilla Creek Ho

9.30am 28 May CO 2 Para hit
④ battle for Goose Green in
the balance

2

12 Goose Green

0 5 10 Km

106

As 2 Para was feverishly toiling to dig trenches in the waterlogged peat on the slopes of Sussex Mountain at about 9.45 am on the 21st, a single- seater, light-attack Macchi 339 aircraft was approaching San Carlos Water. It was one of five such aircraft based at Stanley and it had been scrambled as a result of 1st Lieutenant Estoban's warning of a British landing. His report had been brief and imprecise. Menendez needed to know a lot more, particularly about the size of the force coming ashore. At the controls was Lieutenant Guillermo Crippa, a pilot of the Argentine Fleet Air Arm, who had specifically volunteered for the Malvinas. He was not supposed to be on a solo mission, but his wingman's aircraft had technical problems at take-off so Crippa had flown on alone, as there was real urgency in finding out exactly what was happening around San Carlos. At first a slight mist covered the area so he could see little. He flew north of San Carlos, out to sea, searching for the British ships he had been told to expect. It was not until he headed inland again that he saw a ship, then two, then with the mist thinning Crippa:

> Came face to face with a Sea Lynx helicopter. I was going to attack it when I saw the ships in the distance. I decided to forget about the helicopter and go for the other target. I banked away from the helicopter when I was only a few yards from it, and at that moment the pilot must have seen me because he dived down. I had to laugh, and thought to myself: It's your lucky day today. Obviously I couldn't have missed him from that range. I flew straight to the first ship which was lying at anchor, landing troops [it was the frigate, HMS *Argonaut*]. I don't know which of us was more surprised. I came in for the attack and they started firing at me. I was taken aback by the number of ships there were in the area and I thought to myself: If I go back and tell them there are so many ships they'll never believe me.[17]

Crippa's lone attack was a gallant one, a foretaste of the courage of the Argentine pilots in the days to come. His cannon shells and rockets splattered *Argonaut*'s superstructure, causing damage and injuring two sailors. The mist had gone. Crippa was struck by the sheer beauty of the islands in the sunlight. It seemed so peaceful and lovely. Nevertheless, there was considerable ground fire coming up at this audacious aviator, including, possibly, a few rounds from Colonel 'H''s sub-machine gun, as Crippa banked over the hills and began systematically to count the ships below him. With his ammunition gone he could have fled for Stanley, but he was determined to deliver an accurate report to his superiors. He later dismissed his achievement with the words: 'I circled and came back trying to hug the terrain and I drew a little map on my knee pad before I returned to Puerto Argentino, [Stanley].'[18] Menendez saw him personally immediately he landed. He later became the only pilot of the war to receive the Cruz-La Nacion as his reward for this flight.

Now Menendez knew for sure that a landing was in progress. He knew it was substantial, but as yet he was uncertain whether it was the main one or a diversion. For the next few days, as Thompson strove to establish his beachhead, prepare for the march to Stanley and placate his superiors in London, so Menendez became embroiled in wrangling with his high command as to what should be the Argentine reaction. As Colonel 'H' planned his raid on Goose Green, the Argentines considered using it as the base from which to launch a counter-stroke.

The British had succeeded in confusing their enemy by their diversionary attacks at Darwin, Fox Bay and Stanley, the latter two being by air and naval forces. Menendez contacted Galtieri with Crippa's report. To the obvious query as to the numbers involved in the landing Menendez's response did not inspire much confidence. He told his president not to worry as, 'It [the landing] was within our expectations. They have landed in an undefended place. And well ... we are doing what we can'.[19] As he spoke Menendez had yet to make up his mind if this was the main landing. If it was, should he, or could he, counter-attack or would he be better advised sticking with the strategy of sitting tight around Stanley? To try to get some answers quickly he instructed his staff to study the situation. He made the unusual decision that he wanted two separate studies. One was to be made by his own staff, assisted by Brigadier-General Parada in whose area the landing had been made, and the other by Brigadier-General Jofre, responsible for the Stanley area. A final conference to thrash out the recommended options would be held by Colonel Cervo, the chief of intelligence.

Meanwhile, in Buenos Aires, the Junta met at 9.00 pm. Brigadier-General Lami Dozo, the Air Force Commander-in-Chief, argued convincingly that the beachhead must be attacked at once with whatever units could be assembled. He understood that a landing must not be allowed to consolidate or expand, that it would be at its weakest during the first 24 hours. Thereafter it would grow in strength. There was nothing wrong with this reasoning. It was tactically sound, but with two major provisos. Was San Carlos the main landing, and could an attack be physically mounted in practice? When the Junta contacted Menendez and told him to counter-attack, he objected strongly. His staff had advised him to do no such thing. Like the British in London, the Argentine high command did not seem to understand the realities on the ground.

Menendez struggled with the dilemma. With 5 Infantry Brigade still at sea there was, during the first two or three days, no certainty that it would not land nearer Stanley. If San Carlos was a diversion, and he committed troops from Stanley to embroilment so far away, the second landing elsewhere would catch him badly off balance. All along, the Argentines had reasoned that a landing would be within striking distance of Stanley. San Carlos seemed too far away — a landing to draw off his reserves. He would not be pushed into a premature counter-stroke.

Then there were the practicalities of such a move. What troops could be used? How would they get to San Carlos? Could they be properly supported and supplied? British intelligence had been completely wrong in their assessment of both the strength and location of the Argentine strategic reserve. Instead of a full regiment it consisted of Piaggi's B Company of the 12th Regiment, sitting not at Goose Green or Darwin, but to the north of Mount Kent. Like Thompson, Menendez lacked airborne mobility. He only had sufficient troop-lift helicopters to move a company at a time. Like Thompson he was concerned that neither side had air superiority over East Falkland, so heliborne movement by day was a high-risk venture.

Several other possibilities were considered briefly, but quickly rejected as impractical. It was suggested that the 12th Regiment at Goose Green advance on the beachhead (the precise manoeuvre that 2 Para's occupation of Sussex Mountain was designed to frustrate). This was impractical. It would mean sending a weakened regiment, with no artillery support, on foot to attack a vastly stronger enemy defending high ground under the protection of naval gunfire and aircraft. Ideas of using the units at Fox Bay and Port Howard were quickly dismissed as impossible as there was no feasible or secure way of moving them across Falkland Sound to Goose Green, or any other suitable location from which to coordinate a counter-attack.

Menendez told General Garcia at Comodoro Rivadavia:

> We have studied the possibility of sending a contingent of the 12th Regiment to the hilly area, [around San Carlos]. ... Later we are going to try some limited action. We have a plan to climb the hills but there is a risk that the British with their

helicopters would trap us there in a sort of a sandwich.[20]

This decidedly unmilitary explanation for doing little or nothing was, some years later, put more lucidly:

Initially we thought the landing at San Carlos could have been a diversion. The target [of the British] was clearly Puerto Argentino, and it was there that we had to concentrate our forces because we could not move them around. ... It was almost impossible to prevent the landing by sending troops to the beachhead. Our helicopters could not fly because the British dominated the air.[21]

The most Menendez felt able to do was send two 105mm pack howitzers to Piaggi at Goose Green. They were put aboard the Coast Guard vessel *Rio Iguazu* which sailed before first light on the 22 May.

Initially the Argentine high command had grudgingly conceded that Menendez had a point – a second landing might come elsewhere – but by 24 May Menendez was again under intense pressure to do something about a landing that was now clearly not a diversion. While the British public had been keyed up anticipating a rapid advance, the media in Argentina had been feeding the people with claims that the beachhead was surrounded. On the 24th Galtieri visited the joint operations centre which had just been set up at Comodoro Rivadavia. The Argentine's latest appreciation was that San Carlos was indeed the British base for further operations. The high command was becoming exasperated by what it saw as unacceptable inaction on the part of their forces in the islands. A highly critical cable was sent to Menendez. It called into question the honour of the Argentine Army. It spoke of the Navy as having 'contributed its quota of blood already'. It pointed out that the Air Force risked its 'men and material on a daily basis', whereas:

The Army seems to have only an attitude of static defence which, should it continue indefinitely, will make the men wilt in their own positions even before being able to engage in combat with the mass of enemy troops.[22]

Menendez was told that he should strive to eject the British from San Carlos before the arrival of reinforcements (5 Infantry Brigade), which the Argentines expected between 28 and 30 May, at the very least for 'international and national political considerations'. Both in Britain and Argentina the governments concerned berated their field commanders for alleged inertia.

The beachhead must be reduced or at least contained. Galtieri had discussed the possibility with his chiefs-of-staff of calling up the national strategic reserve, but it was considered unnecessary. Similarly, the idea of paratroops being flown to Goose Green, to attack the landings from there, was mooted. A unit of the 4th Air Mobile Brigade was stood by for this possibility, but it came to naught, frustrated by transport problems and British airpower. Menendez must do something with what he had available. He was ordered to 'immediately adopt an offensive attitude', with a substantial force.

These instructions meant using units deployed for the defence of Stanley. The more Menendez looked at his superior's plan the less he liked it. On the 21st a Chinook and two Pucaras had been destroyed at Mount Kent, followed by three more Pucaras and an Augusta lost on the 23rd on West Falkland. His means of moving was being whittled away. By an odd coincidence, on the 25th, Thompson and Menendez were simultaneously contemplating marching across East Falkland to attack the other's position. Both considered it as a last resort as their helicopter lift capacity had been degraded. As it transpired, Thompson thought it feasible, Menendez did not. Ironically both were correct in their deductions.

For Menendez the prospect, even with additional air transport for some of his equipment and supplies, of

1. Part of the gorse line that bisected the battlefield from Boca House to just south of Darwin. It was a major landmark, it caught fire in many places, and was the scene of heavy fighting by B Company at its western end and A Company in the gully to the east.
The Parachute Regiment.

2. A view of the 'billiard table' sloping down to Goose Green from Darwin Ridge. It was over this open ground that C Company advanced, reminding several soldiers of World War One stories or 'Dad's Army'. It provided the Argentine AA gunners on the airfield (in the distance on the right) with the proverbial 'turkey shoot' opportunity.
Captain J. Peatfield.

3. Looking NE from the entrance to the gorse gully. This photograph was taken just after first light on 29 May and shows 2 Para's forward resupply area, and the large gorse patch, through which Colonel 'H' led his Tac 1 forward the previous morning, still burning. *Lieutenant-Colonel (Retd) R. Miller.*

4. The bodies of Colonel 'H' and Captains Dent and Wood are about to be flown out by Sea King helicopter from the gorse gully on the morning of 29 May. *Lieutenant-Colonel (Retd) R. Miller.*

5. Part of the Argentine trench system on the northern outskirts of Goose Green. It faces NW to cover the airfield. Note the overhead cover and turf camouflage. There are other trenches between the foreground and the hut, and in the centre of the hedgeline. *Lieutentant-Colonel (Retd) R. Miller.*

6. Goose Green settlement as it is today. The community hall, in which all the inhabitants were confined before and during the battle, is the building in the centre with the small spire. *Mr R. Smither.*

7. What Boca House really looked like. Little wonder many in 2 Para were puzzled that they never saw it. The shoreline in the centre is the route used by D Company in its flanking move to accept an Argentine surrender in the area. *Mr R. Smither.*

8. A view of the shoreline along which D Company advanced in its flanking move to accept an Argentine surrender south of Boca House. This photograph was taken from near the ruins of Boca House looking north. *Mr R. Smither.*

9. A view of the spot at which Colonel 'H' was shot taken from the Argentine machine-gunner's position. The white stones mark the approximate place he fell. *Mr R. Smither.*

10. Camilla Creek House and its outbuildings, into which most of 2 Para crammed itself on the night of 26/27 May. *The Parachute Regiment.*

11. Burntside House — A Company's first objective. The company attacked from the higher ground at the top of the photograph, then across the stream and up to the house. *The Parachute Regiment.*

12. A rifleman's view, looking up the gorse gully from near the entrance. It was in this gully that A Company was held up for so long on the morning of 28 May. The Argentine main position was over the crest on the right. Fortunately no Argentines occupied Darwin Hill proper, the lower slope of which is visible on the left. *Captain R. Knight.*

13. The remains of the school (chimney on right) looking north over the small estuary used by 11 Platoon and some of Patrols Platoon as a covered approach to the school. The 2 Para memorial is just visible on the skyline of Darwin Ridge in the centre left. *Captain R. Knight.*

14. The view from Lieutenant Estevez's platoon position on Darwin Ridge, looking north. The open ground over which A Company advanced at dawn and Colonel 'H''s route along the edge of the inlet to the gorse patch on the right are clearly visible. *Captain R. Knight.*

15. The re-entrant up which Colonel 'H' ran before turning left up the slope. He was shot by an Argentine machine-gunner on the right-hand slope. *A Company, 1st Battalion, The Cheshire Regiment.*

16. The view from the Argentine positions on the ring contour (low hill) south of Boca House, looking north. B Company was pinned for several hours along the line of the gorse. It was the hill behind the gorse that reminded Major Crosland of Bowl's Barrow on Salisbury Plain. *Captain R. Knight.*

marching the 80 kilometres 'under constant enemy fire from the air, in an area without cover, wood, drinking water or means of subsistence'[23] was a non-starter. His troops did not even have backpacks for such a move, which he estimated would take eight days. They were certainly unfit for such a gruelling trek, and he rightly foresaw disaster at the end of it. To make such an advance, culminating in a major assault, would necessitate using some 70 per cent of his troops deployed around Stanley. To denude these defences, to abandon his strategy of forcing the British to fight him in prepared positions, for the sake of a foolhardy gamble would, in his view, be madness. He refused to comply with the Junta's plan. He threatened to resign if pressed. He was not pressed.

As Thompson and Menendez disputed with their superiors over what they should do next, the battle for air superiority raged above San Carlos Water and Falkland Sound, watched with fascination by the ground troops of both armies. The period of the most intense air combat was between the 21-25 May. During this time the Argentine Air Forces (naval as well as Air Force units) flew some 180 sorties from Argentina, of which 117 reached their target area. Nineteen aircraft failed to return. One in six of the aircraft joining battle were destroyed. For this sacrifice a destroyer (HMS *Coventry*) two frigates (HMS *Ardent* and HMS *Antelope*) and a supply ship (*Atlantic Conveyor*) were sunk, while another destroyer, two frigates and two supply ships were hit and damaged. Seventy-seven British, mostly sailors, died. Despite their great gallantry the Argentine pilots failed to cripple the British ability to prosecute the ground war for two reasons – one tactical, the other technical.[24]

The tactical error was in concentrating their air attacks on the wrong targets. It was British warships that bore the brunt and suffered the most. The supply ships and landing ships came off comparatively lightly, while the troops on the ground suffered even less. The pilots, in concentrating their efforts, had a choice of three types of target – warships, supply ships, or troops on the ground. They chose the wrong one. From the point of view of the future land battle the key to preventing a British advance lay in crippling their supply system. The sinking of the *Atlantic Conveyor*, by an Exocet missile probably intended for the carriers, had an immediate and dramatic effect on Thompson's plans. Without logistic support and helicopters the beachhead would remain what it was, a small toehold. By dawn on the 22nd 3 Commando Brigade's marines and paratroopers were ashore but their supplies were still on the *Europic Ferry* (carrying 2 Para's landrovers), *Fort Austin*, *Stromness*, *Sir Galahad*, *Sir Geraint*, *Sir Lancelot*, *Sir Percivale* and *Sir Tristram*. Kill them, and you hamstrung the ground force's ability to move or fight. The Argentines made the decision to attack warships which were high profile targets the destruction of which was usually spectacular, and captured the imagination of the public. Success against warships was also seen as an appropriate revenge for the loss of the *Belgrano*, and seemed to indicate ascendency to the wider international audience.

The technical problem was the failure of so many Argentine bombs to explode after striking the target. During the period 12 May - 12 June no less than thirteen 1000-pound bombs failed to detonate after hitting British ships. The most fortunate ship of the conflict was the frigate HMS *Plymouth* which was stuck by no less than four 1000-pounders none of which went off, although they did cause a severe fire on the flight deck by exploding a depth charge. The landing ships *Sir Galahad*, *Sir Bedivere*, and *Sir Lancelot* all escaped serious damage for the same reason. The difficulty was that the bombs were fused, set to explode, after a brief period of time had elapsed to allow for the fall of the bomb and the penetration of the target. In order to attack, however, the pilots had to fly so low — usually below 100 feet — that the bombs often struck their target much sooner than anticipated. It was common for a bomb to penetrate the entire ship without exploding.

At Goose Green Piaggi had reason to be concerned with the landing of 3 Commando Brigade some 25 kilometres to the north. His command was now, unexpectedly, the closest Argentine unit to the enemy. He felt decidedly exposed, with his unit, already something of an under trained hotch-potch, now even more depleted. Estoban's 60-man Eagle Detachment had had their moment of glory and had now disappeared or been taken prisoner. He had lost two platoons, and his B Company was still retained as the so-called strategic reserve. Lack of sufficient supporting weapons was a problem, lack of rations was a problem, the weather was a problem, but the biggest problem of all was lack of artillery support. Piaggi had no guns other than anti-aircraft ones.

As related above, this deficiency was partially rectified at the last moment by the sending of two 105mm pack howitzers on the *Rio Iguazu*. These guns were dismantled and put aboard the ship during the night of 21st/22nd, but there were only two hours of darkness left when she finally sailed from Stanley. At around 7.25 am she was half-way up Choiseul Sound, within sight of her destination, when the first Sea Harrier combat air patrol of the day over the southern end of Falkland Sound spotted her. One aircraft, piloted by Lieutenant Martin Hale, dived down to attack, while the other, flown by Lieutenant-Commander Frederickson, provided overhead cover. Hale's cannon fire raked the vessel, causing it to burst into flames. Two Coast Guard sailors were hit, one of whom died, while the ship went aground on the beach.

For Piaggi this was a bitter blow. He needed both the guns and other stores on the *Rio Iguazu*. He despatched a salvage party by helicopter to retrieve what it could. The Army officer with this party was 2nd Lieutenant Centurion. The precious guns were lifted from the flooded hold, along with some other supplies, and taken to Goose Green. Both had been damaged but one was made serviceable. Piaggi remonstrated with his superiors that one gun was hardly sufficient. Two more were lifted in by helicopter a few days later. Although neither could know it, Piaggi and Colonel 'H' were both destined to be supported in the coming battle by exactly the same number of 105mm guns -- three.

V

PREPARATIONS

'We got word that some pillock back in England had warned the Argies we were coming. This knocked some of the confidence out of everyone.'

Lance-Corporal Bill Bentley MM, describing the BBC announcement on 27 May that the Paras were poised to attack Goose Green.

Six days on Sussex Mountain was enough. Everybody was thankful to be moving at last. A week spent exposed to the wind and weather on those bare slopes, watching the Argentine Air Force hammering the ships below had not been an enjoyable experience. No less than twenty-seven men were evacuated for sickness and injuries to ankles or knees. Of these, twelve had succumbed to trench foot. A seemingly insignificant event like getting wet feet on the landing could, and did, cause severe suffering. The problem was that once wet, boots, socks, and feet could never dry out properly. The issue boot was useless at keeping water out and excellent at keeping it in. The constant dampness, coupled with the freezing cold, could cripple a soldier within a few days if elaborate precautions were not taken. Everybody tended to their feet with the same devotion as that given to their weapons. Every opportunity was taken to remove boots, dry feet, powder feet, and put on different socks. The wet socks were put inside uniforms, in the groin or armpits where, over a period of hours, they would gradually dry out. The distress was compounded by the soggy soil, trenches filled with freezing water when barely half dug, and marching inevitably meant crossing boggy ground. For some this battle was never won. Their feet became white and wrinkled, icy cold to touch. The pain has been likened to one's feet being slowly crushed in a vice.

Other afflictions included minor cuts, burns, dental sick (the medical officer extracted his first tooth), even one case of suspected appendicitis, and one of heat exhaustion — a soldier in C Company had marched too far too fast with too much arctic clothing on.

As day followed day with no sign of the brigade doing anything other than watch the carnage at sea, so resentment mounted. The operation was compared to the infamous landings in the Crimea or at Gallipoli. Inactivity, lack of information on what was happening and why, on top of day after day spent seeking shelter from the biting wind crouched behind flimsy walls of wet peat inevitably dampened morale.

The problems 2 Para had to overcome on Sussex Mountain have been described with great clarity by Sergeant Barrett of 1 Platoon of A Company who, due to his platoon commander injuring his knee, commanded the platoon at Goose Green.

Even on the top of mountains the water table was only a foot or 18 inches below the surface. That meant building sangars out of peat turf, but left us without overhead protection. The wind was a big enemy. It might be still for as much as a day, then blow up to 40 m.p.h. Our main rations were arctic, which need a lot of water. Because it had to be brought in by helicopter we were rationed to about one bottle per man per day. We were frequently short of hexamine [solid fuel blocks] which was not a good morale factor. In that climate, in winter, frequent brews are essential. Ammunition had to be checked every day because it could go rusty very quickly. Bandoliers were also emptied everyday.

Constantly damp and muddy clothing does not help morale. It was an uphill struggle to try to get

118

kit dried out. Every day foot inspections took place. The damp and cold combined in our static position to cause loss of feeling in the feet. At first manpower was not a problem but as our tasks increased and trench foot occurred everybody, regardless of rank, had to work on stag [sentry duty or radio watch].[1]

There were several near 'blue on blue' incidents while the battalion relearnt the importance of attention to detail, and the passage of information.[2] A visit to battalion headquarters could be a risky venture as sometimes the Defence Platoon sentries had not be forewarned. One patrol from 4 Platoon, led by Lieutenant Hocking, was nearly mortared by a C Company OP who was unaware friendly troops were out in that area. By a freak coincidence, not uncommon in war, while Hocking was out on patrol his empty trenches were subjected to a succession of air bursts from the supporting artillery battery. There had been a mix-up with the fuses. In A Company area a patrol sent out to capture a suspected enemy patrol ended by it nearly shooting up a friendly helicopter flight that had been positioned nearby. Although battalion headquarters were aware of this flight the information had not reached A Company.

The commanding officer was incensed by these lapses of coordination on the part of his headquarter staff, and they only served to reinforce his apparent determination to supervise every detail personally. Mistakes occur in war, and it should be remembered that 2 Para's headquarters had been thrown together at the last moment with little chance to train as a team. Major Keeble had only arrived early in 1982, the operations officer just before the battalion sailed, others such as the signals officer and several watchkeepers were new to their jobs, while two (Captain Arnold RA and Lieutenant Thurman RM) joined in the Falklands. The only opportunity for the main headquarters to practice its procedures had been on the voyage south. In the event a proposed two to three day CPX was cut to 12 hours.

Colonel 'H' was similarly frustrated by his inability to probe the nearest enemy at Goose Green. He was only allowed to send out local patrols and set up a line of OPs, the farthest away being just south of Cantera Mountain only half way to Goose Green. This was unsatisfactory in that they were too far forward to alert the battalion of imminent air attacks, and not far enough forward to see what was happening on the Goose Green isthmus. There were, however, moments of intense excitement. These occurred during air strikes. Fortunately for 2 Para it was not a priority target for the Argentine pilots, as they had little protection from air attack due to the lack of defence stores with which to strengthen their positions. Also, after watching the Rapier anti-aircraft missile in action nobody had much confidence in its protective abilities. Great importance was attached to getting these twelve Rapiers into position around the landing area but, as Brigadier Thompson said, 'No one was quite sure what seven weeks in the lower vehicle deck of a vibrating, heaving LSL would do to the Rapier firing posts'.[3] Not a lot. Of those sited in 2 Para's area three generators developed faults and two tracking units failed. Sergeant Rogers, of the Anti-Tank Platoon, described many of the missiles as 'looping all over the place'. In his opinion, if an aircraft was coming in low, straight at you, you could use the Milan. Private Worrall did exactly that. The first time the British Army ever fired a Milan in anger was not at a tank, or even a bunker, but an aircraft. Worrall's aim was good, and he held the missile on course until the Skyhawk pilot saw it with only a split second to spare. A desperate banking manoeuvre just got him out of trouble.

The Machine Gun Platoon fired thousands of rounds into the sky, providing a curtain of bullets through which a number of aircraft were forced to fly. The machine-gunners claimed three hits on different planes. The Defence Platoon, the rifle companies, indeed everybody at some stage, had a go. It was a good way to vent their frustration, and on a number of occasions the firers were convinced their shots went home.

Colour-Sergeant Caudwell claims to have been doused with aviation fuel from an aircraft into whose belly he and his men were firing.

Like many military operations the move to Camilla Creek House was characterized by the 'hurry up and wait' syndrome. The hurry was in getting off Sussex Mountain, the waiting came during the four- or five-hour tab south, as the column concertinaed or stopped frequently for no obvious reason. Then there would be another day of waiting at Camilla Creek House while senior officers made plans and soldiers prepared or tried to rest. Colonel 'H' had dashed back from brigade headquarters to break the welcome news that the Goose Green operation was finally on. He urged speed. Time was short, the main body of the battalion was to be away at last light. There was only time to issue orders to get everybody to Camilla Creek House. The thinking and planning for what was to happen afterwards would be done there. D Company, which was to lead the way and secure the house, had to move off almost immediately. Major Neame recalls the haste:

> My initial brief from the CO for the move to Camilla Creek House took two minutes. The raid was confirmed, I had to get on the road and secure the house as an assembly area. The battalion would follow after last light. I barely got a chance to ask what to take. I was told to centralize my bergens and leave the company's GPMG(SF) kits.[4]

D Company was to be followed after dark by the remainder of the battalion in the order: A Company; Tac 1, with all of battalion headquarters; C Company headquarters, (Patrols Platoon and half of the Recce Platoon were still out manning OPs, and where to join up on the way to, or at, Camilla Creek House); B Company; Support Company.

The battalion almost left without the engineers from the Recce Troop of 59 Independent Commando Squadron. These sixteen men, under Lieutenant Clive Livingstone, just managed to catch the tail of the battalion snake as it disappeared down the hill. This troop, organized into four sections of four men, had not had a good start to the war so far. The day before they had been aboard the *Sir Lancelot* at about 11.15 am when the ship was struck by a 1000 pound bomb which fortunately failed to detonate. There was a scramble to get off before the bomb went off. Troops, including the engineers whose home it had been, came ashore in the clothes they were wearing plus personal weapons. Everything else, including bergens, warm clothing, and sleeping bags, was left behind.

Livingstone, whose men were useless without their kit, tried in vain to persuade brigade headquarters to allow them back on board to retrieve their gear. Undeterred, he scrounged a lift on a landing craft but forgot to tell the coxswain to wait, with the result that he and his party were stranded aboard the ship. Eventually another LCU was obtained so Livingstone and his men toiled through the night to get equipment ashore. Later that day the Recce Troop was ordered to join 2 Para on Sussex Mountain for the Goose Green operation. There was a frantic rush to exchange their soaking kit with that of Support Troop personnel before the exhausted sappers, who had had no sleep, no food and no rest for 36 hours, were lifted up to the summit just in time for another sleepless and gruelling night.

Also in a hurry was Captain Rory Wagon, a former 2 Para medical officer at the Ajax Bay Field Hospital. Given fifteen minutes to get ready to rejoin the battalion as the second doctor, he crammed a haversack with the medical supplies he thought he might need, ran to a waiting helicopter, and was whisked away to meet up with the RAP only minutes before the march started.

Major Hector Gullan MBE, MC, a Parachute Regiment officer serving on the staff at brigade headquarters, was sent forward by the brigadier at this time to act as his personal liaison officer. He had his own direct radio link to Thompson and was to be the brigade commander's main source of information on the operation.

D Company reached the vicinity of Camilla Creek House well ahead of the main body. Major Neame has described the approach:

> After tabbing along for about 12 kilometres over some pretty featureless ground I was not quite sure just how far away the house was. I didn't want to blunder in unprepared so I thought I would call up a fire mission. This would serve a double purpose; firstly it would hopefully neutralize any enemy who might be there, and also it would confirm to us exactly where the house was. Well, the guns duly fired but instead of the shells landing ahead of us they landed about 1,000 metres to our rear. This was not very reassuring as we had certainly not overshot our objective. At that stage we didn't know about the gunners' problems so there were a few caustic comments about the artillery's reputation, and starting the battle with the usual drop shorts.[5]

This inaccuracy caused misgivings, as only the previous day Camilla Creek House had been targeted by the guns, and the shots adjusted by a Patrols Platoon OP. At about this time D Company was joined by Patrols Platoon, under Captain Paul Farrar, who were to be the only members of the battalion to fight at Goose Green wearing their distinctive maroon berets rather than helmets. This had come about as Colonel 'H' had sent them on an area ambush patrol at the head of the valley east of Sussex Mountain, just north of Bodie Peak, on the night of the 25/26th. He instructed Farrar to 'go extremely light'. His words were 'Take food for two days.... I don't mean two days' rations, just some biscuits and brews - enough to last two days.'[6] He was also told not to take either sleeping bags or helmets. Farrar had jokingly remarked to his commanding officer that as they were to undertake the ambush without helmets he had better not send them anywhere else without coming back to Sussex Mountain. Which was precisely what happened. Farrar remembered the night in ambush as 'crystal clear, and, very, very cold'. In his diary he recorded it as a 'desperate night'. They had brewed up for breakfast among the rocks on Bodie Peak before spending the morning 'being pushed around the ridge by battalion headquarters. "Can you see this or that place from your location?". This and that included Ceritos House and Camilla Creek house'.[7] Later they were told to join up with D Company at the house. When they eventually reached their destination it had been many hours since they had slept or eaten.

> We were pretty tired and hungry on arrival at Camilla Creek House. In the room we occupied were some cans of Argentine rations. Imaginations ran riot as to whether it was deliberately planted and poisoned. Needless to say hunger got the better of us.[8]

The rest of the battalion was led by 2nd Lieutenant Guy Wallis, with 3 Platoon of A Company. As battalion headquarters moved off Captain Wood, possibly with a premonition of things to come, looked up at the brilliant night sky and said, 'Just take a good look at that sky - it might be your last'.

'We tabbed off at a horrific pace,' said the medical officer, Captain Hughes, 'which eventually settled down when one of A Company collapsed, causing a long halt.'[9] It was Private Phillips who lay unconscious. Colonel 'H' thought he was dying, but the medical officer was less pessimistic and left Private Clegg to look after him while everybody else pressed on. Those with heavier loads fared worse. The doctor was shortly to have the chance to diagnose and treat his own injury. As he stumbled over a rut in the track he twisted his ankle and felt a sharp stab of pain which he was sure indicated a fracture. His muttered expletives caused some muted merriment to those nearby, but Hughes knew that if he took his boot off the foot would swell, making putting it back impossible. He did the opposite, tightened the lace and hobbled on.

The march soon slowed as initial eagerness evaporated. Most men walked wearily with bowed heads and aching backs, particularly the medics and signallers whose loads exceeded the others. At one moment the column pounded along with those at the rear cursing and stumbling as they tried to keep up, the next it slowed to a shuffle, or came to a halt for some unknown reason. Men began to doze at halts and had to be woken. At one stage a large gap existed between the battalion and Support Company struggling to keep up at the rear. It is a strange but well known fact that in a long column of marching troops those at the back have the hardest time, for ever having to speed up to catch up, while those at the front march at a normal steady pace.

In B Company Major Crosland took the opportunity to put across some of his battlefield experience:

> During the march down, in the usual 'Airborne Snake' you are either running to catch up or waiting to move, and freezing as your sweat goes cold. As we approached CCH the Argentine garrison at Goose Green fired off some harassing fire. Not unnaturally some Toms took cover on hearing the shells, which generally landed well away. One was then trying to explain, make them listen to the noise thereby gauging the direction and so the danger of these shells.
>
> Once having stopped I looked around and saw some shell-holes that were obviously fresh as there was no ice on the edges. I asked a couple of my Toms what they thought these holes were. After a while considering the question, they said they were holes! I said 'Yes, that is a correct observation but what type?' No response. So I suggested that if they were mole hills there 'must be fucking big moles down here'. Much laughter! Then I said shell-holes, and if you look there is no ice round the edge indicating recent shelling. The Toms left this position at a run.[10]

At one point it was noticed that the FAC was missing from battalion headquarters. This was the sole representative of the RAF on the march, Squadron-Leader Jock Penman. Sometime later Captain Peter Ketley, at the head of Support Company, spotted someone on a separate route through his sniper scope. No one could fathom out who it was. Then it dawned that it was Penman with a sprained ankle, on his own, without his weapon, and exhausted. He had done remarkably well to keep moving in his dazed state after a bad fall. Penman was in his middle fifties, a hard drinker, heavy smoker, and unfit for the sort of exertions required of paratroops in war. A medic, Lance-Corporal Bentley, strapped his ankle and helped him hobble along at his own pace.

As 2 Para arrived at Camilla Creek House Colonel 'H' had an immediate decision to make. Should the battalion seek shelter inside the house, out-buildings and sheds, or deploy tactically around the area? He was well aware that his men needed rest and warmth above all else if they were to face a fullscale battle in 24 hours' time. The buildings offered these to some degree; lying in the open did not. 2 Para was told to move in. The risk of Camilla Creek House being registered by the Argentine artillery as a target was appreciated. It was a calculated risk, typical of the sort that occur on operations. As it turned out Colonel 'H' had made the right choice.

Allowing for standing patrols and sentries, to cram 450 men into one house and about ten sheds or outbuildings takes some doing. The house was 'jam packed full, with men sleeping on tables, even in cupboards on shelves'. As the medical officer explained:

There was not enough space for us all to stretch our legs so we piled them on top of one another like pat-a-cake. Then, like pat-a-cake, every half hour one would wake with one's feet at the bottom of the pile, extract them, put them on top, only to wake again half an hour later with crushed legs.[11]

126

Extraordinary ingenuity was displayed in seeking shelter from the elements. Battalion headquarters watchkeepers were crammed in a coal shed, 11 Platoon headquarters fitted into a toilet, while an entire section squeezed into a cupboard. If the conditions were not conducive to comfort at least they generated warmth.

It was still dark as the eight men squirmed on to the forward slope of a hill on the north bank of Camilla Creek from which they hoped, come daylight, to be able to observe much of the Goose Green isthmus. There were two parties of four men, all with faces blackened. One group was led by Corporal 'Taff' Evans, who had joined 2 Para eight years earlier at 17½. He enjoyed his job in Recce Platoon, the independence, the living and working together within a small team. Today could be the climax of his career so far, the ultimate test of all the years of training in fieldcraft and observation. His commanding officer had sent him out to secure information — detailed, specific, tactical information on the Argentine positions that 2 Para must tackle the next night. This information was needed urgently. On it would be based much of the battalion plan of attack. He had all morning and afternoon in which to observe and pass back what he saw. Evans knew that negative information — where the enemy was not — was just as valuable as positive. With less than 24 hours left before the battle, intelligence on the Argentines was still vague, imprecise and much too generalized.

His team was well equipped for its task. Evans carried a rifle, one 66mm, one fragmentation grenade, one white phosphorus grenade, binoculars, and a 352 VHF Clansman radio with a spare battery. His number two, Lance-Corporal Abe Lincoln, was similarly equipped. Lance-Corporal Bob Cole was the radio operator, humping the A16 HF back-up set on the battalion net. It would only be used if Evans could not get through on his. The fourth man was Private Dave Thearle who carried the GPMG light machine gun.

The other four men made up the FAC's party. Captain

Peter Ketley had taken over as FAC from Penman who had been medically evacuated, as he had been previously trained in this role. Colonel 'H' had sent him forward as he wanted to make use of the Harriers during the day to soften up identified enemy positions with air strikes. Ketley's job was to talk the pilots on to their targets. At about the same time as Evans and Ketley were looking for a good hide position another Recce Platoon patrol was doing the same thing some 700 metres away to the SW. This team was led by the platoon commander, Lieutenant Colin Connor. Both OPs had been briefed to try to identify the location of the Argentine 105mm guns that had fired some shells near the battalion as it approached Camilla Creek House. Colonel 'H' was anxious to be able to register enemy artillery positions in advance.

Evans had to select and take up his position before first light. Come the dawn there could be no movement to a better position, so the choice must be made in the dark without knowing for certain how much could be seen, or how exposed to enemy view they would be. Evans was lucky in that, although he knew he was on a forward slope, there were two small knolls nearby with a fair amount of gorse for concealment. The patrol split into pairs. Evans and Cole took the first stag, lying side by side, making the most of the gorse to make a hide, while Lincoln and Thearle tunnelled into a scrub patch a few metres to the rear to rest. Every two hours the pairs would change over. As eight men were too many to conceal on a forward slope Ketley's party withdrew further back, out of sight, leaving the observation work to the OP.

Initially not much was discernible at first light as there was a mist over the creek. In the grey light there was perhaps a last chance to move to a better position, but Evans could see nowhere more suitable. The mist dispersed quite quickly to reveal an amazing sight, a sight that made Evans and Cole catch their breath. Only 400-500 metres away, on the other side of the creek, was an enemy company position dug in on the forward slope and crest of a low hill. Their OP was on higher ground so when they looked through binoculars it seemed as though they could almost reach out to touch the Argentines.

Carefully, Evans began to make notes of what he saw. Certainly the number of trenches and troops indicated a company. The position stretched across the isthmus towards Burntside House, which was clearly visible. Evans recognized the enemy's routine. There had been a stand-to at first light; now soldiers were clambering out of trenches, bunching together in small groups, one or two officers or NCOs appeared to be walking round checking activities. Then Evans heard the sound, instantly recognizable by soldiers, of clattering mess-tins. They were going to have breakfast. The watchers saw a group of about twenty move off towards Burntside House. A closer look revealed some tents and what was obviously a field kitchen not far from the house. The enemy had some military common sense as it appeared only half the troops went for their meal at a time. There were possibly two .50 calibre heavy machine-guns visible on the position, one apparently pointing more or less at the OP, the other towards the track running north to the neck of the isthmus. Quietly and calmly Evans started to pass back information over his radio.

As the sun rose higher so more of the isthmus became visible. Evans' OP was higher than Connor's so he was better placed to see further. The approximate areas of the isthmus that could be seen by either, or both, of these patrols is indicated on Map 8. Throughout the morning, taking it in turns, Evans' patrol scanned the whole area through their glasses. A long look to the SW revealed about five trenches, or bunkers, near where Boca House was supposed to be. Much nearer, between Boca House and the company position opposite him, was what seemed to be a platoon position on a knoll overlooking Camilla Creek. Due south, nothing could be seen of either Darwin or Goose Green settlements, but Darwin Hill was plainly visible with a thick gorse hedge across the top. Sixteen trenches were counted on the high ground west of Darwin

129

Hill. At one stage a lot of tracer shells were fired in the air from the direction of Goose Green. There were no aircraft around at the time so Evans put it down to test firing. There was no sign of any artillery gun position, but a gun, possibly a recoilless one, with a vehicle, was spotted between the track and Coronation Point.

The Argentine company was a perfect target for an artillery or aircraft strike, but Evans was not permitted, to his great disappointment, to fire the guns as Colonel 'H' did not want to risk giving away the gun position. An air strike would, however, be arranged. Colonel 'H' had requested air strikes over the isthmus at about 1.15 am. He had no hard targets at that stage, but wanted Harriers available from 8.00 am through to dusk. Some three hours later he had been annoyed to hear from brigade that, as the brigade log recorded, '0826 [4.26 am local] From Brigade to 2 Para. At present air is out due to weather. No naval gunfire support as ship withdrawn before first light'.

After some time Ketley told Evans he was leaving with his party as he had been called back to battalion headquarters. Evans thought this odd — who was going to control the Harrier strike if, or when, it came? Unbeknown to Evans, 2 Para had put in a further request for air strikes, listing six of the targets described by Evans and Connor. The brigade log records this request as being received at 10.00 am.

Meanwhile the enemy company across the creek was engaged in fairly relaxed routine administration. Some 'stood around looking miserable', others were seen washing their feet. It was also noticed that one or two patrols of about eight men moved off to the left (east) of Evans' position. They were presumably going north via the narrow neck of the isthmus. It was a little disconcerting as they might get behind him, and throughout the morning he never saw any of them returning. At one stage a tractor and trailer came down the track bringing what looked like two recoilless rifles with ammunition containers.

Map 8

2 PARA RECCE PLATOON'S CRITICAL OPs

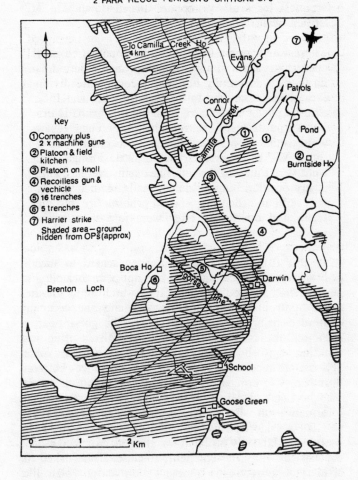

Key

① Company plus
  2 x machine guns
② Platoon & field
  kitchen
③ Platoon on knoll
④ Recoilless gun &
  vechicle
⑤ 16 trenches
⑥ 5 trenches
⑦ Harrier strike
  Shaded area—ground
  hidden from OPs (approx)

To Camilla Creek Ho
4 km

Evans

Connor

Camilla Creek

Patrols

Pond

Burntside Ho

Boca Ho

Brenton Loch

Darwin

School

Goose Green

0   1   2 Km

Suddenly, shortly before 11.30, the Argentine machine-guns and automatic rifles opened fire. Their target was Connor's patrol away to the right (SW) of Evans. Perhaps some small movement had been spotted. Evans heard Connor's contact report over the radio, then his request for artillery support turned down. He later described what followed:

> There was a slight lull in the firing and then they opened up again. I was watching their position as no firing was coming our way. People were diving everywhere, standing-to in their trenches and then climbing back out. There was a lot of automatic fire but I couldn't see the machine-gun. Then I saw white smoke down the valley as Mr Connor's patrol threw WP to cover their withdrawal. Things then went very quiet on the set. The enemy were looking at my position but couldn't actually see us. We lay very still, and then they started probing fire into the scrub and overhead. They were just shooting at random.[12]

After this firing had stopped Evans decided to stay in position as he was certain they had not been located. For perhaps half an hour Evans stayed watching as another enemy patrol went out to his left, and the company continued firing sporadic bursts into the gorse nearby. Although the fire was wild, with the firers often just standing up to shoot, some shots came dangerously close. When Cole received a round though his glove, between thumb and forefinger, Evans decided it was time to go. The hornets' nest had been thoroughly stirred up, all information on what he had seen had been passed back, so he considered his patrol had now outlived its usefulness. His only problem was the lack of a good escape route with a fully alerted enemy so close. Evans asked for artillery support via his company commander which, like previous requests, was rejected, but the battalion would send a platoon from A Company to help get him out. His persistence in asking for indirect fire brought Colonel 'H' to the radio. Evans later commented: 'The net was fairly blue at that stage, and the commanding officer said an air strike was on its way as the weather was clearing.'[13]

Not long after this two Harriers appeared. They flew in low from the NE, heading SW over the isthmus. Ketley had not returned so there was no FAC to speak to the aircraft. As they flew overhead without dropping bombs there was 'pandemonium in the Argentine company position, with a lot of wild firing of small arms tracer into the air'. The Harriers banked, turned, and came over again. Evans told his gunner, Thearle, to open up when he threw a smoke grenade — with the enemy distracted, now was the time to go. He told battalion headquarters what he was doing, threw the smoke, Thearle fired a complete magazine, and they dashed back into dead ground.

They turned in time to see the second air strike. This time cluster bombs rained down but well beyond Burntside House. Unusually, an aircraft returned for a third pass, and this was its undoing. Evans saw it hit. 'The Harrier banked up over Goose Green with the AA guns tracking it. They took the tail off, and I saw the pilot eject.'[14]

Evans and his men got back to Camilla Creek House around 2.30 pm to be debriefed by Colonel 'H'.

When Colonel 'H' arrived at Camilla Creek House his overriding concern had been to find out more about the enemy on the isthmus. He was not happy with the SAS's vague picture of demoralized Argentines whose actual locations they had not pinpointed accurately. He had daylight on the 27th to improve his intelligence and, at last, he could use his own resources to get it. But it had to be done quickly. He needed detailed information in time to make his plan and issue his orders. The result was, as we have seen, the despatch, in the early hours of the morning of the two Recce Platoon patrols and the FAC's party. Colonel 'H' wanted to find the enemy, but he also wanted to hit them from the air. He was reluctant to use artillery fire in case it gave away the gun position, and also the targets were likely to be at extreme range. Harriers should be available so he put in his request for them shortly after 1.00 am. Not for another three hours was he told the weather was unsuitable.

At around 10.00 in the morning battalion headquarters tuned in to the BBC World Service - just in time for an unbelievable shock.[15] The announcer stated that, 'a parachute battalion is poised and ready to assault Darwin and Goose Green'. Robert Fox, from BBC Radio, had been attached to 2 Para to cover its operations since Ascension Island. He has described Colonel 'H's reaction:

> 'H' appeared in the room and started his tirade about suing John Nott, the Prime Minister if necessary, for allowing his battalion's position to be given away so gratuitously. 'Do you think we could do it, Robert?' he asked. 'Sue them. Tell Sara [his wife] she's got to do it. I'll write to her.' Much of this was in fun [although nobody present was laughing], and 'H''s widow tells me this was very much a catch-phrase of his, to sue everyone in sight if disaster threatened.[16]

The listeners at Camilla Creek House were aghast. 2 Para officers were convinced such information could only have come from the Ministry of Defence officials. It was they who knew about the original raid, its cancellation, and now that it was on again. What they could not know was that speculation about the impending break-out and attack on Goose Green had been rife since the beginning of the week. The *Daily Telegraph* and *Express* that morning both indicated that 2 Para were virtually in the settlements already. According to Robert Fox,

> On the Thursday, the day before the attack, at least one defence correspondent mentioned specifically Camilla Creek as a rendezvous point for the attack.

This attack was not scheduled to begin until 0600 GMT on the following morning, Friday 28 May. If they looked at Fleet Street, the Argentinians had more signals about the operation than a troop of Boy Scouts could give at semaphore practice.[17]

The immediate result was that the bulk of 2 Para left the buildings and dispersed into positions in the open.

Colonel 'H''s only consolation was that he had been receiving good intelligence on enemy positions from Connor and Evans since shortly after first light. The intelligence officer's map was showing a rash of red chinagraph symbols. Nevertheless, the BBC had gone a long way towards wrecking the commanding officer's day. It was an extraordinary example of the friction of war over which participants in events have so little control. Commanders have to learn to live with friction and frustration. The mistakes, the breakdowns, the lack of time, the lack of support, adverse weather, and at times even the seeming incompetence of others (of which this radio broadcast appeared a horrendous example) must be borne with robustness. For 2 Para's commanding officer it was not the last discouraging incident that day.

By mid-morning Colonel 'H' had prepared his orders. An 'O' group was to be held at 11.00 but when he arrived a number of officers were missing, among them at least one Company Commander. For people not to arrive at their commanding officer's orders means one of three things — either the person no longer has any regard for his military career, he is physically prevented from attending for some reason beyond his control, or he did not know about it. It is an occurrence guaranteed to cause tempers to rise. With key subordinates absent there is no way a commanding officer can proceed. On a peacetime exercise there can be no life-threatening repercussions, but on the eve of an actual operation with time pressing, a postponed or incomplete 'O' group can be a disastrous start to an undertaking. Colonel 'H' went up in flames. It transpired that the message summoning the 'O' group had not got to all its intended recipients, or not in time for them to make their way from their dispersed locations.[18] Part of the problem was that everybody was still in the process of scattering to the four winds around the House brought about by the BBC's bombshell. Nevertheless, to Colonel 'H' this all reflected on the competence of his headquarters staff. The 'O' group was postponed. It was not to reassemble for another four hours.[19]

An hour before the attempted 'O' group Colonel 'H' had put in another urgent request for an air strike, this time with specific grid references and descriptions of targets provided by the forward patrols. The weather was improving so the likelihood was the request would be met. Captain Ketley with the FAC party would be able to guide in the Harriers — or so the colonel thought. But Ketley was no longer out with the Recce Platoon patrols. Sometime earlier a watchkeeper (an officer doing duty on the battalion command radio net) had summoned him, over the radio, to Camilla Creek House to update himself with the latest information on the enemy. The officer thought he was only 100 metres away instead of nearly five kilometres. Ketley, who did not think to protest or explain where he was, started to trudge back. The problem lay with the passage of information, or rather the lack of its passage, within the headquarters. With inexperience and under pressure errors occur. This was an example. Ketley arrived back shortly after it was known that a Harrier mission was on its way. His appearance in front of his commanding officer at that moment was ill-timed to say the least. Coming just prior to the 'O' group set-back, it did little to improve Colonel 'H''s mood. Ketley was sent back to rejoin the patrols feeling decidedly chastened. The Harriers arrived first and on their initial pass could not make out the Argentine positions; on their second they dropped their bombs anyway and missed; on their third Squadron-Leader Iveson's aircraft was shot down. The friction of war again. An FAC on the ground should have been able to use the laser target marker with which they

136

were equipped to 'paint' the target as the aircraft approached. The bombs would have travelled down the reflected laser beam on to the Argentine position.

Fortune, however, is fickle. Within half an hour of leaving Camilla Creek House Ketley was to redress the balance by capturing the first prisoners of the ground campaign. Lance-Corporal Soane had been attached to the FAC party on the *Norland*, as his normal job of the commanding officer's driver was redundant and he had previous signals training. He had joined the two Royal Signals operators with Penman and now with Ketley, retracing his steps towards the isthmus. He explained what happened next:

As we came down the track we spotted a landrover coming up the slope about 150 metres in front of us. The sun was flashing off the windscreen. It was a farmer's landrover so at first we couldn't identify it, and we couldn't see who was inside. We crouched down on our knees beside the track, weapons in the aim, as the vehicle stopped about 60 metres from where we were. The passenger door opened and the angle of the light changed so we saw helmets. Captain Ketley immediately opened fire with two shots from his SLR, then we all opened up for about ten seconds with our SMGs. The man on the passenger side, who turned out to be a sergeant, leapt out and dived for cover uninjured. There were four soldiers in the vehicle, an officer driving, the sergeant, and two soldiers at the back. Nobody fired back so we pepper-potted forward. As we did so the sergeant fired several shots. Then we were up to the landrover with Captain Ketley yelling 'Manos ariba' [hands up]. The sergeant had run back to the vehicle to try to get on the radio but Captain Ketley put two rounds through the windscreen at close range and that stopped things. One man had been hit in the thigh so I patched him up. He was only a young lad who spoke halting English. When I took a knife to

137

cut away his trousers he thought I was going to kill him and shouted 'Don't kill, don't kill.'[20]

The officer was the Argentine Recce Platoon commander, Lieutenant Morales. Ketley reported what had happened and was told that an A Company patrol would come out to bring in the prisoners. In the meantime one signaller was left on guard while Ketley continued forward. Within a short time Evans was seen and heard withdrawing and the two patrols soon merged to return to Camilla Creek House, collecting the prisoners again en route. The captives were taken to Captain Coulson for questioning with the assistance of the Spanish-speaking interpreter, Captain Rod Bell RM.

The interrogation of the prisoners and the debriefing of Connor and Evans further delayed the 'O' group which Colonel 'H' eventually summoned again for 3.00 pm. 2 Para was about to hear how they were to fight the first battle of the conflict.

As soon as it became obvious that the landings were not a diversion Brigadier-General Parada instructed Piaggi to extend his defences to the northern end of the Goose Green isthmus. He correctly anticipated that if an attack was to be made it was likely to come from the north, over the narrow necks of land at the Low Pass and Burntside House. Block them and you prevented land access to the isthmus. It would be like corking a bottle, deceptively simple.

The problems, however, were manifold. The main one being that Piaggi was not permitted to reduce the area he was responsible to protect. He had to maintain troops south of Goose Green, he still had to watch the beaches, he still had to man a main defensive line west of Darwin, and he still had to secure the airfield and settlements. If he deployed his men at all these locations his defensive perimeter became 30 kilometres long. Even his original area of responsibility shown on Map 4 was too large, with none of his companies able to support each other by fire.

All he had been able to do was put one company looking north from west of Darwin, another looking south from below Goose Green, and keep the third as a reserve. Four kilometres separated A Company in the north from C Company in the south. Mutual support was impossible. Nevertheless, he had laid his mines to obstruct movement across some possible beach landing sites, the airfield, and the main defensive line. His error, in this respect, was in failing to ensure all these minefields were covered by fire. Even the most elaborate obstacles can be cleared easily provided nobody is shooting at those doing the job - the most recent and outstanding example of this being the breaching of Saddam Hussein's deep obstacle belt along the Kuwaiti border.

To comply effectively with his new orders was impossible. There were just not enough men to go round. In the run up to the battle, and for the night fighting of the 27th/28th Piaggi had a maximum strength of 550 infantrymen deployed throughout his area of responsibility. His B Company still remained north of Mount Kent, and Eagle Detachment (about two platoons) had not returned. In terms of rifle platoons Piaggi had nine — three in A Company, three in C Company, two in C Company 25th Regiment, and one from C Company 8th Regiment. To these may be added Lieutenant Morales' Recce Platoon, plus another cobbled together by Piaggi from various administrative soldiers — odds and sods — and placed under 2nd Lieutenant Pelufo, a fourth year cadet at the military academy hastily commissioned for duty in the Malvinas. Eleven rifle platoons maximum — exactly the same number that 2 Para would deploy against them.

The numerical similarity of the two sides at the start of the battle is striking, in direct contrast with the numerical superiority of around 3:1 in the Argentine favour that many media accounts at the time led the public to believe. Certainly, overall, 2 Para was outnumbered. If the artillery, anti-aircraft gunners, some engineers, and all the staff and Air Force personnel are included the entire garrison numbered between 900-1000 men. But in terms of infantry against infantry the numbers were approximately equal at the outset.

This equality of combat strength was also evident in supporting arms. As already noted, both sides were backed up by three 105mm guns. The advantage of HMS *Arrow*'s support for 2 Para was counterbalanced in part by the Argentine's anti-aircraft guns that could be fired against ground targets. Piaggi was seriously short of his complement of support weapons, while 2 Para's Support Company left most of their mortars behind, and could not fire Milans in the dark. In the air 2 Para anticipated Harrier and helicopter support, whereas the most Piaggi could hope for was Pucara sorties. The outcome of the struggle for Goose Green was going to depend, for both sides, on factors other than the number of troops or guns. It would be decided by the quality of the plan, the tactics, the leadership, and above all the spirit of those engaged.

Piaggi had appreciated that the vital ground for the defence of the settlements from the north was the ridge west of Darwin. It was here that the main Argentine line was constructed and occupied by Manresa's A Company. The trenches were dug on the forward slope and on the crest, just north of the gorse line. There had been plenty of time to construct overhead cover, attempt to camouflage the position, and to site mines across the isthmus in the lower ground about 1000 metres to the north (see Map 9).

Still, a number of errors were made with this key position. Firstly, and most importantly, no attempt was made to occupy Darwin Hill itself. Possibly Manresa had insufficient men, or he may have felt that Darwin inlet channelled any attack on to his position, making the defence of the hill unnecessary. Whatever the reason, the fact that troops on top of Darwin Hill controlled both settlements, the airstrip, and approaches, was not acted upon. Had a platoon, or preferably a company, been entrenched on that hill the outcome of the battle would probably have been quite different. Then, again due to a lack of numbers, A Company had strung out their trenches in a more or less straight line. There was little depth to the position, little chance of platoons being able to support each other. Finally, as mentioned above, the protective minefield was too far in front of the position to be brought under fire, or even seen from most of the company's positions. Apart from minefields, no other obstacles, such as barbed wire, had been erected. In the event wire entanglements in front of the trenches might well have been a battle winning feature.

When told to advance his defences Piaggi's predicament became acute. If only he had had his B Company he might have coped, but without it he was forced to move up one of his three companies already committed to a defensive task. He felt compelled to keep one company in the south as he could not be certain there would be no sudden heliborne assault from that direction; he had to retain a reserve centrally at, or near, Goose Green; that left A Company. His solution was to push this company forward, beyond the protective minefield, up to the Low Pass — Burntside House line. This meant hastily dug new positions, this meant no minefield in front, this meant an even greater gap — seven kilometres — between A and C Companies, and it meant denuding the vital ground west of Darwin. It was done recluctantly. In order not to have the original main defensive line completely unmanned the scratch platoon of some forty men under Pelufo was positioned in the trenches vacated by A Company. The final deployment of the Argentines, as Connor and Evans peered through their binoculars on the morning of 27th, was approximately as shown on Map 9. Compare that map with the one depicting what the 2 Para patrols reported, and the accuracy of their final information is seen to be reasonably high.

The Argentines anticipated some sort of attack at Goose Green. The uncertainty lay in its strength, whether it was to be a raid, whether it would be delivered from the sea or from helicopters, whether it would come at night or in daylight, or any combination of these. Like the British

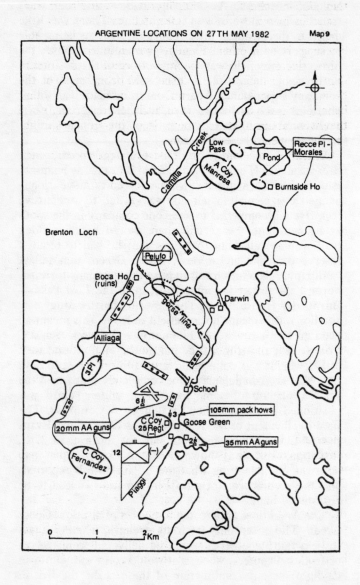

Low Pass

Camilla Creek

A Coy Manresa

Pond

Recce Pl - Morales

Burntside Ho

Brenton Loch

Pelufo

Boca Ho (ruins)

Darwin

goose line

Alliaga

3 Pl

School

6

105mm pack hows

Goose Green

C Coy 25 Regt

3

20mm AA guns

C Coy Fernandez

2

35mm AA guns

12

Piaggi

0   1   2 Km

they also listened to the BBC World Service. Piaggi was just as surprised, but not so infuriated, as Colonel 'H' by what he heard. His superiors in Stanley were also listening, but the announcement provoked no reaction at either location. The Argentines could not bring themselves to believe the British could be so stupid as to broadcast their tactical intentions in advance for their benefit. It must be some sort of bluff. If the British said they were about to attack Goose Green it probably meant the thrust would be elsewhere.

Contrary to some accounts at the time, no reinforcements of any sort were sent to Goose Green as a result of the BBC's blunder. Neither were any dispositions changed. Piaggi's later comment was: 'I did not take it too seriously; I thought it was more a psychological action because it would be crazy for them to announce an actual move. I made no changes because of that broadcast.'[21]

For several days prior to 2 Para's arrival at Camilla Creek House the Argentines had been probing north of the isthmus. Their patrols lacked professionalism. With their raw conscripts this is hardly surprising. Lieutenant Morales was deployed forward with A Company and patrolled up the track as far as Camilla Creek House and beyond. Not that these patrols gleaned much about the British or their intentions. The use of vehicle lights at night near the house had been seen by 2 Para OPs, as had movement around Cantera House.

Once he got his three guns Piaggi deployed them well forward. Their precise location prior to the battle is uncertain, but they had been sited well up towards the northern end of the isthmus. Their most likely position was near the main track, about 1000 metres west of Burntside House. Near there 2 Para's Mortar Platoon was to discover hundreds of discarded 105mm shells still in their boxes. These 105mm pack howitzers had a range of only 10,000 metres, so when their shells burst near 2 Para on its march to Camilla Creek House they could not have been at Goose Green, which is where they were at the start of the battle.

When Manresa's men fired on Connor's OP late in the morning of the 27th Piaggi became highly suspicious that something was afoot. He immediately ordered Morales to go north to investigate. Morales, who knew full well that enemy was close, jumped into the driver's seat of his landrover with three other soldiers and in broad daylight started to drive towards Camilla Creek House. As already related his incompetence was rewarded by capture.

At Goose Green Piaggi waited in vain for information. But, as he explained: 'From midday onwards I knew from various sources — particularly the disappearance of the landrover — that an attack was imminent.'[22]

VI

2 PARA'S PLAN

'I was concerned to, say the least, as this meant there
would be little room for manoeuvre, and therefore
little scope for imaginative tactics - just a straight
slog.'

Major Philip Neame after studying his map of the
Goose Green isthmus on the 27th May. *Above All
Courage*, Max Arthur, Sidgwick and Jackson 1985.

At all levels within the military it is the commander who
has responsibility for deciding upon, imparting and
supervising the execution of an operational plan. This
duty remains the same for an army commander devising
a campaign strategy, down to a section commander
attacking a bunker. The commander is ultimately
accountable for a plan's success or failure. For example,
if a battalion makes a daring or successful assault the
commanding officer would normally expect to receive the
DSO, whereas if his plan collapses with heavy losses he
might be removed from his command with his career
blighted. When men's lives are at stake it is a heavy
burden which has no equal civilian counterpart.

Although few plans survive the first shots in their
entirety, without a sound plan at the outset confusion,
even chaos, may quickly undermine the whole operation.
Because war is such a muddled business the best plans are
usually simple, ones that can be understood by all
subordinates, ones that can be remembered in the tumult
and terror of battle.[1] Military leaders are taught and
practise the planning process. The principles are much the

same no matter what size of unit is undertaking the operation, no matter whether it is a war plan drawn up over a period of months, such as Operation Desert Storm against Iraq, or a platoon attack involving thirty men devised in a ditch in a few minutes. The commander has first to think. In the case of a general he has the benefit of a large staff to gather information, to process it, to study alternatives, and to submit staff papers assessing detailed pros and cons. The platoon or section commander has only the benefit of what his eyes and ears tell him, of trained common sense and initiative. Nevertheless, each commander will, consciously or unconsciously, depending on the time available, make what the military call an 'appreciation of the situation'. This is really a logical thinking process designed to ensure that the resultant action makes some sort of military sense. The appreciation may be written and lengthy, or mental and quick resulting in shouted instructions to a handful of men by a corporal.

When considering his plan the commander is trained to examine certain fundamental factors. They are: the aim of the operation, the enemy, the ground, the time available, and fire support. Some plans will entail considering additional elements such as logistics, transport, and communications, but these five are common to most. They were the key ones that Colonel 'H' had to assess between being told around midday on the 26th at San Carlos that 2 Para's raid was on again, and his giving out his orders at Camilla Creek House at 3.00 pm the next day. In order to understand 2 Para's battle for Goose Green it is important for the reader to know the plan with which action was joined, and why it was constructed as it was, and what bearing it had on the outcome. It has been criticized as being too complex, too rushed, and of being made by too few men with too little support. Even if all these were true, 2 Para still took Goose Green, won the first crucial engagement of the land conflict, and established a moral ascendancy over the Argentines which was never reversed. To judge the worth of the plan it is necessary to know the circumstances in

146

which it was made, and under what constraints the planner worked. The first part of this chapter will attempt to put the reader into Colonel 'H''s shoes as he thought through how best to comply with his brigade commander's orders. The second will explain and comment on the plan itself.

It is almost certainly true to say that Colonel 'H' was unhappy with the original aim of the operation. He did not query it with Thompson because he was so desperately keen that 2 Para should get off the Sussex Mountain and do something — but the concept of a raid was imprecise. The actual orders he received stated that: '2 Para is to carry out a raid on Goose Green isthmus to capture the settlements before withdrawing in reserve for the main thrust in the north'.[2] To the brigade commander it was a re-run of the previously cancelled raid, which had now been forced upon him by his superiors at a most inopportune moment. It was a side-show, of secondary importance to the move, then just starting, towards Stanley. It resulted in the dispersal of units and scarce helicopter resources which Thompson felt to be operationally unsound. At that stage he did not foresee what was actually to happen, with 2 Para becoming embroiled in a long hard stuggle that, at one time, there was a possibility of it losing. Later, with hindsight, Thompson accepted that he probably should have commanded the operation personally, with a second battalion in reserve, and given the task the full weight of support possible, although this would have meant delaying the march east of his other units.[3] In having to do everything at once the Goose Green raid suffered from not being top of the priority pile.

Thompson's original intention was that 2 Para's attack should be a repeat performance, the plan for the original raid already having been accepted. On the first occasion Colonel 'H' only proposed attacking with two rifle companies; D Company was to stay at Camilla Creek House, and Support Company was destined to remain on Sussex Mountain as 2 Para remained responsible for its defence while undertaking the raid. Somewhere along the line a raid now became a full-scale battalion attack to take and hold Darwin and Goose Green. Colonel 'H' must have secured his superiors' authority to upgrade the raid by taking Support Company, as it was relieved on Sussex Mountain by L Company 42 Commando later on the 26th.

One thing that must be firmly grasped about any plan is the aim. If it is woolly, if people are not absolutely clear what the final objective is, the whole scheme will disintegrate. Colonel 'H' was to make no mention of raiding in his orders. It was an operation of war that was unfamiliar to him and his battalion. He was one of the few that understood the calamity of a repulse in those early days of the campaign. He was utterly determined that 2 Para would win. His first step was to interpret 'raid' as 'capture'. This was straightforward, not clouded with implications of withdrawal.[4] It had been well practised by 2 Para on the recent exercises in Kenya. But, despite a now unambiguous objective, he still had doubts as to what might happen afterwards. He felt obliged to tell his company commanders: 'Once we've got there, I don't know if we will stay there or not. That will depend on brigade headquarters.'[5]

Next, he needed to know about the enemy. The information that the 12th Regiment was at Goose Green was correct in so far as it went, but it was not specific enough. Detailed tactical information on exactly where the enemy troops were dug in, where was their artillery, where were the machine-guns, mortars, command posts, and minefields? This sort of intelligence could come from several sources. Aerial photographs could have pinpointed many positions in the rolling, open terrain of the isthmus. Unfortunately, *Canberra* photographic reconnaissance aircraft were not available in the area, and attempts to use the Harrier with a photo-fit pod attached proved only marginally successful. Flying low and fast to avoid detection or anti-aircraft fire was not compatible with good pictures. Another source was from a higher formation, in other words brigade headquarters. It had responsibility for gathering intelligence and disseminating it to all units under command. Regrettably 2 Para was not kept as well informed as it should have been. Afterwards at least one official report was particularly scathing of the lack of good intelligence:

> Throughout the campaign intelligence and the passage of information was particularly poor. Once the battalion moved out of the beachhead only 2 INTSUMS [Intelligence Summaries] and one set of rather poor quality air photographs were received ... at battalion level very little accurate intelligence was received.[6]

Deep penetration patrolling had been the task of the SAS and SBS since the beginning of May. The Goose Green garrison had been under SAS surveillance and had been raided on the 21 May. Because of this, aggressive patrolling by the units of 3 Commando Brigade had been frowned on. This had been frustrating for 2 Para sitting on Sussex Mountain. As Sergeant Barrett of A Company said:

> It was obvious for the first 36 hours that we had to establish a beachhead but after that, if we were to stay in defence, we were keen to go out and find the enemy rather than be patrolled against. Although we were given some limited patrol tasks, more positive patrols were discouraged.[7]

A commanding officer's best means of obtaining local tactical intelligence are his own patrols, OPs, and snipers.

When Colonel 'H' was first told to raid Goose Green he and his intelligence officer were entirely dependent on what others told them. Despite their reputation it seems that on this occasion the SAS's information was less than satisfactory. Their raid on Darwin consisted of little more than some long-range shooting which did no harm and produced a feeble response. From this they deduced that

149

opposition was down to about one company. They belittled the Argentine's capacity to resist. As the brigade commander was later to say: 'The SAS didn't really go and look properly'.[8]

Although by the 26th it was generally accepted that the 12th Regiment plus some Air Force personnel were in the Darwin - Goose Green area specifics were still lacking. At this stage, Colonel 'H''s knowledge of his enemy was as follows: 'Some in Darwin, but now depleted; minefields along the beach [and] on outside of headland; school housed enemy in the past; roads definitely not mined; airfield - 3 AA guns on southern edge; helicopter roost in settlement [Goose Green]; stores area north of airfield, and tented accommodation [stores] at [grid reference] 633550 [SW of Goose Green]'.[9] Not a lot. Certainly insufficient for him to make a satisfactory plan.

Before the battalion left Camilla Creek House on the night of the 27/28 May a lot more information was available thanks to the Recce Platoon patrols of Lieutenant Connor and Corporal Evans, whose activities were described in the previous chapter. At last some meat was put on the few Argentine bones held by 2 Para. Map 10 shows the total amount of information available to Colonel 'H' when he put the final touches to his plan on the late afternoon of the 27th.

The locating of a company at Coronation Point is puzzling. An infantry company, dug in, means at least thirty trenches, probably more. So who reported this position, which in fact never existed? Perhaps it originated as the nebulous strategic reserve reported north of Darwin prior to the landings; possibly it was the location given by the SAS of a position after their night raid on the 21st. The only definite information on this area came from Evans, who reported what he thought to be a recoilless gun and a vehicle near the track. From this meagre evidence the intelligence officer confidently announced a 'company position'. It was to be one of those pieces of misleading information that inevitably occur in war that was to have its effect on both the plan of attack and on the course of the battle.[10]

When Colonel 'H' sat down to decide his plan and prepare his orders on the afternoon of the 27th he was better informed. He knew he was dealing with at least three rifle companies plus other troops and Air Force personnel. There seemed to be a northern line based on a company from Low Pass to Burntside House, then a second line across the isthmus from Coronation Point NW to a platoon on the higher ground overlooking Camilla Creek. There were sixteen trenches on the centre of the ridge NW of Darwin Hill, with more south of Boca House. Further south still defences had been seen, or were suspected, in Darwin, around the airstrip with its AA guns, the school, and in Goose Green itself. Perhaps as much as three lines before Darwin with another, based on the airfield and school, between the settlements. It was 7 kilometres from Low Pass to Goose Green. A long way to go at night, even without an enemy.

The ground favoured the defence. Because it was so open visibility by day from the low hills was excellent. Although individuals could, and did, find shelter behind ridges and folds in the ground there was no way a daylight advance could avoid coming under heavy fire at long ranges. Therefore any attack should be by night. This deduction was reinforced by the problem of Argentine aircraft. Harrier combat air patrols had not won complete air superiority, and in bad weather could not be launched. The risk of being caught in the open in daylight was very real. There was no question in Colonel 'H''s mind but that he should aim to be close to Darwin and Goose Green by dawn.

The narrow 2-kilometre-wide isthmus appeared to preclude manoeuvring. Once the advance made contact it would be obvious from which direction the assault was coming. A frontal attack seemed the only option as heliborne and sea approaches had already been vetoed for reasons beyond 2 Para's control. Major Neame put the problem thus:

151

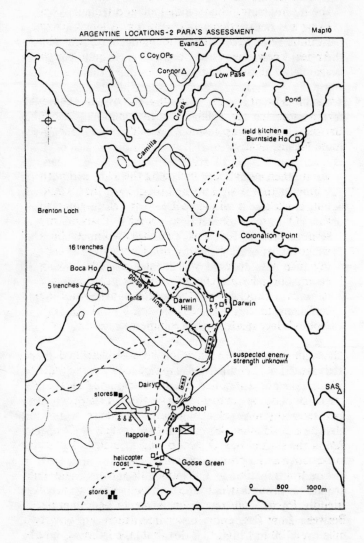

Evans△

C Coy OPs

Connor△

Low Pass

Pond

field kitchen ■
Burntside Ho □

Camilla Creek

Brenton Loch

Coronation Point

16 trenches

Boca Ho □

gorse line

5 trenches

tents

Darwin Hill

Darwin

suspected enemy
strength unknown

Dairy □

SAS△

stores ■■

School

?

flagpole

12

Goose Green

helicopter
roost

stores ■■

0   500   1000m

After the BBC's message we were dispersed all around the house with not a lot to do except think about tomorrow. I had a long look at my map. What I saw was not particularly reassuring. A long narrow isthmus with little chance to manoeuvre, and the Argies knew we were coming. A frontal attack against an alerted enemy.[11]

It was the fervent hope of many that the Argentines would have no stomach for a fight; that the opinion of the SAS that they were not up to much as soldiers was true.[12] To quote Neame again:

Up till then everybody, including the SAS, had been telling us that if we knocked them hard they would fall, crack like a windowpane. Just before going to the 'O' group I said to Nobby Clarke, my sergeant-major, that this was either going to be a walkover or a very bloody do. Coming back later my map was covered with a rash of red showing enemy, or possible enemy positions, all down the isthmus. I chucked it to the sergeant-major with the comment that it looked like being a bloody do. Nobby's face made further comment unnecessary.[13]

Although company and platoon commanders had maps (only issued at Camilla Creek House), and the intelligence officer brought a detailed 1:25,000 scale one to the 'O' group, nobody, apart from the two Recce Platoon patrols, had seen anything of the ground. Reliance would be placed on a detailed description by Lieutenant Thurman RM at the start of the 'O' group, and a quick look at some low-quality aerial photographs.

The military like to talk about dominating and vital ground — ground which needs to be held or secured by friendly forces if an operation is not to be jeopardized. Between Low Pass and Goose Green there are only two hills over 100 feet high that dominate the isthmus. One is 500 metres NW of the Darwin inlet, south of which sixteen trenches had been seen, while the other is Darwin Hill itself. This latter is the largest and highest hill in the area. Beyond it the ground slopes down gently, flat like a snooker table, to Goose Green. To troops wishing to occupy the settlements Darwin Hill is both the dominating and vital ground.

As mentioned above the Argentines had failed to occupy this hill. It was to prove their undoing, and was to save 2 Para from an even tougher fight on the 28th. Strangely, neither of these hills seem to have had much influence on the planning process. Captain Benest, the battalion signals officer, in his written account compiled immediately after the war, says this: 'The Settlement [Darwin] was in a bowl, dominated by the hill ... to the West, and South, covered in gorse and thought to be a likely enemy position'. What is odd is that none of the company commanders recorded suspected enemy on Darwin Hill in their notes taken at the 'O' group.

If Colonel 'H' did one thing more than anything else from the start of the advance from Camilla Creek House to his death it was surely to look at his watch. As the operation progressed so time became more precious, with deadlines to meet, and the moment when daylight would expose the battalion coming ever closer. It was Napoleon who said, 'Ask of me anything but time'. It is the crucial factor in every military undertaking. This is why the military set such store by punctuality, with the importance of timings instilled into commanders and men from the outset of their careers. In battle, starting at the right time, opening fire at the right time, moving at the right time, or arriving at the right time, are normally essential to keep any plan on the rails. Failure to keep to the proper timings can result in confusion, loss of life, and possibly failure. For Colonel 'H' the consideration of time available was fundamental to his planning for the Goose Green battle. In his orders he had to give out precise timings for some parts of the operation while allowing subordinates enough time, and some flexibility, for the completion of their tasks. It was

154

all a matter of judgement, of experience, of arriving at practical answers to time and space problems.

From previous factors it was clear that 90 per cent of the advance on Goose Green needed to be completed during darkness. This immediately restricted the time available to 14 hours – from 4.30 pm on the 27th to 6.30 am the next day. 2 Para spent the day of the 27th at Camilla Creek House preparing and patrolling. They had from last light that evening to first light on the 28th to get to their start line, advance, and be within a whisker of securing Darwin and Goose Green. The distances involved are important. From Camilla Creek House south to the Low Pass, facing the nearest enemy position, was nearly 5 kilometres. An approach to Burntside House, where a platoon was thought to be based, around the pond was nearer 7 kilometres. From there to just south of Goose Green was another 7 kilometres in a straight line. But, as Colonel 'H' was well aware, there were known and suspected enemy positions between the start line and the final objective. In round figures 14 hours of darkness were available to cover the 14 kilometres of ground. It was up to Colonel 'H' to allocate this time to tasks. He had about one hour for every kilometre. It appeared ample, but movement across country at night is seldom fast, and with the advance being resisted it was not easy to judge the speed of progress. This was no longer a raid on the nearest enemy, no longer 'wellie-in, duff-up the garrison and bugger off', but a night advance to contact with the virtual certainty of having to fight through a series of in-depth positions in order to take the settlements.

Colonel 'H''s final key factor was fire support. Back on Sussex Mountain he had had to make a quick decision on what 2 Para should carry into battle or, conversely, what should be left behind. They had to move on foot, nobody could fight bowed down under bergens, and they had a 13- kilometre night march to get to the assembly area at Camilla Creek House, so they must travel light. This conflicted with the need for plenty of ammunition and the requirement for as much fire support as possible.

Supporting weapons and their ammunition are heavy. Helicopters would fly in the three 105mm light guns with their shells, but virtually everything else would have to be manpacked forward. Colonel 'H' rightly decided to move and fight as lightly as possible.[14] No bergens, except for the RAP personnel who needed them for medical kit, 24-hour rations to last two days, entrenching tools at two per section, minimum radios and maximum ammunition. At Goose Green 2 Para communicated via a VHF net only. No HF radios were carried at company level which meant that command, control and administrative messages (about resupply, ammunition, casualties and PoWs) all competed for time on the same net.[15] At company commander's discretion the platoon 2-inch mortars could be left behind (B and D Companies took theirs, A did not). With the battalion's support weapons, the six GPMGs in the Machine Gun Platoon were to be taken in the light role, that is without the heavy tripods and extra barrels needed for long-range sustained fire. Only three Milan firing posts with seventeen missiles were to be carried and, initially, no 81mm mortars. Colonel 'H' had seen how the carriage of mortars and bombs had crippled the battalion in the climb up Sussex Mountain and he wanted no repetition of this.[16] His intention was to rely on the artillery and naval gunfire for support. This decision worried the battery commander, Major Rice. In the end he persuaded Colonel 'H' to agree to taking two mortars with the rest of the platoon carrying bombs. It was suggested that brigade be asked for at least two light tanks from the Blues and Royals to support the advance. Major Keeble's request was turned down as it was felt that the ground would be too soft and boggy, particularly on the route from Sussex Mountain to the isthmus. With only one recovery vehicle in the brigade it was too risky committing them at this early stage of the conflict in an operation that was thought to be of secondary importance. As Brigadier Thompson now readily admits, the terrain was entirely suitable for the Scimitars and Scorpions, and if the battle had had to be refought they would have accompanied 2 Para. At the time it was not appreciated that the CVR(T) can cross virtually any ground that a man can walk over.

The availability of HMS *Arrow* with her 4.5-inch gun influenced Colonel 'H' in his fire support planning. It was a unit with the equivalent firepower of several times the three 105mm guns both in weight of shell and speed of delivery. He had, therefore, two main fire units available to allocate to fire support tasks, plus the two mortars and other weapons of Support Company. The only snag with the naval gun was that HMS *Arrow* would have to leave the area at around 4.30 am to get back into the protection of San Carlos Water before daylight brought renewed air attacks. Captain Arnold, the NGFO, had a few other misgivings. It had been his experience that there was perhaps too much technology, which could not always be relied on. HMS *Antrim*'s tardy response at Fanning Head was an example. His doubts were to prove well founded.[17]

A lot of reliance would have to be placed on the artillery support. Normally a battalion is never allocated less than a battery of six guns to support it. The difficulty was the need to lift them, their crews, and hundreds of shells, forward by helicopter at night. There was only one night in which this could be done — the 26th/27th — and only four sets of PNG equipment for the helicopter pilots.

It was at 3.00 pm that Colonel 'H' finally assembled his 'O' group. In the intervening time since his first attempt the Recce Platoon patrols had returned, and Lieutenant Morales with his three men had been captured and questioned. More information on the enemy was thus available, but this bonus had to be paid for in time. As the officers settled themselves down in the lee of a hedge around the intelligence officer's large-scale map there was little likelihood of 2 Para moving off at last light. During the preliminaries it soon became clear that the commanding officer was getting agitated on this score.

The orders started with a lengthy description of the ground by Thurman. He knew his subject well, almost too well. Some of the detail was of doubtful immediate tactical importance — the quality of the land for farming; the number of houses in Darwin which were empty; which was the manager's residence; the sheep pens near the airstrip; the location of the local dairy. It was taking up time, and as the signals officer later recorded:

> Many people on the 'O' group did not even possess maps due to the haste with which the battalion had moved off from Sussex Mountain. So this detailed description could only be given on the one large-scale map. In the fading light much of the information was thus meaningless unless checked on a map at a later stage. For many it was the very first time that they had studied the geography of the isthmus in detail.[18]

The description of how Darwin might be approached conjures up images of a pleasurable cross-country walk rather than a night advance through the middle of several known enemy positions. 'One possible approach to Darwin he [Thurman] suggested, was along the west side of the isthmus overlooking Camilla Creek as far as the gorseline in front of the ruins of Boca House, and then along the gorseline to the track that enters Darwin from Goose Green.' Alternatively, one could leave the gorseline at 'a gorse-filled re-entrant north of the gorseline provid[ing] cover to the inlet at its western corner, from where Darwin could be approached along the inlet'.[19]

Next, it was the turn of Alan Coulson, the intelligence officer, his duty being to describe everything known about the enemy — their locations, strengths, weapons, minefields, obstacles, morale and, if possible, intentions. It is one of the most crucial parts of an 'O' group. What he described has been marked on Map 10. Like Thurman, Coulson's briefing was long; time was ticking away, and the bulk of the orders had still to be issued. Colonel 'H' felt compelled to urge him to speed up, and eventually to stop him altogether, telling the company

158

commanders to get together with Coulson afterwards over any points needing clarification.

Colonel 'H' stepped forward to give his plan for the battle that was to be the climax of his career.[20] He gave the mission, 'to capture Darwin and Goose Green'. In outline it was to be 'a six-phase night/day, silent/noisy battalion attack'. To his listeners these opening remarks told them a lot. Six phases meant it was going to be an unusually long operation, possibly complicated, as most battalion attacks do not extend beyond two or three phases. With the defensive positions being so deep and the final objective so distant, there were really only two possible general options.

First was to divide the operation into phases, allocating troops to a series of subsidiary objectives, giving companies specific tasks in advance, and controlling everything tightly from the centre. This was the method Colonel 'H' had chosen. The second possibility was to treat the whole thing as an advance to contact, although with many enemy positions known, and to make most of the tactical decisions as and when events unfolded. The problem with the former was unavoidable complexity, and with the latter the need to give considerable freedom of action to, as yet, untested subordinates.

Night/day meant that it would start by night but finish in daylight. Silent/noisy indicated that the advance would start silently to secure surprise, so no supporting gunfire would be put down on the enemy until they became aware of the attack. The guns would be 'on call', ready to fire the moment the advancing troops were seen, or surprise was lost.

Who was to do what and when is best understood by a study of Maps 11 to 13. Each of the rifle companies had an MFC from the Mortar Platoon, and a section of engineers from 59 Independent Commando Squadron RE, attached to it. A, B, and D Companies also had gunner FOOs to control artillery fire once the attack went noisy. Support Company had the sniper section and the NGFO, Captain Kevin Arnold RA, to direct HMS *Arrow*'s gun.

Phase 1 would see the battalion move to their forming-up positions just to the rear of the start lines. It was C Company's task to lead in this phase, moving forward to establish a battalion RV at the bridge over the Ceritos Arroyo stream. While company headquarters manned the RV most of the Recce and Patrols Platoons would go forward to secure the start lines of A and B Companies respectively. A Company were to attack the Burntside House area, while B Company would advance on the enemy positions overlooking Camilla Creek, just south of the Low Pass.

2 Para would move down from Camilla Creek House, along the track, in the order C Company - Support Company - A Company - Tac 1 - B Company - Bn Main - D Company - being checked through the RV before moving to their jump-off positions. C Company was to start almost immediately after the 'O' group, just after last light at around 5.00 pm. A Company was to cross its start line at 2.00 am on the 28th, with B Company advancing as soon as A Company had secured its objective. Support Company was to drop off its two mortars at a baseplate position at the northern tip of Camilla Creek near the RV, while the remainder moved to a fire support base west of Camilla Creek, on rising ground opposite B Company's objective. The Assault Pioneers had the job of carrying the bulk of the ammunition for the Machine Gun Platoon. After they had dumped it at the fire base they were to join C Company at the RV to form a third rifle platoon for that company. During Phase 1 C Company had HMS *Arrow*'s gun on priority call.

Phase 2, starting at 2.00 am, would see A Company take Burntside House and B Company the positions south of the Low Pass. For these attacks A Company had priority call on the three 105mm guns, while the 4.5 inch fired for B Company as required. The rest of the battalion were in reserve.

The third phase would, it was hoped, get under way at 3.00 am. In it A Company would assault the Argentine company thought to be on Coronation Point, while D

Company moved forward to take on the platoon position 1,000 metres SW of B Company's first objective. A Company would retain priority call on the artillery, while HMS *Arrow* was allocated to D Company.

Phase 4 was to start an hour later. In it B Company would advance through D Company to attack the Boca House position. This would entail an extremely long advance of some 2000 metres so Colonel 'H' explained that it might be necessary to halt B Company on the gorse line, and move up D Company to complete the capture of the Boca House area. While this long, and perhaps complicated, phase was in progress A Company would be in reserve at Coronation Point. It was during this phase that Support Company was to vacate its fire base and move up behind the leading companies. Both the ship and the artillery were to support B Company initially, then D Company if it was used.

By 5.00 am it was hoped to start Phase 5. A Company was to exploit forward to the outskirts of Darwin; C Company would clear the airfield; D Company was to advance behind C Company to the edge of Goose Green. B Company was the reserve. By this time HMS *Arrow* would have left so the two mortars, which until now had been in reserve, were to have moved forward to a closer baseplate position and were to support A Company while the guns were on call to D Company. Support Company's Milans and machine guns should also be forward at this stage as the battalion's reserve of fire support.

All should be ready to start the last phase, Phase 6, at first light − 6.30 am. This was to be the daylight part of the battle - the actual taking of Darwin and Goose Green. Colonel 'H' deliberately planned for the settlements to be secured in daylight so that civilian casualties could be minimized. A Company, with the mortars in support, would take Darwin while B Company remained in reserve with the possibility of being used to secure the school. C Company was to exploit well south of Goose Green, with D Company moving into the settlement itself, supported by the guns. On call after first light would be Scout

2 PARA'S BATTLE PLAN – PHASES 1 & 2   Map 11

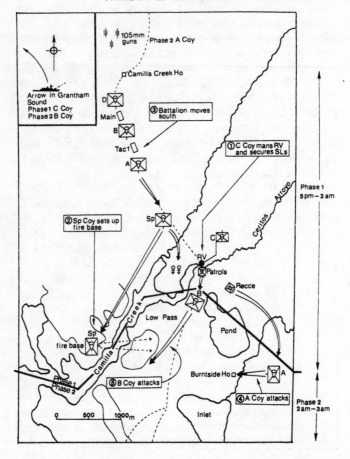

162

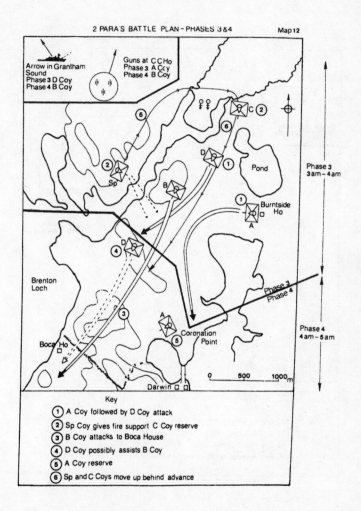

2 PARA'S BATTLE PLAN - PHASES 3&4   Map 12

Arrow in Grantham
Sound
Phase 3 D Coy
Phase 4 B Coy

Guns at C C Ho
Phase 3 A Ccy
Phase 4 B Coy

Pond

Sp

B

D

C ②

⑥

⑥

②

①

①

Burntside
Ho

A

Phase 3
3 am – 4 am

D
④

Phase 3
Phase 4

Brenton
Loch

③

A

⑤

Coronation
Point

Boca Ho

Phase 4
4 am – 5 am

0   500   1000 m

Darwin

Key

① A Coy followed by D Coy attack
② Sp Coy gives fire support C Coy reserve
③ B Coy attacks to Boca House
④ D Coy possibly assists B Coy
⑤ A Coy reserve
⑥ Sp and C Coys move up behind advance

163

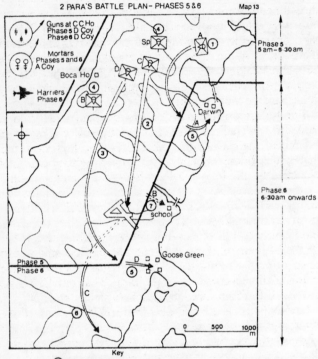

2 PARA'S BATTLE PLAN – PHASES 5 & 6   Map 13

Guns at C C Ho
Phase 5 D Coy
Phase 6 D Coy

Mortars
Phases 5 and 6
A Coy

Harriers
Phase 6

Boca Ho

Darwin

Goose Green

school

Phase 5
5 am – 6·30 am

Phase 6
6·30am onwards

Phase 5
Phase 6

0   500   1000
m

Key

1 A Coy exploits to edge of Darwin
2 C Coy secures airfield
3 D Coy advances to outskirts of Goose Green
4 B and Sp Coys reserve
5 D Coy takes Goose Green. A Coy takes Darwin
6 C Coy exploits south of Goose Green
7 B Coy secures school if required

164

helicopters for casualty evacuation and resupply, with Gazelles armed with SS11 missiles for fire support. Similarly, the battalion would also be backed up by Harrier strikes — weather permitting. For defence against Argentine aircraft the two Royal Artillery Blowpipe detachments would stay at Camilla Creek to protect the gun line, while another (specially requested by Colonel 'H'), operated by the Royal Marines who were much fitter than their gunner comrades, would accompany the battalion. Colonel 'H' concluded his 'O' group with the words: 'All previous evidence suggests that if the enemy is hit hard he will crumble'.

The 'O' group had lasted about one and a half hours, so light was fading fast as the company commanders assembled their own subordinates. It was the time factor that struck home as being crucial to everybody who had crouched by the hedge. 2 Para had a long way to go and a lot to achieve in a few hours of darkness. Nobody was more aware of this than the commanding officer. He had given out timings but had stressed that they were estimates and flexible. With so many imponderables they had to be. Of the 14 hours of darkness available the first nine would be spent preparing for battle and moving forward the five or more kilometres to the start lines. That only left four and a half to reach the outskirts of both settlements.

Unavoidably, as he had been refused permission to try other methods, Colonel 'H' had had to plan a frontal advance/attack, a 'straight slog' down the isthmus at night, taking out known or suspected enemy positions on the way. Because a company could only take on one position at a time, and because they needed time to reorganize after each assault, the plan had to involve passing through the reserve company to take over the lead after each phase. This is not an easy thing to do in the dark in the middle of a battle. It involves not only a high standard of training but also extremely tight control by commanders. Colonel 'H' had been careful to have at least one company uncommitted in each phase. He had tasked a company with attacking known or likely Argentine positions to roll

165

up the defences on the isthmus until the settlements were reached.

Burntside House, the Low Pass position, the platoon to the SW, Coronation Point, Boca House, the airfield, the school and, finally, Darwin and Goose Green were the specific objectives of rifle companies in the battle plan. There was, however, one significant omission — the sixteen Argentine trenches and tented area identified as being west of Darwin inlet. They were in the centre of the isthmus, on part of the dominating high ground west and NW of the settlement, but no company had been detailed to secure this area — unlike every other position. Similarly Darwin Hill. Although no enemy was reliably reported as occupying this vital ground, it was, by its height and location, the key hill from which to secure the area. From its summit troops could control Darwin, the airfield, the school, and the northern approaches to Goose Green, but it did not feature specifically in the orders. Nevertheless, A Company would have to do something about Darwin Hill if they were to exploit to the outskirts of the settlement in phase 5. Although it was not spelled out in the orders, Major Farrar-Hockley was well aware that Darwin Hill sat astride all his routes into Darwin.

Another point of interest arising from the plan was the use of Support Company. Accepting that, for reasons of lack of transport, Colonel 'H' had little option but to leave behind a substantial part of this company's weapons, he did have a choice as to how it was to operate. His choice lay between splitting up the Milans, machine-guns and snipers among the rifle companies, thus giving responsibility for their use to the company commanders, or keeping them centralized. He chose the latter.

Support Company was instructed to set up a fire support base as already explained. As Colonel 'H' knew, the positioning of the fire base on the western flank of the advance, on the far side of Camilla Creek, severely restricted Major Hugh Jenner in providing fire support. His mortars were placed in reserve until phase 5 due to shortage of ammunition, his Milans could not fire in the dark without good illumination, and his machine- gunners could see nothing of Burntside House which was anyway at extreme range. Jenner could only use his machine guns to assist B Company in their advance through the Low Pass, and (possibly) D Company's attack on the next platoon position. After this it would be a question of pick up weapons and walk. During Phase 4 the company faced a 5-kilometre flog to catch up with the war to be in position to assist in the final phases.

The battalion was also trying out a new system for the control of Support Company's weapons. Each rifle company had an officer or senior NCO nominated as a fire support coordinator. He travelled with the company headquarters with a radio on the Support Company net. His job — to locate suitable targets in his company's battle and direct Milan or machine guns to deal with them. In an ideal situation these weapons would be split into two groups so that they could leap-frog forward as the battalion advanced, with one group always ready to fire. The problem with this system was that it was brand new. It had never been practised and, on this occasion, the company commander had not been consulted concerning the possibility of leap-frogging two smaller fire bases forward.

The distance to the final objectives, the number of enemy positions sited in depth, the limited hours of darkness, the unavoidable frontal nature of the attacks, the low level of supporting fire (particularly after HMS *Arrow* left), and the lack of reconnaissance, taken together presented a truly remarkable challenge to 2 Para. What had started out as a raid had developed into a full scale battalion night attack against an enemy whom 2 Para thought were expecting them (via the BBC broadcast).

Colonel 'H' realized the significance of what was about to happen; he understood the magnitude of the task before his battalion. He had devised a plan that he knew had weaknesses, as all plans do, but it was a framework through which to control events. Things would certainly change the moment the start line was crossed, if not before. To succeed he knew he would have to rely far more on aggressiveness, training and forceful leadership than on a set-piece plan. Neither he nor any of his officers doubted that they would succeed. Lieutenant Jim Barry's comment to his platoon was, 'There's only one way out of here [Camilla Creek House] now and that's up that track'.

The battle for Goose Green has often been described by participants as a 'come as you are party'. Perhaps the attitude of most at the outset is summed up by the words of Major Crosland to his own 'O' group: 'These people have nicked our islands - we're going to make them wish they had never heard of the Falklands Islands. Let's get stuck in!'[21]

VII

THE LOW PASS
AND BURNTSIDE HOUSE

'About three minutes after starting our advance we came across an Argy, our first test! There was no face just a helmet and a poncho. I challenged him and told him to put his hands up, but he just said: 'Por Favor'. On the third time his hands moved under his poncho and in unison two riflemen and my two GPMGs opened fire. Not unnaturally he fell over.'

Corporal Margerison, a section commander in 6 Platoon of B Company, describing events shortly after crossing the start line during a brief on Operation Corporate to the Staff College, Camberley, May, 1983.

'It is with artillery that one makes war'. So said that most famous of gunners — Napoleon. After the war Menendez commented on the demoralizing effect of artillery and naval gunfire, saying, 'It was the artillery that beat us'. He was referring to the tremendous hammering his troops took in the battles for the hills west of Stanley prior to the infantry assaults. He was certainly not talking about Goose Green. At this first ground clash 2 Para's artillery support was limited to three 105mm Light Guns from the 'Black Eight' battery – 8 (Alma) Battery of 29 Commando Regiment Royal Artillery. During the 14-hour struggle to reach and secure Goose Green these three guns were in action almost continuously. Frequently calls for fire could only be answered by one gun, so great were the difficulties at the gun position. Despite the desperate efforts of all the crews, who toiled throughout the night and day of the 28th, sometimes under air attack, to keep firing, 2 Para was not always greatly impressed with the results at the receiving end. As will be seen, if there was, at times, a lack of quantity or quality in the artillery support, the reasons lay in the circumstances, both tactical and technical, under which the gunners were compelled to operate.

Because one of the critical lessons re-learnt at Goose Green, and religiously applied thereafter, was that infantry require all possible help from supporting arms, particularly guns, to get them forward, it behoves the reader to know in some detail the artillery's activities at this first engagement. The 105mm Light Gun had only recently been supplied to artillery field regiments in the British Army. It replaced the 105mm pack howitzer, the same weapon the Argentines fired against 2 Para. It has a maximum range, with supercharge (which was not available at Goose Green), of 17,200 metres. Its normal range is 14,500 metres, so, with the guns near Camilla Creek House, the entire isthmus could be covered without having to advance the gun line. With a crew of six its sustained rate of fire is three rounds per minute (rpm). Therefore, with a battery of six guns firing at this rate the infantry would expect to see some eighteen shells arrive in the target area every minute. The gunners describe these rates as Rate 1, Rate 2, or Rate 3 up to Rate 6, of which Rate 1 is the slowest – 1rpm. At Goose Green, with only a section of three guns, the number of shells fired at any rate was half that of a battery.

The arithmetic of ammunition expenditure can be alarming. Using Rate 2 one gun would fire 120 shells in an hour, but all fire missions must have all available guns in action, so with the three supporting 2 Para an hour's firing would require 360 shells. As the gunners knew, the operation was planned to last at least 4½ hours during darkness, while the final phase would be in daylight without HMS *Arrow*'s presence. The problem was accentuated by a shortage of transport – helicopters that could operate at night. There was a maximum of twelve Sea King lifts available to move the section to Camilla Creek House — the gun position. With one for each gun, and one for personnel (28 men), that left eight for ammunition. This translated to one box of 48 rounds slung under the helicopter in a net. Total to be taken 384 shells — enough for one hour's firing at Rate 2.

Then there was the decision as to the type of ammunition to be sent forward. With such a limited amount it was important that the right mix of shells for the task was available at the gun line. Discounting armour-piercing ammunition (Piaggi had no tanks), the choice lay in striking the correct balance between HE, smoke and illuminating rounds. The gunners, on the basis that it was primarily a night operation with HMS *Arrow* available to fire star-shells, and 2 Para's mortars able to provide smoke cover during the daylight phase, opted for 100 per cent HE. The only other shells taken were six coloured smoke for possible target indication tasks for aircraft. The likely targets were infantry in trenches, vehicles, or guns, all vulnerable to HE.

On 27 May, after the BBC broadcast, when there was great anxiety that the Argentines had been forewarned and might reinforce their Goose Green garrison, the commanding officer of 29 Commando Regiment, Lieutenant-Colonel Holroyd-Smith, authorized a further eight ammunition lifts. In the meantime the battery commander had broken open all the crates of shells, discarded the boxes, fuzed up the ammunition and placed them on tarpaulins inside nets. That way 60 rounds could be carried instead of 48. So the three guns were destined to have 320 HE shells each for the battle.

Before artillery can fire effectively the Gun Position Officer, in this case Lieutenant Mark Waring RA, in command of the actual gun line, needs certain basic facts. He must know where the target is, what it is, when to fire, what type of ammunition to use, and how long to fire. This information is passed to the gun position over the radio by the FOOs who are up front with the infantry.

They are the eyes of the guns, they can (hopefully) see the target, they can see the strike of the shells, they can adjust the fall of the shot on to the target if it is inaccurate. The whole system of artillery fire support is built around the FOOs. These officers are usually captains, but with a battery supporting a battalion battle group, which is the normal practice, there are sometimes insufficient officers to provide FOOs to each rifle company. At Goose Green for example D Company's FOO was Sergeant Bullock, while C Company had none.

Also forward with the infantry is the battery commander. Major Tony Rice RA commanded 29 (Corunna) Field Battery of 4 Field Regiment – the Parachute Gunners. This was the battery affiliated to 2 Para within 5 Infantry Brigade, to which 2 Para belonged before the Falklands conflict. The battery commander is the infantry commanding officer's adviser on all gunnery matters. He assists with fire support planning, he travels with the commanding officer in Tac 1. As is usual, Colonel 'H' had designated Rice to take command of 2 Para in the event of his being hit, until such time as the battalion second-in-command (Major Keeble) could get forward. The reasoning behind this is that the battery commander will be the most senior officer up front who is fully in the picture as to what is happening.

During the battle Rice was responsible for controlling the FOOs, deciding target priorities, switching the allocation of the guns to another company if necessary, and keeping track of ammunition expenditure. He had little control over the guns, which reacted to fire orders from the FOOs over the radio. Waring, at the gun position, had to keep him informed of the ammunition state or other critical matters such as guns going out of action. The layout of artillery support to 2 Para is shown in diagramatic form at Appendix 3.

Once the guns were in position Waring's overriding task was to keep them in action. Others included the layout of the guns, local defence arrangements, safety, the preparation and distribution of ammunition, and receiving

172

and disseminating orders from his battery commander. His reaction time to calls for fire was not going to be as fast as it might because the guns were working with FAME (Field Artillery Manual Equipment) instead of FACE (Field Artillery Computer Equipment). This meant that the number-crunching calculations in the command post, that converted the FOOs data into elevations and bearings for each gun, were done manually rather than by computer − still accurate, but slower.

The length of time between calling for fire and the shells arriving was also increased due to all messages having to be channelled through a rebroadcast (relay) station. The problem was that the radios carried by the FOOs were VHF sets, whereas the gun position had HF ones which were not compatible in these circumstances. Waring set up a small relay post on higher ground near the gun position whose vital task was to relay every message from or to the FOOs. It was another link in the communication chain which took time. It also meant that the FOOs could not speak directly to an officer at the gun line. There could be no officer-to-officer conversation to sort out problems quickly.

A similar situation existed with naval gunfire support. Although Captain Arnold was the NGFO he could not do much observing as he was positioned, at the start of the battle, with Support Company at their fire base. He was stationary, and for much of the time would not be able to identify targets or see the fall of shot. The FOOs would actually call for naval fire missions when HMS *Arrow* was in support of their company, just as they did for the artillery. In effect the NGFO was another rebroadcast station, albeit an essential one, that translated the Army FOOs procedures into language understandable to the ship's gun crews.

A greater technical handicap was the lack of meteorological information to feed into the system. High winds, for example, can cause shells to land up to 800 metres in any direction from the target. This would mean total reliance on the FOOs seeing the fall of shot to be

173

able to make corrections, not easy if enemy shells are also falling in the area. How does one tell a friendly 105mm explosion from a hostile one?

With HE rounds there is a choice as to the type of bang available at the sharp end. High explosive artillery shells come as airburst or point detonating. With airburst the round explodes 30 feet above the ground, showering shrapnel over a wide area; exactly what was needed against infantry in the open. At Goose Green, however, 2 Para were the exposed troops, advancing over bare terrain, so for this reason no airburst ammunition was taken forward. For this battle all the shells at the gun position were the PD type.[1] As its name implies, it detonates as the point of the shell hits the ground. Excellent against bunkers or trenches, which is where the majority of Argentines were assumed to be sheltering. There is even a refinement with these rounds. In the fuze is a small screw, the turning of which can delay the explosion for a fraction of a second − just enough time for the round to penetrate into the target. At Goose Green it was found that the soft, soggy soil allowed the shell to penetrate even with PD ammunition, so the effects were somewhat smothered and localized. There was no need deliberately to delay the detonation. The water-logged peat was roundly cursed by soldiers in the Falklands, but many individuals on both sides had reason to be thankful for it when under artillery or mortar fire.

One final technical matter. The section of guns did not have any sophisticated locating equipment designed to detect enemy gun positions with precise accuracy. Reliance had to be placed on somebody actually seeing the Argentine artillery before counter-battery fire could be employed. Colonel 'H' was to give Major Rice a hard time for not being able to neutralize the enemy 105s which, in the event, remained hidden and firing to the bitter end. Cymbeline mortar locating radar could not be brought forward until after the battle. This equipment detects the flight path of a mortar bomb, and rapid computing enables the baseplate to be identified. It can only be used against high trajectory rounds.

3 Commando Brigade had five major infantry units ashore — three Royal Marine Commandos and two parachute battalions — but only four artillery batteries. For adequate support one battery should be allocated to each battalion. 29 Commando Regiment had three gun batteries and belonged to the brigade, the fourth battery, 29 (Corunna) Battery, had joined the landing force with its affiliated battalion — 2 Para — from 5 Infantry Brigade, the main body of which had yet to arrive. While on Sussex Mountain 2 Para had 29 (Corunna) Battery in direct support. All the FOOs came from this battery. These parachute gunners had trained with 2 Para, individual officers had got to know each other as part of a deliberate policy of ensuring that those who might have to fight together had trained together. At Goose Green, however, the guns firing for 2 Para belonged to a different regiment from the battery commander and FOOs giving them fire missions. They did not know each other, and had not been able to develop the same level of mutual respect and trust that had been built up within their own units.

In theory this should make no difference on the battlefield. The guns are the same, the procedures are the same, so the results should be the same. Indeed, afterwards, gunner officers unanimously asserted that it made no difference to performance. But, for all that, there was disappointment that at the moment of truth when action was joined 2 Para did not get its affiliated battery in support. The reason was entirely practical. At the brigade 'O' group for the original raid Lieutenant-Colonel Holroyd-Smith was told that 29 (Corunna) Battery had not practised night flying with its guns for some time, whereas 8 (Alma) Battery from 29 Commando Regiment had recently returned from Norway where they had done exactly that. The battery more experienced in night movement by air was chosen. Major Rice protested without avail. He was upset, but, according to Waring when he reported to Rice, he showed no sign of his disappointment.

27 May was hectic for Waring and his gunners getting ready for their night move to Camilla Creek House from their position near the Ajax Bay meat processing plant. With only one helicopter lift for personnel, giving a maximum of twenty-eight, it only left ten men for duties other than gun crews: ten men to run the CP, the rebroadcast station, and provide for local protection against enemy patrols which Waring had been told to expect. 'There was only room, therefore, to take webbing and small arms with the minimum of gun stores. The men had to wear warm clothing and carry rations in their pockets.'[2]

During the afternoon Waring was told an extra eight flights would be available for shells:

> Time was running out, and we had difficulty preparing the ammunition. We were by now very vulnerable to an attack from any Argentine pilot who may have been in the area by chance spotting the piles of ammunition sitting in the middle of the gun position. By 4.00 pm the section was ready in all respects. The CO [Holroyd-Smith] arrived to wish us well. We were all sitting on a bank listening to the CO when two enemy aircraft screamed past the position. 45 Commando opened up, and the entire gun position was peppered by their small-arms fire. One of my sergeants, Sergeant Jobling, was hit in the arm and had to be replaced.[3]

This raid by Skyhawks was a great Argentine success, killing five men and wounding twenty-seven. No less than three parachute-retarded 1000-pound bombs hit the Ajax Bay Field Dressing Station, but miraculously failed to detonate. Others outside did. As Brigadier Thompson has said:

> The bombs that did explode in the BMA started

among the piles of ammunition stacked close by, mainly 81mm mortar bombs and Milan missiles. These exploded all night a hundred metres or so from the Dressing Station and Logistic Regiment Headquarters sending shrapnel whining through the darkness .... The netted loads of gun and mortar ammunition waiting on the helipad to be lifted forward to 2 Para were also destroyed.[4]

The air raid had barely finished before the Sea Kings from 846 Naval Air Squadron arrived to start moving Waring's guns to Camilla Creek House. He took the first flight as time was desperately short, and it was beginning to look as though 2 Para might start their advance before the GPO arrived. Waring has described his arrival:

It was with great relief, after the longest 20 minutes of my life, that I finally landed at Camilla Creek House. BC 29 Bty [Rice] was found some 800 metres away, where he had selected a gun position well away from the house [to the north], it being a likely DF target. Having given me a final briefing he disappeared into the darkness with the rest of 2 Para.[5]

It took over four hours to get the gun position ready. Each helicopter took an hour for the round trip. The guns were in a shallow valley with a stream in it, making the ground totally unsuitable for digging. Only on the sides of the valley could trenches be dug for the rebroadcast team and machine-gunners. For the 105s protection was confined to low walls of ammunition boxes filled with earth, and camouflage nets. There was some frustration when one gun was found to be inoperable due to a bent breech mechanism lever, damaged during the move. A replacement arrived with a later ammunition lift. There was also some humour. Waring, who had been warned of possible enemy

177

patrols, was moving cautiously round the position visiting the guns

> when I saw what seemed to be an Argentine section approaching. I dived to the ground and lay absolutely still wondering what the hell to do as the enemy came closer. Then I heard what sounded like whispering only a few metres away. I stared hard into the darkness and just made out the cause of my pounding heart — a bunch of geese![6]

By midnight the 'Black Eight' were ready to fire their first shells in anger. They had to wait another three hours for the call to come.

Lieutenant Colin Connor was worried. The responsibility for getting A Company to its start line was his, and he was late. A Company's advance on Burntside House was due to start at 2.00 am from a north-south fence line about 500 metres east of the house. The problem was for Connor to locate the correct fence on a pitch black night, mark out and secure the start line and then send back guides to the battalion RV at the bridge over the Ceritos Arroyo stream. These guides would lead A Company to the fence. From the RV it was a difficult and circuitous route of over 2,000 metres across ankle-breaking ground. Not only were there a number of small, steep-sided streams to be crossed, but the terrain was boggy, the water icy, and what solid ground there was was covered in 'babies' heads', a term the Toms used to describe hard, round tussocks of grass that could turn an ankle or twist a knee with ease, especially in the dark.

The onus for 2 Para launching the attack at the right time from the right place rested on Connor's young shoulders. He had taken half of his platoon, three patrols of four men each from the Recce Platoon, plus his radio operator. Connor was leading, but navigation was not a real problem as the fences on the ground were remarkably accurately shown on his map, while Burntside Pond was an unmistakable feature to his right. The complication was the slowness of the march, and the consequent realization that he was not going to make it in time. As he reached a fence close to Burntside Pond Connor made a decision. He called up the senior patrol commander and whispered his instructions. The corporal was to take the men forward, find the fence, secure the start line and mark the ends and approaches by men with red torches, while he, Connor, went back for A Company.

He appeared to be taking an enormous gamble that his NCO could complete the task unaided, but it was a decision based on knowledge of his subordinate's competence. Connor was certain he was not asking too much. With a soft 'See you later', Connor watched his men move off before he and his radio operator started to retrace their steps. They were both carrying 40-50 pounds, mostly ammunition, but the operator had his set in addition. It was not long before the stumbling but cracking pace began to tell. The radio operator was 'knackered so I eventually had to leave him by the fence and push on alone'.[7] If Murphy was going to apply his law with a vengeance this was the moment. The start of the battalion attack now depended on a corporal searching for a fence in the blackness and a junior officer pounding along in the opposite direction, with an exhausted signaller sitting by a fence somewhere between them. Such is war.

Fortune, however, smiles on the brave, so on this occasion all went well in that Connor got to the RV before A Company, led it back, retrieved his radio operator, found the start line, and with a sense of relief handed over further responsibility to Major Farrar-Hockley. A Company would begin their advance only 35 minutes late.

From the time Colonel 'H''s 'O' group broke up nine hours were planned to elapse before A Company assaulted Burntside House. As this was allowing twice the time to get the battalion into position to start the operation than was allocated to fighting through to the outskirts of Darwin and Goose Green, it is hardly surprising that, with hindsight, the timings have come in for considerable

Map 14

PHASES 1 & 2 — START LINES ARE CROSSED

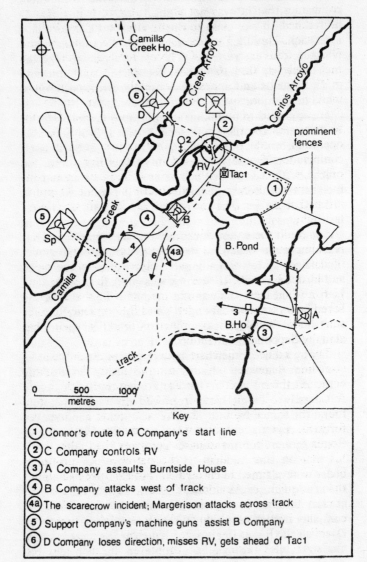

Key

1. Connor's route to A Company's start line
2. C Company controls RV
3. A Company assaults Burntside House
4. B Company attacks west of track
4a. The scarecrow incident; Margerison attacks across track
5. Support Company's machine guns assist B Company
6. D Company loses direction, misses RV, gets ahead of Tac1

criticism. Events proved that Colonel 'H' had accurately estimated the time it would take to get the leading companies on to their start lines, but with only 14 hours of darkness to play with that only left 4½ for the bulk of the attack. Could 2 Para have got to the start lines earlier? Did the delaying of the 'O' group for four hours mean that much less time to achieve the objectives?

With the second question an early 'O' group would merely have meant a less hurried departure for C Company, but, as nobody could move until after dark for security reasons, the effect on the time available for the operation would have been nil. Company and platoon commanders would have had more time for their own briefings, the troops might have snatched a bit more rest, but there was no critical disadvantage in the late 'O' group given that no forward movement could start until after last light.

But could the actual advance have started earlier? That is an important issue. If 2 Para had had an extra two hours of darkness there was a good chance that Darwin ridge would not have stalled the advance as it did. Supposing H-Hour had been at midnight instead of 2.00 am, surely seven hours was enough to get A and B Companies to their start lines? Well, perhaps, but it is unlikely when what actually happened is examined.

The speed with which the leading companies got to their start lines depended mainly on how quickly C Company could get them there. As already related, even nine hours was barely enough; Connor had to resort to desperate measures to get back to the RV and guide A Company forward. Even then they were 35 minutes late. Major Roger Jenner, commanding C Company, had taken both his platoon commanders to the battalion 'O' group in order to save time. Their own 'O' groups were little more than a quick explanation of the company's tasks, 'a cursory briefing' as Captain Farrar describes it, before the company headed south down the track to clear the route, establish the RV at the bridge, and then locate and secure the start lines. Because of the extra distance and the

181

difficult nature of the ground, coupled with the blackness of the night, it was the Recce Platoon that had the toughest task. Had H-Hour been midnight A Company would surely have still crossed its start line around 2.30.

While C Company, particularly the Recce Platoon, was to be continually pressed for time, the rest of the battalion spent hours waiting to move. Support Company was the next off. Although delayed by the realization that its fire base task necessitated the machine guns firing in the sustained fire role and that the gun kits were still on Sussex Mountain, it left the House at 7.00 pm and had set up its position overlooking Camilla Creek by 10.00.[8] It then waited for five hours before it could fire a shot. A Company, the next in the order of march, left Camilla Creek House at 10.20 pm, six hours after last light. There was no point in departing earlier just to sit at the RV waiting for their guides. The RV was meant as a checkpoint through which companies passed on their way forward. A bottleneck at the bridge with the battalion bunched up waiting was not what Colonel 'H' wanted.

For Phase 1 everything hinged on C Company. If Connor's task seemed fraught with problems, Patrols Platoon came close to causing confusion at an even earlier stage. The white bridge over the Ceritos Arroyo was an obvious landmark, difficult to miss even at night. For this reason it had been selected as the battalion RV (checkpoint). However, there had been a report that the Argentines might have a gun position near the bridge, so Corporal McNally had been sent with his patrol to watch it during daylight on the 27th. Nothing was seen. Because McNally was assumed to know exactly where the bridge was, his patrol was selected to lead C Company to it. As his platoon commander, Farrar, was later to say:

Because I was confident that he knew exactly where he was going I didn't pay much attention to the route. After a bit of up and down work we arrived at a re-entrant in the bottom of which was a bridge. He [McNally] indicated that this was to be the RV.

Even though I hadn't been check navigating something told me this was not the right place. I informed Roger Jenner, the OC, that I was not happy and took over the lead — arriving some time later at the correct watercourse, which was carefully checked out by the half section of attached engineers.[9]

Farrar believes that McNally may have spent the 27th watching the wrong bridge, the one over the Camilla Creek Arroyo. Small errors can be dangerous.

For A Company the attack on Burntside House was an anti-climax. The fence line that was its start line had been secured and marked by Recce Platoon soldiers with red torches. Although it was on the correct fence it was some 400 metres north of where it should have been, but Farrar-Hockley was satisfied that the error was not critical so no attempt was made to move further south. The company lay on the ground with 2 Platoon on the right, 3 Platoon on the left, Company Tac in the centre and 1 Platoon to the rear as reserve. They had had an exhausting journey which, 2nd Lieutenant Mark Coe of 2 Platoon recalls, had 'many stops, and seemed to take for ever'. It was pitch black, nothing could be seen of the objective, the ground was sodden, feet were soaked, it was bitterly cold and it started to rain. Although the conditions were miserable, the adrenalin was flowing fast; this was the moment for which they had trained so long and hard — the final rendez-vous with reality.

Major Farrar-Hockley was concerned at the complete inability to see anything, and regretted not bringing the platoon 2-inch mortars. The FOO, Captain Watson, had recorded two targets on his map — Burntside House, and some tents reportedly 500 metres away to the right, near Burntside Pond. As A Company stood up to advance the guns back at Camilla Creek House got their first mission. Watson was as blind as everybody else so called for fire on the basis of the original grid references, hoping to be able to see the flashes and adjust as necessary. Within minutes of H-Hour the silent attack became noisy. It was to remain so for the next 14 hours. Watson 'fired the guns on Burntside House as we crossed the start line, but I have no idea if they were effective because of the darkness; probably not'.[10] As A Company neared the objective the artillery fire was lifted to the second target area.

2nd Lieutenant Guy Wallis led 3 Platoon towards the house, down a long gentle slope, then over a deep and freezing stream only 100 metres from the building itself. The exploding shells had helped with maintaining direction and HMS *Arrow* was now firing star shells for illumination. Burntside House was blacked out, and not a shot had come in his direction when Wallis ordered his 84mm Carl Gustav anti-tank missile to fire. The first shot missed. The two-man team reloaded, the number one squeezed the trigger — nothing; a misfire. The number two gingerly removed the offending rocket and reloaded for a third try. Another misfire. 2 Platoon opened up with 66mm rockets, machine guns and rifles.

Inside the house four civilians cringed on the floor. Gerald Morrison, his wife, his mother, and a friend knew the Paras were coming as they had heard the BBC World Service like everybody else. At around 8.00 pm an Argentine soldier had come across from the nearby lambing shed, where a group of Morales' men were located, to tell Morrison to turn off their generator as it was making too much noise. As he later explained; 'They used to come down, two at a time, pinch the food and then bugger off.' He has graphically described his experience, as Wallis's men opened up, to Martin Middlebrook:

We were all lying in the corners; we would have got under the carpet tiles if we could. It was a wooden bungalow which gave no protection .... We were terrified, but the shelling eased off [the British guns had indeed missed].

Then the house was hit, bullet fire at first all over

184

the place — mother had a row of eleven bullet holes just above her head. A grenade came through the window of one bedroom but luckily there was no one in it. It lifted the roof of the bedroom about five inches, and all the furniture caught fire. We thought we were caught in the crossfire but then we heard them shouting orders in English and a bit of swearing. We started shouting we were civilians .... Jim and I went out and they made us stand with our hands against the house. They were full of apologies then — but it was a bit late. We counted 130 holes in the house afterwards and then gave up counting.[11]

Somebody was surely watching over the occupants of Burntside House. First the artillery missed, then the rocket launcher failed three times, it was grenaded in an empty room, and not one of hundreds of rounds touched anybody. The only casualty was a dog, wounded in the mouth. And the Argentines? There was a lot of tracer flying everywhere outside, but nothing directed at A Company. Coe recalls that any rounds that came his way were 'probably ricochets of our own tracer coming back'.[12] The enemy platoon had pulled out either just before, or during, the assault. Sergeant Barrett took 1 Platoon over to the edge of the pond to where tents had been reported, but nothing was found. It was not until after the battle that two dead Argentines were discovered lying between the house and the pond.

Farrar-Hockley was able to report that his objective had been secured without loss. This was a relief to Colonel 'H' as he could now release B Company to start its advance. Earlier on he had been exasperated by his inability to get a sitrep from A Company. His request was answered by the company signaller with 'Wait out'. This was a normal response to such a question, as the operator could not be expected to describe the tactical situation — an officer was needed. But, as a witness said:

'H' wanted an immediate answer but the signaller

could only reply 'Wait out'. The conversation continued for about 10-15 minutes with 'H' demanding a sitrep and 'Fetch officer'; it was frustrating to listen to and [it] would have been quite understandable if later 'H' had shot the signaller .... Captain Chris Dent (2IC A Coy) was the unfortunate who eventually gave 'H' his sitrep; Chris should have been on the net, and so 'H' ordered him to carry A Company's battalion net radio himself instead of the signaller.[13]

When Dent died on Darwin Hill he was still carrying it.

Sergeant Smith's patrol, with Captain Farrar close behind, had moved forward cautiously down the track to locate and secure B Company's start line. The battalion RV was only 600 metres from possible enemy positions so, unlike Connor, Farrar did not have far to go. Navigation was simple; they just followed the track that led south down the centre of the narrow neck of land between Camilla Creek and Burntside Pond. What follows is Farrar's own account of how B Company was got forward:

Our [Patrols Platoon] advance was extremely slow, and conducted in complete silence. With many listening halts we arrived at a position where we could hear Argentine sentries chatting. Luckily it was quite dark, and I recall slightly overcast. I moved forward to confirm the Argentine position, which I reckoned was no more than 100 metres distant. This decided the position for the start line. I would estimate we had the start line secured by 0400 [midnight]. I left the whole platoon less my own patrol on the start line. Although it would have been SOP to mark it with white tape − I believed it was a little [too] close to the enemy. It was therefore physically marked and secured by my spread out patrols.

Having established the start line I moved with my

team back to the Ceritos Arroyo (the Bn RV). Just before descending into the re-entrant I came across the CO's Tac HQ crouched by the side of the track. I can recall the CO and Adjt [Captain Wood] being there. This was the last time I saw either of them alive .... I waited in the RV for B Company.

Somewhere around this time a herd of wild horses could be heard shuffling around (the occasional whinny giving their identity away). At one stage they moved in the area of the start line because I remember a jumpy Argentinian sentry letting off a few rounds. I remember thinking, 'I hope my blokes on the start line don't fire back and give the game away'. They didn't.

Eventually B Company arrived. I spoke briefly with Major John Crosland and then led him back up the track to the start line .... Having settled them in all my personnel withdrew to the RV in the rear.[14]

B Company had arrived on time, but now they had to wait. First A Company's attack had to go in, and then there was a problem with HMS *Arrow*'s supporting fire that had to be sorted out.

Captain Ash, the FOO, was having difficulties. Both his radios chose this crucial moment to pack up just as he needed to talk to the NGFO. A lot of fiddling around, and the swopping of bits with other sets, finally got one working. B Company had the ship's 4.5 inch gun for this phase, capable of firing 25-30 enormous shells a minute. The plan was first to identify the target and then illuminate it. Having got a star shell over the area, it could be adjusted, then another fired before putting HE on to the target. The infantry advance would follow this procedure. The plan was fine, the practice was not. It was raining, dark, Ash was unable to identify anything, and at the outset his radio was not working. HMS *Arrow* started firing star shells independently. Then, shortly after getting his set back on the air, Ash heard the NGFO's curt and ominous message, 'Gun out'. A mechanical fault in the turret had stopped *Arrow* firing. There was now no naval gunfire for B Company.[15] Illumination would be dependent on 2 Para's two mortars and the hand-held Shermully flares carried in the platoons, or, for those that had taken them, the small 2-inch platoon mortars. There was hope that the fault could be rectified quickly, but meanwhile the attack must continue. A further delay ensued while Ash spoke to Rice to get authority to switch the 105mm guns from A Company to B Company. Permission was forthcoming as A Company now had no need of them – but there were no illuminating rounds at the gun position.

Ash resorted to picking a likely grid reference, firing the 105s, and adjusting by the sound or flash of the explosion. He then ordered continuous fire at Rate 2 as B Company advanced. The idea was to 'roll back' the gunfire as the troops progressed. But there were long delays between the shells arriving and being able to get them to 'roll back', so Ash was apprehensive that the Paras might walk into their own fire. Part of the problem was the need to go through the relay station.

It was around 3.00 am that B Company with bayonets fixed finally clambered to their feet at the start of their long advance with Boca House, their final objective, 5,000 metres away. 6 Platoon under Lieutenant Clive Chapman was the left forward platoon, with Lieutenant Ernie Hocking's 4 Platoon on his right. In reserve came Lieutenant Geoffrey Weighell with 5 Platoon. Major Crosland has described that moment:

> I was walking around my leading platoons and the atmosphere was very like the tension before a parachute descent – but underlying this was a quiet confidence .... At 0700 [3.00 am] the word was given and the company rose as one to start our long assault. My orders were clear – advance straight down the west side destroying all in the way .... The company was tight and prickly, with two machine guns or an M79 per section. We contained a lot of firepower.

This was going to be a violent gutter fight, trench by trench — he who hit hardest won.

He continued:

> The GPMGs suppressed a trench, a grenade L2 [HE] or WP followed, and on they went. There was to be no reorganization as such — once the momentum was started we were going to keep them rolling back ....
>
> We started the attack with about three hours' sleep in the previous 24 hours and with little food. About 3 minutes after crossing the start line the leading sections destroyed an enemy machine-gun post and quickly moved into the first company position. This was rapidly overrun .... The advance continued with our trench-clearing tactics working well ... by now enemy artillery and mortars were firing on to the first position and also along the line of the track .... The advance continued through increasingly heavy DFs, and while doing so the leading platoons missed an enemy position off to our flank. As Company HQ drew level I saw trenches in the gloom and indicated an immediate attack on to this position. It took about 45 minutes to clear this position containing mortars and AA missiles.[16]

If the company commander's account makes it all sound rather simple in retrospect, the actuality was not all that different. Apart from the problem of maintaining control, of knowing where people were in the dark, the Argentines put up little resistance and B Company completed this phase of the attack without a single casualty, despite the close-quarter fighting. Chapman has given a lively account of what happened after his Toms hit the first positions:

> As mentioned previously we were on the start line for a long while because of HMS *Arrow*'s problems. There was no enemy shelling but there was a lot of

tracer being pumped across the western side. I thought from the tracer that it was enemy MGs but it might have been our own MGs [it was]. I reckon we were on the start line for 40 minutes .... We had two sections forward and one in reserve .... I remember that our left-hand boundary was initially the track. I know Margerison's section had to cross this boundary to destroy a couple of trenches....

Our platoon skirmish was initiated by the 'scarecrow' incident. As we were advancing with two sections up someone said, 'Watch out, there's a scarecrow in front'. Although this now seems quite ridiculous it seemed plausible to me at the time, as the ground paragraph of the orders had included something to the effect that the ground we would be manoeuvring over was some of the best arable land in the Falklands (visions of tramping through cabbage fields!). The message was passed around the platoon and then someone else said, 'The scarecrow's moving'. The scarecrow was in fact an Argentine soldier who came towards us and said 'Por Favor' (please) in Spanish. What he actually meant I don't know, but he was wearing a poncho and I said, 'Shoot him' (I had attached myself and Kirkwood [Chapman's radio operator] to the right hand edge of Margerison's section). Private French, one of the GPMG gunners, opened up on the Argentinian and put quite a big burst into him. The enemy soldier literally flew through the air and the tracer ignited as it passed through him. He was hit quite a few times. [Corporal] Eiserman later searched his body and found about five rounds had penetrated a prayer book he was carrying .... I have no regrets about this action as it was then that we executed a platoon frontal attack upon a series of enemy trenches behind the scarecrow.

There was a lot of light in the air at the time from our Schermullys and (I think) from our 2″ mortar. I remember thinking at the time that the fieldcraft of the troops as they attacked was fantastic. They were weaving left and right, covering the bounds of moving men and really getting stuck into the fight. There was little need to hit the ground and people generally knelt to fire between moves. It was a very dark night, and we had closed to (I think) about 20-40 metres from the Argentinians when the fight began.

As to the complete number of trenches and how many enemy were killed I do not really know. Estimates have ranged from eight to well over twenty....

Just about every trench encountered was grenaded .... Kirkwood and myself even took out a trench. There was a continuous momentum throughout the attack and it was very swiftly executed .... The Argentinian resistance was pretty weak. A lot of them were, I believe, trying to hide in the bottom of their trenches and ignore the fight .... They were a scared bunch, and a lot of them were non-participants.

The success of the attack had an electrifying impact on the platoon. I think we believed from there on in that we were invincible. I am a great believer in the force of 'will' in battle, and the fact that we had imposed our will so well and so early made us a better platoon .... On the company level there was a profound faith in John Crosland. As long as he was OK we believed that we, as a collective unit, were also invincible. Both on exercise and in the Falklands it was a case of 'follow the Black Hat' (given Crosland's penchant for wearing a black woolly hat rather than more conventional headgear).[17]

B Company pushed on, although few officers knew

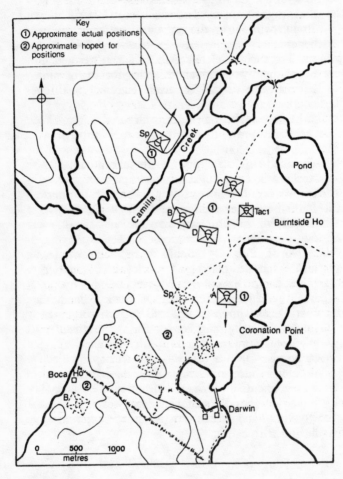

precisely where they were. When asked over the radio for his location Crosland replied, 'Four hundred yards west of the moon for all I know'.

On the right Hocking's 4 Platoon moved up on to the low hill SW of the Low Pass, which was where the bulk of the Argentine company was expected to be but they swept through without a contact. 5 Platoon came across six hastily vacated trenches. Crosland ordered 5 Platoon to push on. More trenches and three prisoners were taken before the platoon came under fire. Sergeant Aird went forward to fire with the M79 grenade launcher but this did not suppress the enemy. Weighell called for covering fire while he and his platoon sergeant dashed forward to grenade and capture the trench from which the fire was coming.

The original plan had slipped well behind schedule. When Crosland started to gather together his scattered company it was around 5.00 am. By this time D Company should have been forward on the knoll overlooking Camilla Creek, with B Company well on its way to Boca House and A Company in reserve on Coronation Point. In other words Phase 4 should have been nearing completion. What had happened was that, although A Company had had no opposition, Manresa's company had succeeded in engaging and delaying both B and D Companies. (D Company's actions will be described in the next chapter.) Once fighting started, once the attackers became involved in taking out trenches on a dark night, time became a casualty as well as men, and its loss was just as difficult to recoup. The approximate situation as at 5.00 am is depicted on Map 15. Although they did not know it the Argentines, despite their poor performance so far, were buying Piaggi time, time to reinforce his thinly held main line of trenches.

VIII

DAWN AT DARWIN AND BOCA HOUSE

'If they had counter-attacked at dawn they would have thrown us off the battlefield because we were totally outgunned and wrong-footed'.

Lieutenant-Colonel Chris Keeble DSO, 2 Para's second-in-command at the start of the battle. *Speaking Out.*

Whether Major Keeble's remarks truly reflected the situation will never be known for certain as no counter-attack was made, but there can be little doubt that as the sun rose that morning 2 Para was still a long way from reaching its objectives. In terms of distance covered the battle group had progressed about half way to Goose Green in the four hours since A Company had crossed its start line. To get there was going to require the momentum being maintained for another ten hours in broad daylight, across bare terrain against an entrenched enemy. As the Paras came up against the Argentine's main defences the climax of the battle had arrived. Undoubtedly, if the attackers could be checked there, if only temporarily, it was the right moment for a counter-attack.

Lieutenant-Colonel Piaggi had been contemplating just such a move for some time prior to first light. He knew that Manresa was in trouble and falling back despite repeated appeals to hold. Piaggi had been reporting progress to Parada at Stanley and urging support. He had been promised some troops and air strikes later that morning, weather permitting, but for now he must hold

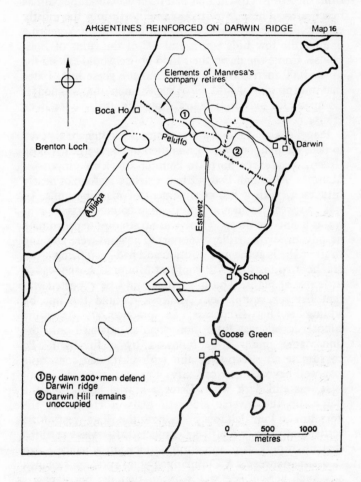

Elements of Manresa's company retires

Boca Ho

① Peluffo

②

Darwin

Brenton Loch

Aliaga

Estevez

School

Goose Green

① By dawn 200+ men defend Darwin ridge
② Darwin Hill remains unoccupied

0   500   1000
metres

195

his own. To do this Piaggi made two moves which were to have far reaching consequences on the battle. The first was to order up 2nd Lieutenant Aliaga with his platoon from the 8th Regiment that had been watching the Salinas beach area. These forty men came north into the mostly empty trenches on the extreme left of the main Argentine line on the low hills south and SE of the ruins of Boca House. Come the dawn their field of fire would extend for up to 1000 metres over and beyond the gorse line. Later that morning it would be Aliaga's men that pinned B Company for over four hours, checking its drive for Boca House.

Piaggi's second move was to instruct Lieutenant Estevez to take his platoon, which was then in reserve near Goose Green, to advance north to counter-attack in support of Manresa. Although Estevez had a strong platoon of nearly fifty men, with a full complement of machine guns, he was too weak to mount an effective counter-attack. Nor was it trained to do so. There was no attempt to coordinate his advance with artillery support. The guns were running short of shells at the gun position and had been firing blind off the map, as their OP south of Mount Usborne was of little use at night. The most that could be expected was that Estevez would help Manresa to hold the line by adding to his firepower. In practice an Argentine counter-attack was little more than an advance until the unit came under fire, followed by a fire-fight. To coordinate an effective assault with ill-trained conscripts was well beyond their capacity.

It was still dark when Estevez moved north past the dairy, up the reverse slope of Darwin Hill, over the gorseline to join Pelufo's platoon on the ridge west of the settlement. The two officers conferred. Estevez explained that his orders were to counter-attack, to advance north to assist Manresa's A Company. Pelufo spoke out against any such action. He was worried that his position was insecure, pointing out that attacking in the present circumstances, when Manresa's men were already withdrawing, would be impossible in the dark. He had a point; so Estevez contented himself with deploying his men into the trenches on the right of Pelufo. Nobody was on Darwin Hill itself, or in the gorse-filled gully that separated it from the ridge running NW. This ridge was now strongly held, and once again constituted the Argentine's main line of defence against an attack from the north. Here Estevez was to meet and check Major Farrar-Hockley's A Company. It was a machine-gunner from his platoon that cut down Colonel 'H' when he made his gallant and desperate effort to organize a breakthrough. Estevez too, would die on Darwin ridge - the only Argentine Army officer to be killed in the battle.

The approximate layout of the Argentine positions is shown on Map 16. With Aliaga on the left, Pelufo in the centre, and Estevez on the right, together with some of Manresa's company who had fallen back, these defences were manned by at least 200 men. They were not a cohesive unit as all three platoons were from different regiments, let alone companies. Nor did they have a senior officer coordinating the defences. The task fell to Manresa who was not in a position to make proper arrangements, or even know who was under his command, as he only arrived back on the position just before first light. At 5.00 am, and for the next hour and a half of darkness, as the Argentines sorted themselves out on the Darwin ridge, the sights and sounds of battle to the north crept steadily closer. Tracer trails curved and crackled across the sky, their own green or white criss-crossing with the red of the British. The flash and crump of bursting shells; the long, endless rattle of belt-fed machine-guns; the stuttered popping of small arms; the thump of grenades, all served to confirm the British had launched a major attack. Up in the sky the parachute illuminating, and other flares, dispelled the darkness over the battlefield for those engaged, but not for the watchers who waited on the ridge. When the fighting died down as Manresa's men were overrun or pulled back the blackness closed in again reducing visibility to a few metres.

Had 2 Para been able to keep to their optimistic time

schedule the assault on the Darwin ridge position would have taken place at night, with the attackers able to close to within charging distance before being discovered, as had happened as Phase 2 merged with Phase 3. In these circumstances the defenders would surely have crumbled. But Manresa stole sufficient time to compel the Paras to face the Argentines' main position in daylight. It was to prove almost enough to swing the battle in the Argentines' favour. Able to see their enemy, to open fire at long range over bare ground, even the reluctant conscripts had the confidence to keep shooting from bunkers and trenches they had had several weeks to prepare.

All this was several hours into the future as Major Neame's D Company, the last sub-unit in the battalion column, made its way warily down the track towards the RV. Neame has given a typically nonchalant description of what happened next:

It was not a particularly ingenious plan. I suppose, in the circumstances, it couldn't have been, but it followed the familiar military thinking with regard to the alphabet — two companies up, A left, B right, and in this case D in reserve. The military mind likes things in the proper sequence. My company set off from the assembly area [Camilla Creek House] forward to the start line at the back of the battalion snake. This should have meant no navigation problems for me; just follow the guy in front. We were to trog along until we met the C Company guides who would lead us to our start line. Part of the problem was that we had the main battalion headquarters in front of us so when they suddenly halted we had to thread our way through this enormous gaggle of bodies, but there were no guides on the other side to meet us — just a mass of tracks. My leading platoon pressed on but it soon became clear that we were lost, and had overshot the main axis track[1].

Exactly how D Company managed to get on to the battlefield without checking through the RV, and then arrive ahead of the commanding officer despite getting lost en route, will probably never be sorted out. These things happen. Captain Farrar remembers how concerned he was when C Company eventually left the RV as D Company had still not passed through. He queried it with his company commander who told him they had somehow got ahead. 'How they did it I'll never know. They certainly never came through the RV[2].' Lieutenant Peter Kennedy, C Company's second-in-command, is equally emphatic: 'D Company never passed through us, though they found their way on to the battlefield. We assumed that they were very wet as we controlled the only crossing over the river! OC D Company later denied this, but couldn't explain how he managed it.'

Neame's account continues:

My concern was not to get ahead of A and B Companies. I turned the platoons around, retracing our steps until we hit what I was sure was the main track. We sat down, and I was thankful we were still behind the leading companies. Unfortunately we had somehow got ahead of 'H'. He suddenly came stomping down the track from behind us. 'What the hell are you doing here?' were his opening words. My response of 'Waiting for the battle to start' did not placate him, and he made it plain that he didn't take kindly to his reserve company being closer to the battle than he was. Feeling somewhat subdued, I continued to sit while he and his Tac HQ disappeared into the blackness.[3]

Colonel 'H' did not get far before coming under fire himself. He retraced his steps to Neame and directed him to advance and clear the track ahead, pointing out where he thought the enemy position was located. Neame's problem 'was that I couldn't really tell exactly where this position was on the map and he [Colonel 'H'] didn't know precisely where it was either.'[4] Thus was the reserve company committed to the battle.

It was a decision that changed the original plan whereby D Company was to advance in Phase 3 after A Company had moved on Coronation Point. It led to a bloody little battle for a trench system that was a part of Manresa's company, and would result in the first 2 Para casualties of the night. It had not been bypassed by B Company, rather the positions now encountered by D Company were those not yet reached in Phase 1. D Company was now out in front, about to engage Manresa's right and rear.

Colonel 'H' was becoming increasing fretful at the delays. This was wholly understandable as by this time the dawn deadline, by which his battalion was to be poised to enter the settlements, was only some 2½ hours away. It was taking longer to regroup scattered sections and platoons than actually to take out enemy positions. Progress thus far measured about 1,500 metres with another 5,000 to go. The commanding officer felt it imperative to push through his reserve to take the lead, to sustain the impetus along the line of the track which was the axis of advance for the battalion.

B and D Companies were now very close. Both were deployed on the right of the track. Within D Company, 12 Platoon under Lieutenant Jim Barry, the young officer who had foregone his yachting trials to be where he was, was in the lead. Behind him and to the right came Lieutenant Shaun Webster with 10 Platoon, and to his left 11 Platoon, under nineteen year old 2nd Lieutenant Chris Waddington, nicknamed the 'Boy Wonder' for his propensity on joining the battalion for taking his men on platoon attack training at 6.00 am.

Webster's platoon, although not in the lead, was the first to come under effective fire. He recalls:

There was suddenly a huge racket and tracer started flying everywhere. We took cover and returned fire. I can remember thinking how strange that they should let us get so close because we must have been

200

only 30-40 metres away. Their tracer was green and white and ours red, the colours were amazing.... Corporal Staddon's section and platoon headquarters were best placed to move closer towards the enemy [so] we crawled in a more or less straight line towards them. Suddenly a heavy calibre opened up and I think that was when Lance-Corporal Cork was hit in the stomach. [Cork, and Private Mort, who was wounded in the arm at the same time, were 2 Para's first casualties of the battle. Mort survived but Cork did not.] Private Fletcher went to assist him and at about that time some mortars started falling on us. Luckily the ground was soft and absorbed most of the blast, but I remember thinking that command and control is all very well but what can you do when you and everyone around you is deaf! I was shouting something but couldn't hear my own voice.

As we lay there an Argie got out from his cover and started to walk very slowly and deliberately away from us, he didn't have a weapon and I think he must have been shell-shocked as their mortars fell amongst their position as well. We continued moving towards their position until we could throw grenades. A few WP and L2s were thrown and ended it.... We did not know what had become of Cork or Fletcher.... I sent Corporal Staddon to look for them but he could not find them. The company had to move on so we informed the CSM ....

This event [the loss of Cork and Fletcher] had a deep impact on everyone because it was the first time most of us had come under direct fire at close range, and obviously the deaths of two in such an apparently random manner brought home the seriousness of the situation. It might sound rather naive to say so, but until then we were quite 'gung-ho' and confident death would only happen to someone else.[5]

A glance at Map 17 will show how this skirmish

progressed. 12 Platoon was leading and had been making straight for a dimly perceived position on a slight rise to their front, when two machine-guns opened up on one of Webster's sections behind and to the right. The situation had suddenly deteriorated, with the leading platoon committed, and 10 Platoon pinned by heavy fire. The company commander described this moment with a degree of wry frankness:

> 12 Platoon was already engaged, then 10 Platoon was hit from the right leaving me with only 11 Platoon uncommitted. However I was worried about B Company as if 11 Platoon moved right it would be attacking towards them. At that point I was being somewhat hesitant, wondering what the hell to do next, when I saw from the flashes of fire that Chris Waddington [11 Platoon commander] had already started to assault towards the right, and 'H' was yelling to find out what was holding us up, so I told him to get on with it. John [Crosland] gave me some flack because our fire was coming his way, but there was nothing I could do about it.[6]

11 Platoon's attack cost two further Para casualties — Lance-Corporal Bingley and Private Grayling. The story of their gallantry is best described by the medic, Lance-Corporal Bentley, who later carried in Bingley's body:

> As daylight approached, we started to search for those of D Coy still missing. Padre Cooper called me over, he had found Gaz Bingley. Gaz had been shot through the head. I helped the Padre carry Gaz back to the RAP in a poncho. I will never forget that short walk, his head kept banging against my knee ... . It was a moving moment for everyone. Gaz was the first of our dead to be recovered. The story of his last few minutes of life had already reached us through Baz Grayling. They had been making a

202

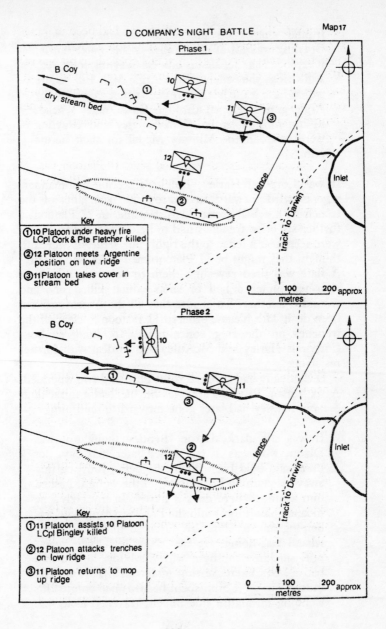

Phase 1

B Coy

dry stream bed

10

11 ③

12 ②

fence

Inlet

track to Darwin

Key
① 10 Platoon under heavy fire
   LCpl Cork & Pte Fletcher killed
② 12 Platoon meets Argentine
   position on low ridge
③ 11 Platoon takes cover in
   stream bed

0   100   200 approx
      metres

Phase 2

B Coy

10

11

③

② 12

fence

Inlet

track to Darwin

Key
① 11 Platoon assists 10 Platoon
   LCpl Bingley killed
② 12 Platoon attacks trenches
   on low ridge
③ 11 Platoon returns to mop
   up ridge

0   100   200 approx
      metres

frontal charge on an Argie machine-gun post. Grayling was hit at close range in his water bottle; it exploded shattering his hip. As Grayling collapsed, still firing, they silenced the Argie MG. But as fate would have it the last few rounds squeezed off by the Argie gunner ripped through Gaz Bingley's head, killing him instantly. Both Bingley and Grayling were awarded the Military Medal for their heroic effort.[7]

It was Corporal Harley, Bingley's section commander, who crawled forward to destroy the occupants of the trench with a WP grenade. Meanwhile, in 12 Platoon, a further six or so trenches had to be cleared. Four figures were seen near a fence to the right, but Sergeant Meredith thought they might be 11 Platoon men so he held his fire. A flare was fired revealing them to be enemy. All four vanished under a hail of shots which killed one and wounded another. To ensure that all the Argentines had been dealt with Neame ordered 11 Platoon to clear all the trenches on the ridge once more. In doing so both Corporals Harley and McAuley had to deal with further resistance.

D Company had suffered three dead and two wounded. A sixth man, Private Parr, was hit but had a miraculous escape. Bentley had later gone forward to tend him:

> It was still dark, Dixon [Bentley thought it was Dixon, who was in fact killed later that day, not Parr] said he'd been hit in the belly, [but] cutting away his clothing I couldn't find the wound. I asked him again, 'Where does it hurt?' 'In my belly,' he moaned painfully. I told the P.T. Sergeant, who was helping me, to shine his torch so that I could see what I was doing. He said, 'You're fucking mad,' but, shielding the light with his body, he did as I had asked. There nesting in Dixon's [Parr's] belly button was a 7.62mm spent head! It had entered his webbing through a side pouch, travelled along the

inside of his 58 pattern belt, burrowed through his clothing and, unbelievably, come to rest without breaking his skin exactly in his belly-button.[8]

Regrettably this story has a tragic ending. Parr was evacuated but soon returned to duty only to die at Wireless Ridge, killed towards the end of the battle by British artillery fire in one of those depressing 'friendly fire' incidents so common in war. Unbelievable good fortune was followed by the ultimate misfortune.

After this tough little action, typical of the sort of close-quarter 'gutter fighting' required to push back Manresa's men, the time-consuming task of reorganizing, of gathering together the company before any further advance was possible, began. D Company was badly scattered, at least one section, Corporal Kinchins', had strayed well into B Company's area. Neame found the only practical, if risky, way was for him to fire flares into the air and tell everybody to close on him. More delay followed while a search was made for Cork and Fletcher who were missing, but not known to be dead at that stage. Neame again:

It took ages to reorganize — I would think at least an hour and a half. Fighting at night is extremely confusing, but at the time we accepted it as normal, as, apart from training, we had no yardstick with which to compare it. It didn't seem much different to the average muddle on a night exercise. The besetting problem after any action in the dark is reorganizing, when your soldiers have been fragmented in all directions. You get very disorientated. It's like being blindfolded, twirled around several times, and then being expected to know which way to go. Both A and B Companies had the same problems during the night. This was the main reason that 'H' had fed us in early, he wanted to keep up the pressure; as the reserve company that was our role.... After this life for us

205

was fairly simple. For the next hour or more we merely followed along behind the leading companies. By dawn we were on a small hill some 1,000 metres north of the gorse line.[9]

To some in C Company, which was also following up behind the action along the axis track, these vicious little fights by both B and D Companies resembled a realistic night exercise on Salisbury Plain. Lieutenant Peter Kennedy recalls:

We moved slowly south down the main track, stopping and starting throughout the night, listening to the sound of battle just ahead, watching the streams of tracer and the flashes of explosions. It appeared to be a very well-organized exercise with plenty of Batsims [battlefield simulations]. We were still on the track as dawn broke. Enemy small arms fire began to fly past us, but buzzed like angry bees rather than the expected crack because they were reaching the limit of their range. They bounced along the track; I remember one soldier being hit, but he only jumped and yelled as the force was probably no more than a stone fired from a catapult.[10]

By about 4.30 am it was A Company's turn to advance again. For over an hour they had crouched cheerlessly in the wet and cold west of Burntside House, watching the progress of the flashes and tracer as the battle moved gradually from right to left down the isthmus. The continuous noise seemed to indicate heavy fighting as first B and then D Companies pushed forward. At last Major Farrar-Hockley got permission to move over the radio. A Company now had the guns again, which the battery commander was having to switch from company to company as the need arose due to HMS *Arrow*'s problems.

The assault on Coronation Point had the makings of a difficult one if the experiences of the other rifle companies were anything to go by, especially if there really was a full Argentine company waiting for them as they had been led to believe. Farrar-Hockley grouped his company on a new start line — another convenient fence that ran east-west from just south of the inlet south of Burntside House. Although it was to be a long advance of 1,000 metres to Coronation Point from the start line navigation was not a problem. On the right 2 Platoon under 2nd Lieutenant Mark Coe had the battalion axis track on its right as a guide, while on the left Sergeant Barrett with 1 Platoon could use another fence that led exactly to the objective. The company commander was well forward in the centre, with 3 Platoon under 2nd Lieutenant Guy Wallis behind. In the circumstances a frontal two up and one back advance was the only practical option.

As the company advanced Captain Watson called for a fire mission on to Coronation Point. Progress was cautious but steady. Within fifteen minutes A Company was once more the leading company, further down the isthmus than the others who were still regrouping in the darkness to the west. As the leading sections closed with their objective without provoking a single shot from the enemy, spirits rose. Where was the Argentine company? There is a slight rise west of the Point itself and A Company manoeuvred up it in the darkness expecting any second to be in the midst of a trench system, and to be blasted by close-range fire — instead nothing. No enemy, not even a trace of their presence. For the second time that night Farrar-Hockley's men had had an easy task. As they consolidated on the northern edge of the Darwin inlet, they were a mere 500 metres across the water from their final objective — the settlement. It was only 5.20 am, with more than an hour of darkness left, yet A Company was not destined to set foot in Darwin until after the final Argentine surrender.

If the rifle companies had had a successful night so far, Support Company's activities had been something of a disappointment. The decision to centralize at a fire support base off to a flank at the start had not proved effective. A lot of effort, physical effort, had been necessary to carry weapons and ammunition to the position, but when the battle started only the Machine Gun Platoon was able to come into action. The snipers could see nothing, neither could the Milan teams, who spent most of their time trying to sleep or rest to the rear of the position. Even the NGFO's efforts had been thwarted by the naval gun jamming early in the proceedings.

The GPMG in the sustained fire role is an excellent gun, but it is a direct-fire weapon. This means that the gunner has to see what he is shooting at to be effective. There must be a direct line of sight to the target. This was not always so with British medium machine guns. Prior to the GPMG the old Vickers gun, which was water-cooled, could pump out streams of bullets to ranges up to 4,000 metres, or twice the distance of the GPMG, in an indirect role. At these distances the firer did not have to see his target, the bullets travelled in a pronounced curve over intervening obstacles, and there was a substantial lethal beaten zone at the receiving end. The problem for the Support Company gunners was they they could not see anything. As the company-sergeant-major, Warrant Officer 2 Jed Peatfield, said, 'It was a pitch black night so we couldn't see properly; we had to keep switching fire - everything was largely guesswork.'[11]

There never had been any chance of the machine guns assisting A Company at Burntside House, and now all that could be done for B Company was to shoot hopefully at where the Argentines were thought to be, at the sources of their tracer, and then switch the fire to the right to ensure the safety of the advancing Paras. The use of the rifle company's fire support coordinators was problematic in the dark. As the leading platoons fought through the enemy trench system the medium machine guns had to fire on other suspected targets to the south. Because of the darkness and dead ground, D Company got no benefit from these guns when they became embroiled west of the track. Despite the difficulties, there was considerable expenditure of ammunition. According to Corporal McCready: 'There were fireworks all over the place. All guns were firing and we got through plenty of ammo. They heated up to such an extent that flash eliminators were melting, and some gas plugs were fired down range. We still kept firing, using 1 in 1 tracer, as there were plenty of spares and two extra barrels per gun kit.'[12]

The system of supporting fire being controlled by company coordinators had not been practised before; the officers or NCOs using it did not have experience of the system. This disadvantage was compounded by the siting of the fire base, and the direction of A and B Companies' initial attacks. A glance at Map 14 will show the problem. Once A Company had secured Burntside House and exploited to the west, the machine guns firing in support of B Company's advance south of the Low Pass were shooting towards A Company — it was in the line of fire. A Company experienced a number of 'overs', although nobody was hit. Once this stage of the battle was complete Support Company could do nothing but await permission to try to catch up with everybody else.

By 4.30 am Major Hugh Jenner realized that he was serving no further purpose in his position so he radioed Colonel 'H' for authority to pack up and rejoin the battalion. He received permission and, by 4.50, was on the move. Support Company had long since lost the services of the Assault Pioneers as load carriers, so they had to carry everything themselves. As the company commander admitted 'a lot of ammunition had to be left behind.'[13]

Although the Mortar Platoon was under Jenner's command as an integral part of Support Company, in the battle for Goose Green it acted independently under its commander, Captain Mal Worsley-Tonks. Worsley-Tonks took his orders direct from Colonel 'H' at the 'O' group and personally moved as part of Tac 1 with his own radio operator to control the fire of the two tubes that were in support of the battalion. Each rifle company had Mortar Platoon NCOs acting as MFCs performing the

209

same function for the mortars as the FOOs did for the guns.

The 81mm mortar can be an extremely effective killer of infantry. It has been said that 30 per cent of British battlefield casualties in World War 2 were caused by mortar fire. Its advantages include the lethality of the bomb against troops in the open, its ability to fire HE, smoke (WP), or illuminating bombs, its very high angle of fire enabling it to fire from behind walls, steep hills, or from gullys, and the speed with which it can come into action. A good crew can get off 12 rpm, with a normal rate of eight. Without a vehicle, the disadvantages are its weight, plus the associated complication, its insatiable appetite for bombs. At the normal rate the two mortars with 2 Para would need eighty bombs to keep them in action for five minutes. Only some 500 bombs were dumped at the first baseplate position. This was the primary reason Colonel 'H' wanted them in reserve initially, relying on HMS *Arrow* and the artillery at least until the later phases.

Two other considerations were to influence the use of the 81mm mortar at Goose Green. The first was the softness of the ground into which shells or bombs tended to sink before exploding, and the fact that the Argentines were dug in. An effective answer to the first was to use white phosphorus. Its property of continuing to burn despite every effort to extinguish it made it devastatingly effective against personnel, particularly in a confined space. The second was the need to ensure that mortar fire was not brought down too close to the Paras when they were in the open. Training manuals specify 200-300 metres, but this safety margin is often cut in action. Nevertheless, there was a real need to restrict close support by both mortars and artillery once A Company had closed up to the enemy, on the Darwin ridge for example. A strong, gusting wind aggravated the problem.

The fortuitous capture of a landrover with Lieutenant Morales partially solved the carriage of ammunition dilemma. Responsibility for getting the bombs forward to the first baseplate position near the battalion RV was that of Colour-Sergeant Pye, the CQMS of Support Company. Initially Corporal Hain, an MT NCO serving with the Defence Platoon, took over the vehicle. He stripped the blue and white landrover of every superfluous piece, including the radio, and stuffed it with mortar bombs 'until the springs turned inside out'. Throughout the night this vehicle was driven backwards and forwards from Camilla Creek House. On the outward journey the cargo was mortar bombs, on the return it was casualties. The ammunition had been dumped at the house by Sea King helicopters on pallets where it was manhandled by Hain's section into the landrover. Hain drove it himself for the first trip, then Corporal Thayer took over, remaining with it for the rest of the battle. Four trips were completed before first light. Without the unexpected bonus of this vehicle the baseplate position would have had a negligible, as distinct from an inadequate, amount of ammunition to support a long battalion attack. 2 Para's landrovers still sitting on the ship were sorely missed. The earliest the Scouts or Gazelles could be available to ferry ammunition forward would be after first light, by which time the battle was supposed to be almost over.

Reliance had been placed on HMS *Arrow* to light up the battlefield with a continuous shower of star shells, but when the gun malfunctioned 2 Para were thrown on to their own resources. The artillery had not brought illuminating shells, so the first fire mission for the Mortar Platoon was to provide light for B Company. This they did, but as only some five per cent of bombs were illuminating it could not last long. Come the dawn the platoon had stockpiled bombs, but were beginning to wonder if they would shortly have to move forward again as the leading rifle platoons were then approaching Darwin Hill — another 800 metres south of the hill and they would be beyond the mortars maximum range.

At first light Worsley-Tonks ordered Sergeant Ian Hastings, who throughout the battle commanded the two tubes supporting the battalion, to move forward. He was not to know that it would be another five hours before any Paras got south of Darwin. Hastings found that at the first new position he selected the baseplates rapidly disappeared into the ground and had to be dug out. He got permission to move again. His next location was about 2,000 metres south of the old RV. From there he could hit anything well to the south of Goose Green. Hastings was not too happy, however:

> I would have much prefered a reverse slope position. Although the ground was hard we were right out in the open. We must have been near an old Argy gun position as we found hundreds of 105mm shells still in their boxes, which we used as wind-breaks. Here we stayed until the fighting died down at the end of the afternoon. I listened in on the company radio net to find out what was happening, so I heard all the contact reports.
>
> Shortage of ammunition was the main problem, particularly WP. We had to organize a runback to the old baseplate position with the blokes staggering along with eight bombs each — two cases on each shoulder. I reckon everyone in the platoon did four round trips. It was a fantastic effort.[14]

Colonel 'H', anxious to keep the advance rolling, had taken his Tac 1 close up behind D Company and had come under enemy artillery fire. One shell landed with a wallop between himself and the adjutant. It failed to detonate. 'Fucking lousy ammunition they're using,' was Captain Wood's comment. Further back, at a prominent track and fence junction with gates just west of the inlet south of Burntside House, the main headquarters had had to deal with some enemy trenches overlooked by D Company before they could organize themselves. One of the watchkeepers, Warrant Officer 2 Fenwick, whipped the blanket from the bottom of a trench to reveal three Argentines — all asleep. Here also the RAP was established.

So far casualties had been light – just D Company's – but a weakness in the system had been revealed. Insufficient thought had been given to finding wounded and evacuating them. Most of the injured in this battle were compelled to lie for hours, one officer for over twelve, a few soldiers for twenty, before they could be brought in. Although, once attended to by the medics, not a single man died, there was much suffering by those unfortunate enough to be hit. Some were probably saved by the cold from bleeding to death as the near freezing temperature tended to contract wounds and further dilate blood vessels.

There were several factors that contributed to the problem. First, it was difficult to find casualties in the dark. When soldiers went missing they had to be left behind when their platoon moved on, as had happened with Corporal Cork and Private Fletcher in 4 Platoon. No proper search could be made until daylight for the missing D Company men. Then, medics or soldiers who found wounded comrades had great difficulty in carrying them to the RAP as there were no stretchers. Use was made of ponchos which are awkward if not useless pieces of kit for the job. Improvisation was the order of the day, with pieces of corrugated iron, metal plates, and even a wheelbarrow being pressed into service at various times.

Sometimes medics had to carry dead bodies single-handed. Lance-Corporal Bentley described one such attempt:

Out of respect for the kid I carried him in first. I was knackered and kept stumbling. Finally I couldn't pick him up any more. I lay down next to him, pulled his arms up over my shoulders and struggled to my knees, then to my feet. As I staggered he slipped, I gripped his wrists tightly but he just rolled off my shoulders on to the floor; I was still holding one of his arms! I just couldn't pick him up again so I spread out my own poncho, rolled his body on to it and dragged him back to the RAP.[15]

As soon as the seriousness of the problem was appreciated, the Assault Pioneer Platoon was removed from C Company to assist with carrying casualties. These men were to spend the remainder of the battle carrying forward ammunition and bringing back wounded. It was one of the crucial lessons learned and applied at Wireless Ridge, where a platoon of thirty-five soldiers was earmarked at the start solely for finding and carrying casualties. It proved a drain on manpower, and the decision not to take the Band to the Falklands was regretted as these men were trained in precisely these duties, in addition to being musicians.

By day Argentine artillery and mortar fire delayed some evacuation, while this, plus the threat from Pucara air strikes, kept the light helicopters from flying right up to the forward area until midday. Back at Camilla Creek House Major Ryan, the officer commanding Headquarter Company, had responsibility for supervising the re-supply of ammunition and coordinating all helicopter flights. The plan was for the larger Sea Kings to bring up the bulk ammunition and off-load at Camilla Creek House from where the Scouts and Gazelles would take over. Sometimes it worked, sometimes it did not. The system of putting in a formal demand to brigade for a helicopter, using the proper procedure, often produced disappointing results. A more effective method was to bribe the pilots back at Ajax Bay with cigarettes or space heaters.

The light helicopters were supposedly controlled by 2 Para. The idea was (by day) for a request for helicopters to be radioed to brigade who would send a pair forward to Camilla Creek House. There they would land for the pilot's final tactical briefing before going south to undertake the mission. This would normally be to land at or near the RAP, which eventually developed into a combined ammunition supply point and casualty clearing centre close to battalion main headquarters. Helicopters

214

were expected to take ammunition forward and bring back the wounded.

When A Company secured Coronation Point to find it deserted the first critical moment of the battle had arrived for 2 Para. It was only 5.20 am, the company had had no casualties and was well in hand, there was over an hour of darkness left and only 1,000 metres at most to Darwin Hill. If they could push on at once the likelihood was they would be on the hill overlooking the settlement by dawn, which was precisely where Colonel 'H' wanted them so that Darwin could be taken in daylight. This did not happen because, unbeknown to the Paras, they were now facing the Argentine main line of defences, and because A Company remained at Coronation Point for almost an hour before continuing the advance. Nothing is certain in war, but, seemingly, there was a chance that if A Company had advanced that hour earlier the prolonged struggle for the Darwin ridge line would have been briefer and less bloody.

So why did A Company sit waiting at Coronation Point? The situation must first be viewed through the eyes of the company commander. According to his original orders he was supposed to secure Coronation Point by around 4.00 am in Phase 3, but, due to the slow progress of B and D Companies thus far, A Company had arrived on its Phase 3 objective an hour and twenty minutes late. During Phase 4, which should have seen B Company, supported by D Company, push on to Boca House, Farrar-Hockley was required to wait at Coronation Point in reserve.

The real position was that the phasing and timings of the plan had been merged, compressed, so that when A Company got to Coronation Point they were well ahead of the other rifle companies on the ground. When Farrar-Hockley went forward to verify his position, he was aware that if he ignored his Phase 4 orders to remain in reserve and advanced on Darwin Hill he could catch up for lost time, and possibly be the only company to achieve its Phase 5 objective on schedule. He radioed Tac

1 for authority to continue the advance. To have pushed on without permission on his own initiative was an option, but, as Farrar-Hockley well knew, Colonel 'H' ran a very tight battalion. He maintained complete personal control and expected strict compliance with his orders. Farrar-Hockley saw the opportunity, but his request to exploit it was met with the order to wait until his commanding officer could come forward to assess the situation.

Colonel 'H' was not prepared to release A Company without his seeing the position first hand. He was surprised that Farrar-Hockley had got as far south as he had, surprised that there were no enemy on Coronation Point, and that the east side of the isthmus appeared undefended in contrast to the centre and west. Possibly he felt that to allow A Company to get yet further ahead of the rest of the battalion as they sorted themselves out in the darkness risked the advance becoming unbalanced. He hurried forward down the centre track, asking Farrar-Hockley to put on his strobe light to facilitate his finding him[16]. Much of the delay at Coronation Point was thus caused by the time it took the commanding officer to reach A Company in the dark.

After conferring with Farrar-Hockley, Colonel 'H' pressed A Company forward with the utmost speed. He now appreciated that there was a real chance of making up for lost time, feeling that the main enemy defences had possibly been penetrated during the night. He told Farrar-Hockley in no uncertain terms to get a move on, becoming irritable as A Company waited while Wallis, with 3 Platoon, moved around the inlet to get into position at the northern end of the causeway leading into Darwin. Farrar-Hockley considered it important to have a platoon able to cover the settlement while the remainder of the company advanced west of the inlet on to the high ground, and thence into Darwin. By the time A Company was ready to continue first light was only minutes away.

It was once again the hurry and wait situation so well

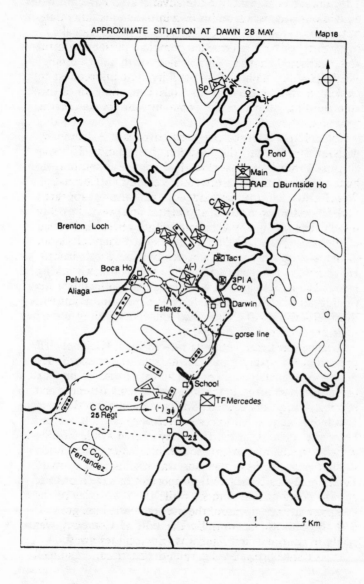

known to soldiers. After the holdup at Coronation Point, A Company was now in a desperate hurry to beat the sunrise. Time was so short that risks had to be taken and tactical principles relating to movement and ground abandoned as the approaching daylight exposed the company's right flank. Farrar-Hockley had the commanding officer on his back demanding speed, so he in turn pressed his leading platoon. The colonel, however, was confident. With a little bit of luck and maximum momentum they might still have a late breakfast in Darwin. The brigade log records the following message from Colonel 'H' at 6.40 am as dawn approached: 'On schedule and approaching PLACE FREE [Darwin]'.

As A Company moved south, just west of the Darwin inlet, they were down to about seventy-five men as the third platoon was then separated from the company by 500 metres of water. Farrar-Hockley was destined to fight his battle with only two platoons, plus the nineteen men in his command group and company headquarters. Had he or Colonel 'H' known what lay in store the approach to Darwin ridge would surely have been conducted differently. At the commanding officer's 'O' group they had been told to expect a company of Argentines on Coronation Point; this was proved false. On Darwin Hill nothing of significance had been reported, although sixteen trenches and some tents were said to be located on the northern slope of the ridge 600-700 metres due west of the Darwin inlet. Sixteen trenches could represent a lot of men, at least a strong platoon, possibly more, but in the rush to get forward this probable position was ignored. There was no specific bombardment planned on this location, no smoke screen was intended to mask A Company's advance, and no sub-unit had been ordered to take this location. Although given out at the battalion 'O' group, it then appears to have been forgotten.

To understand the significance of what was happening the reader is asked to refer to Map 19 which shows the essential features of the ground in the area of A Company's advance. In the centre of the isthmus, WNW of Darwin

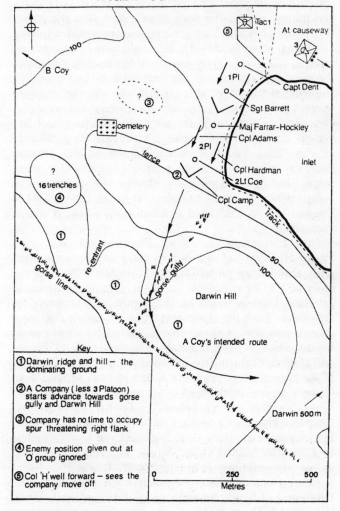

B Coy

100

⊕

cemetery

? ③

⑤ Tac1

At causeway

3

1 Pl

Capt Dent

Sgt Barrett

Maj Farrar-Hockley

Cpl Adams

2 Pl

Cpl Hardman

2Lt Coe

inlet

fence

②

Cpl Camp

? 16 trenches ④

re-entrant

gorse line

①

①

track

50

100

gorse gully

Darwin Hill

①

A Coy's intended route

Darwin 500 m

Key

① Darwin ridge and hill – the dominating ground

② A Company (less 3 Platoon) starts advance towards gorse gully and Darwin Hill

③ Company has no time to occupy spur threatening right flank

④ Enemy position given out at 'O' group ignored

⑤ Col 'H' well forward – sees the company move off

0   250   500
Metres

219

inlet, is a hill, slightly over 100 feet high, with a rounded spur running down almost to the inlet. A Company was to advance close to the inlet without occupying this spur/hill on its right. This was a risk. Had Farrar-Hockley had more time, had he been allowed to follow the tactics text-book, he would have secured this spur before moving on, so that come the daylight he would have had a covering force in position to give support to his leading platoon in the open as it approached the next ridge — Darwin ridge. Immediately south of this central hill was the ridge on which the sixteen trenches had been reported. A Company's right was in the air as B Company were not yet up level with A Company to provide flank security at this stage. Wallis's platoon down at the Darwin causeway was supposed to be the company's covering force, but was completely unable to support the company's move until, or unless, it got to the summit of Darwin Hill. A calculated risk had been taken. It almost succeeded.

2nd Lieutenant Coe's 2 Platoon led the way. Farrar-Hockley had told him to make for the gorse-filled gully that led up on to Darwin Hill. At the head of the gully he was to swing left on to the summit. If he could get there Darwin would be below him, and he would be able to see both the airstrip and Goose Green. The route chosen was one of those recommended by Thurman in his discourse on the ground at the outset of the 'O' group, and afterwards during the informal get-together with some of the company commanders. Coe had put Corporal Tom Camp's section in the lead in arrowhead formation, with himself a few metres behind[17]. To his left rear was Corporal Hardman's section, with Corporal Adams and his section to the right rear. Darkness was dissolving fast as 2 Platoon headed south. Spirits were high, there was an air of confidence in the company. It was four hours since A Company had crossed its first start line. The battalion had fought several tough little skirmishes during the night with negligible losses and were now half way down the isthmus. One more push should do it was the

220

feeling of many. In fact many more pushes were needed. The real battle for Goose Green was about to begin.

IX

THE GORSE GULLY

'Don't tell me how to run my battle.'
Lieutenant-Colonel 'H' Jones OBE to the officer
commanding D Company when Major Neame
suggested trying a right-flanking move along the
western beach of the isthmus to break the deadlock
at Darwin ridge, and in front of Boca House.

Three and a half hours is a long time to spend crawling
around in a gorse gully with the nearest enemy often less
than 100 metres away, but this was about to be the fate
of A Company, or rather two platoons of it. Corporal Tom
Camp had no inkling of what was in store as he led his
section across the open ground towards Darwin Hill.
Visibility was improving with every step he took as the sun
rose to his left. His platoon commander, Coe, had directed
him to make for a gorse-filled gully on the right of Darwin
Hill itself, with the intention of using it as a way up on
to the high ground overlooking the settlement. Once up
there A Company would have completed Phase 5 of the
plan. With 3 Platoon giving support from the causeway,
and the rest of the company on the dominating ground,
the final phase of securing Darwin should be simple.
Neither Corporal Camp nor his platoon, nor indeed his
company, were destined to reach their ultimate objective
during the battle.

Camp's men were well spread out in arrowhead
formation with a GPMG on each flank as they negotiated
a wire fence about 100 metres from the entrance to the
gully. Behind, almost treading on their heels, came Coe

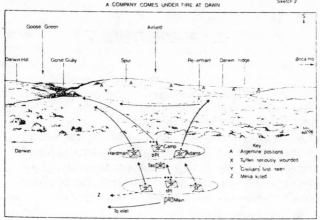

Goose Green   Airfield   S

Darwin Hill   Gorse Gully   Spur   Re-entrant   Darwin ridge   Boca Ho

Darwin   Hardman   Camp   Adams   Key
   2Pl   A   Argentine positions
   Tac   X   Tuffen seriously wounded
      Y   Civilians first seen
   1Pl   Z   Melia killed
Z   Main
   To inlet

with his radio operator. Immediately behind 2 Platoon
Farrar-Hockley's group of seven men was conspicuously
a headquarters of some sort as no less than three soldiers
were humping radios. These sets belonged to the company
commander, the FOO and the MFC. As the light
improved Camp's view of what lay ahead began to take the
shape of that shown on Sketch 2. The ground over which
they walked was bare and covered with grassy hummocks
— more 'babies' heads'. Ahead, a low hill, or spur,
pointed directly at him; on its left was the gorse gully to
which he was heading. A lot of thick clumps of high gorse
clogged this little valley, some of it spreading well up the
right side. The left side was the lower slope of Darwin
Hill. If Camp or his men looked slightly right of the
central spur the entrance to a smaller re-entrant could be
seen. Further right still the outline of Darwin ridge was
just visible against the grey sky.

Suddenly, as the leading section was almost at the gorse
gully entrance, three figures appeared on the slope of the

spur to the right. At first they seemed harmless. Somebody suggested they were civilians. 'Perhaps its a man walking his dog,' said another soldier. Then, Lance-Corporal Spencer, who was a mere ten metres from them, noticed they were armed. He yelled at them in English. They waved, perhaps thinking the Paras were Argentines pulling back from the night fighting to the north, as the Para's helmets looked similar to the Argentines. One shouted back in Spanish. Both sides realized their error simultaneously. One Argentine raised his hands, one ran, the third fell as Camp's men opened up and dashed into the gully. Instantly the main line of the Argentine defences dug in on the spur and the ridge to the right came to life. Heavy automatic rifle and machine-gun fire was directed towards A Company. It was 6.45 am − the start of the only all-day battle of the war.

When coming under effective fire British troops are trained to double forward into the nearest cover if they can, and this is precisely what A Company did. It was an instinctive reaction. Although caught in the open at close range, casualties were few. It is hard to hit a fast-moving man in poor light, especially when he is only visible for a few moments. In these circumstances the tendency is to shoot high, which is what happened on this occasion.

While Camp's section, followed by Corporal Hardman's, made it to the gorse gully with their platoon commander, Corporal Adams was too far away to join them. His section had been at the right rear of the platoon and thus faced the re-entrant to the right of the spur when firing started. Adams did the only thing possible. He led his men in a rush for the re-entrant. His effort was rewarded by a hail of fire. Unbeknown to him he had run straight up against Estevez's platoon position, and was in the same re-entrant in which his commanding officer was to die so gallantly some three hours later. Adams was hit in the shoulder, while Private Tuffen received two wounds in his head which dropped him instantly. He was to lie where he fell for some four hours, less than 100 metres from the enemy trenches. It was known he was down, but he was too far away from the gorse gully, and too exposed for any attempt to get to him to be made. Incredibly he survived[1]. Despite his wound Adams continued to command his men. Realizing the futility of staying in the re-entrant on his own, he led his section back around the spur into the gorse gully.

Farrar-Hockley had also led his tactical headquarters into the gully, followed by the majority of Sergeant Barrett's 1 Platoon. Theirs had been a long run, but the enemy fire was still too high, so they made it without loss. Not so company main headquarters and one or two soldiers from the rear of 1 Platoon. They were too far from the gully to reach it unscathed so they went to ground and became involved in a one-sided fire fight. Lieutenant Livingstone, with his four Royal Engineers (serving in the Royal Marines), was among this group. He found that returning fire merely served to attract an intense response, so he sought to stop his men firing while the group worked their way down to the shore of the inlet to their left[2]. During this process, which lasted about half an hour, Corporal Melia, the Royal Engineers' NCO who was the booby-trap expert earmarked to clear Darwin, was shot dead. Lance-Corporal Shorrock, one of A Company's medics, received two bullets in his spine at about this time. Like Tuffen he was in for a long and agonizing wait. Also like Tuffen he lived.

Private Martin was a rifleman in Corporal Abols' section of 1 Platoon, one of those who failed to make it to the gully at this stage:

> I was at the back of the platoon with part of company headquarters. When firing started we doubled forward a bit, went to ground, and opened fire on the hill. We were soon under mortar fire as well but were saved by the soft ground. One man [Corporal Melia] got hit going forward to the left. It was all chaos with no orders as the section commander had gone into the gully. Gradually we made our way down to the beach by the water [inlet]. Shorrock

225

crawled back and we put a dressing on him. We met a signaller who told us 2 Platoon had been wiped out. I was worried about my brother [Lance-Corporal Martin who was the second-in-command of Corporal Prior's section]'.[3]

The situation was not as black as feared by Martin although Farrar-Hockley was in an unenviable position. With him in the gorse gully were some sixty plus men whose sections and platoons had intermixed in the scramble to get into comparative shelter. Another twelve men, who made up his main headquarters, were 400 metres to his rear, while his third platoon was 700 metres away across the inlet. His only consolation was that there was no enemy on the Darwin Hill side of the gully. Had the Argentines occupied the hill there is little doubt A Company would have been progressively shot to pieces, under fire from positions above it and from either flank.

The most immediate problem was a group of several trenches up on the spur to the right of the entrance to the gully. They were dealt with by an unusual mixture of soldiers who happened to be to hand at the time, including Corporal Camp, several more soldiers from 2 Platoon plus the signaller, Captain Watson the FOO, and Corporal Russell from 1 Platoon. Between them they fought a neat little action that removed the threat. Use was made of grenades, 66mms and a GPMG. The problem with the GPMG was that it could not be elevated sufficiently to fire uphill. Camp and Private Dey (2 Platoon's radio operator) tried lifting it to fire, then Dey resorted to using Private Pain's back as a firing platform. By crawling forward, blasting the bunkers at close range, and hurling grenades, this part of the spur was secured, including the capture of several trenches.

Captain Watson had left his signaller in the gully to become an infantryman, crawling forward with Camp's men. He judged the enemy to be far too close to risk trying to bring down artillery fire, and at that stage nobody had any idea of how extensive the position was. Watson got to within five or six metres of a trench and tossed in a WP grenade. The same at the next; then back into the gully for more grenades and to face the caustic comments of his signaller who was feeling abandoned by his officer.

At the same time 2nd Lieutenant Coe, acting on his company commander's order, had gathered together his number 2 Section under Corporal Hardman to attempt to push on up the gully to do a left-flanking movement around the spur. They came under intense machine-gun fire from further to the right, forcing Coe to give up the attempt at the cost of Private Worrall lying in the open with a wound in his stomach.

Meanwhile, Barrett took several men with a GPMG some way up the left side of the gully, but like Coe's group met with heavy fire, wounding Private Kirkwood in the leg and knocking Barrett off his feet. He yelled for more men to come up, then dropped back and summoned Corporals Abols and Prior to assist in dragging Kirkwood clear. Worrall, however, had still not been recovered.

There now occurred a most outstanding incident of rescuing a wounded comrade under fire. It was to take nearly an hour to complete, involving, at various times, Coe, Sergeant Hastings, six NCOs from both platoons and several soldiers. Tragically, one of the NCOs was killed, but Worrall was saved. It was an example of the absolute determination of the Paras never to desert their comrades and the bond of loyalty and devotion that exists between well-motivated soldiers. Sceptics can say it was also an example of playing into enemy hands, of wasted manpower and time, which tied up a large number of junior leaders when they might have been better employed organizing efforts against the enemy. But this is to ignore the morale factor. High morale wins battles and is built on many things, not least of which is the knowledge that your mates will never let you down. There is a brotherhood between soldiers that have lived, trained and finally fought together that demands and receives absolute loyalty. There exists a powerful bonding that develops through shared danger, an implicit trust in the words 'Cover me'.

The story of Worrall's rescue is best told by Corporal Abols, whose actions won him the Distinguished Conduct Medal:

There was a bank to our front. The three of us skirmished forward. The bank used to be covered in gorse but when we got there it was smouldering from a fire .... When I took cover I had to jump up as I had burnt myself. To fire we couldn't lie down, so we had to stand back and fire. We could see the enemy trenches, the furthest being 350 metres away.... We saw two men on the other side of the bank, one was Private Elliott the other Private Worrall. We shouted to them to get back and we'd give them covering fire. Elliott shouted back that Worrall was hit, so myself and Corporal Prior went out to give assistance while Corporal Russell and Elliott gave covering fire. Once we got out to Worrall we told Elliott to get back. Corporal Prior then began to give Worrall first aid. Corporal Prior didn't know how bad the injury was so the only thing we could think of to do for Worrall was for us to get him back to the other side of the bank....

We knew it would be a hard task as it had to be done on our bellies, and the bank was about 30 metres away. Every time our heads or webbing went above the grass the snipers would open up. We could hear the rounds whizzing past our heads. It took us about half an hour to get about 25 metres. Then we couldn't go any further because of the burning roots from the gorse bush, so we realized we would have to pick Worrall up and carry him to the bank. As Corporal Prior was at the feet end of Worrall and I at his shoulders, I told Corporal Prior I would go over the bank first and organize covering fire. So I skirmished and dived over the bank and saw that Corporal Russell was still there, so I told him what

Corporal Prior and myself planned to do, and would he organize covering fire, he said yes.

I then returned to Corporal Prior and Worrall [but] we couldn't coordinate the covering fire because of the noise of battle, so I skirmished and dived over the bank again to discover that Corporal Russell had been hit by shrapnel from an anti-tank weapon. Then Sergeant Hastings, [2nd] Lieutenant Coe and a few privates assisted us with covering fire, so I returned to Corporal Prior and we decided to throw a smoke grenade, which would be the signal for the covering fire to commence as we moved in. I threw the smoke grenade, then we grabbed Worrall but couldn't move him as his webbing had caught on some gorse roots. By the time he was ready to be moved the smoke had disappeared, so we decided to take a chance and go over the bank with him. Just as we were about to move a sniper shot Corporal Prior in the back of the head; he then fell dead onto Worrall.

Then Corporal Hardman and Lance-Corporal Gilbert came over and we managed to get Corporal Prior over the bank and then returned for Worrall, and managed to get him over too.

Corporal Camp and myself then carried him down the gully to the remainder of the company. I then rested and had a few fags and returned to the battle on the hill.[4,5]

Sergeant Hastings, who had provided much of the covering fire for the rescue of Worrall remembers how in his haste to reload magazines he threw down his gloves which caught fire in the burning gorse, forcing him to use a pair of socks on his hands instead.

Corporal Underwood was A Company's MFC. Shortly after arriving with Farrar-Hockley's group he had been called further up the gully from where he was able to get a better view of the enemy bunkers. He could see fourteen or so stretching away in a line to the west. He called for fire, but was disappointed with the results. The HE rounds tended to bury themselves in the soft ground and, as far as he could see, no trenches had been destroyed. Thereafter he made the maximum use of WP bombs in the anti-personnel role, which had the added advantage of blinding the bunkers even if they were not hit. The problem was the accute shortage of bombs at the baseplate position. After a while enemy mortars zeroed in on Underwood forcing him back down into the gully.

The company commander had decided that concentrated fire was needed to neutralize the Argentine positions along the ridge west of the spur near the gorse line, and close to the cemetery. He got Sergeant Barrett to group six GPMGs up on the spur. It was now clear to Farrar-Hockley that his was a difficult position with the enemy at least in company strength, entrenched on dominating ground, while his force was scattered in small groups and individuals. For nearly an hour Sergeant Barrett kept his guns firing, with belts of ammunition being thrown up from soldiers in the gully, including Farrar-Hockley and Sergeant-Major Price. In some ways this part of the battle was one of strange contrasts – at one moment dramatic bursts of fighting, or courageous action by individuals to rescue a wounded comrade, followed by relaxing under cover for a quick cigarette. 2nd Lieutenant Coe, for example, recalls lying on his back in a hole after coming back down the gully, smoking, discussing cricket with Corporal Camp, and listening sympathetically as his NCO described his concern that his wife had recently bought a car.

At the Darwin causeway Wallis was largely impotent. He could see a battle was raging but the range was excessive, it was difficult to tell friendly from enemy troops, and they had been spotted themselves. This later led to heavy mortaring which forced 3 Platoon down to the shoreline for shelter after firing into a few likely Argentine positions.

Captain Dent, back with the main company headquarters, had been compelled to remain pinned by heavy fire near the inlet shoreline for an hour. There was a convenient bank behind which the headquarters was able to seek cover. Eventually he decided to make his way along the beach and rejoin the company, leaving Livingstone to command the headquarters. The gorse gully battle had become a patchwork of uncoordinated efforts by small groups and individuals. Nothing Farrar-Hockley tried produced startling results. The left-flanking attempts had proved impossible. Although the GPMGs were producing considerable fire, and much of the spur had been secured, the Argentine fire from the remaining trenches did not slacken. *HMS Arrow* had long since departed, while attempts to use artillery proved fruitless as they were primarily tasked to support B Company, which was then trying to advance on Boca House. Despite this Farrar-Hockley repeatedly asked for their help and the FOO tried to fire a mission. He was eventually given authority, and endeavoured to hit several trenches south of the cemetery. However, the shells fell wide of the target, to such an extent that B Company's FOO, Captain Ash, cut in to order 'check firing'. The rounds were landing amongst his company.

At 7.25 Farrar-Hockley called for an airstrike. The long, open ridge would make an ideal target for the Harriers dropping cluster bombs. The request was relayed to brigade, and from there to the carriers. It was turned down as fog at sea was preventing take-offs. A Company had now been stuck in the gully for over an hour and a half. Every effort made to leave the relative safety of the dead ground was thwarted by a hail of fire, there was no ship available to assist, the guns were needed equally by B Company and were anyway firing inaccurately, the weather was preventing air support, and two mortars with limited ammunition could not produce the weight of fire needed. As Major Keeble put it, "Sod's Law' was operating well that morning'.

To make progress reliance would have to be placed on slowly trying to take out the remaining trenches one at a time with 66mms and grenades. Farrar-Hockley later explained: 'Our advance could not be effected by complete platoons closing but by skirmishing in small groups. Control was crude, principally by NCOs shouting to those nearest to move or give covering fire. This was aided by the initiative of individuals such as Corporal Abols.'[6]

Success was likely to be a long, painful, and probably costly business.

A lengthy business was exactly what Colonel 'H' did not want. By 8.00 am his high spirits and confidence that had been obvious as dawn approached had all but gone. It was replaced by frustration and mounting impatience. In the first hour or so of daylight both his leading companies had stalled in front of what was obviously the main Argentine line. (B Company's advance on Boca House is the subject of the next chapter). His exasperation was not helped by the inability of anybody to locate the Argentine artillery, which was now firing continuously, or by the generally ineffective fire from his own guns. With no Harriers able to assist, 2 Para was thrown back onto its own resources — the rifle companies and Support Company. The critical moment of the battle was looming fast, calling for vital decisions from the commanding officer, as Colonel 'H' was assuredly well aware.

Tac 1 had been immediately behind A Company as it moved off from Coronation Point just before first light. Colonel 'H' had watched as the company came under fire, and he had seen the bulk of them dash into the gorse gully. His style of leadership can be summarized as the 'come on' method rather than the 'go on'. He believed passionately in a commander being well forward. This is the tactical teaching within the British Army, it is mandatory in the Parachute Regiment, and Colonel 'H' was its greatest exponent within 2 Para. Exactly how far depends on the circumstances, and personal judgement.

The principle is based on the need for a commander to supervise and not be tied to his command post. The fact that communications work well does not excuse him from intimate contact with his subordinates, or from personal observation of the action. Should radios fail a leader must

232

still be able to influence events. Although initiative must not be destroyed, supervision is still crucial. A simple, workable plan is important, a clear order is important, but supervision to see that the will of the commander is implemented is all-important.

Responsibility for the result of an operation rests squarely with the commanding officer. Of course, a commander cannot be everywhere but he can, and should, weigh the capabilities of his subordinates, determine the critical point or time of the action, and then lend the weight and authority of personal supervision where it is most needed. This was precisely what Colonel 'H' resolved to do.

Colonel 'H' was seldom to be found at his main headquarters in the field, either on exercise or operations. He demanded direct experience of any situation. Information and assessment of the position which a commander receives via his subordinates, being indirect experience, will be coloured by the personality of the person transmitting it. If the latter reports that he cannot advance because of intense enemy fire, the commander at the rear will not be able to gauge to what extent this assessment is made under the strain of battle, and whether it is an unnecessarily pessimistic one. With Colonel 'H' there was never a danger of his lacking direct experience. At moments of crisis it is the drive and energy of the commander on the spot that often counts far more than his intellectual powers. This was the proven philosophy of a renowned battlefield leader — Field-Marshal Rommel. In most great victories in military history these elements of energy and will were present.

There are three ways in which a commanding officer can influence events once his unit is committed to battle. The first is the use of firepower. This entails his coordinating an increased concentration of gunfire — of all types — at the crucial point, on the proven principle that the more you use the less you lose. The effective use of air strikes, naval gunfire, artillery, and the battalion's own heavy weapons, can be decisive — as they were to be at Wireless

Ridge. As has been related 2 Para had problems with all these means of support at 8.00 am that morning, although the Milans and machine guns of Support Company were still a possibility as they moved up behind the advance.

The next method is by the use of reserves. At all stages of a battle the commander strives to keep a proportion of his force in hand as his reserve. It is for use to exploit success or block an unexpected enemy thrust. Colonel 'H' had carefully planned 2 Para's advance so that at every stage at least one company was in reserve; in most phases there were two. The battalion was always balanced as it advanced. Possibly a commander's most important judgement once action starts is when and where to commit his reserve. Having committed it he must immediately form another — to maintain balance. There is, however, a 'golden rule' about the use of reserves that has retained its validity from ancient to modern times. The astute use of even a small reserve force can bring startling results if used to reinforce success rather than redeem failure. Strength should be used against enemy weakness. In monetary terms it is the same principle as not throwing good money after bad. On countless occasions in the past reserves have been committed where an attack has been held up in the hope of achieving a breakthrough. It rarely does more than produce a stalemate in that area. Often the fresh units are merely sucked into a difficult situation without being able to affect the outcome. The key to breaking a strong position is to find the soft spot, then exploit it. Colonel 'H' had both C and D Companies in hand that morning. Would he commit them, and if so where?

The third means of influencing events is by personal example; for the commander to appear at the crisis point personally, to lead the troops himself, to so encourage and inspire the units that his will to succeed is transmitted to his men. At all levels of command from general to corporal this method can be extremely effective. It is as old as warfare itself. Julius Caesar rode forward to grab a shield from a legionary to rally a wavering line in his battle against the Nervii over two thousand years ago. It requires courage, perfect timing and, most crucial of all, that the actions of the commander are seen by the soldiers. These, then, were the choices open to Colonel 'H' as he considered his next move. If he could use them in combination so much the better.

Tac 1 had been caught in the same fire that hit A Company as it headed for the gorse gully. With Colonel 'H' were some twelve men, including the adjutant, Captain Wood, the battery commander, Major Rice, the mortar officer, Captain Worsley-Tonks, their associated signallers, plus his two 'minders' — Sergeant Norman and Lance-Corporal Beresford. Norman has described what happened:

> The amount of fire that came down on us in that first few seconds was thousands of rounds. By firing high in the first burst they gave us time to get to ground. Once they realized their mistake nobody was standing up. Again they brought down fire. We were behind little tufties and in an inlet, so the fire never hit anybody .... The CO stood up and said, 'Right we can't stay here all day', and went into the inlet and, with a mixture of crawling, running, sprinting, and diving we all got out of the killing ground and into the inlet and the protection of a bank, which luckily was not mined.'[7]

Although in cover, Tac 1 was still under fire and had to remain crouched on the tiny beach, where they soon joined up with A Company's main headquarters. At one stage Sergeant Blackburn, the commanding officer's radio operator on the battalion net, had his antenna clipped by a bullet. For a while Colonel 'H' thought they were under fire from Darwin, across the water. There was now a long pause while everybody waited to see how A Company would fare. Colonel 'H' was soon picking up Blackburn's handset to find out. He got a sitrep from Farrar-Hockley, then urged him to press on and sort things out. He was alarmed by the amount of Argentine artillery and mortar fire that was now falling, not only in the A and B Company areas, but also further back among D Company and even battalion main headquarters.

It was also not long after he got to the inlet that Pucaras attacked both Camilla Creek House and the gun line. Nobody had spotted the enemy gun position and it was thought that they must have an OP on high ground to the east able to adjust their fire. Colonel 'H' pressed Rice to get his guns firing, and Worsley-Tonks his mortars. Fire they did, but the mortars with only two tubes and a shortage of ammunition could make little impression. The 105s were still supporting B Company, although they later tried unsuccessfully to help A Company. Part of the problem was the erratic fall of shot due to technical problems at the gun position, lack of meteorological data, a strong gusting wind, and the difficulty FOOs were experiencing in spotting the first strike. The other reason that the rifle companies became critical of their artillery support was the increasing frequency with which their requests for a mission were rejected on the grounds that the guns were not available. It was a question of priorities. As the battle progressed Major Neame in particular suffered from this problem:

> I believe that priority for the guns was counter-battery fire, which is why they were so little use in affecting the battle .... The point on priority is important. We wasted the assets chasing a needle in a haystack [trying to find the Argentine artillery]. Had we had locating assets, or clear intelligence where the enemy battery was, then it would have been totally different. We didn't, and therefore priority should have gone to troops in contact.[8]

At about this stage, with A Company pinned in the gorse gully 500 metres to his SW, and B Company similarly halted 1,000 metres to his west, Colonel 'H'

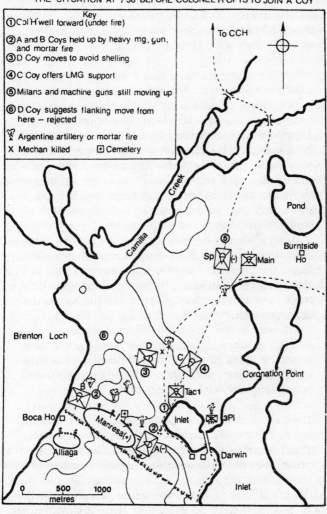

Key
① Col 'H' well forward (under fire)
② A and B Coys held up by heavy mg, gun, and mortar fire
③ D Coy moves to avoid shelling
④ C Coy offers LMG support
⑤ Milans and machine guns still moving up
⑥ D Coy suggests flanking move from here – rejected
Argentine artillery or mortar fire
X Mechan killed   ⊡ Cemetery

To CCH

Camilla Creek

Pond

Burntside Ho

Sp ⊠ (-)   ⊠ Main

Brenton Loch

⑥

D ⊠   X   C ⊠ ④
③

Coronation Point

B ⊠ ②

⊠ Tac1

Boca Ho □

Manresa (+)

①

Inlet

⊠ 3Pl

Alliaga

② ⊠ A(-)

□ □   Darwin

Inlet

0   500   1000
metres

was reminded that he had two companies in reserve. A glance at Map 20 will show the approximate situation at around 7.30 am. Dawn had found D Company atop a long, low ridge 700 metres due north of Tac 1. Major Neame had radioed to give his location, which drew the response - 'Stay put'. Neame has described it:

'H' made it crystal clear that I was not to get any closer to the action. We went to ground and then noticed some Argentinians slipping south along the shoreline to our right [the west coast of the isthmus]. I suppose they were remnants of the force that had been opposing B Company during the night. There were about 20 of them, moving in dribs and drabs rather than in a formed body. Some of my blokes started to use them for a bit of target practice, but I put a stop to it as the range was excessive, and we couldn't afford to waste ammunition.

After a while it became apparent to me that some Argentinian artillery was trying to register us as their target. Shells started to land some way off, and then slowly to creep nearer and nearer. I thought they must have an OP up on Darwin Hill [it was in the mountains east of the isthmus]. I decide to risk 'H''s wrath and move forward a bit into the lee of the next hill where I thought any OP would not be able to see us. This proved a timely decision. Literally within moments of leaving a full fire mission landed precisely where we had been sitting.[9]

It was about then that D Company took its first daylight casualty, Private Mechan, killed by shellfire. Colonel 'H' noticed Neame's men moving forward, thought they were ignoring his previous instructions, and once again told him to keep out of the battle: 'Where the hell do you think you're going?', or similar phraseology. He did, however, then accept Neame's assurance that the move was necessary to get D Company under cover and that it was not going to get involved in his battle.

238

Neame's next suggestion, however, was turned down.

> It was at this stage that I first mentioned to 'H'
> that there could be scope for a right-flanking move
> along the shoreline. But 'H' had other things on his
> mind and said something like 'Stop clogging the net;
> I'm trying to conduct a battle.'[10]

Also coming up at the same time was C Company. It came down the axis track, to the left (east) of D Company, on to the slightly rising ground west of Coronation Point. Lieutenant Kennedy, the company second-in-comand, tells what happened at this juncture:

> A Company had been caught in the open in front of
> Darwin Hill as dawn broke and were now pinned at
> the base of the hill. C Company went to ground in
> extended line with all the company's LMGs [12] in
> a position to engage the enemy. The only problem
> at that range was identifying the correct target. I
> called A Company on the battalion net and asked
> them to identify their exact positions and the
> enemy's so we could assist with our guns. I was
> ordered to stay off the radio by 'H'; he said he was
> trying to fight a battle. So was I, and found it
> frustrating to be ignored when we could so obviously
> help.[11]

Colonel 'H' spent nearly an hour at the inlet before deciding his next move. His judgement appeared to be that it was too soon to commit either of his reserve companies, and Support Company had still not reached the battlefield. He was irked by the delay, by the inability of the guns and mortars to achieve anything, and so resolved to go forward personally — to join A Company. The wisdom of this decision has been the subject of much controversy, although it was absolutely in keeping with his character and style of command. Certainly he had been pushing A Company, certainly he wanted to assess the resistance it was facing first hand, and certainly he must have felt that his presence in the firing line might be sufficient to tip the balance and get A Company on to the spur.

Nevertheless, there is an argument that says he was already far enough forward, already under fire, and that by going so close to the enemy he unnecessarily put at risk the entire forward command element of the battalion. Similarly, how could he be expected to assess the situation, coordinate supporting fire, and the eventual use of his reserves, if he was himself lying in the dirt dodging shot and shell. Perhaps his impatient streak was coming through, perhaps he felt that he could galvanize A Company for just that extra effort. At the time who was to know for sure that he was not right? While the use of his reserves or Support Company had not necessarily been ruled out, Colonel 'H' inclined towards the third option — personal intervention and example.

Something of his commanding officer's mood is evident in Norman's description of his decision to go further forward:

> A Company's attack started floundering after they cleared up the Argentine first platoon position. The CO got on the radio and told them to get a grip, speed up and continue the movement, which they couldn't. So he said: 'I'm not having any of this', and decided to go up and join A Company. To say he got a little pear-shaped would be an understatement. When he made up his mind that a thing was going to be done then it was going to be done, and off he went all the way round the edge of the inlet.[12]

Colonel 'H' set a cracking pace which the battery commander's party found difficult to emulate. When they reached the southern edge of the inlet there was a gap of 200 metres to A Company's position in the gully.

Half-way across this exposed ground was a large patch of gorse. To get to it the commanding officer determined to throw a WP smoke grenade. Typically, he wanted to throw it himself so he turned to ask those with him if anybody had some. One was produced, but a soldier remonstrated - surely if they attempted to run through the burning phosphorus they would all be burnt. 'Bollocks', said the colonel. 'What do you prefer, no cover at all?'.[13] He duly threw the grenade and dashed across to the gorse. There was a large gaggle of assorted soldiers now heading for the gully, a mixture of Tac 1 and A Company's main headquarters, over 20 men, some of them cursing their heavy radios (usually carried in bergens) and spare batteries, as they crouched, crawled and ran along behing the inlet bank.

Major Rice preferred to wait for the smoke to clear before crossing the gap. Soon the entire group was wriggling and pushing their way through the gorse which gave good protection from view, but none from fire. When the gorse gave out another 100-metre stretch separated them from the comparative sanctuary of the gully proper. Sergeant-Major Price and Sergeant Norman threw more grenades, then Colonel 'H' led the final rush. It was around 8.30 a.m.

By the time Colonel 'H' flopped down beside Farrar-Hockley progress had been made in that the nearest seven or so trenches on the right side of the spur had been cleared. The problem was that the trenches further away along the ridge were still able to pour a devastating weight of fire across the top of the spur. All efforts to get up onto, behind, or around the spur had been thwarted. Sergeant Barrett's GPMGs were still in action but without heavy supporting fire from guns, or better still aircraft, there seemed no way to get out of the gully. Farrar-Hockley knew this, but his commanding officer had still to be convinced.

After talking to the company commander Colonel 'H' turned to 2nd Lieutenant Coe.

'Can you get up to the gorse line?' [at the top end of the gully].

'Well yes, but its pretty hairy,' he replied.

'Can you get into a position where you can get mortar fire down on the trenches?'

'Yes, but that would be fucking hairy.'

'Well, will you take Mal [the mortar officer] up there?'

As the two officers started off, Farrar-Hockley took issue with his commanding officer, convinced that both officers would be killed. At first Colonel 'H' was reluctant to accept this advice asking, 'Are they really taking their lives in their hands if they go any further?' The answer was emphatically affirmative. Colonel 'H' called them back.[14]

A new tack was attempted. Farrar-Hockley told Coe to attempt to go round to the right along the side of the spur, since all efforts to move on the left were doomed to fail. Coe's men started to leave the gully but the volume of fire was too severe. They too were pulled back.

The stalemate continued. Individuals fired or rested, Barrett's guns were fed with more ammunition. Even the battery commander sat for a while making up linked belts of bullets, while enemy mortar and artillery rounds landed incessantly in the open ground in front of the gorse, which was now burning well to add to the confusion. Wounded were carried down to near the entrance to the gully for treatment.

It was during this phase of the battle, with Colonel 'H' now in the gully, that both D and Support Companies suggested ways of assisting.

D Company had moved closer to the west coast of the isthmus and halted between two hills only 300 metres from the shore. Neame still considered the beach offered a possible route for outflanking the whole Argentine line. Although he could not know it at the time, he had discovered the soft spot in their defences. He radioed his commanding officer:

242

With both A and B Companies obviously not getting anywhere quickly I was getting more and more convinced that the right flank beach approach was worth a try, or at least my going to have a look. It could offer the possibility of turning the whole enemy position on the ridge. I reported to 'H' on the radio, told him my location and again suggested my idea. He was still not very receptive as he was clearly having a difficult time in the gorse gully. In fact 'H' gave me pretty short shrift and was in no mood to commit his reserve yet.[15]

Colonel H's words were: 'Don't tell me how to run my battle!'

Shortly after 9.00 am Support Company's Milans and machine guns had arrived at the same low rise that D Company had occupied at dawn, some 1,200 metres from Darwin ridge. They were told to wait there. Captain Ketley, who was now back with his Milans, was able to see movement along Darwin ridge and wanted to come forward better to identify targets and then bring his missiles into action. Major Hugh Jenner made the suggestion to Colonel 'H' but received the response: 'No, I don't want anyone to come forward until we sort this thing out. We have enough trouble up here ... its a difficult situation'.[16]

He seemed determined that A Company would win, would roll up the enemy line along the central portion of the ridge. One officer who was with him later said he thought the commanding officer was 'mesmerized' by the need to get A Company forward. The company was slowly making progress, but Colonel 'H' had the time factor very much on his mind. His original schedule was now in shreds. 2 Para had been halted for some two and a half hours so far, and if a counter-attack was to be launched the battalion was at its most vulnerable. Had A Company been attacked from Darwin Hill, or even come under heavy fire from its summit, there was little anybody could do to save it. The Argentine failure to occupy this hill was a fatal flaw in their defences, but at the time there was no way Colonel 'H' could know an attack was not imminent.

His forthright dismissal of Neame's outflanking suggestion was almost certainly made for two reasons. Firstly, the time factor; he wanted to break the deadlock quickly, and D Company might take a long time moving round. Secondly, and probably more importantly, Colonel 'H' was then right in the firing line himself, he was physically committed to A Company. He was in no position to check out whether Neame's idea was sound or not. To allow the flanking move would be risky, it would mean trusting his subordinate's judgement at a crucial moment in the battle. This would have been uncharacteristic, given the situation at the time. As there was no way he could go and see personally he opted for another try himself.

2 Para's commanding officer understood, indeed was a fervent exponent of the belief, that combat is a battle of wills, that you have to be stronger-willed to win. He turned to Farrar-Hockley and said, 'Dair, you've got to take that ledge [top of the spur]'. The company commander cobbled together a force of about fifteen men to assault the summit, although the reality was far from a coordinated advance or charge, rather a disjointed scramble up the slope with individuals crouching, crawling and squirming forward.

Worsley-Tonks had arranged for the mortars to fire smoke, which they did, but the baseplate position had only started with 40 per cent WP bombs so stock was now very low. Also the wind whipped the screen away quickly, so it was not effective for long. At about 9.00 am the mortars stopped firing – temporarily out of ammunition. Among the group attacking were Captain Dent still carrying the radio, Lance-Corporal Gilbert in Corporal Hardman's section, and the adjutant, Captain Wood, who was determined not to be left out and followed up behind. Gilbert recalls the attempted attack:

I can't remember anybody organizing anything; we

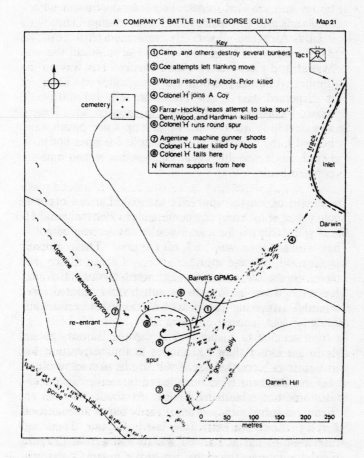

Key

①Camp and others destroy several bunkers
②Coe attempts left flanking move
③Worrall rescued by Abols. Prior killed
④Colonel 'H' joins A Coy
⑤Farrar-Hockley leads attempt to take spur.
   Dent, Wood, and Hardman killed
⑥Colonel 'H' runs round spur
⑦Argentine machine gunner shoots
   Colonel 'H'. Later killed by Abols
⑧Colonel 'H' falls here
N Norman supports from here

Tac 1

cemetery

Track

Inlet

Darwin

Argentine trenches (approx)

Barrett's GPMGs

re-entrant

spur

gorse gully

gorse line

Darwin Hill

0   50   100   150   200   250
        metres

245

just went. We were walking initially, then crawling at the top. As we went forward round the slope I was in time to see Captain Dent killed. He was hit in the chest, fell back on to his radio, and was then hit again. I crawled passed the adjutant who was on his hands and knees encouraging us saying: 'That's it lads, Airborne all the way; remember Arnhem!' After ten metres I looked back and he was dead too. Myself and Corporal Hardman worked our way to the left while the position was being smoked. Then it dispersed and I saw Hardman fall. He didn't move. I crawled over to him and checked him. He was obviously dead. I had to take up a fire position behind him, using his body as a rest. I felt his body twitch as it was hit again. I took his ammo and crawled back.[17]

To remain up on the spur was suicidal. Lance-Corporal Toole yelled at his company commander, 'For fuck's sake, sir, if you don't get back now you're not coming back.'[18] They winkled their way back off the crest. There was no way forward over the spur.

It is impossible to know what went through Colonel 'H''s mind when he saw the assault he had ordered fail. Certainly witnessing the deaths of three soldiers in an assault he had insisted on must have hit hard. Nothing he tried seemed to succeed. A Company did not appear able to get closer than 100 metres to the nearest enemy still fighting. Nevertheless, outwardly he was as resolute as before. Sergeant Blackburn heard him say, 'We've got to do something about this.'[19] But what?

From his subsequent actions it seems likely that Colonel 'H' felt that one last effort, one last push, and the enemy would crumble. If he himself was to lead a quick assault round the spur to the right, up to the nearest trenches, that might be sufficient. Bearing in mind what he had witnessed, bearing in mind the time that had been lost and the possibility of an enemy counter-attack at any moment, and bearing in mind the courage and character of the man, it is not surprisingly that Colonel 'H' opted for setting a personal example at the very forefront of his battalion. He knew better than anybody how close 2 Para had come to stalling, perhaps to failing. It was his battalion, his plan, his battle, and now it was his decision.

At about this time both 2nd Lieutenant Coe and Corporal Abols heard him shout something that sounded like, 'Come on A Company, get your skirts off!' to the nearby elements of company headquarters. Shortly afterwards Colonel 'H' got to his feet and yelled 'Follow me', before setting off on his dash round the spur. What happened is recounted in the Prologue. Sergeant Blackburn's feelings on his boss's actions were summarized as: 'It was a death before dishonour effort; but it wouldn't have passed junior Brecon.'[20]

For 10-15 minutes after Colonel 'H' was hit Norman lay on the exposed slope of the spur for what was probably the longest quarter of an hour of his life. The battle for the ridge continued unabated, but gradually A Company were getting the upper hand. The great potential of the 66mm rocket as a bunker buster at close range was a lesson well learned in the gorse gully. Sergeant-Major Price fired one at the trenches on the west side of the re-entrant, but missed. Then Corporal Abols, who was lying with his section and several company headquarters personnel, had a go. It was his shot that avenged Colonel 'H's death and started the Argentine surrender on that part of the battlefield.

Sergeant Norman was the first to reach his commanding officer. He was barely conscious and obviously in deep shock. Norman turned him over, removed his webbing, found his wounds and applied field dressings. 'What struck me was that there was very little blood, so that meant a lot of internal injuries. He was slipping into shock and we carried a drip containing saline solution for that sort of thing. I administered the drip .... He took the whole litre of my drip and then I used his.'[21] Others gathered round to assist. They endeavoured to construct a makeshift stretcher from a piece of corrugated sheeting from the Argentine trench he had been attacking. The aim was to carry him up over the spur to a suitable helicopter landing site from which he would be evacuated. The first attempt to carry him failed when the 'stretcher' collapsed, causing Colonel 'H' to fall to the ground. It was another example of the problem of actually carrying wounded without the proper equipment. They tried again, this time successfully taking him to the proposed landing site. There, at about 10.00 am, Colonel 'H' died. There is no doubt among those who were present that, doctor or no doctor, helicopter or no helicopter, their commanding officer had but a short time to live from the moment he was shot.

Immediately it was known that Colonel 'H' had been hit, Farrar-Hockley, who had been asking for at least an hour on behalf of his other wounded, again radioed for a casualty evacuation helicopter to fly forward. This message was passed to brigade, but it was not for over another hour that the news was received that two Scouts were on their way to Camilla Creek House for briefing. They were both from 3 Commando Brigade Air Squadron, 'TWA', (Teeny Weeny Airways). By this time the commanding officer had been dead for at least half an hour. The signals officer, Captain Benest, personally briefed one of the pilots, Lieutenant Richard Nunn RM, on the whereabouts of Colonel 'H' and the other wounded. At 10.45 am he took off from Camilla Creek House, almost three quarters of an hour after the commanding officer had died. Benest was unaware that Colonel 'H' was dead when he assured Nunn that the battle at the gully had died down and it was all right to fly forward, although it would have made no difference to his briefing if he had.

There has been some uninformed speculation that it was only because the commanding officer had been hit that the Scouts were despatched, or that had it been known at Camilla Creek House that he was dead by the time they arrived they would not have gone forward. 2 Para had been clamouring for casevac helicopters from well before Colonel 'H' was wounded. They had not come because the

248

hazards of going up to the gully while the battle still raged on the ridge were unacceptable. It was nothing to do with air raid warnings as has been suggested in some accounts. As Sergeant Belcher RM, Lieutenant Nunn's crewman, later explained, 'If we had not flown every time there was an air raid warning red I doubt if we would ever have got airborne that morning. As it was, by the time we went forward to pick up Jones my log records we had already clocked 4½ hours flying.'[22] These flights had been back to Sussex Mountain for refuelling, and from Camilla Creek House forward to the RAP (which was at that stage still some 2,000 metres north of the gorse gully) with small arms and mortar ammunition, returning with some of the men wounded during the night advance.

Belcher's account puts the record straight:

> There were two Scouts and two Gazelles from 3CBAS under command of 2 Para, Captain Niblett was in command of the section of Scouts with Sergeant Glaze as his crewman, while I flew with Lieutenant Nunn. We were all tasked as airborne landrovers. Initially we had been armed with SS11 anti-tank missiles but had taken them out on the 26th to make room for stretchers. From shortly after first light we had been ferrying forward ammo and casualties back. Mortar bombs in particular were needed. I remember hearing the CO yelling over the net for more mortar ammo. Sometime a bit later I heard that he had been hit. This was while I was on the ground at Camilla Creek House waiting for Nunn to return from a refuelling trip. He had left me behind so that he could carry that much more fuel forward. It was all a question of taking on the maximum payload. At about 10.30 am both Niblett and Nunn landed back at Camilla Creek House, and we began to load up with small arms ammo for another trip to the RAP area. Then the decision was made by Niblett to take it all off again and go forward with empty aircraft for casevac. We briefed

249

ourselves, and it was agreed that initially we would only go as far as the RAP. Once there we could decide whether it was OK to get further forward. We had heard it said that the Goose Green airfield had been taken, but we didn't accept this. We took off around 10.45 with Niblett leading, following the track south, and our aircraft about 500 metres behind.[23]

Even if they had known that Colonel 'H' was dead, even if they had decided not to make this an entirely casevac trip, both Scouts would have been airborne at this time resupplying ammunition. Within minutes two Pucaras pounced on the Scouts. Despite frantic manoeuvring, Nunn's helicopter was blasted out of the sky. Nunn died instantly, but Sergeant Belcher survived appalling leg injuries that later necessitated the amputation of his right leg mid-thigh. He was fortunate that the impact of the crash threw him clear, so he was able, despite the shock and agony, to inject himself with painkiller. Belcher again:

The cloud base was very low, about 300 feet, while we were barely 20 feet above the ground. I was at the rear of the aircraft, not strapped in the front with Nunn, in order to accept stretchers. It also facilitated my seeing what was happening at the rear because that was a blind spot for the pilot. Suddenly two Pucaras appeared, approaching head on. They split up and so did we. Nunn turned about and we were hit by a burst of cannon fire from six o'clock [directly behind them]. I was hit in the right leg above the ankle which took me out. I lay across the back and started to pull out the aircraft's first aid kit to patch myself up, while at the same time trying to watch the Pucara and tell Nunn where it was, what it was doing, when it fired, talk him through the situation so he could take evasive action. It flew past our starboard side, turned on its left wing, and came at us head on firing its 7.62 machine-gun.

250

Nunn was struck in the face, dying instantly, and I was hit again, this time above my left ankle. We crashed, bounced, turned through 180 degrees, the doors burst open and I was flung clear. The Scout went up in flames and I lost consciousness for a few moments. The attack had lasted some 30 seconds.

I injected morphine into my left leg, then tried to apply a shell dressing from the medical kit that was still clutched to my chest. Then I saw a Gazelle approaching so I raised my arms to wave at it. This was not very sensible as for us it's the signal not to land as it's not safe. In my state I had forgotten this. The Gazelle flew away for a bit, but to my great relief not for long. It landed nearby and I was given more morphine while we awaited the arrival of Captain Niblett's Scout to take me out. They had to do this as the Gazelle didn't have a stretcher on board at that time. Even so I don't think I was on the ground for more than ten minutes.[24]

Niblett had had a narrow escape after a hair-raising flight weaving and ducking as a Pucara persued him, firing every weapon it had. With a display of superb flying, and not a little luck, he dodged his attacker and landed back at Camilla Creek House.[25] A Gazelle, piloted by Captain Pounds, was sent forward to locate the crashed Scout. Niblett then flew to the site, some 1,500 metres SE of the house, and evacuated Belcher to the Field Hospital at Ajax Bay.

Back at the gully it was discovered that ninety-two Argentines had been defending the centre portion of the ridge and the spur from some twenty-three trenches. Of these eighteen enemy soldiers had died and thirty-nine been wounded. One of these had been lying injured at the bottom of the first trench attacked by Corporal Camp at the outset of the action. For the entire battle he had been within A Company's area. 2 Para had suffered severely as well. Three officers and three soldiers had died in the struggle for the gorse gully and the spur; another eleven were wounded - 20 per cent of those involved in this fighting became casualties.[26] As the company reorganized and dug in the process of casualty treatment and evacuation took priority with helicopters now coming up to join the the medical officer, Captain Hughes, who had walked forward. At long last Tuffen was able to be retrieved and treated after lying near the entrance to the re-entrant for at least four hours. Private Styles reached him, dressed his wound, and then remained with him for hours afterwards, constantly talking to him to keep him from falling into a coma.

During this reorganization period Argentine artillery shells and mortar bombs continued to fall. One mortar splinter hit Lance-Corporal Gilbert, whose story of the incident illustrates how even wounds could not destroy the Toms' sense of humour:

> The battle was over and we were dished out with more ammunition. I was digging in with Lance-Corporal Spencer, but we didn't have enough digging tools so I went over to an Argy trench for some kit when a mortar round landed about 40 metres away. I felt something like a sharp kick in the right side, but which was otherwise not particularly painful. I was really pissed off after getting through the whole battle unscathed. I turned to Spencer to tell him I had been hit, to which he replied, 'Don't be bloody stupid'. He did, however, pull up my clothing and thermal vest to take a look. 'Fucking hell, Jerry, you're pissing with blood.' To which I said something like, 'Where is all the calm, rest, and reassurance?' Spencer made some comment about it being all right as it was only a small hole, and he could see it moving. We then had an argument as to whose field dressing to use. In the end he used his.[27]

Gilbert went back to start digging, but after a couple of shovels his wound began to hurt and he sat down to brew tea. This supposed idleness drew the attention of the sergeant-major who had him moved into the gully to await a lift out.

The question of whether the commanding officer's gallantry tipped the balance and brought about A Company's final success and the Argentine surrender on the ridge is one of the disputed issues of Goose Green. It was some 15 minutes after he was shot that the Argentines started to come out of their trenches waving white cloths, immediately following Corporal Abols' destruction of the trench from which his commanding officer had been killed. Did Colonel 'H' intend to lead A Company in a last attempt to break what he percieved as a deadlock? It is possible he did, in view of his shout to the company heaquarters just before he dashed off. We will never know for sure. More probably his intention was to use his tactical headquarters in a flanking attack — but that was not what happened. He made a solo charge, with only one man close enough to be able to give him support — Sergeant Norman. He had rushed off without gathering together any men, without informing the company commander, and without checking to see if anybody was following. Some were, but they were few and far behind. Significantly, not a single A Company soldier followed, and only two or three from Tac 1, for the simple reason that they did not know he had gone. Farrar-Hockley has described Colonel 'H's contribution thus:

It cannot be said that 'H''s courageous sortie — or whatever he had in mind — inspired the soldiers at that moment, because few, if any, were aware of what he was doing. But his enterprise on our right did distract the enemy there to one degree or another. I do not agree that a particular piece of ground was taken on this account. Most important was 'H''s standing and drive in the Battalion. He put us to a difficult task; he inspired us in the undertaking; he was up front from the beginning and hence provided the dynamic needed for the impetus of attacking and continuing to attack until

253

we had succeeded. His inspiration and example were to remain with us for the rest of the campaign.[28]

The view of the soldier who strove so bravely to support him in his last moments, who stayed the closest to him, Sergeant Norman was: 'My own opinion was that he shouldn't have been there, but being 'H' Jones he was always going to be there because he was that type of CO'.[29]

X

BOCA HOUSE

'At daybreak the enemy could sit back in bunkers
and engage us at a range of 900-1400 metres with
guns, mortars, heavy machine guns and snipers.
The ground was very similar to Salisbury Plain
and we found ourselves grovelling at the base of a
hill not dissimilar to Bowls Barrow. Here we
fought and grovelled for nearly seven hours.'

Major John Crosland MC, Officer Commanding
B Company, summarizing the battle for Boca
House.

The weather that halted Harrier sorties hindered, but
did not prevent, Pucara operations that morning.
Despite the low cloud and high winds a handful of
aircraft took off from Stanley for the Goose Green
isthmus to assist Piaggi. Contrary to some British
accounts after the war, there were no Pucaras based at
Goose Green on 28 May. All had been withdrawn to
Stanley.

Just before 8.00 am Captain Roberto Villa was
approaching Camilla Creek House with two
accompanying Pucaras flown by Lieutenants Cimbara
and Arganaraz. They had been badly buffeted by the
wind en route and were now flying extremely low, well
under the 300-foot cloud base. This made them
vulnerable to ground fire, even from small arms, and in
danger of crashing into a hillside. Nightmare flying.
Villa and Arganaraz swooped down on the British at
Camilla Creek House spraying the area with 2.75-inch

rockets. On the ground A Echelon and headquarters personnel scrambled for cover but no real harm was done. It persuaded the signals officer to do some more serious digging:

> Rather stupidly I had set up a relay post in a shed when the attack occurred. It galvanized us into digging in properly beside a nearby hedge! We used empty ammo tins to build up a wall and dig down.[1]

A few moments later Cimbara, followed by Arganaraz, flew low and fast straight up the valley towards the British artillery gun position. When Cimbara was only 200 metres from the forward gun, about to fire his rockets, a Blowpipe detachment from 32 Guided Weapons Regiment engaged. Cimbara narrowly evaded the missile but his rockets went wide of their target. Almost simultaneously another Blowpipe was launched at Arganaraz. This one misfired into the ground, although Arganaraz was so low that the explosion flung his aircraft upwards, turning it upside-down as it rose. Its pilot did not panic, the knowledge that a downward ejection would be fatal keeping him in his seat. To his astonishment the Pucara righted itself and was still flyable. The British gunners jubilantly claimed a kill and both his companions initially thought Arganaraz was lost. This was not the case; he was able to limp slowly back to Stanley. He had been extremely lucky, and his luck was to hold when he made his second appearance over the Goose Green battlefield later that afternoon. Although Blowpipes did not come up to expectations in the campaign Argentine Pucara pilots had a healthy respect for their killing power if they hit home. Lieutenant Micheloud later commented:

> With the gunfire our planes would return to base with holes, but the Pucara proved able to take quite heavy battle damage. We had two engines so we could return with one shot out. But a hit from a Blowpipe was another matter; it would always

destroy sufficient of the aircraft to make it unable to continue flying.[2]

Not until nearly three hours later were the Pucaras able to return. This time a section of two aircraft, led by Lieutenant Gimenez, with Cimbara back on his second mission as wingman, was tasked with attacking any targets of opportunity on the battlefield. The pair had reached the Camilla Creek House area when first one, then another, British Scout helicopter were seen. Although the Argentine pilots probably did not know it, neither of these Scouts had been fitted with any means of defending themselves. They were the ones piloted by Niblett and Nunn on their way to pick up Colonel 'H'. As Nunn took violent evasive action Gimenez caught him with a burst of cannon, then machine-gun fire. The latter killed the pilot causing the helicopter to plummet into the ground. The second Scout escaped.

Both Pucaras turned for Stanley, Cimbara flying so low that the front of his cockpit canopy was splattered with stones and mud from the compression wave of his aircraft. Within minutes both became separated in the low cloud and Cimbara and Stanley lost radio contact with Gimenez. He was never seen again, nor was any trace of his aircraft found until 1986. That year the wreckage was discovered on Blue Mountain. Gimenez had flown straight into the mountainside in the poor visibility. He was still strapped to his seat, with his pistol on his belt twisted out of shape by the force of the impact. He was subsequently buried at Goose Green. His family were the first group of Argentine relatives to visit the settlement after the war. Despite their dangerous reputation, the shooting down of Nunn's Scout was to be the only confirmed success of the Pucaras during the conflict.[3]

The 200-plus Argentine infantry opposing A Company in the gorse gully and B Company opposite Boca House fought surprisingly long and hard for ill-trained conscripts. They had some advantages in weaponry. Their rifles were automatic, they had a number of powerful .50

calibre heavy machine guns, plus excellent optical equipment. If the British could be kept at arm's length these weapons were superior to their enemy's SLRs and GPMGs. They had also had weeks to prepare. 2 Para were later amazed to see how much ammunition and food was stocked in the forward trenches. Their clothing was adequate while their boots, which did not let in water, were the envy of the British, some of whom 'won' pairs from prisoners or casualties as the war progressed.

Come the daylight the tactical balance of the situation swung from the attackers to the defenders. It is not too difficult to sit in a bunker and shoot at an enemy you can clearly see several hundred metres away across open ground. It does not demand great nerve, or a high standard of training. The attacker's usual answer to this problem is to pound the enemy with guns and aircraft, to soften him up, before and during their advance. The fact that the Argentines were able to stand up in their trenches to fire their weapons for over six hours is indisputable evidence that the British artillery and mortar fire was woefully inadequate for the situation facing 2 Para that morning. Shortage of ammunition and the wind combined to render serious attempts by the Paras' mortars to put down effective smokescreens impossible, while the spongy ground meant that a trench needed a direct hit to put it out of action. Any British shells that did this were the result of a fluke, not accurate shooting.

As has been seen, with A Company's own short-range weapons, and will be seen again with B Company, it was the direct-fire weapons that eventually tipped the scales against the Argentines. Not until the British brought up their Milans in a direct-fire, bunker-busting role, did the defences in the Boca House area collapse. Hence the significance of the quote at the start of this chapter by the Para officer most involved in this part of the battle.

Another factor favouring the defenders was the inability of the British to locate and destroy the Argentine artillery or mortars. Of the four 105 pack howitzers from A Battery 4th Air Mobile Artillery Regiment only three could be used, but they were handled with skill. Earlier in the action, as 2 Para advanced from Sussex Mountain, these guns had been deployed well forward at the north end of the isthmus in order to get within range of the British. They were pulled back before the start of the battle to a position on the northern edge of Goose Green. Their gun line was in a shallow hollow, sufficiently deep to conceal them from ground observation unless the observer was within 100 metres. From the air it would have been a different matter but no British aircraft overflew the battlefield until long after Darwin ridge had fallen.

There were periods when the Argentine gunners ran short of shells, but there were reserve stocks nearby at the settlement. Throughout the fighting A Battery's three guns, like the British three, kept firing. Like the British they were not particularly effective in producing heavy casualties, but their target was troops exposed in the open so their shelling was a considerable deterrent to movement across the ground in front of the Darwin ridge. Their activities were enhanced by an OP on the high ground well to the east of the isthmus.

Piaggi had placed mortars in the outskirts of Goose Green, on the tiny peninsula east of the settlement, in Darwin, and elsewhere in the front line. Like the artillery they were continually in action; like the artillery they were never located or neutralized. It was with the guns and mortars that the Argentines' equipment was inferior to the British. Their pack-howitzers had a shorter range than the 105 Light Gun, while their mortars were obsolescent American models. Sergeant Hall, a section commander in 2 Para's Mortar Platoon, later examined the captured mortars with professional interest. He described the 81mm bombs 'as the old bulbous type, lots of blast which knocked you over, but not nearly as effective as ours in terms of causing casualties. Their 120mm mortar was pretty ancient, using the old type of brass sights.'[4]

During the period from around 7.30 am to 10.00 am 2 Para was acutely vulnerable to a counter-attack, particularly in the area of the gorse gully. This exposure had worried Colonel 'H', but Piaggi was never able to exploit the opportunity. Perhaps he never saw it, but more likely he saw it and was unwilling or unable to grasp it. To do something, he needed fresh troops. They could either come from those already on the isthmus or from reinforcements flown from Stanley. He had pestered Parada for help since early that morning, but apart from the Pucaras nothing was forthcoming until about noon, by which time his main line had fallen and 2 Para was on the move again. The struggle for the gorse gully and Boca House would be decided by the troops already deployed.

Piaggi could, in theory, have used his C Company sitting south of Goose Green awaiting an attack that would never materialise, or his reserve platoon of C Company 25th Regiment, still near the settlement. In the event both these sub-units were used, but their efforts had no bearing on the battle for Darwin ridge. Probably the real reason there was no counter-attack was that Piaggi knew his men could not undertake one. As conscripts their training, morale and leadership were not up to it. Realizing this, their commander resolved to conserve his reserves, await reinforcements and hang on.

Boca House was something of a misnomer. There was no house. All that remained of the building were the foundations and a few stones. It featured in the British battle plans as a useful reference point, an objective even, but there was nothing there to capture, or to defend. The Argentine defence of the western half of the Darwin ridge and the Boca House area was entrusted, in the main, to 2nd Lieutenants Pelufo and Aliaga. The former was on the ridge, while the latter defended the high ground SE and south of the Boca House ruins. They both came under the command of Manresa and were assisted by some of his officers and men from A Company.

Pelufo, on the ridge, had a good view of the battle as it developed and was involved, first, in fighting A Company, then B Company as it came over the high ground 500 metres to his front. He has confirmed the misunderstanding on both sides as A Company of 2 Para approached the Darwin ridge:

> It was a very confusing situation when we saw troops approaching. At first we were not sure whether it was the enemy or part of our 12th Regiment that was withdrawing towards our line. We thought they could be our troops. They knew what route to take through the minefields. In fact, they were British troops.[5]

The Argentines opened up all along their line. Pelufo comments on the rain of mortar bombs that soon fell all around, but not of artillery fire. 'There was shooting all over the place, intense fire raining on both sides. ... We carried on like this for about three hours [it was longer].'[6]

At the height of the battle Lt Estevez died, the only Argentine Army officer to be killed at Goose Green. He was hit in the leg, arm and left eye while crouched with his radio operator, Private Carrascul, trying to adjust supporting artillery fire. Carrascul continued to fight the battle over the radio himself until he too was killed. Both were posthumously decorated. It is an interesting example of the closeness that often develops, despite the differences in rank, between an officer and his operator. The officer relies heavily on the competence of his radio operator. He must listen on the set, have a grasp of tactics, understand what is happening, remember messages accurately, act as a relay station for the transmitting of critical information, and at times answer for his officer to senior commanders. At all levels from the platoon upwards the commander depends on his signaller for his ability to communicate to command. Little wonder that a bond develops between the two in training or on operations when they work as an inseparable pair – wherever the officer goes his operator is usually only five paces behind. Examples in 2 Para during this battle are numerous. Sergeant Blackburn tried to follow Colonel 'H' in his dash round the spur; Captain Watson's signaller was most upset when his officer left him to go grenading trenches; and we have the yet to be related activities of Lieutenant Chapman and Private Kirkwood.

Not until just before midday did the defenders' morale begin to collapse on the west of the line. Pelufo again:

> The Paras got closer and closer. They were trying to outflank us [along the beach]. They avoided a frontal assault .... However, their fire was very precise. I remember seeing a corporal receive a direct hit from a wire-guided missile [the Paras Milans were in action by then].[7]

The end for Pelufo was then not far off. He later related how he heard the Paras yelling at them in Spanish and English to surrender and then he fell to the bottom of his trench, hit in the head by a bullet:

> At first I thought I'm dying, but when I fell to the bottom of the trench I realized I was still alive ... the soldier treated me and when he saw the wound he said, 'Don't worry sir, its only a flesh wound'. I tried to stand up and pick up a rifle but I couldn't. I felt very dizzy .... I finally understood that it was useless to continue sacrificing lives .... I told a soldier to tie a napkin to his rifle and wave it. He was shot at and they hit the rifle. He got back into the trench very frightened. I told him to go up and wave it again, so he came out of the position and then we saw the British coming out into the open.[8]

2 Para had finally, some two hours after Colonel 'H' had died, taken the entire Darwin ridge and the Boca House area. The battalion was on the move again, the real crisis had passed.

First B Company, then D Company, then Support Company were eventually involved in the battle for Boca House. It was a complicated engagement, the great bulk

262

of it conducted at long range. It started at the same time as A Company made its rush for the gorse gully, just as it got light, and finished with the surrender of the Argentines south of Boca House some six hours later. To understand the problems facing the commanders on both sides it is necessary to know something of the ground over which the action was fought. Map 22 shows the main features. Because it played a key role, and because it has no real name, the 100 foot high hill 600 metres NE of Boca House is referred to as Hill B on the map and in the text. It was the hill occupied by B Company for much of the time. Other features that influenced the tactics included the thick gorse line that bisected the battlefield from NW-SE, the series of tiny valleys or re-entrants due south of Hill B, the 50 foot hill 500 metres SW of the Boca House ruins and the rocky beach that formed the western boundary. The entire area was a rectangle with the longer sides measuring 1,200 metres and the shorter ones 700. At the northern end was Hill B, to the south the 50 foot hill. To the west was the sea, and in the east the Darwin ridge feature with the main Argentine positions. In the centre was the open, shallow Boca House valley completely devoid of cover except for small folds in the ground, slight undulations. Plate 16, taken from the Argentine position on the 50-foot hill looking north to Hill B over the gorse line, demonstrates why Major Crosland was reminded of Salisbury Plain.

As it got light B Company was starting its advance over the crest of Hill B, down its southern (forward) slope heading for Boca House.[9] Two platoons were forward, 4 Platoon under Lieutenant Ernie Hocking on the right, Lieutenant Clive Chapman with 6 Platoon on the left, Major Crosland, conspicuous in his black hat, well forward with his command group in the centre, and Lieutenant Geoffrey Weighell's 5 Platoon in reserve. When the Argentine line opened fire B Company were caught in the open on the forward slope of Hill B. The entire company dashed for the nearest cover. There was precious little. A few folds in the ground or grassy hummocks were all that were availabe. In 4 Platoon a machine gun firing from the left was spotted, and as visibility improved Corporal Kenyon picked out bunkers and another machine gun 800 metres away on the 50-foot hill. Hocking's men returned fire, but as the enemy shooting became more accurate they could not continue the advance. It was difficult to see targets at the long range and Hocking had quickly to restrain his men from wasting ammunition.

Meanwhile Crosland had made a quick decision on what to do. Both the leading platoons were to work their way down the slope to the gorse line, while 5 Platoon was told to pull back on to the crest of Hill B as soon as the rest of the company had reached the gorse.

For Clive Chapman the next few minutes were the only occasion he felt really frightened during the battle:

> The only time when I was frightened was when we were skirmishing up to the gorse line. As I took cover on a bound there were a number of splashes in a puddle to the left of my head. They were splashes from bullets and it was the first time I had considered my own mortality.[10]

6 Platoon worked its way in bounds towards the gorse line which was situated on top of a slight rise. The first problem was a bunker just north of the gorse. Lance-Corporal Dunbar in 4 Platoon had spotted it. He proceeded to destroy it with a 66mm rocket, despite Chapman's yells at him not to fire, as he feared for A Company over to the left. Chapman has described what happened:

> We were not under heavy enemy fire from Boca House [the 50-foot hill south of it] until we were fairly close to the gorse line, maybe 40-60 metres. The bunker that Dunbar had fired at was cleared and we reached the gorse line intact .... We then proceeded to try to neutralize the Boca House

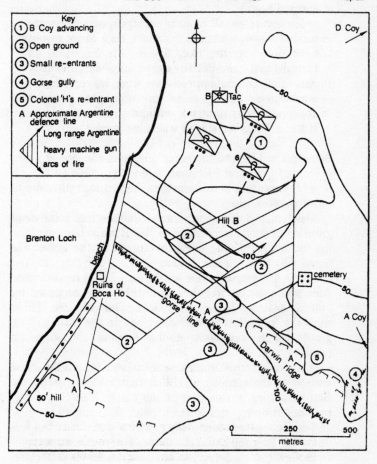

Key

1. B Coy advancing
2. Open ground
3. Small re-entrants
4. Gorse gully
5. Colonel 'H's re-entrant

A Approximate Argentine defence line

Long range Argentine heavy machine gun arcs of fire

D Coy

B Tac

Brenton Loch

beach

Hill B

Ruins of Boca Ho

gorse line

cemetery

A Coy

Darwin ridge

50' hill

50

100

100

50

50

0   250   500
                metres

position with well controlled fire control orders. Privates Lewis and Connor reckon they managed to hit an Argentinian who got out of a bunker .... The gorse line certainly provided us with some good protection as the sections we were behind had earthen banks.

However, to all intents and purposes we were pinned down; we could not move back as we would be exposed to the Boca House fire again; to go forward to try and destroy the position was obviously part of my combat appreciation when we reached the gorse line, but I came up with the negative conclusion that to attack without support would be suicide. Thus we stayed where we were.[11]

Being pinned behind the gorse unable to advance or retire prompted Corporal Eiserman to enquire, 'What the fuck is the DS solution to this one then?' For some time nobody could think of one.

Weighell had managed to get 5 Platoon into some dead ground on the forward slope of Hill B while he waited for the remainder of the company to get to the gorse. He noted that much of the Argentine fire was being directed towards A Company. He could also see three machine guns and thirteen trenches (probably those occupied by Pelufo's platoon) in the centre of the Darwin ridge. These were the 'sixteen trenches' described in the battalion 'O' group which were now giving A Company so much trouble.

It was when the time came to move back up the slope and on to the summit of Hill B that 5 Platoon took the first casualties of this part of the battle. The choice was between running, quicker, but with the runners exposed and easily spotted, or crawling, which was slower but less obvious. Weighell chose the latter. To provide some cover from view Private Street, an old sweat nicknamed 'Strasse' who was the 2-inch mortarman, fired several smoke bombs but was hit twice in the left leg. Corporal Standish and Private Brook came up under fire to assist. They took

Map 23

B COMPANY'S BOCA HOUSE BATTLE, 6:30 A.M. – 9:30 A.M.

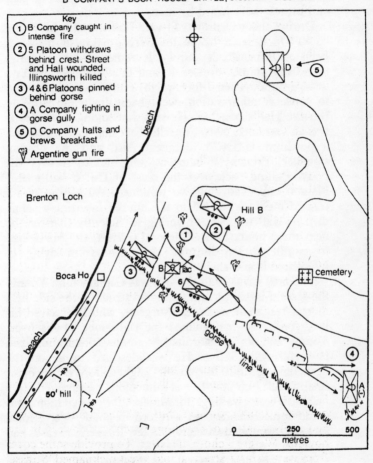

Key
1. B Company caught in intense fire
2. 5 Platoon withdraws behind crest. Street and Hall wounded. Illingsworth killed
3. 4 & 6 Platoons pinned behind gorse
4. A Company fighting in gorse gully
5. D Company halts and brews breakfast

⚐ Argentine gun fire

Brenton Loch

Boca Ho

beach

beach

50' hill

Hill B

cemetery

gorse line

0   250   500
metres

a chance, grabbed Street and began staggering up the 70-metre slope towards the crest and safety. They could only go five or six metres before having to fling themselves down to avoid the bullets that their efforts attracted. Street came in for some very rough handling. His yells of pain and protest were heard by many.

During this withdrawal Private Hall was also hit in the back. Once again his mates were quickly at his side. Privates Illingsworth and Poole removed his webbing, found his wound, dressed it, and then dragged him into dead ground. Then Illingsworth, remembering the need to conserve ammunition, went back down the slope to retrieve Hall's pouches. He was shot, dying instantly. It was an extremely brave, unselfish act that was to win him a posthumous DCM. Sergeant Aird and the platoon signaller, Private Williamson, went out to recover the body. Pulling back over the crest of Hill B had cost 5 Platoon one dead and two wounded. Aird, who was a trained medic, attended to the injured inserting a saline drip in Hall who was shivering so violently that for the next three hours Lance-Corporal Garrett, the MFC, had to cuddle up to him to keep him from dying of hypothermia and shock.

The next casualty in the area was Captain John Young, the second-in- command, who was struck in the side by a mortar fragment which the surgeon, who later saved his life, confirmed had gouged the right lobe of his liver. Young had an extraordinarily tough constitution and powerful will to live. He was destined to lie on the battlefield until 10.00 pm that night before a helicopter finally took him out. It was miraculous he survived. In a battle where waiting for hours for evacuation was commonplace Young set a record of about twelve for a seriously wounded casualty — a few less serious cases had to wait twenty.

There was now a long lull in the battle on the western side of the isthmus which lasted until Colonel 'H' was killed and A Company secured their part of the Darwin ridge. Aliaga's men on the 50-foot hill and Pelufo's on the ridge were able to keep B Company at a distance. The commanding officer did not want to commit his reserve companies, expressly forbidding them to move closer. In the gorse line soldiers rested, had a quick smoke, fired when they saw worthwhile targets, but otherwise conserved ammunition. Hill B was under continued enemy mortar and artillery fire, both on its summit and forward slope. The frustration of being unable to influence events was humorously expressed by Chapman's radio operator, Private Kirkwood, who was lying in a patch of gorse that had caught fire. He suddenly came up on his set:

'Hello two [company headquarters] this is two three [6 Platoon], over.'
'Two, send over.'
'Two three, for fuck's sake beam me up, out!.'[12]

He was obviously a Star Trek fan and felt it would be nice if, like Captain Kirk, he could be instantly transported from his present position to one of safety.

If an infantry unit cannot go forward the answer is often artillery. At Boca House the protagonists were separated by long distances so there was little danger of 'friendly fire' casualties, unlike the situation in the gorse gully. The guns at Camilla Creek House had plenty of missions, hundreds of shells were fired, but their effect was disappointing.

The FOO with B Company, Captain Bob Ash, did his best. He successfully brought down sixty rounds onto the hill south of Boca House for example, but getting effective fire missions was a frustrating business. At the start Ash took cover on the crest of Hill B. Within a few minutes his signaller, Gunner Comley, yelled for a medic when a machine-gun bullet struck his leg. His trousers were cut away but there was no wound, the round having gone through his pocket and hat without touching him.

Ash found that spotting the enemy trenches in daylight was easy, hitting them was not. Observation was tricky.

Having asked for a fire mission the FOO hears the word 'shot' from the gun position on the radio. This indicates that a shell is on its way. The observer has then to stick his head up to watch it arriving, as he needs to check the accuracy to adjust the fire if it is off target. Normally, with a direct radio link to the guns, the observer would be able to wait under cover for about ten seconds after hearing 'shot' before he needed to raise his head. At Goose Green, with the messages being repeated through a relay station, there was no way of accurately assessing the time of flight of the shell. So 'a lot of time was spent with one's head up or scurrying about as one couldn't stay long in the same position'.[13]

Even more exasperating was the problem of identifying the 'friendly' shell landing. It was vital to see the strike. As Ash has explained:

> At Boca House the guns were firing up to 800 metres out of line, left or right. It was almost impossible therefore to distinguish between theirs and ours. Enemy shells were landing all over the place. We had no meteorological data to feed into the guns to compensate for the strong wind, and it's possible that the gun position at Camilla Creek House was not plotted with absolute accuracy. For some of the time at least one gun was firing short due to a loose sight bracket. I had to try deliberately firing adjusting rounds into the sea to be sure of identifying them. At one stage, when A Company had control of the guns, some shells were landing in B Company area as the enemy positions they were engaging were as close to us as they were to them. I had a bit of an argument over the radio as I ordered the guns to check [stop] firing.[14]

If things were difficult up front, the gun position was not without its problems either. Like the infantry the gunners had started the battle not having slept for 36 hours and, as 2 Para's night advance developed into an unexpectedly long all-day struggle, so the demand for sustained fire from the guns led to severe crew fatigue. Under the camouflage nets space to work became cramped as piles of loose containers and cartridge cases built up around the guns. Waring could hear the firing, the explosions, the yelling and screaming over the radio. The drama of what was happening 12 kilometres away was absolutely clear. As the requests for fire missions built up after dawn so the inadequacy of three guns became progressively more apparent. Waring found it increasingly difficult, sometimes impossible, to keep them all in action. On occasion only one gun was able to respond to a fire mission. In the soft peat the guns tended to jump sideways after firing, so throughout the action crews had to carry out check-bearing drills. This necessitated the gun being taken out of action for about 15 minutes. It was common to find the gun 20 mils off the correct bearing. One gun developed an oil leak in a buffer but there was only one spare can at the position. Waring had to resort to collecting rifle cleaning oil in a mess tin from all the crews; it was not the right type but better than nothing.

Even had all three guns always been available, even if meteorological data had been included in the calculations, the artillery found themselves being asked to do the impossible once HMS *Arrow* had gone. Throughout the action they fired about 900 shells. For the 14-hour battle this gives a rate of slightly over one shell per minute, falling into an area of 12 square kilometres. Naturally these 900 rounds were concentrated, both in time and space, but long periods without support and vast areas of ground that never saw a shell were inevitable.

As the morning wore on Crosland sent Corporal Robinson, from 6 Platoon, forward to take out a bunker that was giving trouble not far from the gorse line. Crosland was later to describe how this little skirmish had an amusing ending:

Corporal Robinson and his section moved in and he himself fired a 66mm LAW and scored a direct hit on this bunker. Much excitement and they pressed home the attack, only to discover a further position in depth giving mutual support. As they crested the initial position they were caught in covering fire and Corporal Robinson came running back holding his balls. All I could get out of him was that his wife "would kill him if he had lost his nuts". Fortunately he had only received a ricochet in the balls resulting in severe bruising, and much laughter from the rest of us.[15]

Shortly after this Crosland determined to pull back 6 Platoon from the gorse line to a shallow re-entrant. Some mortar smoke was provided as a screen, although the platoon commander was uncertain where it came from:

> With our hearts in our mouths we took a couple of suicidal bounds back into the re-entrant. The enemy fire was pretty heavy at the time. ...[Corporal] Margerison was the only one wounded in my platoon .... It occurred during the withdrawal from the gorse line and he was either hit by two bullets or a single bullet that entered his shoulder and then hit him in the face, smashing out a number of teeth before exiting from his mouth.[16]

Margerison had fallen on the exposed slope while his section had continued into the dead ground. Someone then shouted that Margerison was hit. His second-in-command, Lance-Corporal Bardsley, dashing back under heavy fire, dragged Margerison under cover. For this gallantry he was to receive the Military Medal.[17] His company commander detailed the medic, Private Smith, 'to get a drip in him and send him out'. Smith was able to keep Margerison alive despite a suspected punctured lung and deep shock. With his company now regrouped, Crosland took control of trying to get the artillery and mortars on to the enemy positions giving the most trouble. It was during this period, at about 10.00 am that he heard that Colonel 'H' had been hit.

The brief but emotional message 'Sunray is down' from Sergeant Blackburn was heard by Major Keeble 1,500 metres north of the gorse gully at main headquarters. For a moment he was disbelieving and asked for verification. 'Sunray is down for Christ's sake,' Blackburn's usually impeccable voice procedure slipped under the stress of the moment. Keeble later admitted to a wave of fear, of apprehension that he would not perform well, would not make the right decisions. The feeling was fleeting. There were things to do — he was now the commanding officer.

Normally it would have been Major Rice, the battery commander, who took control of the battle until the second-in-command could come forward with Tac 2. But on this occasion Rice was in no position to know what was happening outside the immediate vicinity of the gorse gully. Keeble therefore made the decision to put Crosland temporarily in charge. After some 30 minutes on the radio trying to sort out what was happening, he assembled his command group for the move forward. In addition to Tac 2, Major Hector Gullan, the brigade liaison officer, accompanied him with his direct radio link (via the signals officers' relay station at Camilla Creek House) to Brigadier Thompson. As they left, the RSM, Mr Simpson, called him back: '"What is it?" I asked sharply. He looked me in the eye and said, "You are going to do fucking well, Sir!". I felt a million dollars!'[18] With everyone loaded down with extra ammunition Tac 2 set off. As they walked down the track they all had to scramble for cover as the Pucaras on their way to shoot down Nunn's Scout roared overhead. It was 10.45 am, about an hour since Colonel 'H' had been hit. It would be well after eleven before Keeble could reach B Company.

2 Para's being stalled for several hours in front of stubborn Argentine defences, culminating in the death of

the commanding officer caused acute anxiety at brigade headquarters. The bulk of the other units were marching towards Stanley, there was no way that reinforcements could be lifted in quickly enough to cope with an enemy counter-attack should it materialize, the appalling weather kept the Harriers on the carrier decks, and it was impossible to bolster artillery support. For a while it looked as though the start of the land campaign was going to suffer a severe set-back. But Thompson did not go forward to assess the situation, neither did he attempt to send even a company of reinforcements, and he did not try to influence Keeble to halt or withdraw.

He made his decision on the basis of the confident reports he received from Gullan. In Keeble's mind, in Gullan's (he had served in 2 Para), and indeed throughout the battalion there was never any doubt that they would win. If anything, Colonel 'H's death stiffened the will of everybody. Gullan assured his brigadier that it would be sorted out, and Thompson trusted his judgement. It proved to be sound. In theory the options of halting and holding until more troops could arrive, or even of pulling back, existed. Some, perhaps many, battalions might have been content with the former, taking advantage of the original brigade concept of the whole thing being a raid. Within 2 Para they were never considered. Despite the slowness of the advance, the long delays, despite the lack of support, and despite their commanding officer dying, there was no question of doing anything other than pressing on, of finding a way forward – of winning. But how?

In fact, as Keeble came south the crisis had passed; 2 Para's situation was improving. A Company had at last won their struggle for the gorse gully and the spur, the Argentines had finally surrendered in that area, and the eastern side of their main defence line had now fallen. Additionally, neither of the two reserve companies, C and D, had yet been committed, nor had the heavy weapons of Support Company been utilized. 2 Para had a lot of punch left untried. At about this time air

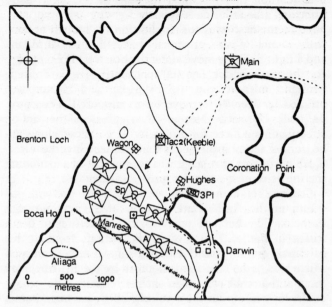

support was also available in the form of an armed
helicopter. The brigade log records a request for an armed
helicopter strike on Boca House being sent by 2 Para at
10.21 am. It was sent forward to Camilla Creek House but
never used. At 1.00 pm brigade asked whether it was still
needed – the response was 'no'. The fact that it was never
used is puzzling. According to Major Benest, who was the
signals officer at the time:

It was around this time that I relayed a request for
HELARM [an armed helicopter]. It was made
available by Brigade but battalion headquarters then
said there was no task for it. I never really got to the
bottom of why it was stood down. It was at Camilla
Creek House ready to go.[19]

275

The position was approximately that shown on Map 24. The solution that unlocked the door in the west, as A Company's hours of close quarter fighting had eventually done in the east, was the application of the two options that Colonel 'H' had previously rejected – use of Milans and a right flanking move along the beach by D Company. As the commander on the spot until Keeble arrived, Crosland initiated the use of Milan and Neame was ordered by Keeble to move up to support B Company. As will be seen Neame then pressed the acting commanding officer for authority to go ahead along the beach and accept a surrender that was seemingly on offer. Keeble's task at that stage was simply that of sanctioning the initiative of his two company commanders.

Corporal Hanlon was about to win his bet with his friend in the Anti- Tank Platoon of 3 Para, Sergeant Colbeck. The bet was who would be the first to fire a Milan in battle. The shot at the aircraft from Sussex Mountain did not count. Although an anti-armour weapon Milan was to be first fired in anger by the British Army in an anti-aircraft role, then against bunkers.

Hanlon was up on the crest of Hill B, his target was a troublesome bunker in Pelufo's position about 500 metres away. He was lying down with the firing post resting on its tripod. He checked his line of sight, identifying the bunker. His number two took a missile, removed the 'elephant's feet' (end covers) and the central plastic strip that runs the length of the tube to keep out the wet, placed it on the guide rails on the firing post, pushed it home, and tapped Hanlon's shoulder – he could fire when ready. Hanlon put the cross-hairs in the sight over the bunker, pressed the firing button and the missile was on its way with a violent flash from the rear of the firing post. Had the target been moving, Hanlon would have had to steer the missile, which was visible like a huge tracer round, until it hit. This, however, was static so he had little to do other than watch it sail across to strike the front of the bunker, penetrate, explode, and destroy its target. His success was greeted with a spontaneous cheer from all who saw it. There was at least one survivor 'who scurried out, performed a quick pirouette and ran like a greyhound to the cover of a second bunker, only to have a second viewing of the missile flare when that bunker was destroyed'.[20] Within a few minutes the Argentines had retaliated with a successful mortar strike, one bomb of which landed near the firing post wounding Privates Binns, Grant and Taylor.

If there were doubts in the minds of the Argentines still defending the ridge as to what to do next, the Milan decided them. Only about four missiles were fired but their accuracy and destructive power produced a flurry of white cloths. As Crosland put it, 'Milan took over from Anadin as a painkiller.' Keeble later said, 'That was the end of it — it really upset them.'[21]

The story of D Company's role in the Boca House battle began with breakfast. It was just after Colonel 'H' had declined Neame's suggestion of using the beach approach that he decided that as his company was not destined to go anywhere for a while it was time for a brew:

This was not the sort of thing one did on a School of Infantry exercise, and some of my blokes thought I had gone over the top a bit, but there didn't seem anything else worth doing. I was fairly certain that with 'H' not wanting me involved we were in for a long wait, and that as far as we were concerned nothing very dramatic was going to happen for the next half an hour or more. So what better time to have a brew? Needless to say I was tempting fate because just as my porridge came to the boil we heard that 'H' had been hit.[22]

Shortly afterwards Neame was told to find Crosland to see if he could assist.

Well I was buggered if I was going to waste my porridge so the entire company got on the move with most of the blokes holding their weapons in one hand and their mugs or mess-tins in the other, trying to take sips of tea or spoonsful of porridge as they moved along. What a ridiculous sight we must have looked.[23]

Neame took his tactical headquarters and platoon commanders up on to Hill B in an effort to meet up with Crosland to discuss their next move. 10 Platoon came up the hill with him while the remainder stayed tucked in behind, only 300 metres from the sea. On the crest Neame could clearly see the enemy positions on the 50-foot hill (Boca House) feature, but Crosland was not available as he was still well forward down the slope nearer the gorse line. Feeling secure at that distance (1,200 metres) he moved on, only to 'feel this thing zip past my leg'. A bullet had grazed his knee and shot away a pouch from the belt of his signaller Private Willoughby. They scurried hastily back behind the crest. They had had a personal demonstration that the Argentine .50 calibre heavy machine guns outranged the Para's GPMGs.

Meanwhile artillery fire missions were being directed at the enemy positions. The FOO, Sergeant Bullock, used his laser binoculars to get an exact range to the 50-foot hill, but most shells only landed harmlessly out to sea despite Bullock's repeated attempts to direct the shoot. Neame still felt that the beach offered the best alternative to a frontal attack but Crosland was still nowhere to be seen. 'There seemed no point in continuing to risk getting killed trying to find Crosland; much better to develop the right flanking idea rather than to get bogged down with B Company.'[25]

He determined to test his proposal with a reconnaissance along the shoreline. He radioed to Keeble to tell him what he proposed. It was agreed.

Taking Corporal Elliott's section from 10 Platoon, Lieutenant John Page, the company fire support coordinator, his signaller, and Bullock, Neame moved down to the shore. The beach was very hard and rocky which made mines unlikely. There was also a small cliff and strip of rock which gave good cover from the enemy provided they kept low. After about 300 metres Neame halted at some boulders on a low spur that were a good position in which to set up a fire base to cover a further advance. It was some 700 metres from the Argentines and several were seen moving about on their position (these were Aliaga's men). From the beach Private Laker, the GPMG gunner, tested the gun's effectiveness on the enemy. A few bursts and the movement ceased.

Neame's plan was now to leave the two sections of 10 Platoon under Lieutenant Shaun Webster back on Hill B, together with his second-in- command, Captain Peter Adams, acting as a radio relay link to Keeble. He would advance with 2nd Lieutenant Waddington's 11 Platoon and Lieutenant Barry's 12 Platoon under covering fire from B and Support Companies back on Hill B, plus his own GPMGs fire base near the beach. He radioed for his two platoons to join him. As they arrived their six GPMGs were positioned on the nearby rocky spur under Waddington's control.

At this stage the Milans came into action. Coupled with Neame's GPMGs on the shore, this combination of firepower had immediate and visible effects on the defenders of Darwin ridge. White cloths started appearing all over the place. Watching through his binoculars Neame was convinced that 'these buggers were packing it in; they had clearly had enough'.[26] But another half an hour was to pass before Neame was allowed to continue his flanking move.

Keeble and Tac 2 had by now arrived to the rear of Hill B where they were joined by the battery commander, the mortar officer, together with Sergeant Norman and Lance-Corporal Beresford. Keeble approved of the action taken by both Crosland and Neame, but would not yet give the go ahead for D Company to move forward to take the likely surrender until B Company had been replenished with the ammunition he and his party had brought up. This took some time.

Back on the beach Neame's patience was running out.

He urged that he be allowed forward to take advantage
of the situation, but radio links were poor, with the
frustrating business of having to have all his messages
relayed and then being told to wait. He was ready in all
respects to go; the delay was worrying. The longer he
waited the more chance there was that the enemy might
have a change of heart regarding the surrender, or he
would get caught by artillery fire.

> It was a boulder beach with the water in between the
> rocks, and beginning to lap round our feet. I had
> managed to keep my feet dry up till then and I had
> no wish to get them wet then, so I had the bright
> idea of telling Chris [Keeble] that if we didn't go
> soon the tide would cut us off. I'm sure it would
> never have come to that, but it worked − we got
> permission to move.[27]

What was about to happen was not, in the event, the great
tactical masterstroke that finally turned the Argentine
flank and won the battle that some accounts would have
their readers believe. It did not involve an assault as such,
with the enemy resisting and having to be winkled out of
their trenches. Most of the opposition were indicating that
they wished to surrender; the Milans, plus the GPMGs
of B and D Companies, had broken their will to continue
the fight. Certainly it was a calculated risk, as a few
Argentines were still firing, and there was always the
possibility that some might change their minds half way
through the surrender process. Neame's initiative, if
permitted earlier in the battle, might have won the day
but that is speculation. At this stage it was a sensible, and
the quickest, way of clinching a victory that had been won
by the close-quarter fighting of the Toms in the gorse
gully, and then the long-range application of heavier
weapons at specific targets.

While waiting on the beach Neame had spoken briefly
about the value of accepting surrenders if at all possible,
with the proviso that no unnecessary risks be taken.

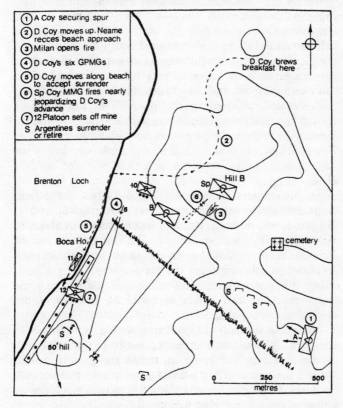

① A Coy securing spur

② D Coy moves up. Neame recces beach approach

③ Milan opens fire

④ D Coy's six GPMGs

⑤ D Coy moves along beach to accept surrender

⑥ Sp Coy MMG fires nearly jeopardizing D Coy's advance

⑦ 12 Platoon sets off mine

S Argentines surrender or retire

D Coy brews breakfast here

Brenton Loch

Hill B

Boca Ho.

cemetery

50' hill

0   250   500
metres

Having said all this, when the time came to move he felt obliged to take the lead, but as he stood to do so Corporal Harley dashed ahead saying, "'You wait here Sir. We don't want to risk you on this. This is Tom's work".[28] Neame admits to always having a soft spot for him after that.

Up on Hill B the Machine Gun Platoon had taken up fire positions. Initially they had been told not to fire. Organizing a surrender on the battlefield is an extremely delicate undertaking. The nerves of both sides are raw and tense. The man surrendering is frightened that if he exposes himself too soon he may be shot, or one of his comrades may fire and thus bring about renewed fighting with himself exposed in the open. The troops going forward to take the surrender are worried that they too are vulnerable to an enemy position not willing to give in, or that someone on their own side, not understanding what is happening, may open up and thus provoke another clash.

To his surprise Lieutenant Hugo Lister, the officer commanding the machine-guns, was ordered to open fire. He protested, pointing out that a surrender was about to take place. He was overruled. He engaged. From 10 Platoon Webster yelled over the radio to the company second-in-command to get the guns to stop. They did so, except for one runaway gun that continued to fire some thirty more rounds before it could be brought under control.

Along the shoreline D Company were now right out in the open. 12 Platoon had elected not to follow the beach as directed but had come up on to the ground inland behind the beach. They walked straight into a minefield. Sergeant Meredith, Barry's platoon sergeant, has given an amusing account of what happened next:

We could see the mines, anti-tank ones that had not been buried properly, each about four or five feet apart and connected by orange cord which was also pretty easy to see. I yelled at the blokes to watch out, and we started to move cautiously through them. They were not hard to avoid. We had only been going a few moments when there was an almighty bang. It knocked me flat, along with several blokes nearby [including Corporal Barton and Privates Spencer and Curran]. We were lying on the floor with ringing ears wondering what the hell had happened. Then I saw Spencer sitting up with a bit of the orange cord wrapped round his foot saying, 'It wasn't me, it wasn't me!' Some of the lads started to come across to get him out but I shouted, 'Leave him in the bloody mine field, he tripped it'. Nobody was hurt but one of the company HQ blokes was moaning. He was OK, so he got a boot in his ribs and was told to 'Get fucking moving'.[29]

Thinking that 12 Platoon had come under fire, another machine-gunner opened up again on to the 50-foot hill bunkers. A Milan was fired. Had the Argentines decided to retaliate the probability was that a number of D Company would have been hit. 'For fuck's sake stop firing.' The anger in Neame's voice over the radio was unmistakable. Some witnesses of this misunderstanding were convinced that the enemy were in fact still firing at Neame's men. 12 Platoon, who were very close, were emphatic they were not.

D Company reached its objective with no further incident. Aliaga's platoon had collapsed with, according to the Paras, twelve dead and fifteen prisoners, many of whom were horribly wounded.[30] Some ten or so had run off towards the airfield. It was after midday and 2 Para had been fighting almost ten hours. Although the main Argentine positions had now been taken it was to be another twenty-two before the battalion finally liberated Goose Green.

XI

ACTION FOR THE AIRFIELD

'We weren't quite sure what to expect, but it seemed quite comical as we advanced forward, like a scene from World War 1. It reminded me of the closing scene from 'Dad's Army' and I began whistling the theme tune'.

Major Peter Kennedy, the former second-in-command of C Company, describing to the author the start of his company's advance towards the airfield.

First Lieutenant Estoban had been standing by at Stanley to return to Goose Green since early on the morning of the 28th. He, and the reinforcements he would take, had been waiting for the weather to clear sufficiently for the helicopters to risk the journey. He would be taking his old 'Fanning Head Mob' survivors, together with more men scraped together from various administrative duties – in total 84 soldiers of the 12th and 25th Regiments.[1] The only other officer was 2nd Lieutenant Jose Vasquez. Estoban was anxious to be off, but it was not until around 11.00 am that clearance was finally given for the flight.

The nine helicopteis flew together as a group. One Puma and six UH-1Hs (Iroquois) carried the fully equipped troops, with two A-109As as gunship escorts. They hugged the south coast past Fitzroy, then up Choiseul Sound to land just south of Goose Green settlement after a 30 minute, 90 kilometre flight. By the time Estoban had organized his command and marched north to report to Piaggi it was around midday, with the surrender of the Argentines in the Boca House area virtually complete.

Throughout the morning Piaggi's perimeter had been shrinking. This was brought about by 2 Para's inexorable advance down the isthmus, by the loss of the Darwin Ridge/Boca House positions, and also by Piaggi's own deliberate contracting of his defences. The latter included the bringing of C Company, under Fernandez, closer to, and west of the settlement. By the time 2 Para started their advance towards and around the airfield the Argentine defences were approximately as shown on Map 26. Piaggi was now defending a large semi-circle, whose base was the sea in the east. In the centre of the diameter was Goose Green. In every direction inland the ground rose gently to the rim of the circle. Northwards, for 700 metres, the grassland stretched to the school and, slightly to its west, the low undulation which marked the beginning of the flat plateau on which the airfield was sited. Both the school, which blocked a bridge carrying the shoreline track over the estuary, and the flagpole position on the higher ground immediately east of the strip, which controlled the main north-south track, were key locations. Attackers approaching down the track, which up till now had been 2 Para's main axis of advance, would need to seize both positions in order to get to Goose Green. Troops pushing south, taking the flagpole area, could not leave the school unsecured only 300 metres to their left.

Piaggi reinforced both these areas in time for the next phase of the fighting. To Estoban's surprise he was told to hand over command of the bulk of his reinforcements to Vasquez, who was sent to bolster the school position. Estoban himself was not to rejoin his men until much later, after he had organised some 200 Air Force personnel as infantrymen to defend the settlement. The flagpole position and the airfield were reinforced by 2nd Lieutenant Centurion with his platoon from C Company 25th Regiment. Beyond these positions, to the north, was another 1000 metres of 'billiard table' terrain that gradually climbed to Darwin Hill.

To the NW was the airstrip, and westwards another 1000 metres of almost flat ground, rising imperceptibly to

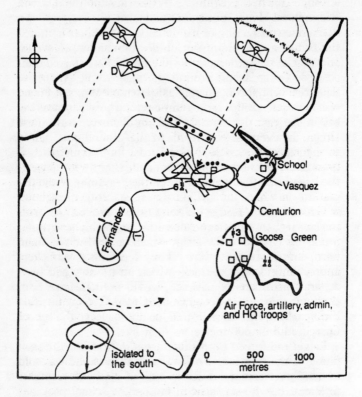

the low plateau in the centre of the isthmus. The airfield was protected by a number of bunkers and, to its immediate south, by six 20mm Rheinmetall twin anti-aircraft guns. They had a range of 2000 metres, could fire 1000 rounds per minute per barrel with a 360 degree traverse. In whatever direction the Air Force crews looked they had an unobstructed line of sight out to maximum range. It was these guns, firing horizontally rather than vertically into the sky, that were to cause consternation in 2 Para's C Company in the next stage of the struggle. The

286

Argentine's C Company 12th Regiment had taken up positions to the west and south of Goose Green, although it only had two platoons. Its third platoon had been helicoptered down to the extreme southern tip of the isthmus in response to a rumour that British troops had landed there. The helicopter left these men there, they had no radio, and were unable to join the battle.

Goose Green itself played an important role during the afternoon of the 28th. Piaggi had his command post in one of its houses, all the civilians were still in the community hall, and Argentine mortars and bunkers were positioned around its perimeter, close to the buildings. These arrangements were deliberate in order to deter the British from firing into the settlement. In this they were largely successful in that none of 2 Para's heavy weapons, mortars, artillery, or later airstrikes were ever targetted at Goose Green. The two 35mm twin-barrelled Oerlikon anti-aircraft guns were located on the tiny peninsula on which the eastern part of Goose Green is built. In the open, just beyond the houses, these guns were to come into action in the ground role. Their range was twice that of the 20mm Rheinmetall but with half the rate of fire, although they made a bigger bang at the receiving end. Firing due north they could hit the southern slope of Darwin Hill with ease.

As with Colonel 'H', so for Piaggi, Goose Green was a make or break battle. As soon as reinforcements arrived he had put them into the perceived weak spots in his defences, but it was difficult for him to know what was happening minute by minute. Although in constant touch with Parada 100 kilometres away, he was frequently out of touch with his troops only one kilometre from his headquarters. Without adequate radios reliance was placed on runners and landrovers to get messages around his sub-units. At one stage during the Darwin Ridge/Boca House engagement Manresa had driven back to Piaggi's command post personally to brief him, and then take ammunition forward. Not long after he had committed his reinforcements Parada came on the radio to instruct him to launch a major offensive effort. He must attack. As he later told Middlebrook:

> 'I was in a raving fury at that order. Counterattack! With what? God help me. I remember I picked up an aluminium mug and threw it at the wall. Normally I am a very placid character, but that order was impossible to carry out. I told him it was not possible and I told him why not - politely but firmly'.[2]

Despite his indignation at the time Piaggi's performance at Goose Green was to cost him his career.

At this stage it is revealing to digress a little to consider the effect that lack of transport was having on 2 Para's logistics, and therefore its fighting capacity as it moved further and further from Camilla Creek House. By midday the leading platoons were 12 kilometres from A Echelon at Camilla Creek House, and almost 40 from B Echelon back at the Brigade Maintenance Area. 2 Para had been fighting hard for over nine hours and, although they did not know it then, had another five hours in front of them. To sustain the effort the paratoopers needed food, radio batteries and ammunition, primarily the latter. They also needed medical attention and evacuation for the wounded. The requirement was for a two way flow — supplies forward, casualties back, over the 40 kilometre gap between the base area and the firing line. If the Toms at the front had to look over their shoulders for ammunition, or their injured comrades had to lie for hours before being evacuated, it indicated something remiss with the system.

To state the obvious, supplies and casualties are heavy, so to move them quickly requires transport. Up until about noon, forward from Camilla Creek House, 2 Para's land transport consisted solely of one captured civilian landrover. It became committed to carrying mortar bombs from Camilla Creek House to the baseplate positions. Without it the two tubes would have run out of

17. 2 Para's memorial on the southern slope of Darwin Hill, with Goose Green in the background. *Captain R. Knight.*

18. Burntside House from the east, near the stream over which A Company advanced. *Captain R. Knight.*

19. The surrender on the 50' ring contour south of Boca House. The Argentine wounded and prisoners are from 2nd Lieutenant Aliaga's platoon of the 8th Regiment. Note the flimsy overhead cover and white flag on the headquarters bunker/trench. The Paras are from D Company. Corporal Barton (12 Platoon) faces the camera with an SMG slung round his neck and an M-79 grenade launcher in his right hand. *Colour-Sergeant W. Owen.*

20. D Company move up from the beach towards 2nd Lieutenant Aliaga's CP, which is flying a white flag, to take the surrender south of Boca House. Note the leading section well spaced out on the skyline, and that only about one man in three carries a shovel. *Colour-Sergeant W. Owen.*

21. The Boca House battlefield as seen by 2nd Lieutenant Aliaga's men as they looked north from their position on the 50' ring contour south of Boca House. Compare this photograph with Map 22. The skyline beyond the gorseline is 1,000 metres away. This is where B Company was caught in the open as it advanced south earlier that morning. The photograph is of the Argentines surrendering to D Company. Note one Argentine is wearing Wellington boots to keep his feet dry, and the attempt to keep rain out of a trench by erecting a poncho tent – thus giving away its position. *Colour-Sergeant W. Owen.*

22. A group of 2 Para waiting for the final surrender near the airstrip. *Left to right* – Major Keeble, David Norris, Robert Fox, Corporal Elliot, Private Hanley, Major Keeble's radio operator, CSM Clark, Captain Bell RM (interpreter), an Argentine, Lance-Corporal Osborne (OC D Company's radio operator). *Colour-Sergeant W. Owen.*

23. Snow-covered bodies of Argentine dead lined up near Goose Green on the morning of 29 May. Note how the houses have remained untouched by the battle. The community hall is the building with the small spire in the centre. *Colour-Sergeant W. Owen.*

24. A detachment of Argentines marches away to captivity on the morning of 29 May, having dumped their helmets and personal weapons. The other large group awaits its turn to complete the formalities of the final surrender. *Colour-Sergeant W. Owen.*

25. A solitary Para picks over the abandoned Argentine helmets and weapons left on the ground after the final surrender.
Colour-Sergeant W. Owen.

26. Corporal Staddon (10 Platoon) turns away after examining the remains of a burnt-out Pucara on the edge of the airstrip.
Colour-Sergeant W. Owen.

27. This Pucara, seen here on the edge of the airstrip, had in fact crashed on take-off before the battle, and was left by the Argentines as a decoy to attract fire. *Colour-Sergeant W. Owen.*

28. 2 Para sorts out its administration in front of the community hall on 29 May, watched with interest by a small boy. The vehicle on the extreme left is the civilian landrover captured from Lieutenant Morales the day before the battle. The other vehicle is one of the tracked oversnow Volvo BV 202s later commandeered by 2 Para at Sussex Mountain to help bring up supplies and ammunition. *Colour-Sergeant W. Owen.*

29. The 2 Para flag flies over Goose Green on the 29th May. The building with the spire is the Community Hall.
Colour-Sergeant W. Owen.

30. Colonel 'H''s grave near San Carlos. *Mr R. Smithers.*

31. *Left to right:* Major Tony Rice RA, the battery commander, Colonel 'H' and Captain Alan Coulson, the Intelligence Officer, onboard a landing craft at Ascension Island. *The Parachute Regiment.*

32. The strain of 'tabbing' with bulging bergen and radio set shows on Sergeant Graham Blackburn's face. Blackburn was Colonel 'H''s radio operator during the battle, who was to announce that his Commanding Officer had been hit with the message 'Sunray is down'. *The Parachute Regiment.*

33. Major Chris Keeble who as 2 Para's second-in-command, took over command of the battalion after Colonel 'H' was hit. *Lieutenant-Colonel C. Keeble, DSO.*

34. Major John Crosland, OC B Company, on Sussex Mountain just prior to moving to Camilla Creek House. Despite the order that helmets were to be worn Crosland persisted in wearing his famous black hat. *Lieutenant-Colonel J. H. Crosland, MC.*

35. Captain Paul Farrar, Patrols Platoon commander at Goose Green. *Major P. Farrar.*

36. The only Royal Engineer officer at Goose Green, Lieutenant Clive Livingstone. Livingstone took over as second-in-command of A Company after Captain Dent was killed in the gorse gully. *Major C. R. Livingstone.*

37. A brew-up on Sussex Mountain before the battle by some of Support Company's headquarters. *Left to right* Mayor Hugh Jenner, OC; Warrant Officer 2 Ged Peatfield, CSM; Private Lukowiak, the company clerk; and Lance-Corporal Thayer, the storeman.
Colour-Sergeant F. Pye.

38. 2 Para's medics assembled in the gorse gully prior to moving into Goose Green on 29 May. *Left to right* Signaller Pete Hall, Corporal Taff Jones, Lance-Corporal Bill Bentley, Captain Steve Hughes, Private Mark Polkey, Private Phil Clegg, and Private Irvine Gibson. Note how all medics were fully armed, and that Bentley, Polkey, and Gibson had 'binned' their SMGs and taken Argentine automatic rifles.
Mr Bill Bentley MM.

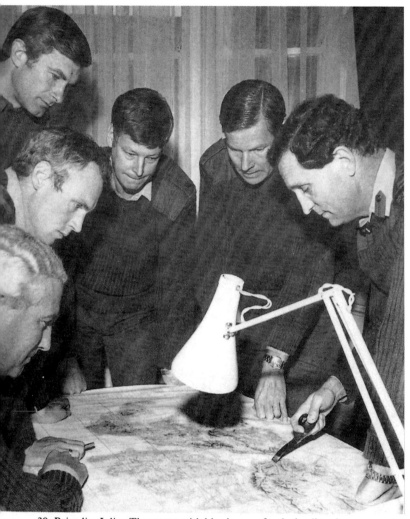

39. Brigadier Julian Thompson with his planners for the landings in the Falklands. *Left to right* Major Southby-Tailyour RM (expert on the Falklands coastline), Major Macdonald RE (combat engineer support), Captain Lowe RM (GSO 3 Intelligence), Major Wells Cole RM (DAA & QMG), Major Chester RM (brigade major or chief-of-staff), and Brigadier Thompson. The only person missing is Thompson's chief artillery officer Lieutenant-Colonel Holroyd-Smith.
3 Commando Brigade.

40. Major Roger Jenner, OC C Company, studies his map on Sussex Mountain. Note the rank badge worn on the chest rather than the normal position on the shoulders.
Major R. D. Jenner.

41. Major Phil Neame, OC D Company, on the deck of the *MV Norland* during the battalion sports day en route to the Falklands.
Colour-Sergeant W. Owen

42. Brigadier Julian Thompson escorts Vice-Commodore Wilson Pedroza to 3 Commando Brigade headquarters at San Carlos shortly after Pedroza had surrendered the Argentine garrison at Goose Green.
Mr R. Boswell.

ammunition long before they did. Even with the almost superhuman efforts of Colour-Sergeant Pye and his men, plus the light helicopters in daylight, the bombs had run out at the crucial moment of A Company's attack on the spur. The Defence Platoon, the Assault Pioneer Platoon and all the Mortar Platoon except for the section manning the mortars spent their entire time lugging ammunition. Sixty soldiers out of 500 is a lot of men — two platoons worth — to have to use on manual resupply and casevac activities.

Even getting supplies forward to Camilla Creek House, where the battalion's staff could sort them out into priority loads, was fraught with difficulties. The only method was by helicopter, and these were now desperately scarce with virtually the whole brigade on the move. Dependence on helicopters had several drawbacks. Movement, except on foot, stopped at night; availability by day of the Sea Kings was often curtailed by air raid warnings or bad weather, while the urgent need for lifts by every unit led to frequent 'hijackings', with consequential chaos to planned schedules. Heavy-lift helicopters frequently failed to turn up, with problems compounded by a shortage of nets and chains for large loads. At B Echelon Captain Banks Middleton was just able to keep adequate stocks moving forward due to his being co-located with the Naval Air Squadrons, plus his ready supply of cigarettes and space heaters. As a good quartermaster he looked after his battalion; if that entailed a bit of judicious bribery so be it. When you cannot beat the system you have to join it.

Part of the problem was that, although two Scout helicopters were in direct support of 2 Para for the operation, all requests for their use had to be sanctioned by brigade. These aircraft were part of 5 Flight of 3 Commando Brigade Air Squadron commanded by Captain John Greenhalgh who was well known by 2 Para. In fact these helicopters were normally part of 656 Squadron Army Air Corps then temporarily attached to 3 CBAS. Colonel 'H' had specifically requested that 656 Squadron accompany the battalion to the Falklands as they had trained together in Kenya the previous year. He actually asked for those pilots by name who had been on this exercise as an excellent working relationship had been established. Being Colonel 'H' he got what he wanted. These Scouts (and the two Gazelles) were usually ATGW helicopters, designed to shoot at tanks with their French SS11 missiles, but as there was no armoured opposition to 2 Para in this battle they flew re-supply and casevac missions with the rear seats ripped out of the Gazelles to make more room, like the Royal Marine aircraft. Neither type had armaments.

It was not until after Colonel 'H' was killed that any Scouts ventured further south than the RAP, when it was located alongside 2 Para's main headquarters, and not far from the second mortar baseplate position to the SW of Burntside House. The first attempt had resulted in the shooting down of Nunn's aircraft and the narrow escape of Niblett's. This was to have been the first casevac flight of the battle forward to the gorse gully. When Niblett returned to Ajax Bay with the badly injured Sergeant Belcher he was able to apprise the brigade staff of the urgent need for casevac in 2 Para. It was then decided that both AAC Scouts (Captain Greenhalgh's and Sergeant Walker's) should be used for casevac tasking.

By the time the first casualty (Worrall) was lifted out from the entrance to the gorse gully it was well after midday. Prior to this all those wounded during daylight had to lie on the battlefield awaiting collection. Some could be carried to makeshift company aid posts, others, like Captain Young and Private Tuffen, had to lie where they fell indefinitely. That so many survived was due to the devotion and instant attention given them by their comrades and medics, whose training was of such a high standard, and the fact that 2 Para had two medical officers who came forward leading two separate teams as soon as practical. The RAP was co-located with main headquarters, but during the night Captain Hughes had led it forward as soon as he heard D Company were taking casualties. They came under prolonged mortar, artillery and later, sniper fire. Hughes readily admits his fears: 'at one stage a round whistled inches above my head. We were asked to move forward. I was petrified, especially of the sniper as I was wearing a waterproof, the lining of which glowed white from its snow camouflage reverse'.[3]

After advancing about 400 metres the first casualties were found — Parr with a bullet lying harmlessly in his umbilicus, and Grey whose only injury turned out to be bruising after a round had struck his webbing. The RAP caught up briefly with Tac 1. Hughes had watched incredulously as a shell landed between Colonel 'H' and the adjutant without doing either any harm. It was the last time he saw either of them alive. Shortly afterwards they were joined by main headquarters. Both remained at that location until after A Company's battle in the gorse gully.

Hughes heard the news that Colonel 'H' was down and that medical assistance was urgently needed forward by both the leading companies. As there was no practical means of getting the casualties to the doctor the doctor had to go forward to them. The RAP personnel were split into two teams - Lance-Corporal Bentley has described them as 'over qualified Company Aid Posts'. The A Team was the largest, with four medics (including Bentley), a signaller, plus the padre and his escort. Team B was under Captain Rory Wagon and had three medics with a signaller. Hughes approached Keeble to suggest both teams go forward but as 'Chris was busy, I didn't get a reply but took it as a tacit agreement'.[4]

Hughes, with his enormous bergen full of medical supplies, accompanied by his signaller, Private Hall, set off immediately for A Company to try to reach the colonel. Bentley was to bring on the rest of A Team, while Team B headed for B Company. Bentley has described how ammunition supply, indeed fighting, was almost as much his duty as tending the injured:

The RSM appeared, 'Load up with ammo, as much as you can carry; they need every bullet!' We were

291

going forward to A Company. It was only about 1,500 metres, just follow the track. Some GPMGs were next to the ammo pile, so I took one and about 1,000 rounds of belted ammo. I stowed my SMG in my rucksack. Each medic now carried about 200 lbs altogether. It wasn't far, but we had overdone it with the ammo. Bit by bit as it slowed us down it was being left behind. We were about half way there when a Pucara light attack aircraft flew low over the ridge towards us. I let rip from the hip with the GPMG. I was getting a bad feed and having to recock. I screamed at Gibo [Private Gibson] to come and feed the belt. As he raced towards me he dropped like a stone, I thought he was hit but continued to fire. Gibo lay under his enormous rucksack arms and legs straining trying to get a grip. I had to laugh, he looked like a tortoise on its back.[5]

Meanwhile Hughes pressed on as fast as his injured ankle and crippling load would allow, passing Major Rice on his way back to join Tac 2. At the gorse gully A Company's wounded were waiting. There was Shorrock, one of the company medics, who had been hit five hours earlier and whom Hughes almost missed as he had a piece of corrugated iron over him to keep the rain off, Adams, Kirkwood, Tuffen, Worrall, and a large number of Argentines. Immediately Hughes started to categorize the casualties into priorities for treatment (triage). As he finished, Bentley and his group staggered up, dumped their ammunition with Sergeant-Major Price, and set to work under Hughes' guidance. Bentley's account of what he did is a revealing glimpse of battlefield medicine:

Also there was Paul Shorrock, one of my dearest friends. 'I'll take Paul, Gibo with me. Mark, Cleggy, see to Monster [medics Mark Polkey and Clegg were to look after Corporal Adams] and that kid (Doc Hughes had already started on Worrall);

get to the others as soon as you can.' Strictly speaking under the circumstances Paul's injuries [he had been hit in the back] didn't justify the attention of the two best medics in the battalion. Unlike the doctor who treated people strictly according to medical priorities.... we were soldiers first with specialist training as medics so we had other priorities based on friendship....

If we didn't get it [the needle in a vein] right the first time Paul wouldn't believe he could make it. We needed to be careful but fast. I cut away his clothing while Gibo set up a drip. We each carried one litre of IV fluid in our smock to keep it from freezing. Gibo pulled open his [own] shirt and put the still ice cold package against his naked abdomen, wrapping his smock over it to maximise the warming effect. I was looking for a vein. We don't like to use joints because of the movement problems, splinting and associated flow restrictions, but there's a big vein near the elbow and I dared not miss! We couldn't move Paul, or strip off too much clothing, he was like a block of ice already. I went in. 'See Paul, piece of piss - first time!' 'I love you Basha, and you Gibo', cried Paul.[6]

Within minutes Greenhalgh's and Walker's Scouts touched down nearby. At last a speedy evacuation was under way for the remaining hours of daylight for casualties at the gully. Naturally, 2 Para's own casualties had priority but all Argentine wounded received medical attention, cigarettes, and hot brews of tea. Lance-Corporal Framlington and Private O'Rourke used some 40 shell dressings on the wounded prisoners. Undoubtedly many lives were saved by the prompt treatment given by 2 Para to their enemy. It was very much in accordance with Colonel 'H's instructions, and a great surprise to the Argentines. Large numbers of prisoners had to be disarmed and assembled for their long walk north. To Bentley the morale of the majority seemed shattered.

Many of them prayed, clutching rosary beads or looking at pictures of the Madonna.

From midday and until dark the gorse gully area was to become decidedly overcrowded. It was occupied at various times by A Company, the RAP, battalion main headquarters, Keeble's Tac 2, elements of Support Company, numerous wounded from both sides, while at its entrance was the helicopter landing site. No wonder it continued to attract the attention of the Argentine artillery. Later, Bentley observed:

> Whether by intention or mishap, when the next large group of prisoners came in they were 'paraded' conspicuously in the open on the chopper landing site. This seemed to go on for ages, till it was fully dark.... The effect was impressive. I don't remember any more shelling [in that area] for the rest of the battle.[7]

Whether this was just good luck or not will never be known.

With the Boca House position now secure and the Argentines either surrendering or running it seemed there was now a good chance of clinching a complete victory if the momentum could be kept up. After six hours of stubborn defence the gates had been forced open and 2 Para could now flood through. For this tactic to work speed was vital; the retreating enemy must not be given time to recover. There were rumours that Argentine reinforcements had arrived, but no knowledge of the detailed disposition of the defences around the settlements. The only major obstacle remaining of which 2 Para were certain was the airfield, together with the possibility of a position around the schoolhouse near the coast. For Keeble and the company commanders the opportunity to press on had at last presented itself and they resolved to take it.

Keeble did not hold any formal 'O' group. It was now

a question of rapid radio orders to point the companies at their objectives, coordinate their movement and arrange fire support. It was around midday. The next stage — 2 Para had reason to hope the final one — of the battle was about to begin.

In Colonel 'H's original plan the battalion was now about to undertake Phase 5. It was six hours later than intended, but part of it had been accomplished — the securing of Darwin Hill, and with Boca House now in the hands of D instead of B Company. If the next phase was to be the same A Company would be in reserve on Darwin Hill, B Company would be in reserve at Boca House, while C Company headed for the airfield and D Company for the outskirts of Goose Green. Support Company would provide fire support for C Company, the mortars for A Company, and the guns for D Company. Keeble made little change. It should be stressed, however, that at this stage, with victory thought to be in sight, nobody was thinking in terms of slavishly following Colonel 'H's original orders. The need was to keep going; it happened to be convenient to stick with the companies' original objectives - with the exception of B Company.

At the suggestion of Major Crosland B Company would now advance south along the west of the isthmus, by-pass the airfield, and then swing east to arrive near the coast south of Goose Green. It was a thrust of over 4,000 metres which, if successful, would complete the surrounding of the settlement. Otherwise A Company would go firm, C Company was to take the airfield, while D Company closed on Goose Green. There was only one slight hiccup in putting these movements into effect: C Company was heading off in the wrong direction — towards Darwin.

Some time after Colonel 'H' was hit, C Company had received orders to move up to the gorse gully to join A Company. This made sense as its next objective was still the airfield. As the company headquarters personnel came into the area, with the evidence of intense fighting all around — prisoners, wounded, dead bodies, burning trenches and gorse — they sought out the company commander. Farrar-Hockley had been out of touch with events elsewhere for some time, and had no contact with Keeble as to what was to happen next. He greeted the C Company officers somewhat formally. 'The commanding officer's dead, the adjutant's dead, my company second-in-command's dead. What are we going to do?' The situation was explained to him and they quickly settled down to discuss the next move.

Darwin settlement had always been A Company's final objective and the securing of the gorse gully was only a means of getting there. Nevertheless, at this point in time Farrar-Hockley's main concern was securing the immediate area, checking all the trenches, and ascertaining whether any enemy remained nearby or on the approaches to Darwin. The two company commanders agreed that C Company would assist in this process with Jenner sending his men to check towards Darwin. At this stage Jenner had yet to receive orders to continue advancing south so he told both his platoons to move down towards the settlement. This arrangement was short lived. After the platoons had advanced only a few hundred metres they were recalled over the radio. Keeble did not approve the diversion. Darwin could wait, the important thing was to keep pressing south. Farrar- Hockley, who had had no instructions from Keeble for some time, was now told to release 3 Platoon to give C Company a third platoon for its move on the airfield.

To have all the rifle companies, with the exception of two platoons of A Company, on the move simultaneously was a bold manoeuvre. The objectives were to keep the enemy on the run, seize the airfield, and surround Goose Green. If the Argentines were crumbling, and so many recent surrenders seemed to indicate they were, then speed and impetus were surely the answer. There was, however, a proviso. If the Argentines' back was not yet broken, if they had been able to deploy their recent reinforcements, and if the troops as yet uncommitted were still prepared to fight, then Keeble's initiative could run into serious difficulties. It did.

Against an enemy determined to fight it out 2 Para's quick follow-up plan had several potential flaws. The first of these was that the ground still favoured the defence in that troops on the airfield, or dug in around Goose Green, had uninterrupted fields of fire of at least 1,000 metres, to the north nearer 2,000. That is a long way for infantry to go on foot if under effective fire. To do so requires substantial indirect and direct fire support, probably augmented by smoke screens. 2 Para still lacked effective indirect support, no air strikes were yet forthcoming, the guns performance had not improved, and the two mortars were low on ammunition and were now nearing their maximum range as there was virtually no supercharge ammunition. They would need to advance their baseplate position once more if the advance got much beyond the airfield.

Next, if C Company was heading for the airfield and D Company the ground overlooking Goose Green, or indeed the settlement itself, there was a strong possibility that both companies would become inter-mixed. D Company's route towards Goose Green crossed, or went close to, the airfield which was C Company's objective. Unless D Company went south for 2,000 metres before turning east to the settlement it was likely to meet C Company on or near the airfield. It was unlikely to do so as this was the route now to be taken by B Company (see Map 26).

Even with direct fire support from the Milans and machine guns grouping on Darwin Hill the situation was far from ideal. The range was long, and would lengthen as the rifle companies advanced. B Company could get no support from them whatsoever. With C Company these Support Company weapons would have to fire over the heads of the platoons, as they advanced so this became more and more dangerous. Just at the time when fire support should be increasing it would need to stop to avoid hitting their own troops. At ranges in excess of 1,000 metres it is extraordinarily difficult in the confusion and rapid movement of battle to be able to differentiate between the good guys and the bad guys. In summary, the nearer 2 Para got to the enemy the less likely it was to get effective direct fire support from its own heavy weapons.

Finally, there is always a calculated risk in having all the rifle companies on the move heading for different objectives simultaneously. Not only are they widely spread, but there is no reserve. In this case A Company was still recovering from its long battle in the gully, and had released 3 Platoon to C Company, so was not much use as a reserve. In army parlance there was no 'foot on the ground'; everybody was on the move; every sub-unit was committed. Should hard fighting develop the battalion might be caught off balance and scattered over some 4,000 metres.

Undoubtedly these problems were considered by Keeble before he gave the go-ahead to press on. Risks must be taken, decisions must be made and at the time the prospect of a quick victory if only the pressure could be maintained was very real. In the event final success was to elude 2 Para for another 18 hours as the Argentines still had some fight left in them.

C Company, with Wallis' 3 Platoon from A Company as its third rifle platoon, filed through a gap in the gorse line on Darwin Hill to start its 1,500 metres advance to the airfield a little after midday. The company immediately spread out into open formation and Lieutenant Kennedy ordered bayonets fixed. Farrar (Patrols Platoon) was on the left, Connor (Recce Platoon) was to the right with Wallis behind in reserve. Kennedy has described the moment:

We reached the highest point of the ridge between Goose Green and Darwin [Darwin Hill] and could clearly see Goose Green about two kilometres to the south. We looked over a thick gorse bush but that appeared to be the last piece of cover before the settlement. In fact the slope from the gorseline down to the area of the school house looked like a sloping billiard table. Roger [Jenner] ordered two up one

298

back [two platoons forward, one in reserve] but
without the normal 'bags of smoke'.[8]

To most of those who participated in this advance it
evoked images of what World War 1 was supposed to have
been like. Kennedy thought of the Dad's Army film,
Corporal Evans of his grandfather in World War 1, while
Captain Farrar speaks of 'those of us who were there still
talk about going 'over the top'.[9]

From the start C Company were unaware of what the
rifle companies were doing. Farrar did not know that C
Company's route was about to converge with D's.
Speaking of D Company he says, 'We had observed them
first from the gorse line. I recall having a brief discussion
with Roger Jenner as to whether they were British or
Argentinian. I commented that looking at the way they
moved they must be British'.[10] In fact none of the C
Company officers had much idea of what D Company
were supposed to be doing, and still less of why they were
moving into what they thought was their area of action.
Kennedy's views are very clear on this issue:

At some point during this period, it may have been
before we crossed the gorse line or on the slope, D
Company crossed in front of us from the right flank.
We weren't expecting them. It was a dangerous
move, and indicated that command and control in
Tac HQ/Tac 2 was not all that it should have been.[11]

To the Air Force crews of the 20mm AA guns around the
airfield it was an incredible sight. Nearly 100 paratroopers
were seen as little dots moving slowly down the open
slope. For a few moments they stood and watched. Then
there was a rush to depress barrels to get the guns into
action. Mortars and heavy machine guns joined in. There
was, at that stage, little or no incoming fire, and even by
the end of this action the Air Force had had only three
men killed. From the Argentine point of view it seemed
too good to be true — a turkey shoot.

For the Patrols Platoon commander it appeared that:

> Suddenly all hell broke loose. The weight of fire was
> incredible. Small arms whizzed past, anti-aircraft
> cannon ploughed up the turf around us as we
> skirmished along.[12]

Further back up the slope Lieutenant Kennedy's
whistling of the Dad's Army theme tune was cut short:

> The comical side soon changed as the enemy opened
> fire with a large number and variety of weapons.
> Falkland Islanders who witnessed the scene later
> said they couldn't imagine how anyone survived it.
> The enemy weapons included mortars, artillery, .5
> heavy machine-guns, AAA 30mm [20mm] in the
> ground role, and small arms. A soldier is always
> concerned with the question 'How will I react under
> fire?' As I lay on the ground I realized that the choice
> was not too difficult, it was either move forward and
> do something or die. The weight of fire was
> incredible. I moved forward a few metres to the
> company's two MFCs, Corporals Walters and
> Collins, and joined them in bringing mortar fire on
> to the enemy AAA 30mm [20mm] which was
> engaging the company from the western end of the
> airfield. The AA gun was put out of action and I
> told Corporal Walters to try and switch fire on to the
> enemy artillery at the western edge of the settlement.
> We were told it was too close to the village and might
> endanger civilian lives.[13]

C Company had been caught flat-footed, trying to do an
advance to contact over open ground from a long way
away, without supporting fire. It had been a gamble that
did not pay off. It so happened that fresh troops under
Centurion and Vasquez had just arrived in the area, and
that the AA guns and .50 machine-guns could make the
maximum use of their long range. The Argentines were

still prepared to fight at a distance, particularly as they had not been softened up by indirect fire. C Company provided them with an irresistable target.

What had happened to B Company in front of the Boca House position was now repeated with C Company. The company was split, with a long expanse of open, fire swept-ground between the two elements. Recce and Patrols Platoons dashed forward, along with company headquarters, while 3 Platoon dashed back. Jenner took what cover he could find and got on the radio for fire support. He spoke to Keeble, who told him that none was available. This was one time when artillery fire for a rifle company was surely an absolute priority, but it was not available. Jenner could actually see smoke rings from the barrels of the Argentine 105s near Goose Green, although without direct or indirect fire support he was asked if he could keep going. Jenner tried. His company headquarters reached the half-way point on the slope when it was hit by a shell which bowled over Private Russell, a GPMG gunner, inflicting chest and neck wounds. The company commander's signaller, Private Holman-Smith, dashed forward to grab the GPMG but was hit and killed outright as he did so. The blast that had injured Russell had also wounded both Jenner and another radio operator, Private Holbrook, although not so severely. Jenner later spoke of the AA guns with justifiable sentiment: 'You could feel the guns zeroing in on you'.

Despite being dazed and wounded Jenner tried without success to get through to his leading platoons on the radio. He could see them moving forward but he had lost control over them. Holbrook had reported the situation and loss of contact to battalion headquaters and had been told to get the leading platoons to switch to the D Company net. This order never got through. There was little he could do but make his way painfully back to the gorse line, to rejoin 3 Platoon which had had Sergeant Beatty and Privates Thomas and Tunn wounded in the process of withdrawing.

Keeble was now forward on the gorseline where he

could see the seriousness of the situation. He told Jenner
to get medical attention, although Jenner was determined
to carry on, wanting to go forward again to get his platoons
back on the net and control the action. He was not allowed
to move. In the circumstances this was perhaps fortunate
as the company had already had twelve casualties on that
open slope.

By now Support Company was deploying its Milans and
machine-guns on the forward slope of Darwin Hill. They
had an excellent view but the range was extreme. Corporal
Rogers, in the Anti-Tank Platoon, remembers the Milan
coming into action against the two 35mm Oerlikon guns
on the Goose Green peninsular that had joined in shooting
up C Company:

> At Goose Green two firing posts fired, first Corporal
> Hanlon at the bunkers then Corporal Titley at the
> AA guns. The others were not firing, so only three
> or four missiles were used. We saw the AA cannons
> near Goose Green and Titley fired a missile at them.
> Unfortunately the missile's wire is only 1,750 metres
> long so his shot fell into the water about 75 metres
> short. It was effective though as the crew ran off.[14]

A few of company headquarters had got down the slope,
among them Lieutenant Kennedy (whose party, unlike
the rifle company seconds-in-command, had no signaller)
and Sergeant-Major Greenhalgh. Patrols Platoon
commander has described his experience in getting
forward:

> We had got approximately half way down the slope
> when we went to ground. There was a shallow dip
> in the ground across our front. Most of us got into
> it. Meanwhile 3 Platoon retreated back over the
> gorse line into relative safety. The obvious feature
> in front of us was the schoolhouse, which we had
> been told was an enemy strongpoint. At this stage
> it was still some 400 metres distant. Command and

control was proving extremely difficult. It was clear that most of us came to the same conclusion - move forwards or die. I suppose it must have looked quite impressive from the enemy point of view. A wave of paratroopers moving relentlessly forward. It was in this dash forwards that Lance-Corporal Tighe received a severe gunshot wound to his upper arm and Private Gray subsequently lost his leg.[15]

Gray's shrapnel injury was horrific in that one leg was shredded from the knee down. He was a patrol medic who had been hit as he went to help Tighe.

Some time later Lance-Corporal Cole had staggered back to the gorse line, almost in tears as he reported to the medical officer that his best friend (Gray) was dying on the exposed slope. Captain Hughes knew he would have to send a medic forward. Lance-Corporal Bentley heard himself volunteering. His actions were to save Gray's life and gain himself the Military Medal. He went forward with Cole as a guide while Hughes got together a follow-up stretcher party under Captain Ford. Eventually they found both Tighe and Gray, who was in a desperate condition:

The shell had blown about ten inches of his tibia clean away and shattered what was left of both legs ... obviously he had also lost a critical amount of blood. I applied a tourniquet just below the knee and whacked some morphine into one of his arms. I tried to dress what was left of his leg but the fibula [had] disintegrated. I concluded that there was no way we could move him quickly without dressing the wound without killing him. Someone down in Goose Green must have spotted me moving and a few rounds started to plop into the peat in our general area. I got out my Swiss army knife, I always keep one blade razor sharp ... 'Hang on Dave', then I severed what was left of his leg. He didn't scream, he just cringed into the crater.[16]

The stretcher party arrived and got Gray and Tighe back to the RAP under a hail of fire. The medical officer had great difficulty finding a vein to give Gray an infusion. He got him away on the next helicopter. A blood transfusion at Ajax Bay brought him miraculously back to life.

The Recce Platoon had not escaped unscathed either. Corporal Evans was hit in the lower back which bruised his kidneys; Private Crockford remained with him to dress his wounds. He lost all feeling and was paralysed from the waist down. Private Smith was wounded in the stomach. Evans later remembers watching his evacuation: 'I saw Corporal Raynor with a wheelbarrow pushing Smith back up the track. Smith had been hit in the stomach and Raynor doubled 200 metres pushing this wheelbarrow in full view of the enemy. He deserved a medal'.[17] The platoon's third casualty had been Private Russell.

By 12.30 pm C Company's two leading platoons were down at the foot of the slope near a footbridge that carried the main track to Goose Green over a stream estuary. The company had had one killed and eleven wounded in as many minutes, about 15 per cent of the troops who had crossed the gorse line. The frontal attack on the airfield had been checked some 600 metres short of its objective.

When Lieutenant Webster brought 10 Platoon along the beach to rejoin his company near the 50 foot hill he found:

a real sense of urgency. We were disarming prisoners, getting them to lie down, seeing to their wounded, getting ammo, grenades, etc. from their positions, and at the same time we could see the airfield and feeling that if we pressed on quickly we could finish this thing soonest. The OC gave quick orders. 10 Platoon were to [lead the] advance with all speed towards the right hand [northern] edge of the airfield and then sweep [on] towards Goose Green settlement.[18]

Keeble had come up on the radio to congratulate D Company on securing the Boca House position and telling Neame to head straight for Goose Green. Neame was able 'with some smugness' to inform his new commanding officer that he was already on the move. His assessment of the situation he faced was:

> We were clearly well forward of C Company, almost on the northern edge of the airfield, and faced with an enemy we could see running away before us. This included an officer (?) on a farm tractor with several soldiers attempting, but failing, to clamber aboard! The situation called for 'hot pursuit', and I do not believe anyone at this stage saw the slavish pursuit of H's original plan still as the only way forward. My personal view is that the plan went out of the window at Phase 3/4.[19]

Be that as it may this phase of the battle was to be characterized by confusion, poor communications, intermingling of sub-units and little evidence of tactical control at battalion level. If you draw a line on the map between D Company's starting point and its objective, Goose Green, the line runs through the centre of the airfield - C Company's objective. In the haste to keep snapping at the enemy's heels this potentially disastrous 'blue on blue' possibility was either ignored or overlooked. There was no disaster as C Company never reached their objective and D Company only sent one platoon up on to the airfield, the remainder keeping to a shallow valley to the north of the landing strip. Even so, both lines of advance eventually crossed in the tangled fight for the schoolhouse and flagpole position which are the subject of the following chapter.

Unaware that his route was going to converge with C Company's, Neame chose a line of advance that headed SE, following the shallow valley of the stream that ultimately became the schoolhouse estuary. He would pass north of the airfield and, to get to Goose Green, would need to turn south when he hit the main track about 600 metres north of the settlement. B Company were doing the wide sweep west and south of the airfield. The airfield, as such was not his objective, and he had received no instructions as to what route to take. Shortly after the company advanced so too did C Company. When the AA guns on the airfield opened up D Company found that by keeping to the valley they were in dead ground to the Argentine gunners. Neame kept going until the enemy minefield in the valley was encountered. It was poorly laid, with the mines mostly visible, but it slowed the pace, gradually pushing the leading platoon further to the left (north) so that they were virtually following the stream.

Prior to this, after going for about 500 metres, Neame had noticed what looked like a deserted enemy headquarters off to his right on or very near the airfield. It needed to be checked out so he ordered 10 Platoon to investigate. The other two platoons, with Barry (12 Platoon) in the lead, continued down the valley, watching with some anxiety as they saw C Company getting hammered on the hillside to their left front.

Webster had only two sections with him as the third, under Corporal Owen, had been left behind to assist the sergeant-major dealing with the prisoners. As he looked towards the (to him) right edge (north) of the airfield he could see several trenches or sangars. Webster was uncertain whether they were occupied; although nobody was firing at them they were well within range. He could see what appeared to be a command bunker with radio aerials and a small tent alongside it. 10 Platoon were about to become the first and only 2 Para sub-unit actually to attack on to the airfield. Webster's account well illustrates a number of the uncertainties and difficulties a platoon commander can encounter. Map 27 shows in outline how this small action developed.

As we moved down the hill towards the airfield (Platoon headquarters, Corporal Elliott, and

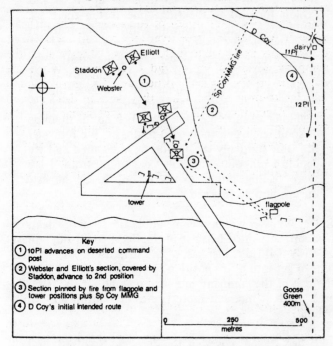

Key
1 10 Pl advances on deserted command post
2 Webster and Elliott's section, covered by Staddon, advance to 2nd position
3 Section pinned by fire from flagpole and tower positions plus Sp Coy MMG
4 D Coy's initial intended route

Corporal Staddon's sections) it became obvious that the command post was not occupied. But, more alarming, there seemed to be some activity on the ridge [airfield] and a lot of other small sangars at various points around the airfield. As yet no one was firing at us, but we were very much in the open and I think we all felt a bit exposed.

On reaching the first line of positions I decided that Corporal Staddon's section should take up fire positions before advancing further with Corporal Elliott's. Corporal Elliott's section and platoon headquarters moved towards the next line of positions about 100 metres further on. These positions also looked empty and I was planning to get Corporal Elliott's section into fire positions, thus

307

allowing Corporal Staddon to come up to us and exploit forward to the ridge line. From there we could sweep left and join up with the company on the outskirts of Goose Green.

Unfortunately, just as we neared the position we came under fire from the ridge. Initially it was not heavy, not as intensive as the previous night's contact, but enough to discourage us from a headlong assault. We took cover behind the mounds of spoil left when they tried to dig in. We returned fire, but suddenly the fire on us intensified and we couldn't pinpoint where it was coming from. I lay there feeling rather exposed and, to be honest, unsure how to proceed.[20]

In fact Webster had now come under fire from the flagpole position, so named because of the flag flying from a mast on the small ridge just east of the strip itself. Neame told him to get into a fire position, go no further, and wait as the rest of the company intended making for the flagpole area. At that moment more fire came pouring in - from behind.

I had taken cover with Privates Bradford and Lambird. The next thing was Bradford told me some fire was coming from behind us. I looked round and sure enough an arc of red tracer was coming at us. The guys all seemed to realize this at once and we climbed over the banking into the trenches. The fire around us seemed to intensify. Corporal Elliott, in the next trench, seemed to think an Oerlikon was also firing. I got on the radio to the OC to see if he could get the MGs to stop firing at us.

I remember at one point we took our berets out and waved them above our trenches, hoping to attract the attention of our Machine Gun Platoon. While we were doing this I felt rather stupid because it was like something you read about in the 2nd WW, surely not in today's modern army? As the

three of us cowered in our trench waving our berets
on the end of our rifles we saw what a stupid
situation we were in, and for some reason took a
fit of the giggles. In retrospect I guess our
situation was not only stupid but very alarming,
and it was as much fear as anything that inspired
the giggles! But, I can assure you, that is exactly
what happened.

Corporal Elliott suggested firing a 66mm at a
sort of 'tower' in the hope that it would create
smoke and provide us with cover to withdraw. I
cannot remember if the 66 misfired or missed but
either way the 'tower' remained intact.
Fortunately, throughout this incident no one was
killed or injured and therefore I can look back and
treat it with a sense of humour, but believe me if
one of my platoon had been killed by our own
MMGs I would have viewed the situation very
differently.[21]

Back on Darwin Hill the machine gunners had
eventually seen the waving berets through binoculars
and ceased firing. At about that time the Argentine's
fire also slackened, thus permitting Webster to regroup
and set off to rejoin his company. By the time he did so
the schoolhouse battle was over and his friend,
Lieutenant Barry, dead.

While C and D Companies converged on each other
from the north and west respectively, B Company
undertook its long looping move around the airfield. It
was a decidedly less eventful journey than the others,
but not entirely without incident. 6 Platoon had the task
of suppressing the Argentines on the airfield while 4 and
5 Platoons bypassed it to the west.[22] Chapman's job was
easily accomplished: 'The suppression of the airfield was
accurately done and there were many enemy scurrying
about. The enemy Oerlikons [in fact Rheinmetall guns]
were clearly visible and firing'.[23] The leading platoons
had some minor brushes with some Argentines as they

309

left their positions to head for the settlement. Many of the bunkers near the airfield and to its south were deserted. The company had rounded up over twenty prisoners by the time it halted as dusk approached only 400 metres from the SW of the settlement.

XII

ACTION FOR THE SCHOOLHOUSE

'The thing was to kill them as fast as we could. It was just whack, whack, and the more I knocked down the easier it became, the easier the feeling was. I was paying them back.'

Sergeant John Meredith DCM describing his reaction after his platoon commander, Lieutenant Barry, Corporal Sullivan and Lance-Corporal Smith were killed in trying to arrange an Argentine surrender. Max Arthur, *Above All Courage*.

The Argentine defensive line from the school on the east coast westwards across the airfield can be likened to a partially opened door, whose hinges were the school and the flagpole position. Behind the door was Goose Green. B Company's wide outflanking move in the west pushed the door further open and it slipped through the gap heading for the southern outskirts of the settlement. D Company gave the centre of the door a hard push with 10 Platoon at the airfield, but the bulk of the company got deflected towards the hinges. Part of C Company never got near the door (3 Platoon of A Company), part approached the door near the hinges but had not the strength to exert pressure (the Recce Platoon), while Patrols Platoon became involved in smashing through at one hinge (the school) with 11 Platoon of D Company.

Keeble had hoped that with the door opened there would be little resistance to hold it, that a quick kick would cause it to fly open. He could not know that more men had been sent forward to put their shoulders behind it, soldiers who were to hold it for another four hours until, with darkness, C and D Companies stopped pushing altogether, in fact pulled back despite having destroyed the hinges at both the school and flagpole positions.

The fighting for the school and the flagpole area was some of the most confused of the battle. Not only did different sections and different platoons become intermingled but the attack on the school was carried out by a mixture of ad hoc groups from two companies. Neither of the main groups carrying out the assault were initially aware that the other was to attack the same objective. They met by accident en route to the school. There was no overall coordination, no communications on the C Company net, so the success achieved was due to the initiative of D Company commander, junior leaders, and the unflagging determination of the Toms, who had now been marching or fighting non-stop for over twelve hours. This stage of the struggle was also to be marred by the surrender misunderstanding near the flagpole, which resulted in three unnecessary Para, and a number of Argentine, deaths. At the end of it all at last light both Goose Green and Darwin remained in Argentine hands.

Nobody wanting to force entry through a partially open door would intentionally do so by smashing the hinges which are obviously its strongest part. The school was never a specific objective of either C or D Company, yet both became involved in its destruction. It and the flagpole position were mutually supporting localities which defended Goose Green from an attack from the north down the line of the main track. C Company had been launched in a frontal advance to contact, aiming for the airfield. D Company's objective was Goose Green but it had been deflected along the outside of the door by the enemy AA fire and a minefield until it too ended up attacking the hinges with C Company. Because of the complexity of the moves they have been shown in simplified diagramatic form on Map 28.

After 10 Platoon had been despatched to the airfield the remaining two platoons continued SE with 11 Platoon in the lead followed by 12 Platoon. Neame's difficulty was that the route he was now compelled to follow pushed him further and further from the settlement. By shortly before 1.00 pm he was approaching a bridge that carried the Goose Green track over the head of a small estuary. Nearby was a dairy. D Company was then 1,000 metres north of its objective. There was still intense enemy fire from the airfield, both artillery and mortar.

Two positions in particular required immediate attention. First, there seemed to be a position of trenches and bunkers near a flagpole, just east of the airfield. It was on rising ground, a low ridge, and sat firmly across the track to Goose Green. Neame had to turn south (right) along this track if he was to get to the settlement. From this flagpole position he would be able to see his objective. From where he was he could not do so. Somehow the flagpole position must be secured. An immediate attack on it was prevented by the Argentine defences in and around the school. If Neame turned on to the track to advance towards the flagpole area his left flank would be exposed to the fire from the school only 300 metres away. His deduction: the school must be neutralized first. To do this he needed one platoon in a fire position while the other attacked. Barry was told to take 12 Platoon up the slope towards the flagpole and get into a position from which he could shoot up the school area and neutralize the flagpole position. Waddington's 11 Platoon would assault the school by moving along the stream bed or estuary. Neame has summarized his position at this stage:

> We were in a pretty uncomfortable situation. A lot of small arms fire was hitting us from the flagpole area as well as from the school. Then, even worse, the enemy guns seemed to locate us and the shelling became intense. We were cut off from the rest of the battalion by the long slope to our left which was being raked by the Argentine AA guns.[1]

It was the shellfire that shortly afterwards was to take the

Map 28

THE FIGHT FOR THE SCHOOL AND FLAGPOLE

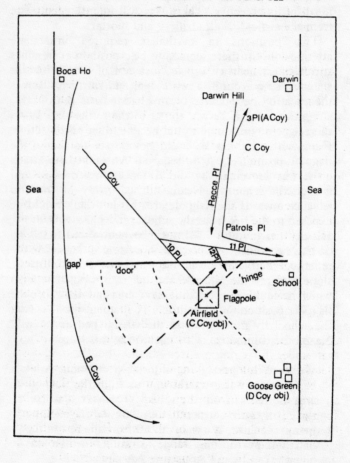

life of Private Dixon who was hit in the chest by shrapnel, dying in the arms of his platoon sergeant.[2] It was a traumatic moment, heightened by the impossibility of arranging a casevac. Just as Neame was getting ready to attack the school he got the news that 12 Platoon commander, Jim Barry, had been shot as he had gone forward to arrange a local surrender near the flagpole position.

It is doubtful if the exact circumstances of the 'surrender' incident will ever be completely established. There are three versions, two British and one Argentine, each given by participants or witnesses. Barry had taken his platoon up the track a short distance towards Goose Green. Looking up the hill, he saw what he thought to be a white cloth waving near the flagpole. Barry had deployed Corporal Barton's and Corporal Kinchen's sections to fire on the school while Corporal Sullivan's remained back in reserve. Barry resolved to take Sullivan's men up to accept the surrender. He told Sergeant Meredith what he intended to do. A message to this effect was sent to company headquarters. Neame was concerned that this was not a good time to accept any possible surrender with the school battle about to start and the still confused situation all round. Although he did not speak personally on the radio Neame told his operator that Barry must wait. On the battalion net he got Captain Adams to tell Tac 2 what was going on. Back at Boca House Neame had stressed the difficulties of taking surrenders, emphasizing that under no circumstances should the Paras expose themselves. While the taking of prisoners saved lives, and for this reason was preferable to a fight, he had also stressed the risks involved and the imperative need to be covered. It was also at about this time that the Support Company machine guns on Darwin Hill were firing indiscriminately at long range, causing 10 Platoon a mixture of anxiety and amusement on the airfield.

For some reason the order to wait never reached Barry. He started to walk towards the Argentines, with his runner, Private Godfrey, just behind him. Meredith yelled at the radio operator, Private Knight, to go with them, and for Corporal Sullivan to take his section up as well. Sullivan moved off with the words, 'He's going to get me killed'.[3]

The distance to be covered was less than 100 metres. As Barry approached up to five Argentines appeared holding their weapons above their heads as if to surrender. Barry and Knight continued forward with Godfrey following. As the distance narrowed Godfrey sensed danger, while Sullivan got his GPMG team, Privates Carter and Mountford, to take up a position to cover their platoon commander. Other enemy trenches could be seen to the right. Barry was now going forward to meet the Argentines face to face. Sullivan shouted up to Knight, 'What's he doing now?' 'I don't know. He must have gone mad,' replied Knight.[4]

While the Argentines still held up their weapons Barry was using his own rifle to demonstrate that the Argentines should put theirs down. The situation was viewed with horror by Knight and Godfrey. Both correctly anticipated the worst. Godfrey's account of the incident is informative.

> There was a group of three or four Argies with a white cloth wanting to surrender. They definitely wanted to pack it in, I've no doubt about this group. They were less than 100 metres from us, but the ground was open like a football field. They were up this slope by a fence with a gap in it. Mr Barry and his radio operator, Geordie Knight, were in the lead with myself a short distance behind, then came Corporal Sullivan's section in support. When we got to the top I saw there were more Argies in trenches nearby. The first group still seemed to want to give up, but I was worried about the others as they were not leaving their trenches.
>
> Mr Barry went right up to the fence, only a few feet from the Argies. I was about 20 feet behind him.

He started to demonstrate to the Argies that they were to surrender by putting down their weapons. He went through the motions of putting down his own. I reckon we were there only a matter of seconds, less than a minute, when this long burst of SF [sustained fire, meaning machine-gun fire] came cracking overhead from behind. Suddenly there were bullets everywhere. All the Argies opened up. Mr Barry was hit at point-blank range by the Argies in front of him.

I fell flat. There was fire from everywhere, I could see rounds striking the ground all round; a lot was coming from the trenches. I was in a bit of a state as the strap of my medical bag was wrapped round my neck. My rifle barrel was stuck in the dirt. A bullet went through my sling and another through the heel of my boot. After a bit I sort of sprinted sideways and dived into a rut made by tractor tyres. It was only a foot deep. Corporal Sullivan's section was firing. Knight was trying to get through on the radio and Brummie Mountford was firing his GPMG. The next thing I knew was Sergeant Meredith coming up with another machine gun. After that we seemed to get the better of the Argies and worked our way back up to where Mr Barry had been hit. Sergeant Meredith did a great job.[5]

The most likely source of the tracer that precipitated the shooting was a machine gun back on Darwin Hill, whose gunner had seen movement near the flagpole position, not knowing that Paras were there, and being unable to distinguish friend from foe at that distance. The Argentines' reaction had been immediate and lethal. They had opened up at point blank range, killing Barry instantly, whereupon the firing became general on both sides.

As Godfrey made his dash for the rut, Knight shot and killed two of the enemy who were skirmishing forward, and Private Carter fired coolly and continuously into the nearest trench. Knight then got on the radio to report, 'The boss is seriously injured or dead'. Corporal Kinchin yelled to Knight to stay where he was as he was bringing his section up to assist. Lance-Corporal Smith aimed his 66mm rocket, but as he did so he was shot at the moment of firing. The rocket exploded in a flash of flame on his back; he died instantly. In the general confusion Corporal Sullivan was also hit and killed while Private Shevill was badly wounded.[6]

Sergeant Meredith's version differs only slightly. According to him two Argentines came forward, unarmed, towards Barry. Another five or six stayed behind, sitting in cover. The two men had their hands in the air and one had a white handkerchief. As they came forward they pointed towards the battle that was now underway near the school, and were ducking as odd rounds came over. Barry is alleged to have told Knight to get a grip on company headquarters to stop the fire. He then went as if to lean his rifle against a fence. At that moment the long burst of machine-gun fire whipped near their heads. The Argentines to the rear and in the trenches nearby opened fire, cutting down Barry.

Meredith knew his platoon commander was down but was unaware he was dead. He now took charge of the situation and opened fire himself. He saw the injured Shevill crawling back and sent Private Wilson across to give assistance. Meredith directed rifle fire on to the trench near the flagpole on the right, but it was not heavy enough to suppress the enemy's response. He then took over a GPMG and opened up with long bursts on the bunker ahead and some Argentines who were lying in the open. Corporal Barton assisted with an M-79 grenade launcher. Gradually Meredith worked his way up the track to where Barry had fallen. He found him dead. The force of the bullets had spun him round and he was in a sitting position leaning against the fence. Meredith removed his map, radio and ammunition, but had to leave the body for the time being. At about this stage a large bunker of ammunition exploded nearby and Meredith was forced to pull back to reorganize.

The Argentine account, given several years later to Martin Middlebrook in Argentina when he was researching for his book *The Fight for the Malvinas*, gives a different slant on what may have gone on in the few moments when Barry conversed with his enemy. The Argentine officer in the area was 2nd Lieutenant Centurion who had been sent forward less than an hour earlier to stiffen the resistance in the area of the airfield and flagpole position. According to the Argentines three British soldiers had come forward, with weapons lowered, to talk. Centurion went up to speak with Barry. This was possible as he spoke good English, having lived for a time in Washington when his father was military attaché there.

Barry suggested that the Argentines surrender, which came as a shock to Centurion who thought the reason for the British approach had been for them to surrender. He had no intention of giving in, and he made this plain to Barry. He finished the brief conversation by telling Barry that he had two minutes to get back to his position before the Argentines opened fire again. As the three paratroopers started to withdraw a British machinegun fired, hitting several of Centurion's men. The Argentines returned fire, killing Barry and the other two soldiers as they were climbing over a wire fence.[7]

The incident is a classic example of how fraught with danger are surrenders taken in isolation in the heat of battle. There was no treachery; both sides agree to that. It was brought about by Barry's honourable misjudgement in exposing himself and his men before making absolutely certain everybody knew what was happening. His platoon was angry at the Argentines, but also angry with him. Meredith personally fired his GPMG with such effect not only to exact revenge for the loss of his officer, but because he felt helpless and frustrated at 'Barry for being so stupid', as it had so recently been impressed on them that Argentines surrendering must be the ones to expose themselves, not the Paras.

It was the third clear example in the battle of how difficult it is to coordinate medium machine-gun support if the guns are well over 1,000 metres to the rear. At this distance supporting fire should come from a flank, not overhead. The initial decision to centralize the heavy weapons had not worked at Goose Green where Support Company was out of the action for most of the time, and when it did catch up the ranges were excessive and plenty of friendly troops were between, and often close to, the gun's targets.

Major Neame had made a definite decision that the school area must be taken before D Company could make progress down the track towards the flagpole position and Goose Green. Accordingly, Waddington was sent to carry out an assault with 11 Platoon. This would involve the securing of a small FUP near the bridge and dairy before clearing several outbuildings which were located between Waddington and the school itself. C Company's involvement in the attack was more haphazard. In the event not less than three separate groups became involved in assaulting the school. All were to choose the same approach route, none were able properly to coordinate their efforts with the other two, and each ended up using its own initiative in partial ignorance of what others were doing. It was a most confusing episode. In the words of Captain Farrar, 'I suppose, being honest, the schoolhouse fight was a free for all.'[8] To establish who did what and when is not easy as the participants themselves are sometimes far from clear. But the struggle for the school is important in that it illustrates the chaotic nature of infantry fighting at close quarters, of how sub-units can become intermingled, and of how, in the absence of coordination at battalion level, junior leaders can still contribute to eventual success.

The three groups involved were: 11 Platoon of D Company, in particular 2nd Lieutenant Waddington and Corporal Harley's section; Sergeant-Major Greenhalgh with Corporal Graham plus eight men from Patrols Platoon; and Captain Farrar with another four men from his platoon including Corporal McNally. It should, however, be remembered that C Company platoons were now fighting as a rifle company, whereas their speciality was reconnaissance. Neither Recce nor Patrols Platoons were trained or organized to fight as rifle platoons. Map 29 shows the approximate moves of the platoons involved in the action. The experiences of each of the group commanders are described separately, but at the time they were happening alongside and simultaneously with the others. The battle for the school started around 1.00 pm and took place during approximately the same period of time during which 10 Platoon was fighting on the airfield, and Barry was killed near the flagpole position.

The common starting point for each group as it moved off towards the school was the bridge at the western end of the stream estuary. Nearby was a dairy. The ground channelled both C and D Companies to this area, which was in dead ground to the enemy and marked the start of a covered approach along the foreshore to within 100 metres of the building.

Waddington's platoon had already gone into action on the outbuildings west of the school when Neame received the news of the failed surrender incident with 12 Platoon. His company was now somewhat off balance with 10 Platoon still away on the airfield, 12 Platoon in some difficulty near the flagpole position, and 11 Platoon committed to an assault on the school. Neame admits he 'dithered a bit' before deciding that, on balance, his presence was required with 12 Platoon. The situation was complicated by the presence near the dairy of elements of the Recce Platoon who were having problems looking after several casualties. Neame considered this group needed assistance so he sent his second-in-command, Captain Adams, over to help. Then, leaving Waddington to continue his action, he headed SW to assess the situation there.

11 Platoon started its attack by firing four 66mm rockets at a shed west of the school; three missed. While others provided covering fire Corporals McAuley and Harley rushed the building, grenaded it and set it ablaze. No enemy came out. As the platoon moved on towards the next small building heavy shellfire came in on the edge of the stream. Waddington then led a group which included two GPMGs along the side of the inlet while the rest of his platoon took up a position from which they could shoot at the main school building. At the bottom of the inlet they met up briefly with Captain Farrar's and Sergeant-Major Greenhalgh's groups. There appeared to be enemy in the upper floor of the school, plus more in outbuildings to the east. There now occurred what might be called a spontaneous joint attack as Waddington's platoon, assisted by Patrols Platoon, assaulted the school from positions along the foreshore of the estuary, supported by fire poured in from GPMGs controlled by Corporal Harley, and by Corporal Bishop from the Patrols Platoon. In Waddington's group Private Francome threw a WP grenade into a room while his platoon commander blasted it with fire. Then Waddington hurled in another grenade which landed harmlessly inside the building. Removing the pin always helps.

The combined assault cleared the main building and set it alight with the enemy in it or nearby fleeing south towards the settlement. At about this stage the AA guns on the Goose Green peninsula started shelling the school with great accuracy. Several holes appeared in the roof and one shell passed clean through the building, narrowly missing Private Trick in the sergeant-major's group. This gunfire forced Waddington to take cover behind a tractor. From this position he observed several bunkers to the east of the school and resolved to attack them, not knowing that Farrar had cleared them earlier. Waddington and Francome went forward, but instantly came under heavy fire. Waddington dived for cover, straight into a pool of

322

Map 29

C AND D COMPANIES MERGE AGAINST SCHOOL AND FLAGPOLE POSITIONS

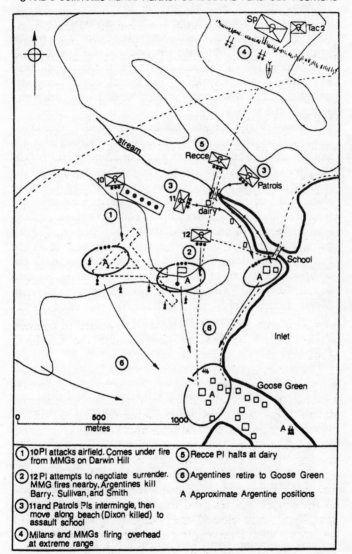

① 10 Pl attacks airfield. Comes under fire from MMGs on Darwin Hill

② 12 Pl attempts to negotiate surrender. MMG fires nearby. Argentines kill Barry, Sullivan, and Smith

③ 11 and Patrols Pls intermingle, then move along beach (Dixon killed) to assault school

④ Milans and MMGs firing overhead at extreme range

⑤ Recce Pl halts at dairy

⑥ Argentines retire to Goose Green

A Approximate Argentine positions

icy water where he remained pinned down for the next 15 minutes.

Eventually the cold became too much for him and he decided to dash back to the tractor. Under covering fire from Privates Francis and Stevens he made it to the vehicle unscathed but with his pockets and boots heavy with water. He then noticed that the tractor's fuel tank was leaking petrol, making its use as cover decidedly unhealthy. He withdrew his men back to the inlet and along to the track.

Sergeant-Major Greenhalgh had been with C Company headquarters when, like the rest of his company, he was caught on the open southern slope of Darwin Hill by the fusillade of fire that greeted the renewed advance. Like the rest, he dived for cover. He was about half way down the slope and had no idea that his company commander was wounded and the signaller killed. Yelling to those nearby, who happened to be mostly Patrols Platoon men, to keep going, Greenhalgh worked his way to the stream at the bottom of the slope. He was one of the first to reach the comparative safety of the re-entrant. Following his lead came Corporal Graham, Lance-Corporals Jackson, McHugh and Walsh, plus Privates Myers, Jones, Trick, Wheatley and Yourston. Apart from Lieutenant Kennedy, who arrived later, Greenhalgh was the senior representative of company headquarters to get that far forward.

Greenhalgh found himself the senior rank in the vicinity so he took command, moving left (east) to the bridge and dairy. The confused nature of events from then on comes through clearly in Greenhalgh's own words:

The Patrols Platoon was behind me. We had no support, no smoke, and when we reached the stream I turned left and stopped to organize my group and get all the 66mms (six) and two GPMGs up behind me. We headed towards the north-south Goose Green track. As we got there [near the bridge] we saw a platoon from D Company [11 Platoon] and they started to merge with us into our area. I got hold of the senior NCO and told him to hold his men there to give us covering fire. I moved my two GPMGs on to higher ground from where I could see the school, a tent, and a brick building about 100 metres beyond the school. On the right of the track [leading to the school] were two outbuildings which had not been neutralized. The Argies at the school were in trenches nearby, beyond the school, and to the south, as well as some in the building.

I got the guns [GPMGs] to cover left while the 66s destroyed the two outbuildings. As D Company was somewhere on the right I forgot about that and moved across the track and took out the outbuildings and tent with grenades. One GPMG fired at the AA guns, but there was no enemy in the buildings we attacked. At this stage I bumped into Corporal Harley [11 Platoon] with his gun group firing towards the school. I told Harley to cover us while we took the school.[9]

We then got back to the stream and moved in single file along its bed until we came level with the school. We advanced up from the stream to a hedge line in a slight dip in the ground, about 40 metres from the building. Then from somewhere on our left Captain Farrar appeared with about six men and joined us. I told everyone to give fire support while I and two men went to the outer walls of the school. We collected all the grenades before moving forward. It was an inverted L-shaped building, with one leg pointed north towards us with four or five windows. We lobbed L2s [fragmentation grenades] and WPs through the windows and raked the rooms with our SLRs, then grouped on the right side to decide what next. There was no fire coming from the school, although enemy mortar bombs were coming from the direction of Goose Green, but I was concerned about fire from our own troops, particularly our machine guns back on the gorse line.

We couldn't see Goose Green from where we were so I crawled up the ridge to have a look. We came under small arms and sniper fire and we couldn't move. I thought I had located them and I wanted to bring down artillery fire but although I had a signaller with me I couldn't raise company headquarters despite trying for at least 30 minutes. Eventually I got D Company and passed a fire mission for them to relay to battalion headquarters. D Company acknowledged. I could see what I thought was the enemy CP in Goose Green with radio aerials alongside a building only about 400-500 metres away. The artillery didn't fire because of the danger to civilians.

We were pinned down there for a long time with no contact with other troops. Eventually, as the light began to fade Captain Farrar and I decided to pull back.[10]

Farrar's story of this action gives an insight into the thinking of a platoon commander caught up in a muddled battle out of touch with his own headquarters.

WO2 Greenhalgh swept up the right-hand elements and led them forward. At one stage he was about 75-100 metres in front of me until I realized what was going on. Luckily, at the foot of the 'billiard table' was a re-entrant. This offered reasonable cover from fire. I think there was a shed [the dairy] hereabouts. From the re-entrant we had two choices, the track leading straight on towards the airstrip and thence to Goose Green, or to move half-left towards the schoolhouse. Diagramatically, I suppose it would have been as in the sketch.

When I had re-assessed the situation it became clear that WO2 Greenhalgh had already selected B, and was heading off towards the school. I led my group slightly lower down towards the foreshore, taking advantage of the dead ground. Either way we

MAJOR FARRAR'S SKETCH OF ATTACK ON SCHOOL

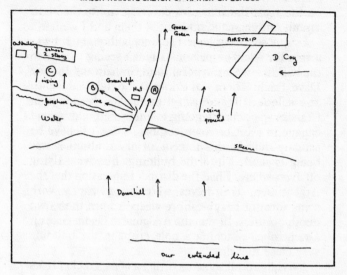

both arrived at about the same time at point C. As we crossed from the re-entrant towards the schoolhouse the enemy barrage continued, some from the school, some from elsewhere. It was at this stage that the Patrol Platoon sergeant, Eric Smith, was blown off his feet and smashed his knee on a boulder towards the shoreline. He was unable to take a further part in the campaign. He became the third Patrols Platoon casualty of the attack.

Somewhere along route B, quite near the hut, I passed what I believe was D Company headquarters sheltering in a small hollow. Captain Peter Adams, the company second-in-command, was definitely there [this was the elements of the Recce Platoon].[11]

The activity at C was confused. Somewhere in there was 2Lt Chris Waddington of D Company, along with a section commanded by Corporal Harley. Corporal Russ Bishop [Patrols Platoon],

327

using his initiative, had assembled all the LMG gunners, i.e. six from Patrols Platoon and moved up on the right flank to give covering fire to the close assault on the schoolhouse.

I suppose, being honest, the schoolhouse fight was a free for all. The persons I recall seeing closest to the building were Corporal John Graham and Private Dave Trick. There was a door at the right hand end, and it looked for an awful minute as though John Graham was actually going to enter the building and engage in a bit of room combat. I don't believe he actually did. At this stage a lot of ammunition was being expended into the building. Bits were flying off everywhere. I had the distinct impression that the Argentinians themselves were firing into it with some form of heavy-calibre weapon from their own depth positions [it was the AA guns at Goose Green]. I remember watching a hole erupt in the building very close to Trick.

I vividly recall someone firing a 66mm rocket from the prone position. The back blast went very close to my legs. White phosphorous grenades were used. The building was soon alight. The assault backed off, and I recall engaging fleeing enemy who ran off along the shoreline.

Meanwhile, my attention had been drawn to our left front where there was a school outbuilding and three enemy bunkers. These seemed to have escaped attention. Due to the narrow frontage at the schoolhouse itself I left WO2 Greenhalgh plus Chris Waddington to get on with that (I didn't order them, just left them to it), and took four soldiers back down on to the shoreline with a view to circling around to the outhouse and bunkers. The four were Corporal Bob McNally, Lance-Corporal Kev Sissons, Privates Ed Stokes and Mark Sleap.

We were able to crawl quite close to the outbuilding and then engage it with small arms and grenades. I can recall throwing my L2 grenade, but it was a blind - no, I definitely did **not** leave the pin in! We did not enter the building, but certainly flushed out the enemy who retreated around the coastline towards Goose Green. I was able to despatch at least one as they broke cover.[12]

Farrar then made his way back along the beach to join Greenhalgh's group on the foreshore just below the school.

After a brief discussion, the CSM and I decided to move up on to the high ground again, to the right of the burning schoolhouse, in order to establish a fire support base for D Company, whom we presumed would be attempting to advance along the main track towards Goose Green. During a momentary lull in the firing the 15 of us were able to move on to the crest line and belly crawl into two shallow Argentinian shell scrapes, which afforded an excellent view of the Goose Green settlement.

From this vantage point CSM Greenhalgh called for artillery fire on to the enemy positions around Goose Green [but did not get it], while I concentrated on organizing harassing fire down into the same area. I say harassing because I estimated that we were at least 600 if not 700 metres from the settlement. I had my sights on the 600 setting and even then was aiming high. I actually zeroed on to a window in the gable end of a house - firing until I broke it.[13]

Before long an enemy sniper was obviously tasked to neutralize these two shell scrapes and began to put down a constant and very accurate fire which effectively pinned us down completely. His rounds were literally skimming the grass between the two scrapes, extremely close indeed.

This stalemate continued for some two hours. We had lost all radio contact with everybody at this stage. Our initial attempt to direct artillery had petered out without causing any particular damage

— it was almost as though the gunners had a red box around Goose Green into which they were not allowed to fire — presumably because of the known civilian hostages.

Towards the end of the afternoon it became increasingly apparent that the temporary advantage gained by neutralizing and occupying the schoolhouse area would be to no avail. We were also at this time being subjected to mortar fire which was creeping steadily closer and beginning to shower us with earth and debris. Luckily the light was beginning to fade slightly so I decided to withdraw back into the re-entrant where I hoped to link up with other elements of 2 Para.[14]

The other platoon caught on the slope was the Recce Platoon. It went to ground and worked its way forward down the slope. Corporal Evans and Privates Smith and Russell were badly wounded. As the platoon sheltered briefly in a dip in the ground, Connor had only about fourteen men with him. When Lieutenant Kennedy, the company second-in-command, caught up with them they seemed uncertain what to do. Kennedy's account is of interest:

I decided to move forward to join the platoons. As I ran down the slope the fire opened again. I dived into a shell hole just as something exploded next to me. I felt the blast but was not hit. It was very exhilarating as the adrenalin flowed…. At the bottom of the slope, in dead ground, I was surprised to find the Recce Platoon in a group arguing. I told them to keep quiet and follow me. I led the platoon, with Colin Connor just behind me, around to the bridge.

The situation at the bridge was unclear; to the left (SE) I could hear the battle at the schoolhouse taking place; in front, about 150 metres towards the village, was a group of soldiers in cover. At first we thought they were the enemy, but soon realized they were ours. In fact they were Jim Barry's platoon from D Company. I said to Colin that we should move up the track to join D Company, and then beyond to our objective the airfield; Colin declined and said he was staying where he was. As far as I know the Recce Platoon spent the remainder of the battle in that spot. I took one of his sections [patrols] and moved forward.[15]

There was really no room for more men attacking the school and Connor's presence would have only added to the confusion there, on top of which he was having difficulties with his injured. He consolidated in the dairy and attempted to treat the wounded. Then Private Boland was badly hit by anti-aircraft fire. He was dragged into the dairy on a piece of metal plate. It took four men, including Captain Adams from D Company whom Neame had sent, to pull Boland into the building. There they stayed. Gradually other casualties began to arrive — Sergeant Smith with his injured knee and Private Davis of D Company hit in the shoulder. The renewed intensity and accuracy of the enemy fire forced Connor to evacuate the dairy, leaving the wounded inside, while the rest of the group sought cover nearby. Recce had been unable to contribute to the schoolhouse action. Kennedy's story continues after leaving the Recce Platoon:

The D Company platoon [12 Platoon] appeared to be in some disarray. ... I had a shouted conversation with the platoon sergeant who was sheltering behind a building; everyone was flat on the ground as there was a great deal of fire. He told me his platoon commander was dead, he was pinned down and had been ordered by his company commander to remain in position. I told him who I was and that I was taking some of his men with me up the hill.

The section on the track was commanded by Corporal Kinchin. I explained that I wanted to

331

capture the airfield that was at the top of the hill. We began skirmishing up the hill, firing at likely enemy positions. We were in two groups, I had Privates Slough and Sheepwash with me. Sheepwash had a GPMG. There was still a lot of fire. I wasn't sure where it was coming from or who it was aimed at, but we took advantage of every piece of cover as we moved up the hill along the track.

On top of the hill a large ammo dump was on fire. The ammo was exploding and flying in all directions. Half way up Corporal Kinchin said he had been ordered back by his company commander [Kennedy, from C Company had taken a D Company section]. I told Slough and Sheepwash [also both from D Company] that I was carrying on, they both agreed to stay with me. We moved past the exploding ammo dump and crawled towards a bunker on the top of the hill. We cleared the bunker but it was empty. Just before the bunker we had passed a pile of large, grey pods with inflammable stickers. I thought they were possibly fuel, but had a suspicion they were napalm. Fifty metres south of the bunker we were able to look through a gap and down into the village. The Argentinian flag was flying at the edge of the airfield about 100 metres away, and a couple of damaged Pucara aircraft [were] even closer.

A few troops were wandering around the village. The range was about 500 metres. I fired a few rounds from my rifle and they scattered. I decided not to use the GPMG into the village because of the civilians. A stream of soldiers was moving from the far side of the airfield into the village. At first I thought it might be our own troops, but then realized it was the enemy. They were in disarray and seemed to have dumped their weapons. I believe about 100 enemy crossed in front of us and presented an excellent target. I decided not to fire. I was to question myself on this decision many times later

and believed I should have opened fire. I am now
glad I didn't as it would have been a pointless waste
of life as the enemy surrendered the next morning
without any further fighting.[16]

By mid-afternoon the intensity of the fighting around the
school, flagpole and on the airfield had abated somewhat
as the Argentines pulled back into Goose Green, and the
Paras paused to catch their breath. The next series of
spectacular events were to occur in the sky.

At Stanley the urgency of providing Piaggi with more
air support was appreciated, but efforts to do so were
being frustrated by the weather, although three additional
Pucaras had been ferried in from the mainland. At about
2.00 pm two naval Aeromacchis had been launched to
attack and demoralize the British troops. Both pilots flew
over the isthmus but reported cloud cover down to ground
level, compelling their controller to order them back to
Stanley. Not long after their touchdown another combined
Aeromacchi and Pucara sortie was planned using two of
each type of aircraft.

Although the Pucaras took off earlier the faster naval
jets reached the battlefield first, shortly after 3.00 pm.
They approached from the south heading north, using the
Goose Green track and the burning ammunition dump and
school as guides. On the ground Major Neame, who had
been instructed by Keeble over the radio not to try to
exploit any further forward but rather to regroup into a
reverse slope defensive position, was expecting a Harrier
strike. He felt particularly vulnerable as he had grouped
his platoons together too tightly for comfort to avoid fire
from Goose Green on one side and the minefield on the
other:

In point of fact my company was strung out along
the main axis track presenting a perfect target from
the air. Then this aircraft roared over churning up
the ground with cannon fire. It was certainly no
Harrier. It was the only time in the battle that I was

really scared. I was sure I had really fucked things up, and I imagined massive casualties among my blokes.[17]

He later added: 'It was a miracle nobody was hit. It all seemed in slow motion, with the cannon shells stitching up the ground and coming straight at us. I felt that if I stuck my hand out it would have been knocked off.'[18]

Within the company everyone leapt for cover, firing up at the plane as it screamed overhead. Private Knight, 12 Platoon's radio operator, yelled at the wounded Shevill to get up and run. Earlier Shevill, with enormous guts, had crawled back down the slope from the action near the flagpole and had by now lost a great deal of blood. He had been given treatment and morphine. His trousers were at half-mast and two saline drips were in position in his backside. He got up to run clutching the drips in his rear and with his trousers round his thighs. Even in his dire circumstances he summoned up enough energy to leap over a fence. Shortly afterwards he lost consciousness and later could remember nothing of the incident.

On the gorse line Support Company had also been expecting a Harrier strike. Then, soon after 3.00 pm, two aircraft were seen approaching. Sergeant-Major Peatfield's account of what happened is slightly at variance with the official version which has one of the planes blasted from the sky with a well-aimed shot from a Blowpipe fired by Marine Strange from the Brigade Air Defence Troop.

We saw two specs in the distance coming from over Goose Green. This was great, marvellous, air support at last. The only trouble was they were coming from the wrong direction. The blokes, and the Royal Marines in the Blowpipe detachment, started cheering and waving. Then one aircraft peeled off and dived on us. The marine holding the Blowpipe tried to get it into his shoulder to aim but in the panic of the moment fired before he could do so. The missile soared up, missed the aircraft

334

completely but so scared the pilot that he swung to avoid it, and in so doing went straight into the deck. Meanwhile the back-blast from the Blowpipe hit the company clerk [Private Lukowiak] who ran around screaming he had been hit. In fact all he had was a bump on the back.[19]

The dead pilot was Sub-Lieutenant Miguel who died instantly when his aircraft smashed into the ground among 4 Platoon of B Company near Goose Green. Part of the plane hit Lance-Corporal Dunbar, removing two belts of ammunition clean out of his hands.

Ten minutes after the Aeromacchis the two slower Pucaras arrived. The section was led by First Lieutenant Micheloud, whose aircraft was loaded with napalm canisters; his wingman, Lieutenant Cruzado, was carrying rockets and incendiary bombs. They had been briefed to find and destroy the Para's mortars if at all possible. Micheloud has recounted his approach:

We came in over the sea from the NW against a headwind, hoping the wind would cover the sound of our approach. When I was within range I opened fire on the enemy's positions, which were shooting at us fiercely. I had to overfly them in order to drop my bombs; it seemed an endless run ... tracer ammunition coming from all directions. I released my bombs where I had previousiy picked my target. Feeling hits on my plane I came even lower. I made a slight turn to observe the impact of my bombs, and the smoke columns were a proof that they were no longer with me.[20]

Again D Company was at the receiving end on the low ground west of the track. The two large containers seemed to fall agonizingly slowly before exploding in a mass of flames within 50 metres of 10 Platoon. The heat was so intense that breathing was difficult as the napalm sucked the oxygen from the air. Corporal Owen remembers 'the heat on my face and hands. Somebody near me said to my platoon commander [Lieutenant Webster], 'They're using napalm, sir,' to which came the reply, 'What am I supposed to do?' Once more the company's luck held and nobody was injured.

Micheloud's plane had flown directly over Lieutenant Kennedy as he lay observing Goose Green from the rising ground just east of the flagpole position.

As we lay on the hill an enemy Pucara flew low over the village and directly towards us hugging the ground. I saw two large grey pods under the wings and decided it was napalm. The Pucara flew directly over us, very low. I could see the pilot's face. I could have shot him in the head. We could certainly have brought it down with the GPMG. Within seconds I regretted not doing so when he dropped the napalm on C and D Companies behind us. I was relieved to be told later that he missed; I certainly made the wrong decision.[21]

Cruzado's aircraft was greeted by a veritable storm of small arms fire. The Pucara was struck many times and its pilot quickly lost control. Unable to fly his plane Cruzado ejected immediately and floated gracefully down to become a prisoner of war, although not before some Toms had taken a few pot shots at him as he hung helplessly in the air. His pilotless Pucara described what Captain Farrar called 'a graceful arc' and impacted, like the Aeromacchi, among the unfortunate B Company. The aircraft cartwheeled, miraculously hitting nobody but showering many with aviation fuel.

Micheloud's Pucara was seriously damaged and, as he started his long flight home in the evening gloom with his engine warning lights flashing, he was convinced he would have to eject long before Stanley. Nevertheless with considerable skill and not a little luck Micheloud made it.

Finally, within moments of the Argentine aircrafts' departure or demise, three Harriers arrived. It was then nearly 3.30 pm with the light beginning to fade. Two were intending to drop CBUs while the third was primarily loaded with 2 inch rockets. The original request had been made by 2 Para shortly after two o'clock with the principal target the two 35mm Oerlikons on the peninsula west of Goose Green which had caused such grief to C Company and had systematically smashed the school. All available information had been passed to the pilots as to the best approach. Captain Arnold, acting as FAC, had given them the precise height at which to drop the CBUs for maximum effect. The AA guns were a difficult target because of their proximity to the settlement. If the pilot released his load either too soon or too late the bombs would fall uselessly into the sea. The aircraft had to approach over the water roughly north-south or south-north if the danger of hitting civilians in Goose Green was to be minimized.

The leading Harrier came in to drop its CBU into the sea — a miss, although the way the bomblets churned up the water over a wide area, as though a giant had thrown a fistful of gravel into the sea, was an impressive demonstration of the violence of these weapons. The second plane repeated the performance. Coming in from the NW it registered another miss into the water on the left of the target north of the point. The third attacked from a different direction — the NE — and scored at least partial success, with a number of shells striking the target area. Unfortunately the 35mm guns continued to fire.

Despite the apparent failure of the Harriers' sortie, they did, seemingly, have some shock effect on the Argentines. Afterwards civilians in the community hall spoke of continual screaming by some soldiers whilst under air attack. The third strike had caused casualties, and there is a strong belief within 2 Para that what the Argentines witnessed from the Harriers played an important part in persuading them take the surrender option the next morning.

XIII

THE ARGENTINES' SURRENDER

'Look we've done bloody well today. Okay, we've lost some lads; we've lost the CO. Now we've really got to show our mettle. It's not over yet, and we haven't got the place. We're about 1,000 metres from D Company; we're on our own and an enemy has landed to our south and there's a considerable force at Goose Green, so we could be in a fairly sticky position.'

Major John Crosland MC, briefing B Company shortly after dark on 28 May. Max Arthur, *Above All Courage*.

An accurate assessment or an exaggeration? A brief look at the companies shortly after last light would seem to reveal Crosland's remarks as almost spot on. Viewed from the perspective of 2 Para at the time the situation was still critical (see Map 30).

A Company was still on Darwin Hill near the gorse line alongside Tac 2. It was to remain there throughout the night. Darwin settlement was not to see paratroopers until the following day.

B Company had completed its sweep south and ended up only 400-500 metres from Goose Green, where an abandoned Argentine platoon position was occupied. Here they came under fire from the settlement and the promontary to its east. The platoons engaged the enemy with machine guns. Shortly after last light the company had an unpleasant shock. An Argentine Chinook helicopter, a Puma, and six Hueys were landing

Map 30

SITUATION DURING NIGHT 28TH–29TH MAY

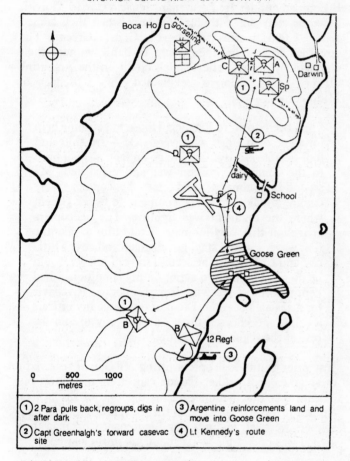

1. 2 Para pulls back, regroups, digs in after dark
2. Capt Greenhalgh's forward casevac site
3. Argentine reinforcements land and move into Goose Green
4. Lt Kennedy's route

reinforcements to the SW of their position.

There were about 100 men of the so-called strategic reserve, known as Task Group Solari, under the overall command of Captain Eduardo Corsiglia, an administrative officer on Piaggi's staff. These men were Piaggi's long-lost B Company under 1st Lieutenant Ignacio Gorriti. Gorriti, however, was not with his company when they landed some 1,000 metres south of Goose Green. The circumstances of his men going to battle without their commander do not reflect much credit on the Argentine officer corps. Gorriti explained his absence to Middlebrook:

I had been down to Estancia House to get some help for some men I had who were sick — frostbite and foot trouble mostly. I had to go on foot.... I got back to the company position wet and exhausted. My second-in-command told me helicopters were coming to take the whole company to Goose Green, where the regiment was fighting. The helicopters arrived at that very moment. I told him to take the first wave. I would stay, get changed and have a little rest and come in on the second wave. I knew I would be no good going into action in my condition. I had kept a bottle of red wine from Comodoro Rivadavia for a special occasion. I took it out, gave my officers a drink and cheered them on their way to join the rest of the regiment in battle.[1]

Just prior to the helicopters lifting off Gorriti received a message from Brigadier Parada cancelling the move, but despite a soldier hammering on the side of the nearest aircraft it was too late to stop them departing. Some forty soldiers were left behind. For Lieutenant Chapman their arrival was one of his worst moments in the battle:

The arrival of the enemy helicopters ... was a very frightening moment as I thought it might alter the course of the battle. I remember being with John

Crosland at the time and saying to him, 'What the fuck do we do now?' His reply was, 'It looks like Arnhem — day three'. I was scared because I thought there was likely to be a big Argentinian counter-attack on our position.... Contemporaneous with the arrival of the helicopters were some battalion casualty figures. These were wrong but I believed (from what source it came I do not know) that we had had seven officers killed. What worried me was the thought that if we had had seven officers killed we must have lost a whole load of soldiers. I thought at the time that we were the only coherent company left (probably a lack of passage of information here) and that was a frightening proposition.[2]

Lieutenant Weighell had been the first to notice these unwelcome arrivals and quickly called for an artillery fire mission. For once the guns were available and accurate and fifteen shells landed in the area of the disembarked troops, just too late to catch the helicopters which took off as they started to explode. But Crosland could not stay where he was, virtually sandwiched between the settlement and the enemy reinforcements, isolated so far from the rest of the battalion. He quickly called an 'O' group.

We were on our own some 1,000 metres from D Company who were to the north of Goose Green [D Company was in fact nearer 2,000 metres away]. A counter-attack force had possibly landed to our south. We were short of ammunition and had been fighting for nearly 16 hours. I gave orders to withdraw to the high ground in order to dominate Goose Green and also to block any counter-attack should it materialize. We searched old enemy positions and carried back some 7,000 rounds. Once on the hill we dug in as best we could [using bayonets, knives, and mess-tins as very few men had carried entrenching tools] and continued digging until 0200 [10.00 pm]. By now the company had been on its feet for over 36 hours and had fought for the majority of this period. Sleep and food had been minimal and in addition snow was falling. The cold was intense as we lay huddled together in an attempt to get some rest.[3]

If things seemed fairly grim from B Company's point of view a number of C Company officers were feeling pessimistic about the situation as well. Among them was Captain Farrar as he made his way back from observing Goose Green with Sergeant-Major Greenhalgh to try to find his company:

It has always puzzled me as to why the impetus of the attack seemed to fizzle out after the schoolhouse. In capturing the feature we were in an ideal position to support D Company in an advance against the settlement itself. In fact after I last saw Chris Waddington, Corporal Harley and [his] section at the schoolhouse I did not see any of D Company again that day.

You can imagine, therefore, that I felt somewhat dejected as we retraced our steps back over the gorse line to Darwin Hill, where A Company and battalion headquarters seemed to have gone firm. Until we met up with them I felt sure the attack had failed and we would in fact be going all the way back to Camilla Creek House and beyond .... On reaching battalion headquarters I was informed by Chris Keeble that Roger Jenner had been sent back to Ajax Bay to have his wounds dressed and that Peter Kennedy was 'missing — presumed killed.' That left me as OC C Company![4]

Gradually, C Company platoons came back to re-group near the gorse gully. The Recce Platoon had temporarily attached itself to D Company before it too was told to

342

withdraw back to Darwin Hill. With the company commander injured, no radio contact, and the platoons scattered with 1,200 metres between those at the school and the third (3 Platoon A Company) it was perhaps not surprising that they had received no orders for several hours.

It seems that Keeble may not have been strictly accurate when he told Farrar that Roger Jenner had been flown out. Jenner had gone for treatment at the RAP but had not been evacuated. Instead he returned to his company as it started to trickle back. He got it accounted for with the exception of Kennedy, then attended Keeble's 'O' group where he was again told to get himself flown out, then hid for the night. The next morning Keeble, somewhat peeved to see his company commander still at the gorse gully, made Jenner 'an offer I couldn't refuse', and at last he was evacuated to Ajax Bay.[5]

The company second-in-command was still unaccounted for. He had last been seen with two D Company soldiers up on the ridge overlooking Goose Green, not far from the flagpole. Kennedy and Private Slough had been able to get forward to within 25 metres of the Argentine howitzers on the very edge of the settlement. It was the closest anyone from 2 Para got to Goose Green during the battle. Their story is best told in Kennedy's own words:

> We were only about 800m away and looking down on to the target [Goose Green], so we had a spectacular view. The enemy gunline was behind a large shed at the edge of the village. We saw the smoke from the barrels over the top of the shed 500m away. I considered opening fire through the shed (which on reflection I should have done), or moving behind the shed and taking the guns out from close range. Night was not far away and I decided to wait before going down, the guns had just about ceased fire by this point.
>
> When it was dark I left Sheepwash on the hill

with the GPMG covering us. It was pitch black but we had lined up the GPMG with the shed in daylight. Leaving our webbing behind and taking only rifles and grenades, Slough and I moved down the hedgerow into the village. At the end of the hedgerow we were at the edge of the village and probably within 50m [the next day when he went into the settlement he realized he had been within 25 metres] of the guns. We stayed there for about five minutes looking and listening but without success; it was so dark I could only see Private Slough a metre away and there was no noise. We had no night sights except my rifle sight which was not designed to function in almost total darkness. I wasn't keen to hang about. I decided to return to Sheepwash and try to make our way back to the battalion.

After picking up Sheepwash we went to the flagpole and I cut down the Argentinian flag and stuffed it inside my windproof.[6] We moved cautiously down the track to the building where we had left the D Company platoon [12 Platoon], expecting a challenge or gunfire at any moment. There was no one in the area of the bridge where I had left the Recce Platoon. We saw some troops gathered around a fire about 100m to the west of the track [almost certainly D Company], but assumed they were enemy as our soldiers wouldn't do that! We then headed towards Darwin Hill and the gap in the gorse line that we had crossed earlier that day. As we approached the gap I whistled 'Ride of the Valkyries' [the Para's Regimental March] as recognition to avoid being shot .... There was no one about ... and I began to believe that the battalion had somehow been beaten back or had withdrawn. We spent the night huddled in a gorse bush and at first light headed north with Camilla Creek House in mind. We soon came across A Company and within minutes were re-united with C Company ....

Slough and Sheepwash were soon re-united with D Company. Slough was later tragically killed on Wireless Ridge.[7]

About an hour before dusk D Company had been told to regroup for the night. There was to be no further advance on the 28th. Neame gathered together his platoons into a defensive position west of the dairy. Corporal Owen's section from 10 Platoon, which had been left behind near Boca House to look after prisoners, was trying to find the company in the dark. On the track just north of the dairy Owen stumbled upon some of the C Company casualties awaiting evacuation, including Corporal Evans and Privates Boland and Smith. In desperation Owen fired a green very light to attract attention. He and Evans moved away from the spot just seconds before a shell landed where they had been.

D Company, like most of the others, was in for a miserable night. It was freezing, snowing, the Paras were utterly exhausted, hungry, without water, and seriously short of ammunition. Lack of entrenching tools hampered efforts to dig in. In 11 Platoon Lance-Corporal Sykes began to suffer from exposure. Two comrades had to cuddle close to him in an effort to provide some warmth. There were no sleeping bags and no spare clothing, although over in 12 Platoon good use was made of the captured pilot's parachute as a sleeping bag, while unbeknown to the company sergeant-major he had sat himself and his prisoners in the middle of a minefield.

After dark Neame was able to organize the recovery of the bodies of Barry, Sullivan and Smith. Later they were taken out by one of the two Snocats that had come forward with some ammunition. These cross-country vehicles had been hijacked by 2 Para back on Sussex Mountain and sent forward without the authority of brigade headquarters. They arrived just in time, and were a godsend for vital resupply and to take out some casualties. They had brought rations and water as well as ammunition, plus some thirty sleeping bags for the casualties. Food was distributed on the basis of one ration between two men in A and C Companies but there was little hope of getting any to B or D, the former being over 3,000 metres away.

Captain Hughes, at the gorse gully, had worked on getting 2 Para injured away on available lifts during the afternoon and had treated a large number of Argentine wounded. The worst was in need of urgent surgery.

The problems for all casualties on the Goose Green battlefield were identical — it usually took forever to get them out. As Hughes was later to say:

> We had a couple of problems. Dressings were not applied very efficiently, despite all the training. Most were ineffective at stopping the bleeding — all they did was to hide the wound from frightened eyes. If the cold weather had not helped to close down blood vessels we would have been in trouble. He added, 'Evacuation on the battlefield was bloody difficult. There were no proper stretches and very few men to move the wounded'.[8]

Just before last light Captain Greenhalgh undertook a particularly daring casevac flight to pick up C Company injured lying on the long forward (southern) slope of Darwin Hill. It was the only time a helicopter ventured so close to the enemy, exposed to direct fire, during the battle. Lance-Corporal Bentley was the medic who flew forward from the RAP with Greenhalgh.

> Doc said, 'Bill, I've got another job. Do you fancy a chopper ride?'... The Doc gave me a slip of paper with a grid reference on it. 'It's the lads from the schoolhouse; they've had some casualties and need help.' I went to the chopper ... and gave the paper to the jockey, Captain Greenhalgh. He checked his map and laughed. 'No way, that's in Goose Green, you've got it wrong.' 'Check with Tac HQ,' I said .... [Greenhalgh] spoke over the radio to Tac HQ,

then over the intercom to his co-jockey. They belted up tightly and took off — I was right. I was just a passenger in a box. There was nothing I could do except wait …. Lights to the right of us I thought, then it started to hit us. The jockeys didn't seem to notice, so I whacked them in the back and pointed to the gunfire flashes in Goose Green. I almost fell out of the bloody box as they dived in evasive action. It was like being in one of those fair-ground waltzers.[9]

Greenhalgh took his helicopter back over Darwin Hill and came in again slowly, hugging the ground. It was now dark and he was uncertain of exactly where to land. Bentley again:

One of the jockeys spotted a torch … so the jockey took us in to a close hover …. We had found what was left of our Patrols Platoon [the helicopter had landed about 150 metres north of the bridge and dairy]…. Someone helped me load one in each pod; we jammed three in the back …. The chopper was already overloaded, but Dave Smith was still waiting perched in a wheelbarrow, gut-shot, and boy was he moaning. The co-jockey must have had a moment of madness, he got out of his seat and we piled Smith in. The co-jockey straddled the pod and they tried to take off but the chopper just wouldn't climb.

Several of us on the ground lifted the runners up, and she was burning fuel, losing weight. Eventually, slowly, she started to climb. Half a dozen backs heaved and strained to lift the runners higher, up, ever so slowly up, and then at last she began to climb up and away …

That's when I realized no one had asked me if I wanted to walk back!
We used prisoners to carry a couple of our wounded on stretchers [Corporal Evans was one]. It was a weird sight, like some ancient funeral procession

347

followed by the few warriors still able to bear arms
.... This was my third night with almost no sleep,
hardly any food, and with continuous physical and
mental strain.[10]

In comparison with the B Company casualties with
Captain Wagon's medical team north of Boca House, the
other companies' wounded had received comparatively
prompt evacuation. Although one Gazelle had removed
several sitting casualties, by nightfall six more were still
in need of urgent evacuation. One was Captain Young and
the other a young Argentine prisoner. Part of the problem
was the fact that after dark the great majority of
helicopters could not fly. But even allowing for this 2 Para
did not seem to be getting much priority for the four
PNG-equipped Sea Kings. It was not for want of trying.
The brigade radio log records:

6.00 pm - From 2 Para 6 casualties outstanding....
6.40 pm — Casualty evacuation task accepted by
brigade. Should be in soon.
6.44 pm — From CO 2 Para. Victor callsign (Sea
King) must be on 60 minutes call as not all casualties
are in yet.
7.37 pm — From 2 Para. No helicopter has been
forward. 4 casualties suffering from cold.
7.50 pm — Report from 2 Para. A helicopter came
over and hovered for 15 minutes.
7.59 pm — Brigade report they have located the
helicopter (a Sea King) but were unable to get it in
again.
9.00 pm — From 2 Para: one of the wounded
casualties will not survive unless evacuated [Captain
Young]; also two enemy require evacuation.
9.12 pm — Brigade agree to one more run only.

It was Captain Greenhalgh who volunteered for the final
flight of the night. Captain Benest's account states:

John's helicopter approached Rory's [Wagon's] RAP and he used a green light to guide the helicopter in. John Young was evacuated, having been hit some fourteen hours earlier. The remainder of Rory's casualties were not so lucky. All that he and his medics could do was to sleep as close to the patients as possible to try and keep them warm. These patients were not evacuated until first light, some twenty hours after receiving their wounds.[11]

Just four minutes before 2.00 pm, with the stand-off after the schoolhouse battle just beginning, brigade headquarters was beginning to think 2 Para might not make it unassisted. The radio log states: '17.56 — Brigade Commander asks if reinforcements are required. No, but 2 Para will let him know if they are'. Just in case, J Company of 42 Commando was stood by to move, and then flown forward to Camilla Creek House where they arrived just before last light. Thompson was taking no chances; if more troops were needed they might be required in a hurry.

Meanwhile the brigade commander finally confirmed that 2 Para was to clear the enemy positions, hold on and not to withdraw unless so ordered by brigade headquarters. The question of whether 2 Para's attack was a raid or not was at last laid to rest. But Brigadier Thompson had other pressing problems on his mind apart from Goose Green. Mostly they involved logistics.

45 Commando and 3 Para had been pressing on with their 'yomp' east, and by last light the former were at Douglas and the latter closing on Teal Inlet, while D Squadron 22 SAS was now located close to Mount Kent. Both units were some 40 kilometres away from the BMA and had been without a ration resupply for 36 hours. Thompson wanted to open up a forward supply base at Teal Inlet as quickly as possible, and he was worried that, with his units so far east, the Argentines could react with a counter-stroke which would catch his brigade off balance and without artillery support forward. The solution lay in

off-loading supplies, moving stocks by sea to Teal Inlet, and flying guns, ammunition and troops forward immediately.

On the evening of 28 May Thompson's position was far from favourable. 2 Para had not yet secured its final objective, indeed the Argentines there had been reinforced so there was no guarantee they would capitulate the next day. They might even mount a counter-attack. Should they do so the move towards Stanley, which was his priority, could be in jeopardy. His logistic conference that night highlighted:

> grave shortcomings in the stock situation at the Brigade Maintenance Area; only eighty-three rounds for each 105mm light gun; a total of thirty Milan missiles for the whole Brigade; no one-man ration packs; two days' supply of ten-man packs — totally unsuitable for carriage by marching troops; no hexamine for cooking ... no spare clothing; three days worth of medical stocks.[12]

The difficulty was in getting the stores off the ships. Because of the Argentine Air Force, to concentrate the supply ships in the anchorage by day was impossible. Off-loading had to be done at night, which was much slower as the number of Sea Kings able to operate in the dark was so few. All the ships had to leave before first light in order to get as far east as possible before daylight. As Thompson says, 'It was a race against time, to get as much off the ships as possible before they weighed anchor.'[13] The combination of these factors, coupled with the demands of 2 Para's battle and the march east, meant that ships often left San Carlos Water with much of their urgently needed cargo still onboard. Lieutenant-Colonel Hellberg, the commanding officer of the Commando Logistic Regiment responsible for solving these problems, has described the situation as 'a nightmare.'[14]

Huddled in the falling snow, trying to seek some warmth from the burning gorse, Keeble too was facing a potentially dangerous situation. On the credit side was the fact that 2 Para had achieved everything asked of it except the securing of Darwin and Goose Green. The settlements were now surrounded. Set against this was a long list of debits. The companies were exhausted, hungry, miserably cold, low on water and ammunition, and had suffered sixteen dead and thirty-one wounded – one and a half platoons out of eleven. His command was scattered, with B Company over 3,000 metres away to the south, and the Argentines had been reinforced by a full company. These extra troops had slipped through into Goose Green in the darkness, and Keeble's concern was that they might be used offensively, or would at least stiffen Piaggi's resolve to continue the fight next morning.

Major Keeble had seen the C Company advance come unstuck in the face of the AA gunfire; he had seen the school taken, but had felt unable to coordinate any further advance in the remaining hours of daylight; he had seen the Harrier strike miss its target. Then another Argentine company had arrived. Clearly the night must be spent resting and refurbishing, but what was to happen come daylight on the 29th?

Shortly before last light Keeble held an 'O' group. Of the company commanders both Crosland and Neame were unavoidably absent. He outlined his thoughts for the next day. He would go for a surrender, persuade the Argentines they were in a no win situation, and back it up if necessary with a massive firepower demonstration. If all this failed, the only option would be to flatten Goose Green and then assault it. To do these things he needed fresh troops and a lot more artillery and air support. He spoke to Thompson on the radio, putting his proposals and requesting reinforcements and the additional firepower. The brigade commander 'also agreed that Goose Green could be destroyed, if necessary, should the Argentines not surrender in the morning.'[15] J Company of 42 Commando was alerted to move down to join 2 Para at first light.

The idea of getting the enemy to surrender was

decidedly the best option; but would they? The Argentines still had a fairly strong hand with their reinforcements and 114 civilians — potential hostages with which to bargain with the British. How could the British go ahead, in any circumstances, and pound Goose Green to pieces, thereby probably killing many of the people they had come to liberate? It was really unthinkable, and certainly not a decision for Major Keeble to take. The problem, however, would only arise if Piaggi refused to surrender. He must be induced to do so. At the very least he must release the civilians before renewing the battle in accordance with the 'rules of war'. Keeble talked through the options and ways and means with Major Gullan, one or two company commanders, and Robert Fox, the BBC representative.

The initial plan was to use Patrols Platoon to escort some prisoners to both Darwin, which had still not been formally occupied, and Goose Green. Captain Farrar was approached by Keeble:

Chris Keeble came to me with words something like, 'I want you and your patrol, and your very best other patrol, to stand by for an extremely important mission …. I cannot stress how important it will be'. He then went on to tell me of his plan.

At that time the idea was for each patrol to be given an Argentinian PoW. These PoWs were to be 'armed' with a white flag and then escorted by the patrol through the British lines to the edge of Goose Green (in my case), and Darwin (in the case of Lance-Corporal Dick Walshe). We were told that the PoWs would have been briefed to then move into the settlements under the white flag. We were to wait one hour for them to return. The PoWs had been given the 'Keeble ultimatum'. If they did not return within the hour we were to withdraw and assume the battle was to continue. If, on the other hand, the ultimatum was accepted then we would escort the PoWs back to battalion headquarters to learn the response.

I will confess that I was a little uneasy at the prospect not only of negotiating our lines, but also of sitting in 'no-man's-land' at the edge of Goose Green for one hour!

Chris Keeble said that the above was his outline plan, and that all I should do in the interim was prepare two white flags. I asked Walshe to do this and waited for confirmatory orders.

The orders never came and we spent a very cold and sleepless night (our fourth in a row) ... ambush night, Camilla Creek House, start lines, and now after the battle[16].

A better way of alerting the Argentines to accept a flag of truce had been discovered. Keeble had again spoken to the brigade commander concerning the offer of surrender terms. Thompson had accepted that they should agree the terms or be destroyed. He also consented that, as a final resort to convince them, it might be necessary to lay on a fire-power demonstration. This would involve a Harrier strike, artillery barrage and a bombardment by all eight mortars sufficiently close to the settlement to impress the Argentines that surrender was their best option. Whether or not the target area selected − over 3,000 metres away across Choiseul Sound − would have been sufficiently close to impress the audience was not put to the test. Thompson undertook to organize the aircraft and fly the remainder of 8 Battery, plus plenty of shells, to join the section at Camilla Creek House. These guns and aircraft would also be essential if, in the worst case, 2 Para had to attack again. He also undertook to get a radio message to the Argentines in Goose Green that a flag of truce party would approach them shortly after dawn.

This was achieved by use of a short-wave radio link between Mr Alan Miller, the manager at Port San Carlos, and Mr Eric Goss, the Goose Green farm manager. By this means the message was conveyed to Piaggi. He agreed to receive the delegation. Patrols Platoon was not needed.

During the night two captured Argentine senior NCOs were selected to convey the ultimatum to their commanders in Goose Green. The terms had to be thrashed out, written down in Spanish, and explained to the two prisoners. Robert Fox has recorded a glimpse of this process:

> I recall passing by a huddle of officers beside the gorse bushes, still blazing and throwing shadows across the men's faces. In the middle of the circle were two Argentinians. I heard Chris Keeble say slowly, 'I am Catholic. You are all Catholics. We are all Christians. I do not believe in killing unnecessarily. I have many many men here and we will fight again at daybreak.' There was a pause as Captain Rod Bell translated. Chris Keeble resumed, 'I have many paratroopers here. Do you know what a paratrooper is?[17] There was a hitch in the translation and the explanation began again: 'You know red berets. There are many of these men here. They are the finest fighting soldiers in the world.'

The real worry was whether they would release the civilians or use them as hostages. Fox, who knew something of the Italian character and that a high proportion of Argentines had Italian connections, stressed to Keeble that in his view there was a good chance of their agreeing to surrender if they could also preserve their honour. A face-saving ceremony might be the answer rather than dire threats. If they were allowed a formal parade with their officers in command of their men, a ceremony of saluting and the senior officer handing over his sidearm to Keeble, this would seem to show to the watching world that the Argentines had fought well and honourably, that their military dignity was still intact. It was agreed that this approach would be tried.

Eventually, a simple ultimatum was drawn up that the

prisoners would take to Goose Green. If the Argentine NCOs returned still carrying the white flag by 8.30 am it would signify a surrender had been accepted in principle; if they came without the flag it meant the battle was still on. In either event Keeble underlined that responsibility for the safety of civilians rested entirely with the Argentines. The full ultimatum is at Appendix 4. Shortly after daylight both prisoners set off.

Keeble was in no hurry. In fact he needed time in order to regroup, for J Company to join him, for the extra guns to be positioned, the remaining six mortars to be flown forward, and for ammunition to be replenished. It was possible the enemy might use the offer to ambush 2 Para's commander, or would be reluctant to give up their hostages. The possibility of further talks for clarification being necessary was very real. It might also be necessary to lay on the firepower demonstration. There were many uncertainties even if the Argentines seemed willing to give in.

From first light the brigade commander was standing by with his tactical command group to fly forward himself if necessary. He was in constant touch via Major Gullan, and had asked him if he thought his (the brigadier's) presence was required. The answer was no, Keeble had the situation well in hand.

Also at this time the lift of the three additional guns to Camilla Creek House began. So few helicopters were available that it was nearly 2 o'clock in the afternoon before the battery was ready in all respects to open fire. Seven hours to move three guns and restock ammunition. Another example of how critically restricted Thompson was by transport shortages.

Well before the deadline the Argentine NCOs had returned carrying the white flag. Their commanders had agreed to meet a British delegation near the airfield to discuss a surrender. Keeble assembled his group. He would take Major Gullan, Major Rice, Captain Bell, the interpreter, and Corporal Shaw, his signaller, plus his media men − Robert Fox and David Norris of the *Daily*

355

Mail who had both shared all the discomforts and dangers of the battle with 2 Para. All seven were to look as unwarlike as possible — no weapons, no helmets, no equipment, not even belts with pouches. D Company was moved up closer to the airfield as a precaution but had to remain out of sight.

The press and television film crews with the Task Force would have dearly liked to get in on the surrender. An Argentine surrender on tape and film would have been a scoop worth having, but although they may have got wind of what was going to happen only Fox and Norris were allowed anywhere near Goose Green. Not only was this an appropriate reward for them for what they had been through with 2 Para, but Keeble and the others rightly felt that putting the media spotlight on a surrender ceremony would be humiliating for the Argentines, and might easily jeopardize the proceedings. The event was to confirm this reasoning as, at the first meeting, Vice-Commodore Pedroza was unhappy when Fox and Norris were introduced, and insisted that Fox should not use his small cassette recorder.

Nevertheless, a television news crew did get as far forward as the gorse gully later that morning. They, including ITN representatives, had arrived at Camilla Creek House, where they were informed that if they wanted to get further forward they could walk. Several managed to hitch a lift on a casevac helicopter. On arrival they began to take a morbid interest in filming 2 Para's dead who had been collected together and were lying in a row nearby. Captain Hughes, the Medical Officer, was furious and, 'sent Bill [Bentley] to see them off'. It was a job that Bentley relished.

> Back down the hill a group of reporters had come in the choppers. They were running around like vultures filming, photographing, recording everything. Some shiny-arsed officers (brigade staff officers etc) had come forward now that it was safe, probably so they could tell their grandchildren how

they'd won the battle of Goose Green. They congratulated us and kept saying important things like 'Splendid effort, splendid'. A reporter asked the Doc ever so concernedly, 'And where are your dead, doctor?' The Doc pointed out a line of bodies wrapped in ponchos. We watched the reporters rush down and start to unwrap our dead. ... Doc said 'Stop them Basha! STOP THEM'. I trotted down and said loudly 'Eh!' I had their attention. 'If you touch them again, or take one fucking picture, you'll be lying there next to them in one second.' I brought my SLR up to cover them; and they looked straight into my eyes and believed me. Suddenly finding something else very interesting they hurried away.[18]

Although 2 Para had been unable to clinch the victory by dark on the 28th, from Piaggi's point of view there seemed little point in continuing the battle on the 29th. Despite the fact that he had been reinforced, both he and Pedroza felt that as they were now surrounded there was little point in inviting complete destruction. At no stage did they consider using the civilians as hostages. They were completely cut off by (they believed) a superior force and the arrival of the white flag gave them an honourable alternative. Contact was made with Menendez in Stanley. He later explained that the decision on whether to surrender or not was to be made by the commanders at Goose Green. 'That night, when we discussed the possible courses of action with the commanding officer at Goose Green, he was authorized to surrender whenever he thought it necessary. There was not really much point in continuing resistance against an enemy who was far stronger and had him completely surrounded.'[19] What was particularly galling was the fact that 29 May was the Argentine Army's National Day.

As Vice-Commodore Pedroza was the senior officer present he would have formally to surrender first with the Air Force contingent, followed by Piaggi with the Army units. It was these two officers, plus the Coast Guard

Officer, Lieutenant Canevari Gopevich, who spoke halting English, who would go to the airfield to meet the British to discuss arrangements. They arrived at the small corrugated iron hut before the time set.

Keeble and his party had a long walk of some 1,500 metres to the meeting point. Keeping to the track to avoid the minefield they felt decidedly naked as they moved down the slope on which C Company had been caught the previous afternoon. Thoughts turned to how easy it would be for the Argentines to shoot them all as they came closer. The weather was appalling, lashing rain that turned to hail. By 9.30 they were approaching the airfield and spotted a white flag flying over a hut. The three Argentine officers came out. Handshakes were exchanged and the talking began inside the shed.

The Coast Guard officer, Gopevich, who had been the captain of the *Rio Iquaz*, introduced his two senior officers. Fox has described him as having 'a heavy black moustache through which he grinned continuously with a gap-toothed, Bugs Bunny expression'.[20] Bell introduced the British delegation which prompted Pedroza to make it clear that nothing should be recorded when he understood two press representatives were present.

Keeble then spoke. He emphasized his concern that no harm must come to the civilians in the settlement, and that although the Argentines had fought long and hard they now had no sensible option except an honourable surrender. To continue would be to waste lives. Whatever happened – a surrender or renewed fighting – Keeble insisted on a guarantee for the safety of the civilians. Pedroza replied that the fate of the garrison and the civilians could not be separated. Then, to the great relief of the British, he added that no hostages would be held and that civilian lives were not endangered. According to Fox:

The Air Force commander was looking for an escape route of surrender with honour; his whole feline approach to the discussions was that of a military politician. I realized that we had to sell him the idea that he had given up with great dignity, which would be respected by his fellow officers in Argentina, and that he had fought against terrible odds.[21]

Piaggi wanted more time to consult Stanley but Gullan interjected that this would not be allowed unless a British officer was present to hear the conversation. This could not be agreed. Considerable time was spent thrashing out details such as the housing of prisoners after a surrender. The Argentines wanted immediate repatriation. Keeble promised this would be done as soon as practical. Minefields were a sticking point. Keeble needed to know their exact location and insisted on technical assistance on how to lift them. He was horrified to learn that the Argentines had not the faintest idea. They had been strewn around various areas by a corporal as he saw fit. All Keeble could do was to demand that the NCO was made available after the surrender.

Eventually the procedure to effect the capitulation was agreed. The Argentine officers returned to Goose Green while the British stood around shivering, anxious that there would be no last-minute hitches, particularly no trigger-happy soldier. A shot at this tense time could ruin everything.

After some 30 minutes troops were seen assembling near the settlement's church. They were marched up to form a hollow square in a nearby field. The officer in command was Pedroza, the 250 or so troops his Air Force personnel. He harangued the parade. His men then sang their national anthem. Fox thought it sounded 'like a dirge, then the chant of a doleful football crowd'. Arms were grounded. Pedroza turned, stepped up in front of Keeble, saluted and handed over his pistol and belt, saluted again and walked away. He was later flown to San Carlos where Thompson took him formally into custody. Pedroza, who spoke perfect English, told his captor that he had enjoyed visiting England. When

Thompson responded that he would like to visit Argentina. Pedroza said, 'You are here already'.[22]

Next, Piaggi marched up the Army garrison. To the watching 2 Para officers and soldiers it was a staggering spectacle. The column seemed endless as more and more men poured from the houses and sheds. There were too many to count accurately, but not less than 800 troops finally assembled in front of Keeble. Weapons were grounded and the soldiers dispersed back to the settlement to collect their belongings before going into captivity. This was later accepted as an error as it was during this period that considerable looting, smashing and defiling of property took place. June McMullen was (like Sergeant Norman) disgusted with what she saw when she got back to her home.

> It was a terrible mess. They had pulled things out of cupboards and drawers, just scattered them all over the place and walked all over them. They hadn't used the toilet − they had gone on the beds, on the floor, in the bath, everywhere ... I was very depressed with what they had done. It was pretty sickening. But the troops helped us clear it all up.[23]

But even this disgraceful behaviour could not spoil the moment of liberty; the Union flag was raised over the settlement; the Paras received a wonderful welcome.[24] June McMullen again:

> One fellow, a paratrooper, asked if he could have his photograph taken with baby Matthew. I think when they saw little Matthew that's when they thought it had all been worthwhile. They could see then what they had been fighting for. One Para, only a young fellow, gave Matthew his capbadge.[25]

POSTSCRIPT

'It is not the number of soldiers, but their will to
win which decides battles.'
Lord Moran, *The Anatomy of Courage.*

2 Para's victory at Goose Green was outstanding, even
unique. It is difficult to find in modern military history a
similar story of a single, isolated infantry battalion fighting
its way forward over seven kilometres, against a series of
in-depth defensive positions. This is precisely what 2 Para
had to do.

In the event just about everything seemed set against
these paratroopers. Most were physically tired and hungry
at the start; it was to be a frontal attack through a series
of enemy positions, with the final objectives seven
kilometres away; the timings proved wildly optimistic
with the result that 75 per cent of the action was fought
in daylight on bare, undulating terrain; the enemy had the
advantage of prepared positions; ammunition resupply
was at best ad hoc, at worst non-existent; casualties had
often to lie where they fell for hours. The battalion
succeeded despite meagre and frequently inaccurate
artillery support; despite dreadful weather conditions that
prevented any air support until the fighting was over;
despite the fact that the naval gunfire upon which so much
reliance was placed failed at the outset; despite its own
heavier supporting weapons either being left behind (six
mortars), or not being able to bring effective direct fire to
bear until two- thirds of the way through the battle; and
despite the death of the commanding officer at a critical

juncture. In other words it was a triumph for the riflemen and junior leaders.

It is hardly an exaggeration to say that Goose Green was fought and won by the rifle sections and platoons of A, B, C and D Companies. The rest of the battalion, Support Company, and the supporting arms, even battalion headquarters, played their part as best they could but their influence in the final result of the combat was marginal. It is very doubtful if any battalion will ever be asked to carry out an operation like this in similar circumstances again. The victory was a complete vindication of the Parachute Regiment's training, toughness, aggressive spirit and junior leadership cadre (both officer and NCO). Having said all this, it is important to clarify some misconceptions, to discuss some myths perhaps, about Goose Green. Firstly, it was not a victory against heavy odds in the numerical sense as many accounts would have us believe. If the number of Argentines, including the Air Force, Coast Guard and administrative personnel, who surrendered are added to those already killed, wounded or captured a total in excess of 1,300 is reached. But only a fraction of these fought, many did not fire a shot, remaining hidden in Goose Green. Added to this was the platoon of forty at the southern end of the isthmus that never participated in any capacity. At most four rifle companies, probably nearer three, fought against 2 Para's three and a half (C Company was only fifty-five strong). About 400-plus paratroopers assaulted a series of positions defended by roughly the same number of Argentines.

Then there is the question of reinforcements either before, during or after the battle. After the BBC's warning to the world that Goose Green was about to be attacked the Argentines did not reinforce their garrison. This has been said earlier but it bears repeating as it is a longstanding myth. At the start of the battle Piaggi had lost sixty men to the 'Fanning Head Mob'; he did not get them back until about midday on the 28th, after the Darwin Hill-Boca House positions had been lost to him. Strictly speaking Estoban's return can be counted as a reinforcement, but it can also be argued that his arrival merely brought the Argentine strength back to what it was before the battle. There can be no dispute that both sides reinforced *after* the battle. At long last B Company 12 Regiment arrived just after dark, and 2 Para got a company of Royal Marines at first light on the 29th. In neither case did they play any part in the outcome.

The claims that 2 Para killed 250 Argentines during the battle appear highly exaggerated. The official roll of honour produced much later by the Argentines, of which I have seen a copy, records a total of fifty-five killed at Goose Green. This specified the 12th Regiment-32; C Company 25th Regiment (Estoban)-13; the platoon from the 8th Regiment (Aliaga)-5; the Air Force -4; the Navy-1. Of these three were officers − Estevez, and two pilots (one shot down, the other killed by the Harrier attack). The Argentine figure for the wounded is something under 100. 2 Para may dispute these figures but I can see no reason why the Argentines should deliberately exclude so many names from their roll of honour.

2 Para lost sixteen dead during the battle. Two others died at Goose Green, Lieutenant Nunn RM, and Corporal Melia RE, making the British deaths almost exactly one-third of the Argentines. Fifty per cent of 2 Para's killed belonged to D Company which is perhaps not surprising as they were in action on four separate occasions — during the night advance, in the latter stages of the Boca House battle, on the airfield and in the fight for the flagpole position and schoolhouse. Ironically it was to be D Company which bore the brunt at Wireless Ridge as well. Here they faced the only Argentine counter-attack, and of the three 2 Para dead in that battle two were from this company.

Some accounts have seemed to imply that there was a monumental intelligence failure on the part of the British in assessing the Argentine strength at Goose Green before the battle. They imply that, had it been known they were so strong, 2 Para would never have been sent alone with so little support to attack them. This version is inaccurate.

While it is true that up to the 27th all intelligence sources appeared to indicate that the enemy would quickly crumble if hit hard, and that at one stage the Argentines' strategic reserve was thought to be on the isthmus, by the time 2 Para crossed its start lines, a reasonable picture of the enemy was available. Colonel 'H' knew he would be attacking a force of 3-4 rifle companies with Air Force and some other support. Thanks to the detailed reporting of the Recce Platoon on the 27th, he also had a fair idea where many of them were located. His knowledge was, of course, imperfect (a company on Coronation Point for example) but in war a battalion commander could hardly expect to know much more about his enemy's positions than Colonel 'H' did. Coronation Point excepted, 2 Para's estimates of Argentine strengths and locations were not that different from reality. Although the numerical odds were never stacked against 2 Para, almost every other factor was – terrain, time, distance, weather, inability to manoeuvre, available support and the virtual impossibility of achieving surprise.

Goose Green was not won as a result of any tactical brilliance; there was no decisive manoeuvre that clinched the victory. Those who claim that D Company's move along the beach past Boca House outflanked the Argentines' main line of defence and brought about the collapse in that area have, I believe, misread the situation at that stage. When D Company advanced they did so to accept a surrender, a surrender that had been brought about by the devastating effects of direct-fire weapons, particularly the Milan which had at last been brought into action, albeit in an unusual role. The immediate follow up by B, C and D Companies was the obvious course to adopt at the time, as all indications were that the Argentines were on the verge of collapse. This advance came unstuck on the open southern slope of Darwin Hill, and 2 Para was unable to press forward after securing the school. Come the night of the 28th/29th most in 2 Para were far from convinced the fighting was over.

There remains the action of Colonel 'H' in the

re-entrant west of the gorse gully. Did his death tip the balance in 2 Para's favour as many have claimed? Most readers will probably agree that it did not, for the simple reason that he was alone when he charged the trench; there was no follow up, no ground was taken, no Argentine surrender resulted, and only a tiny handful knew what he was doing or where he had gone. Colonel 'H''s gallantry as such did not win the battle for Goose Green but his leadership of 2 Para during the year he had been in command, and in the days and hours prior to his being shot, did. The commanding officer had imbued his battalion with his dedication, with his spirit, with his belief that, given the necessary will, anything was possible. He led by example. He set extremely high standards, and his battalion reflected this, particularly at platoon and section level. Colonel 'H' had made 2 Para into what it was at Goose Green — a first rate fighting force. During this battle he may have made tactical mistakes, but his example, his will, his leadership lived on after his death. Some, like Major Farrar-Hockley, believed it remained with 2 Para through to the end of the campaign.

As to the award of the Victoria Cross to Colonel 'H' there can be no doubt as to his personal courage, his total disregard for danger, but he would surely have been the first to agree, had he lived, that this supreme reward was in recognition of his battalion's achievements as well as his own.

APPENDIX I

2 PARA BATTLE GROUP ORGANISATION AT GOOSE GREEN

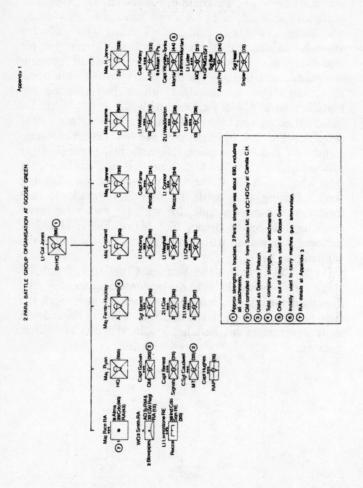

366

APPENDIX II

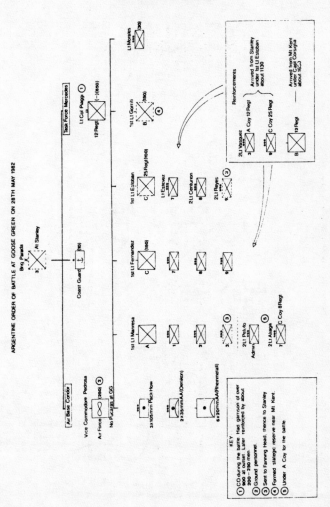

ARGENTINE ORDER OF BATTLE AT GOOSE GREEN ON 28TH MAY 1982

APPENDIX III

THE ARTILLERY SUPPORT AT GOOSE GREEN

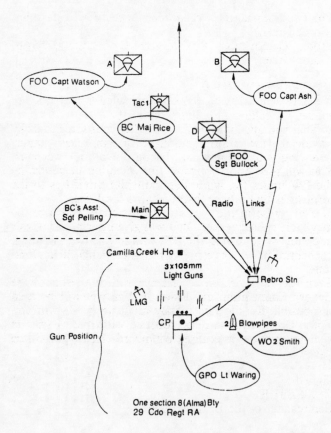

Goose ■ ■ Green

e n e m y

A

B

FOO Capt Watson

FOO Capt Ash

Tac 1

BC Maj Rice

D

FOO Sgt Bullock

BC's Asst Sgt Pelling

Main

Radio   Links

Camilla Creek Ho ■

3 x 105mm Light Guns

LMG

CP

Rebro Stn

2 Blowpipes

WO 2 Smith

Gun Position

GPO Lt Waring

One section 8 (Alma) Bty
29 Cdo Regt RA

APPENDIX IV

MAJOR KEEBLE'S SURRENDER ULTIMATUM

To: The Commander Argentinian Armed Force (Darwin) (Goose Green)
From: Commander British Armed Forces (Darwin) (Goose Green)

MILITARY OPTIONS
We have sent a PW to you under a white flag of truce to convey the following military options:
1. That you unconditionally surrender your force to us by leaving the township, forming up in a military manner, removing your helmets and laying down your weapons. You will give prior notice of this intention by returning the PW under the white flag with him briefed as to the formalities by no later than 0830 hrs local time.
2. You refuse in the first case to surrender and take the inevitable consequences. You will give prior notice of this intention by returning the PW without his flag (although his neutrality will be respected) no later than 0830 hrs local time.
3. In the event and in accordance with the terms of the Geneva Convention and Laws of War you will be held responsible for the fate of any civilians in Darwin and Goose Green and we in accordance with these terms do give notice of our intention to bombard Darwin and Goose Green.

Signed
C. KEEBLE
Commander of the British Forces

APPENDIX V

2 PARA'S ROLL OF HONOUR
FOR GOOSE GREEN

Officers and men of the 2nd Battalion, The Parachute Regiment killed in action at the battle for Darwin and Goose Green, 28 May, 1982.

Lieutenant-Colonel 'H'. Jones OBE	Commanding Office
Captain C. Dent	A Company
Captain D. Wood	Adjutant
Lieutenant J.A. Barry	D Company
Corporal D. Hardman	A Company
Corporal R.S. Prior	A Company
Corporal P.S. Sullivan	D Company
Lance-Corporal G.D. Bingley	D Company
Lance-Corporal A. Cork	D Company
Lance-Corporal N.R. Smith	D Company
Private S.J. Dixon	D Company
Private M.W. Fletcher	D Company
Private M.H. Holman-Smith	HQ Company
Private S. Illingsworth	B Company
Private T. Mechan	D Company

Attached Arms

Lieutenant R.J. Nunn	Royal Marines
Corporal D. Melia	Royal Engineers

APPENDIX VI

HONOURS AND AWARDS

The awards listed below were received by those who fought at Goose Green on both sides. Except for those awarded posthumously, members of 2 Para received theirs for their actions during Operation Corporate as a whole.

2nd Battalion, The Parachute Regiment

Victoria Cross

Lieutenant-Colonel 'H'. Jones, OBE (posthumous) - Commanding Officer

Distinguished Service Order

Major C.P.B. Keeble - Battalion Second-in-Command

Military Cross

Major J.H. Crosland - Officer Commanding B Company

Major C.D. Farrar-Hockley - Officer Commanding A Company

Lieutenant C.S. Connor - Recce Platoon Commander

Distinguished Conduct Medal

Sergeant J.C. Meredith - Platoon Sergeant, 12 Platoon, D Company

Corporal D. Abols - Section Commander, 1 Platoon, A Company

Private S. Illingsworth (posthumous) - 5 Platoon, B Company

Military Medal

Sergeant T.I. Barrett - Platoon Commander (at Goose Green) 1 Platoon, A Company

Corporal T.J. Camp - Section Commander, 2 Platoon, A Company

Corporal T.W. Harley - Section Commander, 11 Platoon, D Company

Lance-Corporal S.A. Bardsley - 6 Platoon, B Company

Lance-Corporal M.W.C. Bentley - Medical Orderly, Regimental Aid Post

Lance-Corporal G.D. Bingley (posthumous) - 11 Platoon, D Company

Lance-Corporal L.J. Standish - Medical Orderly, 5 Platoon

Private G.S. Carter - 12 Platoon, D Company

Private B.J. Grayling - 11 Platoon, D Company

Mention in Despatches

Major P. Neame - Officer Commanding D Company

Captain the Reverend D. Cooper, Royal Army Chaplain's Department - Battalion Padre

Captain P.R. Farrar - Patrols Platoon Commander

Acting-Captain M.S.H. Worsley-Tonks - Mortar Platoon Commander at Goose Green, then Adjutant.

Captain S. J. Hughes, Royal Army Medical Corps - Battalion Medical Officer

Lieutenant J.D. Page - Fire support coordinator in D Company at Goose Green, then 12 Platoon Commander

Lieutenant G.R. Weighell - 5 Platoon Commander, B Company

2nd Lieutenant G. Wallis - 3 Platoon Commander, A Company

Sergeant I. Aird - Platoon Sergeant, 5 Platoon, B Company

Corporal D. Hardman (posthumous) - Section Commander, 2 Platoon, A Company

Lance-Corporal N.J. Dance - Section Commander, 5 Platoon, B Company

Lance-Corporal K.P. Dunbar - 4 Platoon, B Company

Private S.J. Alexander - 1 Platoon, A Company

Private M.W. Fletcher (posthumous) - 10 Platoon, D Company

Private D. Gray - Medical Orderly, Patrols Platoon

Private A. Mansfield

Private R.P.G. Morrell - Medical Orderly, Recce Platoon

Private E. O'Rourke - Medical Orderly, A Company

Awards to other British personnel present at Goose Green
Member of the Order of the British Empire
J.R.R. Fox Esq - British Broadcasting Corporation
Distinguished Flying Cross
Captain J.G. Greenhalgh, Royal Corps of Transport - attached Army Air Corps
Captain J.P. Niblett, Royal Marines - Helicopter pilot, 3 Commando Brigade Air Squadron
Lieutenant R.J. Nunn, Royal Marines (posthumous) - Helicopter pilot, 3 Commando Brigade Air Squadron
Mention in Despatches
Major P.H. Gullan, MBE, MC - HQ 3 Commando Brigade
Lieutenant C.R. Livingstone, Royal Engineers - Recce Troop Commander, 59 Independent Commando Squadron, Royal Engineers

NOTES

INTRODUCTION

1. All three battalions of the Parachute Regiment participated in Operation Musketeer, the Suez Canal crisis, in 1956, but there was no battalion night attack that in any way resembled Goose Green. To find a parallel it is necessary to go back to the Korean War, and even then there is no exact equivalent.
2. The ships lost during the period 21-27 May were:
   HMS *Ardent* (frigate) 21 May
   HMS *Antelope* (frigate) 23 May
   Atlantic Conveyor (container ship) 25 May
   HMS *Coventry* (destroyer) 25 May
   Ships seriously damaged:
   HMS *Argonaut* (frigate) 21 May
   HMS *Antrim* (destroyer) 21 May
   RFA *Sir Galahad* (supply ship) 24 May
   RFA *Sir Lancelot* (supply ship) 24 May
   HMS *Broadsword* (frigate) 25 May
3. The previous lieutenant-colonel to win the VC was Lieutenant-Colonel James Power Carne who commanded the Glosters at the Imjin River battle in Korea. On that occasion he survived the three-day struggle against overwhelming odds, spent many months as a prisoner of war, and was awarded his country's highest decoration for gallantry for his outstanding leadership which had ensured the battalion held out for so long and checked the Chinese thrust to cut off the division.
4. Lieutenant-Colonel Jones did not much like his name of Herbert so everybody called him 'H'. In keeping with this custom I have referred to him throughout as Colonel 'H'.
5. Northwood is the underground command post in Middlesex from which the British high command controlled the

Falklands War. Here was the overall military commander, Admiral Sir John Fieldhouse, who was also C-in-C Fleet; Air Marshal Sir John Curtiss, the air commander; and Lieutenant-General Sir Richard Trant (from 21 May).

6. British paratroopers always refer to themselves as 'Toms', Royal Marines as 'Booties' (or, when wanting to deride, 'Cabbage Heads' from the green berets they wear), and soldiers from other regiments as 'Crap Hats'. I have used 'Toms' throughout the book.

PROLOGUE

1. Private Tuffen from A Company was seriously wounded in the head, but despite lying unattended for several hours he survived. His recovery was little short of miraculous. He married in 1989 and lives in Kent.

2. Captain Wood was a popular officer with a great sense of humour, never at a loss for a wry or cynical comment on a situation. He had come to the Parachute Regiment via the RAF Regiment, with which he had served in Dhofar. Although his place was in the gully with his commanding officer it was not strictly necessary for him to join the A Company assault. No one will ever know for sure why he did so, but it was a courageous act typical of the man. Several soldiers have commented to me that he was still wise-cracking and encouraging others up to the moment he was hit.

3. Interestingly the painting by Terence Cuneo depicting Colonel 'H''s final charge, which hangs in the School of Infantry Officers' Mess at Warminster, shows him firing his sub-machine gun in bursts from the hip, but Norman did not see him fire at all as he closed with the trench. Artistic licence perhaps.

CHAPTER I

1. Not quite every battalion gets to Northern Ireland, for example the Irish Guards and Gurkhas are not allowed to serve there.

2. It was a considerable disappointment to the Parachute Regiment that there was no role for it in the Gulf War. The

need was for infantry experienced in operating from Warrior armoured personnel carriers — 'heavy' infantry rather than the 'light' variety such as paratroopers. Nevertheless, some individuals did get to the Gulf as staff officers, seconded to US formations, in the SAS, or as bandsmen on medical duties.

3. Throughout I have referred to the battle as Goose Green. The Parachute Regiment prefer Darwin-Goose Green as they were tasked with securing both settlements; however, for the sake of brevity I have omitted Darwin when writing of the battle in general.

4. In the event the logistical support system for 2 Para had to be divided into three elements, not two, to cope with the distance involved in supplying the battalion at Goose Green. During the battle B Echelon was at San Carlos, A1 Echelon on Sussex Mountain, and A2 at Camilla Creek House.

CHAPTER II

1. In January, 1991, Seineldin was sentenced to 20 years in jail by a military court for leading an unsuccessful uprising of 'carapintadas' (painted faces), a group of rebellious Army officers. He was obviously a highly dissatisfied officer as he had been forced to retire from the Army in 1988 for involvement in a previous coup attempt. He was later placed in custody for writing a threatening letter to President Menem. It was from prison that he masterminded his second revolt. One wonders if Estoban was pleased to be out of his clutches at Goose Green.

2. An interesting point is that while the local inhabitants used landrovers extensively on the islands, 2 Para was led to believe, en route, that the terrain was unsuitable for any vehicles (including tracked ones). An extraordinary piece of misinformation.

3. The only exception to this confinement seems to have been Eric Goss who was permitted to remain in his house at Darwin. He had established a working relationship with the Argentines, and they used him as an intermediary in their dealings with the local community.

4. Michael Bilton & Peter Kosminsky, *Speaking Out*, Andre Deutsch, London, 1989, p. 137.

5. Martin Middlebrook, *The Fight for the Malvinas*, Viking, London, 1989, p. 51.

6. Perhaps this was part of the reason for the generally poor and rusty condition of so many weapons that 2 Para captured.

7. These claims to be seriously deficient in heavy weapons were made some five years after the event to Martin Middlebrook when he interviewed Piaggi in Argentina. They should, I believe, be treated with caution as they do not match up with the number of such weapons captured by 2 Para after the battle.

8. They were correct in anticipating such landings. A number of British SAS and SBS patrols were positioned inland on the 1st of May, and thereafter in the run up to the landings. The Pucara sorties, however, did not discover them.

9. Jeffrey Ethell and Alfred Price, *Air War South Atlantic*, Sidgwick and Jackson, London, 1983, p.78.

10. Martin Middlebrook, *The Fight for the Malvinas*, p. 125. These notes turned out to be of little significance or value to the Argentines. Flight-Lieutenant Ball's description of the aircraft exploding in a ball of flame seems to contradict Estoban's account. I have been unable to ascertain which version is correct.

11. Taylor's grave remains near Goose Green and is beautifully kept by the local people.

12. Martin Middlebrook, *The Fight for the Malvinas*, p. 92.

13. *Speaking Out*, p. 256.

CHAPTER III

1. Steven Hughes, *Combat and Survival* Magazine, April 1990.

2. That a crash programme was required was due to insufficient thought and time being devoted to the subject of battlefield casualties over the previous months. This type of training is mandatory for Northern Ireland but 2 Para had concentrated on other skills as it was scheduled for a tour in Belize before the Falklands blew up.

3. The entire battalion had to be trained on the new Clansman radios during the voyage south. They were issued only after the troops were on board the MV *Norland*. Most units in the Army had had this radio for months, if not years, as priority was for units in, or destined for, NATO, rather than those

earmarked for AOA operations. The Clansman sets are insecure, apart from the VHF brigade command net. This means reliance must be placed on the use of nicknames, report lines, and encoding. A staggering amount of paper work was necessary to get 2 Para prepared to use its new sets, in addition to individual training. The Signals Platoon clerk spent virtually the entire voyage typing out signals instructions to cover 28 days' use. These were eventually brought ashore in large sacks. The signals officer, Captain Benest, also had a quantity of special codes which he had to carry on every lifeboat drill, weighed down with radio batteries, to be dumped in the Atlantic in the event of any risk of capture. Even the Paras cannot operate without plenty of paper.

4. The MV *Norland* ended up awash with beer. Back in Aldershot the adjutant had been asked how much beer to put on board. He told the enquirer (NAAFI), to think of the average adult consumption per day – and treble it. This advice was followed.
5. Julian Thompson, *No Picnic*, Leo Cooper, London, 1985, p. 24.
6. *Speaking Out*, pp. 223-224.
7. 3 Commando Brigade Operation Order dated 12 May, 1982.
8. Major Paul Farrar, letter to author July 1990.
9. Major Benest's manuscript p. 19.
10. Ibid p. 22.
11. *Speaking Out*, pp. 217-218.
12. Major Benest's manuscript p. 25.
13. *Speaking Out*, p. 226.
14. Interview in February 1990.
15. Interview in January 1990.
16. Major Benest's manuscript p. 29.
17. *Speaking Out*, p. 131.
18. Major Benest's manuscript p. 30.
19. Ibid.
20. Corporal Abols, presentation to the King's Own Border Regiment, October, 1982.
21. Major Paul Farrar, letter to author, July, 1990.
22. *Speaking Out*, p. 111.
His flying helmet is a prized exhibit at the Fleet Air Arm museum.

CHAPTER IV

1. *Speaking Out*, p. 227.
2. *No Picnic*, p. 74.
3. Robin Neillands, *By Sea and Land*, Weidenfeld & Nicolson, London, 1987, p. 247.
4. Lawrence Freedman and Virginia Gamba-Stonehouse, *Signals of War*, Faber and Faber, London, 1990, p. 366.
5. Ibid p. 366.
6. It is difficult to overemphasize the importance of the heavy lift helicopters on the *Atlantic Conveyor*. One Chinook has a ten-ton capacity, five times that of a Sea King.
7. Lieutenant Thurman had avoided capture when the Argentines invaded in April as he was on holiday in Venice with his fiancée, the daughter of the governor of the Falkland Islands.
8. *No Picnic*, p. 77.
9. It is uncertain if the brigade commander sanctioned this alternative plan of Colonel 'H''s. To send just one company by helicopter in daylight with no indirect fire support on the off chance of causing trouble with any enemy in the area seems a questionable venture. Also picking D Company to do it after a sleepless and tiring night was asking a lot, but was probably because 12 Platoon was still forward at Cantera House.
10. *Signals of War*, p. 365.
11. Ibid, p. 368
12. This solitary Chinook continued to fly, frighteningly overloaded, without adequate maintenance or spares for the rest of the war.
13. *No Picnic*, p. 78.
14. Ibid p. 80.
15. *By Sea and Land*, p. 247.
16. Max Hastings & Simon Jenkins, *The Battle for the Falklands*, Michael Joseph, London, 1983. Colonel 'H' was referring to the intense Argentine air activity, heavy British naval losses, and seeming inactivity on land.
17. *Speaking Out*, p. 117
18. Ibid p. 117.
19. *Signals of War*, p. 357.
20. Ibid p. 358.
21. *Speaking Out*, p. 218.

22. *Signals of War*, p. 363.
23. Ibid p. 364.
24. The daring of the Argentine pilots has been acknowledged by all participants and observers of the Falklands conflict, although at times their tactical skills were questionable. Flight-Lieutenant Paul Barton's comments in Jeffrey Ethell and Alfred Price's *Air War South Atlantic*, published by Sidgwick and Jackson in 1983, are worth repeating:

'Their pilots are not bad. Any guy who can fly at 60 or 70 feet above the waves, picking his way between ships' masts, is a pretty skilful pilot. But basically they had not been trained sufficiently in tactical flying. Nothing their fighter or attack aircraft did struck me as being particularly clever or original. That said, however, I would give them 9½ out of 10 for sheer guts and courage.'

CHAPTER V

1. Sergeant T.I. Barrett in a brief on Operation Corporate to the Staff College, Camberley, 1983.
2. 'Blue on blue' originates from the military's use of blue symbols on maps to represent friendly forces ('own troops'). The enemy is always marked in red. So if friendly forces accidentally clash, blue units have attacked blue units.
3. *No Picnic*, p. 62.
4. Interview, March 1990.
5. Interview, August 1991.
6. Major Paul Farrar, letter to author, July, 1990. A small illustration of Colonel 'H''s determination to supervise details personally. He kept everybody on a very short rein, not allowing a great deal of initiative from the majority of his officers.
7. Ibid.
8. Ibid. A few remarks on the arctic ration packs issued during the campaign may be of interest. Generally the troops regarded them as the best, provided adequate water was available for their preparation. Perhaps surprisingly this was not always the case in the islands, and the use of water from muddy pools or soggy peat did not make for an appetizing supper. If eaten without water this food tended to soak up fluid from the stomach causing dehydration and a severe

thirst. Mostly rations were mixed up as an all-in stew, with perhaps a Mars bar to follow. These were extremely popular, although they had to be carried close to the body as otherwise they became as hard as small ingots of iron.

If anything kept the paratroopers going it was the ability to brew tea at every conceivable opportunity. These brews were real lifesavers, and veterans soon appreciated the value of plastic mugs if cracked lips were not to be scalded as well. The commonest complaint related to diet during the conflict was constipation. Many men went for a week without the luxury of a bowel movement.

9. *Above All Courage*, p. 226.
10. Lieutenant-Colonel John Crosland, letter to author July 1990.
11. *Above All Courage*, p. 227.
12. Interview with author, March 1990.
13. Ibid.
14. Ibid. The lack of an FAC on the ground at the crucial time may well have contributed to this strike missing the target.
15. There is some confusion over the time of this broadcast. Benest's account makes it shortly after first light (about 6.45 am), while Thompson describes it as about midday (local). I have taken Robert Fox's time of 1400 GMT or 10.00 am as being correct in that, being a BBC man, he was perhaps more likely to make a note of these things.
16. Robert Fox, *Eyewitness Falklands*, Methuen, London, 1982. p. 156.
17. Ibid p. 157.
18. At this stage Colonel 'H' was, apparently, beside himself with rage at his headquarters staff. Several of those present feared he might lose control of himself. Fortunately he had calmed down by the time he gave out his orders several hours later. It should be remembered that the strain under which any commanding officer would be working before a crucial operation had been multiplied threefold by the BBC's broadcast. For all Colonel 'H' knew he was now about to lead 2 Para against an enemy that was totally alert to an impending attack, and had time to reinforce. With that sort of responsibility on his shoulders it is perhaps not surprising that slipshod staff work, minor mistakes, or the general friction of war caused outbursts in a man of his temperament.
19. At first sight, if the commanding officer was ready to give

out his orders at 11.00 am, it seems strange that it was another four hours before he finally held his 'O' group. Surely the missing officers could have been assembled within half an hour or so? Although the sequence of events that morning is not easy to unravel, it appears that, after the postponement, news came in of the capture of Morales and the landrover, shortly followed by Connor's enforced withdrawal, and then Evans pulled out. It then made sense to await their arrival back at Camilla Creek House to hear what they had to say. The prisoners also might reveal important information during their interrogation by the IO. Colonel 'H' himself debriefed both Connor and Evans in case he needed to revise his plan. I believe it was these activities that consumed most of the time between the two 'O' groups.

20. Interview, February 1990. Corporal Soane was then the Pony-Major with responsibility for the Parachute Regiment's mascot — a tiny pony called Pegasus with the rank of 'sergeant'.

21. *The Fight for the Malvinas*, p. 180.

22. Ibid p. 181.

CHAPTER VI

1. It may be that the ground plan for Operation Desert Storm in early 1991 is one of the exceptions that prove the rule. This vast and complex plan succeeded without any major hitches or alterations way beyond expectations. Nevertheless, it would be foolish to draw too many conclusions from this other than that military operations are not too taxing if the enemy has little or no intention, or ability, to resist. The ground forces in the Gulf were not tested in the same way as those in the Falklands. It was a huge success rather than a huge victory — there is a difference.

2. Major Benest's manuscript p. 55.

3. Interview, February 1990.

4. I have seen an extract from 3 Commando Brigade's situation report for the afternoon of the 27 May, which makes it plain that it was the intention for 2 Para to withdraw after an attack on Goose Green and Darwin airfield.

5. Major Benest's manuscript p. 58.

6. 2 Para's Post Operational Report.

7. Sergeant T.I. Barrett, presentation to the King's Own Border Regiment, October, 1982.

8. Interview, February, 1990. With this comment 2 Para were in agreement. Lieutenant Connor's remarks to me in January, 1990, are worth repeating: 'The battalion's patrol activity was seldom directed and coordinated by higher formation, and the activities of the SAS were particularly frustrating. SAS operations both before Darwin/Goose Green and Wireless Ridge inhibited the battalion's own patrolling activities, and yet no proper debriefing of the SAS patrols was ever made available to the battalion.'

9. Copied directly from Major Neame's notes made at the time.

10. Nobody I asked could come up with a convincing answer to the question of why it was believed an Argentine company was located near Coronation Point. I was unable to speak to the former intelligence officer Captain Coulson. The only possible clue I found was in Major Neame's notes taken at the 'O' group. Under the heading 'Reported from Harrier sortie' is a grid reference for troops dug in near Coronation Point.

11. Interview, August, 1991.

12. The SAS had, on occasion, spoken of the Argentines as 'military pygmies', which turned out to be something of an understatement.

13. Interview, August, 1991.

14. Major Neame later described to Max Arthur how Colonel 'H', while still on board the MV *Norland*, had decreed that all bayonets should be left behind as the battles ahead would be won by firepower, and therefore they were so much excess weight. Neame disagreed with this decision and persuaded his commanding officer to rescind the order on the basis that bayonets make good tin-openers.

15. At the Wireless Ridge battle a separate HF administrative net was used by 2 Para as a result of its experience at Goose Green.

16. It should be stated that it was bergens *plus* mortar bombs that crippled the battalion on the march up Sussex Mountain. In fact the rifle companies could probably have carried mortar bombs forward to Camilla Creek House, and possibly beyond, as all bergens had been left behind.

17. A great deal was expected of the 4.5-inch gun. It could throw its 46lb shell up to 22,000 metres at a rate of 24 per minute. It is controlled by digital computers with fully automatic

loading, giving it an extremely fast response time. Target details are stored in its computer so that the same target can be engaged again quickly much later. The shells are not spread out in the target area like ordinary artillery, making it particularly effective against buildings, bridges, bunkers or fortified positions that might survive other types of gunfire.

18. Major Benest's manuscript p. 76.

19. Ibid.

20. It is worth adding a few comments on this 'O' group. It had been extremely long, somewhat complicated, rushed, with the commanding officer himself obviously impatient as time ticked away. It was not perhaps an ideal atmosphere for queries or further explanations. At least one officer present felt that nobody was prepared to ask questions for fear of having their head bitten off. It must be added, however, that as is normal practice several officers stayed behind afterwards to sort out details with headquarters staff.

Lieutenant Livingstone felt happier discussing his problems with Major Miller, the operations officer, while the system of report lines and nicknames to be used to report progress by the battalion's rear headquarters to brigade were worked out and agreed without reference to Colonel 'H'.

21. *Above All Courage*, p. 200.

CHAPTER VII

1. At Goose Green this decision had some disadvantages. Air burst shells can be effective against hastily dug positions such as those occupied by Manresa's A Company well forward of Darwin ridge, or those adopted by some reinforcements later in the battle. Also, in the event, because of the soft ground deadening the effect of the PD ammunition, plus the inaccuracy of much of the shelling, air burst would have been preferable for many of the fire missions.

2. Lieutenant Mark Waring, *Commando Gunner* journal, 1982.

3. Ibid.

4. *No Picnic*, p. 83.

5. Lieutenant Mark Waring, *Commando Gunner* journal, 1982.

6. Interview, April, 1990.

7. Interview, January, 1990.
8. There is some disagreement now as to whether all six machine guns actually got their sustained fire kits, or only three.
9. Major Paul Farrar, letter to author, July, 1990.
10. Interview, February, 1990.
11. Martin Middlebrook, *Task Force*, Penguin Books, 1987, p. 259.
12. Interview, January, 1990.
13. Major Peter Kennedy, letter to author, January, 1991.
14. Major Paul Farrar, letter to author, July, 1990.
15. I could find no confirmation that HMS *Arrow* ever got back into action. She had to leave well before first light so in effect played no worthwhile part in the battle at all. This was to be a serious setback. Murphy's law again.
16. Major John Crosland, Operation Corporate brief to the Staff College, Camberley, 1983.
17. Captain Clive Chapman, letter to author, February, 1990.

CHAPTER VIII

1. Interview, August, 1991. To be fair it should be pointed out that Colonel 'H' had probably kept D Company in reserve as it had had an especially tiring time during the first attempt to advance on Goose Green.
2. Major Paul Farrar, letter to author, July, 1990.
3. Interview, August, 1991.
4. Ibid.
5. Lieutenant Shaun Webster, letter to author, February, 1990.
6. Interview, August, 1991.
7. Martin Bentley, letter to author, June, 1990.
8. Ibid.
9. Interview, August, 1991.
10. Major Peter Kennedy, letter to author, January, 1991.
11. Interview, January, 1990.
12. Interview, March, 1990.
13. Interview, March, 1990.
14. Interview, March, 1991.
15. Martin Bentley, letter to author, June, 1990. All 2 Para medics were armed, and on occasion had to become involved in combat like any other Tom. Searching Argentine bunkers or trenches for injured paratroopers or enemy after the

advance had moved on was a particularly dangerous time. Bentley has described what could happen in these circumstances:

'Mark [Polkey] came with me; it was a large area so we split up to cover it more quickly. We both had SMGs (useless in this open ground). The Argy trenches were well sited with a very effective killing area. As I approached one of them I saw movement. I opened fire immediately and sprinted to a nearby trench to take cover. Leaping in, I felt movement under my feet, so I fired the rest of my mag into it. An Argy had been hiding at the bottom of the trench, now he was dead.'

16. A strobe light is a small battery-operated light, often used by paratroops at night to facilitate locating individuals who may have become scattered over the drop zone, or casualties.

17. Corporal Tom Camp should not be confused with his brother who was also a corporal in 3 Platoon. Tom Camp was to earn an MM later that morning, and has done exceptionally well since the battle, rising to the rank of major in the Royal Artillery.

CHAPTER IX

1. When Tuffen was eventually attended to, Lance-Corporal Bentley thought he had little chance of life. Tuffen was unconscious and Bentley has described his initial reaction:
   '"What do you think?" asked Cleggy [Clegg]. "Fill him with morphine and help somebody else," was my reply [as] there were still at least six untreated casualties waiting, "but check with Doc first". While Cleggy went for the Doc I started to dress and clean up Tuffen's head. It was a delicate job as much of the top of the skull was shattered, like a boiled egg that had been hit with a spoon. The Doc said, "If he can survive an hour he's still got a chance".'

2. After the Burntside House action, when Captain Dent took over carrying the radio himself he also swapped maps with Lieutenant Livingstone, as his was of a larger scale that would be better for Dent's coordination duties. It was also agreed that Livingstone should take over the tactical control of the bulk of A Company's main headquarters. With his

own engineers this amounted to about twelve men, who moved thereafter a short bound behind Dent.

3. Interview, January. 1990.
4. Corporal Abols, presentation to the King's Own Border Regiment, October, 1982. Abols comes from a most unusual military family. His father was born in Latvia and, as a young teenager and fervent anti-communist, found himself fighting the Russians and fleeing his home in Riga to join the German Army. He rose to the rank of platoon sergeant in a reconnaissance unit and was awarded the Iron Cross 1st and 2nd class. Later he was captured by the Americans, taken to the US before eventually arriving in Britain, where he managed to join the Merchant Navy. Thus he finished the war serving his former enemies. Abols tells me that he believes his grandfather was decorated by the Czar shortly before the Russian revolution in 1917.
5. An interesting sidelight on the stress of war was the marked increase in smoking during the conflict. Soldiers were given a free issue of either 1,000 cigarettes or ten chocolate bars. Platoon sergeants gave the chocolates to the non-smokers. When it was found that these did not last as long as the cigarettes many took up smoking. Corporal Tom Camp, for example, had given up, started again in the Falklands, then stopped once more on the voyage home.
6. Brigadier Farrar-Hockley, letter to author, February, 1990.
7. Michael Bilton & Peter Kosminsky, op. cit., p. 137.
8. Interview, June, 1991.
9. Interview, August, 1991.
10. Letter to author, June, 1991.
11. Letter to author, June, 1991.
12. *Speaking Out*, p. 133.
13. Major Benest's manuscript, p. 120.
14. Ibid.
15. Interview, August, 1991.
16. Major Benest's manuscript, p. 119.
17. Interview, February, 1990.
18. Major Benest's manuscript, p. 120.
19. Ibid p. 122.
20. Interview, September 1990. The reference to junior Brecon was to the section commander/junior NCO tactics courses held at Brecon in Wales.
21. *Speaking Out*, p. 136.

22. Interview, August, 1991.
23. Ibid.
24. Ibid.
25. This was the first attempt to get helicopters to lift out casualties from as far forward as the gorse gully. It illustrates how vulnerable they were to Pucaras, although it was to be the only confirmed Pucara success of the campaign. Had their flight not had the misfortune to coincide with an Argentine sortie the likelihood is they would have been able to extract some wounded, although they would have been too late for Colonel 'H'. Both Captain Niblett and Lieutenant Nunn were awarded the Distinguished Flying Cross (Nunn posthumously) for their exploits that morning.
26. The dead were: Lieutenant-Colonel 'H'. Jones, Captain C. Dent, Captain D.A. Wood, Corporal D. Hardman, Corporal S.R. Prior, and Corporal D. Melia RE.
27. Interview, January, 1990.
28. 1 bid.
29. *Speaking Out*, p. 136.

CHAPTER X

1. Interview, July, 1991.
2. *Air War South Atlantic*, p. 162.
3. Sergeant Belcher, who was invalided out of the Royal Marines, has pieces from both his helicopter and Gimenez's Pucara mounted as mementoes at his home.
4. Interview, September, 1990.
5. *Speaking Out*, p. 152.
6. Ibid.
7. Ibid.
8. Ibid p. 153.
9. A number of officers were somewhat puzzled by the fact that Boca House did not exist. It had been there when the maps were made, it featured in the orders for the attack, but all that remained on the ground was the foundation, which was invisible unless you were virtually standing on it. It certainly puzzled Lieutenant Hocking. Even after the battle he still felt that somehow he had missed it in the confusion.
10. Captain Clive Chapman, letter to author, February, 1990.
11. Ibid.

388

12. Ibid. Private 'Beast' Kirkwood's brother, Tom, was also a platoon radio operator in 1 Platoon of A Company. He was wounded in the gorse gully fighting as related earlier.

13. Interview, January, 1990.

14. Ibid.

15. Lieutenant-Colonel John Crosland, letter to author, July, 1990.

16. Captain Clive Chapman, letter to author, February, 1990.

17. Bardsley, then a sergeant, was one of only two 2 Para soldiers who were present at Goose Green, who are officially acknowledged to have fought in the Gulf as well. He was on attachment to the US 82nd Airborne Division, and his meritorious service gained him a British Empire Medal. The other was Major John Page, who at Goose Green had been D Company's fire support coordinator, and later replaced Jim Barry as 12 Platoon commander. In the Gulf he had the unusual experience, for an infantry officer, of commanding a squadron of Challenger tanks. Afterwards, when asked if he had fired his main armament he is rumoured to have replied, 'Yes, but only out of sheer vandalism'. He too was on secondment — to an armoured regiment.
   Unofficially it is known that several other Goose Green veterans fought behind the Iraqi lines as members of the SAS. At least two were decorated.

18. *Above All Courage*, p. 192.

19. Major David Benest, letter to author, July, 1991.

20. *Pegasus*, October, 1982 p. 44.

21. Major Benest's manuscript p. 139.

22. Interview, August, 1991.

23. Ibid.

24. An aside on laser binoculars. They are large and bulky, and although useful to look through are decidedly uncomfortable to lie on. Captain Ash, the FOO with B Company, exchanged his for a normal pair early on in the battle as 'with them hanging round your neck they prevented you from getting nice and close to the ground'.

25. Interview, August, 1991.

26. Ibid.

27. Ibid.

28. Ibid.

29. Interview, August, 1991.

30. See Postscript for a discussion of Argentine casualties.

CHAPTER XI

1. One report suggests 106 men.
2. *The Fight for the Malvinas*, p.192.
3. *Above All Courage*, p. 229.
4. Ibid. p. 230.
5. Martin Bentley, letter to author, June, 1990.
6. Ibid.
7. Ibid.
8. Major Peter Kennedy, letter to author, January, 1991.
9. Major Paul Farrar, letter to author, April, 1991.
10. Ibid.
11. Major Peter Kennedy, letter to author, January, 1991.
12. Major Paul Farrar, letter to author, April, 1991.
13. Major Peter Kennedy, letter to author, January, 1991.
14. Interview, March, 1990.
15. Major Paul Farrar, letter to author, April, 1991.
16. Martin Bentley, letter to author, June, 1990.
17. Interview, March, 1990.
18. Mr Shaun Webster, letter to author, February, 1990.
19. Lieutenant-Colonel Philip Neame, letter to author, May, 1990.
20. Mr Shaun Webster, letter to author, February, 1990.
21. Ibid.
22. This suppressive fire on to the airfield was another example of a lack of coordination between the companies as they pressed towards their objectives. B Company was uncertain if the airfield was still C Company's objective, or that D Company was likely to cross it on its way towards Goose Green. Neither was it known that 10 Platoon was moving on to the strip. It might be added that Support Company did not seem to realize that troops on or near the airfield might be friendly, as otherwise the MMGs would not have kept Webster pinned there. The airfield was the objective of one company, on the route of another, and was fired at independently of the others. Luck was running with 2 Para at this stage.
23. Captain Clive Chapman, letter to author, February, 1990.

CHAPTER XII

1. Interview, August, 1991.
2. The Royal British Legion have recently launched an audio-cassette record in aid of its Poppy Day appeal on which one of the songs is dedicated to Private S.J. Dixon.
3. Interview, WO2 John Meredith, October, 1990.
4. Major Benest's manuscript p. 163.
5. Interview, August, 1991.
6. Corporal Sullivan had been selected for promotion to sergeant, and had ordered his mess kit uniform before departing for the Falklands.
7. The Argentine version of the circumstances of Lieutenant Barry's death has been given by Martin Middlebrook in a letter in the April, 1988, issue of *Pegasus*. A book, published in Argentina, caused considerable confusion by wrongly assuming that the 'British commander' who approached Centurion to discuss a surrender was Colonel 'H'.
8. Major Paul Farrar, letter to author, April, 1991.
9. I am aware they this account differs in some respects from D Company's version. Neame is emphatic that he and 11 Platoon were already at the bridge/dairy area when Greenhalgh and his party arrived. According to Neame they merged with D Company, not the other way round. Similarly he emphasizes that the elements of C Company in the area supported 11 Platoon's assault, which was part of the plan initiated by Neame before any of C Company arrived, including the clearing of the outbuildings west of the school. These differences underline the confusion of the moment.
10. Interview, September, 1990.
11. The Recce Platoon had been joined by Captain Adams by this time.
12. Major Paul Farrar, letter to author, April, 1991.
13. The October, 1982, *Pegasus* makes an amusing reference to Captain Farrar's marksmanship during this incident when the writer refers to him as, 'Captain "I've shot at Bisley so I know what I'm doing" Farrar'.
14. Major Paul Farrar, letter to author, April, 1991.
15. Major Peter Kennedy, letter to author, January, 1991.
16. Ibid.
17. Interview, August, 1991.
18. Ibid

19. Interview, May, 1990.
20. An extract from the unpublished English translation of *Dio y los Halcons*, quoted by Martin Middlebrook *The Fight for the Malvinas*, p. 191.
21. Major Peter Kennedy, letter to author, January, 1991.

CHAPTER XIII

1. *The Fight for the Malvinas*, p. 193.
2. Captain Clive Chapman, letter to author, February, 1990.
3. Major John Crosland, brief to Staff College, Camberley, May, 1983.
4. Major Paul Farrar, letter to author, April, 1991.
5. Major Roger Jenner, letter to author, June, 1991.
6. This Argentine flag still belongs to Major Kennedy but it has been on loan to the Parachute Regiment's museum at Aldershot.
7. Major Peter Kennedy, letter to author, January, 1991.
8. Steve Hughes, *Combat and Survival* magazine, April, 1990.
9. Martin Bentley, letter to author, June, 1990.
10. Ibid.
11. Major Benest's manuscript, p. 188.
12. *No Picnic*, pps. 96-97.
13. Ibid p. 96.
14. Ibid p. 97.
15. Ibid p. 93.
16. Major Paul Farrar, letter to author, April, 1991.
17. *Eye Witness Falklands*, p. 194.
18. Martin Bentley, letter to author, June, 1990.
19. *Speaking Out*, p.219.
20. *Eye Witness Falklands*, p. 194.
21. Ibid.
22. Julian Thompson, letter to author, August, 1991.
23. *Speaking Out*, p. 259.
24. This Union flag is now held in 2 Para Sergeants Mess.
25. *Speaking Out*, p. 258.

BIBLIOGRAPHY

Arthur, Max, *Above All Courage*, Sphere Books, 1985

Bilton, Michael & Kosminsky, Peter, *Speaking Out*, Andre Deutsch, 1989

Burden, Rodney A. and Others, *Falklands The Air War*, Arms and Armour Press, 1986.

Ethell, Jeffrey and Price, Alfred, *Air War South Atlantic*, Sidgwick and Jackson, 1983

Fox, Robert, *Eyewitness Falklands*, Methuen, 1982

Freedman, Lawrence and Gamba-Stonehouse, Virginia, *Signals of War*, Faber and Faber, 1990

Frost, John, *2 Para Falklands*, Buchan & Enright, 1983

Hastings, Max, and Jenkins, Simon, *The Battle for the Falklands*, Michael Joseph, 1983

Jolly, Rick, *The Red and Green Life Machine*, Century Publishing, 1983

Middlebrook, Martin, *Task Force*, Penguin Books, 1982

Middlebrook, Martin, *The Fight for the Malvinas*, Penguin Group, 1989

Neillands, Robin, *By Sea and Land*, Weidenfeld & Nicolson, 1987

Perrett, Bryan, *Weapons of the Falklands War*, Blandford Press, 1982

Thompson, Julian, *No Picnic*, Leo Cooper, 1985

INDEX

Coronation Point, 130, 151, 160, 161, 166, 193, 200, 206-7, 215, 216, 218, 239, 364
Corsiglia, Captain E., 340
Cotton, Colour-Sergeant M., 37
Coulson, Captain A., 98, 138, 158-9
Coventry, HMS, 113
Cow Bay, 71
Crimean War, 7, 17, 118
Crippa, Lieutenant G., 107-8
Crockford, Private, 304
Crosland, Major J., 25, 31, 86, 125, 168, 187, 188-9, 191, 193, 202, 255, 263, 264, 271-2, 273, 276, 277, 278, 295, 338, 341-2, 351
Cruzado, Lieutenant, 335, 336
Curran, Private, 283
Cymbeline, 174-5

Daher, Brigadier-General, 53
Daily Express, 134
Daily Mail, 355
Daily Telegraph, 134
Darwin Hill, 7, 11, 14, 34, 44, 129-30, 140, 151, 154, 166, 197, 211, 215, 218, 220, 222, 223, 226, 238, 243, 287, 295, 302, 309, 317, 324, 338, 342, 343, 346, 347, 364; Argentines fail to occupy, 154, 226, 243-4
Darwin inlet, 140, 153, 166, 207, 218
Darwin ridge, 2, 11, 13, 42, 44, 140, 151, 181, 197-8, 210, 215, 220, 222, 223, 243, 253, 259, 260, 262, 266, 268-9, 279, 285, 287
Darwin settlement, 1, 12, 43, 56, 76, 79, 108, 129, 138-9, 149, 154, 158, 161, 166, 207, 212, 215, 218, 235, 259, 265, 266, 312, 338, 352
Davis, Private, 331
D-Day, 74, 81, 93
Decorations and Medals, 371-3; al Valor, 44; Cruz La Nacion,

44-5, 108; DCM, 2, 228, 268; DSO, 2, 145; GSM (Northern Ireland), 22; MBE, 20; MC, 2; MID, 2; MM, 2, 204, 272, 303; VC, 2, 5, 17, 31, 365
Dent, Captain C., 14, 186, 230-1, 244, 246
Dey, Private, 226
Dhofar, 40
Dixon, Private S., 204, 315
Douglas Settlement, 90, 349
Dozo, Brigadier-General L., 109
Dunbar, Lance-Corporal K., 264, 335

Eagle Detachment, 63, 79, 115, 139
East Falkland, 6, 42, 43-4, 66, 79, 110, 112
Echelon, A., 40, 256, 288
Echelon, B., 40, 288, 289
Eiserman, Corporal, 190, 266
El Palomar, 47
Elliott, Corporal, 278, 306-7, 308-9
Elliott, Private, 228
England, 117
Estancia House, 340
Estevez, Lieutenant R., 12, 44, 196, 197, 224; death of, 197, 261, 363
Estoban, 1st Lieutenant C., 42-4, 51, 54, 57, 61, 62, 63, 115, 284, 285, 363; at Fanning Head, 63-4, 79, 80, 88-9, 90, 107
Eton, 19
Europic Ferry MV, 114
Evans, Sergeant, 90
Evans, Corporal T., 127-33, 135, 138, 141, 150, 299, 304, 330, 345, 347
Everest, 31
Exocet, 103, 114

FAC, 126, 127-8, 133, 136, 337
FACE, 173
Falkland Islands, 19, 42, 66-7, 168, 174
Falkland Islanders, 300

399

ν